INSIDE

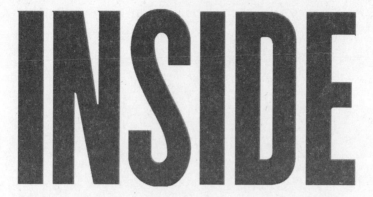

A Top G-Man Exposes Spies, Lies,
and Bureaucratic Bungling
Inside the FBI

I.C. SMITH

FORMER SPECIAL AGENT IN CHARGE

NELSON CURRENT

A Subsidiary of Thomas Nelson, Inc.

Published in Nashville, Tennessee, by Nelson Current, a subsidiary of Thomas Nelson, Inc.

Library of Congress Cataloging-in-Publication Data

Smith, I.C. (Ivian C.)
    Inside : a top G-man exposes spies, lies, and bureaucratic bungling in the
FBI / I.C. Smith.
        p. cm.
    ISBN 0-7852-6061-7
    1. United States. Federal Bureau of Investigation—History. 2. Law
enforcement—United States—History—20th century. 3. Criminal
investigation—United States—History—20th century. I. Title.
    HV8144.F43S655 2004
    363.25'0973—dc22

2004021786

Printed in the United States of America
04 05 06 07 08 QW 9 8 7 6 5 4 3 2 1

To Mattie and William Smith,
the grandparents who reared me with unconditional love.

CONTENTS

CHAPTER 1

TERROR IN THE SKY

*"The facts so far on the public record do not
support the conclusion that these tragic events could
have been prevented by the FBI and intelligence
communities acting alone."*

Former FBI Director Louis Freeh, testifying before Congress,

October 8, 2002

In early January 1995, police in Manila responded to an apartment fire caused by a bomb-making attempt gone bad. One of the two tenants escaped, but the other, a Pakistani named Abdul Hakim Murad, eventually cooperated with Philippine police. His computer database ultimately helped them even more.

The police were awestruck at the digital treasure trove: plans to kill Pope John Paul II, who was to visit Manila in about two weeks; and Project Bojinka—literally "big bang" or "loud bang" in Serbo-Croatian— a plot to blow up American airplanes en route from Asia to the United States. The plan called for terrorists to load explosives in their shoes, change shoes during the flights, then get off the planes during stopovers, leaving the shoe bombs to explode after takeoff. A trial run a month earlier killed a Japanese passenger on a Philippine Airlines jet, though the plane managed to land in Okinawa safely.

Two other discoveries by the police were potentially even more important. First, the plots were planned and carried out by a terrorist group called al Qaeda, funded by Osama bin Laden, a radical Islamic millionaire whose brother-in-law ran a nongovernmental organization in the Philippines that was a front for terrorist activities. Second, Murad's escaped roommate was Ramzi Yousef, the mastermind behind the 1993 World Trade Center bombing, who was eventually apprehended in Pakistan in February 1995.

The police also learned that Murad, who had trained as an airplane pilot, was part of a plot to fly an explosives-laden airplane into CIA headquarters in Langley, Virginia. For the 1993 WTC bombing, the terrorists had parked a truck packed with explosives in an underground garage near a structural support column, set the timer, and left the truck. There were similar plots to set off explosives in a "stalled" vehicle in the Holland Tunnel under the Hudson River between Manhattan and New Jersey, and to bomb the United Nations, the George Washington Bridge, and other federal buildings. These plans were evidently put on hold after observing the rapid law enforcement response to the WTC bombing.

But there was a chilling difference in the plan to crash into CIA headquarters: it was a suicide mission, perhaps designed for Murad himself. This was an alarming new development. As a section chief in the Intelligence Division of the FBI, I was briefed on the threat in the weeks before I left FBI headquarters for my new assignment as special agent in charge of FBI operations in Arkansas, President Bill Clinton's home state. When told of the emerging information out of Manila, I responded, "That changes everything!" It was clear to me the terrorist threat had entered a new and more dangerous phase.

In the aftermath of the September 11, 2001 terrorist attacks, it was revealed that not only had the CIA and the FBI been alerted to the Project Bojinka intelligence but also that several boxes of documents had been turned over to the FBI. Like documents of other investigations, they were never thoroughly examined or analyzed. On the day Islamic terrorists destroyed the twin towers of the World Trade Center, more than six years after the fire in Manila, these key warning indicators of the tragedy and essential information about its masterminds sat ignored in cardboard boxes, still in Arabic.

On that September morning, three years into my retirement after twenty-five years with the FBI, I was sitting at the computer working on this manuscript with *Imus in the Morning,* featuring New York news/talk legend Don Imus, on a television around the corner from my office. Fragments of a newsbreak got my attention, and after a couple of minutes, I walked over and saw the horrific image of an aircraft crashed into one of the World Trade Center towers. I knew instantly that it was an act of terrorism. The second plane crashing into the other tower only served as an exclamation point to my belief.

I spent most of the rest of the day watching the news unfold and fielding calls from acquaintances and the media. One of those calls was from Alice Stewart of KARK-TV in Little Rock, where I had spent the last three years of my FBI career. I told her that in my view the attacks were the result of three events: an intelligence failure in the U.S., principally by the FBI; an intelligence failure abroad, principally by the CIA and NSA (National Security Agency); and a security failure at U.S. airports. I explained further that if any one of those three failures had not occurred, the destruction of the twin towers by terrorists could never have happened.

Nothing since then has caused me to change my mind; indeed, subsequent events have reinforced my belief. The FBI and CIA, in particular, dragged their feet, begrudging the release of crucial information. An acquaintance in the FBI called a few days after 9/11, stating the hierarchy at FBI headquarters was more interested in "circling the wagons" than finding out the cause for the failure to prevent the attacks from occurring. The CIA maintained its stance of noncooperation, even to the 9/11 Commission, while the FBI made a show of being, at long last, more cooperative.

In 1998, the FBI pilot in Oklahoma City had been concerned enough at the number of Middle Easterners taking flying lessons at the airport where he flew that he submitted an official memorandum about it. Unfortunately that information was never shared with FBI headquarters, though in theory it should have been accessible under the FBI's Automated Case Support System.

In July 2001, Special Agent Kenneth Williams, an experienced agent with sound investigative instincts, sent a five-page memo to FBI headquarters expressing concern for the number of Middle Eastern residents taking flight lessons in the area. Further, based upon his personal contacts with some of them, he had determined they were Islamic fundamentalists who openly expressed a great hatred for the U.S. He even reported that one of the students displayed a photograph of Osama bin Laden in his room, and that another had been in contact with Abu Zubaydah, a Palestinian responsible for operating bin Laden's terrorist training camps.

Though Williams clearly showed a tie between several of the students and al Qaeda or other radical groups closely aligned with bin Laden, his memorandum received little attention. In fact, Williams recommended that the FBI canvass flight schools nationwide to determine if there were similar instances of such activity. The request was declined.

On September 24, 2002, Michael Rolince, a deputy assistant director for the FBI's Terrorism Division, testified that it would have taken seventeen months for the FBI to make contact with the flight schools, obtain the names of Middle Eastern students, and collect visa information on them. That assertion is both absurdly wrong and misleading. There were often times during my career when field offices would receive a directive to conduct a nationwide investigation—for example, to contact all the dealerships of a particular make of a car. Each field office would quickly identify all those dealerships in its division and immediately dispatch agents to each one. The whole process took a day or two at the most, and I suspect there are far fewer flight schools in the U.S. than any number of organizations or businesses that the FBI had to contact in the past. Perhaps the verification of visa information would have taken longer, but certainly the seventeen months cited by Rolince is simply wrong.

Then there was the Minneapolis information on Zacarias Moussaoui, which was essentially an open letter from Special Agent Coleen Rowley to FBI Director Robert Mueller saying that FBI headquarters' failure to act on available information had led to the 9/11 tragedy. In August 2001 the owner of a Minneapolis flight school had expressed his alarm at Moussaoui's attitude while taking flight lessons: he wasn't interested in learning how to take off and land, only how to steer large jet aircraft.

That alarm was ignored. The Minneapolis request to search Moussaoui's computer after his arrest for INS violations was not granted until after the 9/11 attacks. While I am certain, given the swiftness of the approval to grant the search warrant for Moussaoui's computer, that there was no real change of probable cause, apparently someone decided (too late) that the predication was sufficient after all. Moussaoui was later arrested and charged with being the twentieth hijacker and is awaiting trial.

"THE FACTS SO FAR on the public record do not support the conclusion that these tragic events could have been prevented by the FBI and intelligence communities acting alone," FBI Director Louis Freeh said in his testimony before Congress on October 8, 2002. That was the first public statement he had made in the thirteen months following the attacks. What Freeh is essentially saying is that some terrorist attacks are simply not preventable. I do not accept that argument. For if the intelligence community had considered all the available information—and I am certain that all such information has not been made public—and if that information had received proper analysis, the attacks could have been prevented. While the 9/11 Commission, due to the political expediency of reaching a consensus by its members, refused to address the essential conclusion, I am convinced the attacks of 9/11 could have, and should have, been prevented, based on the information that has been publicly released, alone. Further, no one has suffered from the management and operational failures that led to the attacks being successful, an abhorrent situation that is simply unacceptable.

What exactly did the analysts have at their disposal? They had information going back to 1993 and the first World Trade Center bombing, indicating the existence of al Qaeda cells in the U.S. They had Operation Bojinka, proving al Qaeda's interest in aircraft as suicide weapons. There was even information from the French intelligence agency DGSE on a plot to crash an aircraft into the Eiffel Tower. Combine that with other reports from Oklahoma City, Phoenix, and Minneapolis, and I am convinced that even an average analyst would have concluded that al Qaeda was planning to use aircraft against U.S. targets. Admittedly, the evidence does not point specifically to September 11, but it would have given the FBI sufficient information to disrupt the project, if only by arresting those with INS violations and interviewing the others. And these terrorists have had a remarkable propensity to talk once arrested, certainly at a much higher rate than, for instance, members of the Mafia.

The embarrassments did not stop there. Michael Isikoff reported in the September 16, 2002, issue of *Newsweek* that in September 2000 an FBI informant had actually been living with two of the hijackers, Khalid Almihdhar and Nawaf Alhazmi, in San Diego. But the FBI had never made inquiries into their informant's roommates, a fact demonstrating, as I was quoted by Isikoff, "a lack of investigative curiosity." I could not imagine how anyone an informant was living with, regardless of what he was reporting on, would not be the object of some interest. In fact, it was the *informant* who told his contact agent in San Diego that he had roomed with the hijackers after he heard their names listed among the casualties when a plane hit the Pentagon.

As information began to develop about the hijackers, I became convinced that they were not the accomplished terrorists they were made out to be. In fact, I began to believe they were simply incredibly fortunate, not good. Seymour Hersh wrote an insightful article in the June 3, 2002, issue of the *New Yorker* detailing how actor James Woods had taken one of the same flights the terrorists later hijacked on 9/11. Woods noticed four individuals in first class who seemed so out of place that he expressed his concern to the cabin staff that the plane was going to be hijacked. The flight attendant shared his feeling, the captain was notified, and Woods was told that a report was made to the Federal Aviation Administration; whether it was or not is unclear.

The article reinforced my belief that the hijackers weren't particularly good compared with the spies I'd encountered personally during the

Cold War. They were far too obvious. They traveled in public together as a group; they got speeding tickets; their visas were expired; they flashed large wads of cash at their flight schools. All of this careless behavior brought attention to them. The good spy blends in with his surroundings and goes about his business unnoticed. He goes to great effort to not do anything that would attract attention. The hijackers violated virtually every precept of undercover operations, yet there was, particularly early on, an effort to make them into something they weren't.

I was quoted in the *New Yorker* about the "superman scenario." This is the idea that it is better to claim you have been beaten by accomplished terrorists than by a scruffy bunch of lucky amateurs, who accomplished their mission because of their willingness to die, as had been previously determined from Operation Bojinka, not because they were skilled operatives. Hersh also correctly quoted me stating, "These guys were not superhuman, but they were playing in a system that was more inept than they were." Nothing since then has changed that opinion either.

FBI Director Freeh's testimony before a congressional panel was preceded by a succession of agents from field offices who recounted their frustrations and anguish that their warnings about domestic terrorism were ignored. An agent from the New York field office, who testified behind a screen to hide his identity, had e-mailed lawyers in the FBI's National Security Law Unit on August 29, 2001—less than two weeks before the terrorist attacks—stating, "Someday someone will die—and [legal] wall or not—the public will not understand why we were not more effective and throwing every resource we had at certain 'problems.' Let's hope the National Security Law Unit will stand behind their decisions then, especially since the biggest threat to us now, UBL [Usama, or rather, Osama bin Laden], is getting the most 'protection.'" The agent had searched unsuccessfully for Khalid Almihdhar, one of the hijackers who crashed into the Pentagon.

Then there was the comment from a Minneapolis supervisory agent to his counterpart at FBI headquarters that the purpose of trying to get someone to pay attention to Zacarias Moussaoui was to ensure that

Moussaoui did not gain control of a plane and "fly it into the World Trade Center."

From behind his identity screen, the New York agent testified that after the 9/11 attacks he had seen the passenger lists of the flights and observed Almihdhar's name. He testified that he had yelled out, "This is the same Almihdhar we've been talking about for three months!" His supervisor simply responded, "We did everything by the book." I doubt the agent, and certainly the families of the 9/11 victims, found any consolation in that remark.

CHAPTER 2

THE RECRUIT

"By God, he does look like old [name of store owner]."
Officer Marvin Johnson, Monroe Police Department

I never considered a career with the FBI until shortly before I left my home in Monroe, Louisiana, for the new agent training facility at Quantico, Virginia, in the spring of 1973. But it was a career choice I felt comfortable with, because in my eyes the FBI stood for the ideals I had been raised to respect and those I believed the American people respected: honesty, patriotism, self-sacrifice, and justice. I felt fortunate, perhaps even unworthy, to have been accepted into the ranks of such an esteemed organization.

I grew up in rural Ouachita Parish, Louisiana, raised by paternal grandparents. I had gone to live with them when I was two, after my parents divorced at the end of World War II. I did not see my mother for the next thirteen years and only on rare occasions afterward; and though my father lived in adjoining Morehouse Parish, I saw him only infrequently. For all practical purposes, neither had any influence on my life.

We were poor in strictly economic terms, but our home was rich with love and laughter (especially from my grandfather) and guided by a strong sense of right and wrong. I learned the value of hard work and that, while there may be material rewards, the greatest reward was the sense of satisfaction in putting everything into a task and knowing I'd done everything I could to succeed.

I was taught a respect for others, especially for my elders, and even today I am prone to use "Sir" and "Ma'am" when addressing anyone I don't know well. I was also taught that the complete truth was the only answer to a question. There was a great love of country and respect for governmental institutions in my grandparents' household. They thought too that I should be prepared to serve my country in some capacity. While neither of them had ever been in public service, they laid the foundation for my career in public service by teaching those values. It was where I learned that to serve one's country is a small price to pay to live in this greatest of nations.

I joined the FBI after taking a rather torturous path from adolescence to adulthood. After my grandfather died in 1958, my grandmother and I lived with an aunt and uncle until I graduated from Calhoun High School in 1960. While we may have lacked in equipment and supplies, the teachers overall were simply excellent in imparting the fundamentals of education. Mr. Berlin Heck was a former boxer who taught literature. Through him I gained an appreciation for the subject as he read Shakespeare's *Julius Caesar* and made it so exciting and alive. And it was the librarian, Mrs. Aubyn Hayes (who also taught English), who encouraged me to read and recommended such classics as *The Count of Monte Cristo* and *Moby Dick* that revealed a much greater world outside insular and isolated Calhoun.

I was senior class president, had leading roles in class plays, and was a well-known basketball player under Coach Jerry Lovett, a transplanted Indiana native. Lovett had been a basketball star at Louisiana Tech and found a wife and home in northern Louisiana. I was the youngest member of my class, only a few months past seventeen. While I did not live in the stereotypical, harmonious 1960s nuclear family, I was familiar with one through my friend and classmate Clifton "Bunny" Gilliland and his sister Jenny, who was also my high school sweetheart. Though certainly not as perfect as the idyllic families of *Leave It to Beaver*, *Ozzie and Harriet*, *Father Knows Best*, and other TV shows of the time, the Gillilands gave me a family life to aspire to.

I learned lessons then that have lasted a lifetime: hard work and a sense of humor could offset the advantage of others financially better off; the more I knew the more I realized there was to learn; and telling the truth does not always have its immediate rewards. Once several of us pulled a few harmless pranks on a school trip. While I readily admitted my role, others lied about theirs. The principal knew they were lying, yet punished only those of us who confessed. I was suspended from the basketball team until the community created such a storm that I was reinstated. The couple of games I missed probably caused me to miss scoring over a thousand points in my career. While I never regretted being truthful, I did wonder at the inequity it brought.

After high school, I entered Northeast Louisiana State College on a partial basketball scholarship. The problem was that I couldn't pay the rest of the costs for room and board and other expenses. Though an acquaintance offered to pay them for me, I was not comfortable with the arrangement. Finally, in my second year, I decided that I had to either give up basketball and work my way through school or delay completing my degree. To be honest, I was restless and bored with college life. So I joined the U.S. Navy.

THE NEXT FOUR YEARS, one month, and twenty-seven days did indeed satisfy the curiosity I had for the world beyond where I grew up. I served on a destroyer escort, a submarine, and two destroyers, went to the Far East, and visited the great cities of the Midwest and West Coast of the United States: first Chicago and Milwaukee for training, then San Francisco, San Diego, Honolulu, and Hong Kong, as well as exotic countries including Guam, the Philippines, and Japan. My assignment aboard the *USS Razorback*, a World War II vintage diesel-electric submarine, was especially colorful and had an unexpected tie-in with my FBI service years later. Working conditions on submarines were grimy, space was cramped, hours were long, and I loved it. I worked hard and played hard, grew a mustache and goatee, and plied the sailor bars in San Diego and other ports where submariners were known for stirring things up whenever they arrived.

In San Francisco my crew members and I frequented the Horse and Cow, a seedy bar where no act of debauchery was off-limits. Later when I became familiar with counterintelligence matters, I thought of the Horse and Cow and how it would have been a tempting target for the Soviet military intelligence organization, the *Glavnoye Razvedyvatelnoye Upravlenie,* or GRU. Many times it was the last place crews gathered before embarking on secretive patrols and the first place they met to unwind after they returned. There was plenty of intelligence for well-trained ears: time at sea, itineraries, other ships encountered, and so forth. I'll always wonder what secrets might have been discovered in that dingy place.

When I was assigned to FBI headquarters in 1995 and the John Walker case broke open, I had a nagging feeling that his name was familiar. The Walker case, arguably the single espionage case that placed the U.S. in the greatest jeopardy during the Cold War, consisted of John Walker, a career Navy man and master Navy communications expert, his brother, son, and best friend. Together they passed more than an estimated one million secrets to the Soviet Union that included such items as communication codes, ship movements, weapon developments, plans, and tactics that compromised much of the U.S. and NATO advantage in technology and battle expertise in the crucial days of the Cold War. I knew he had been assigned to submarines and wondered if our paths might have crossed on the *Razorback.* I went to Bob Wade, assistant section chief of the Soviet section, who had a list of ships Walker had served on that showed he had indeed served aboard the *Razorback,* though he had gone by the time I arrived in January 1964. While I had no specific recollection of Walker, I did recall laughter about the "crazy radioman" who had been a member of the crew some months before I reported aboard.

AFTER MY ENLISTMENT I returned to Louisiana to be near my grandmother, even though I'd been approached by a scout from a small college in Washington state about playing basketball there. I reenrolled at Northeast Louisiana State College (today the University of Louisiana at

Monroe), drove a school bus, and began to work toward completing my degree on the GI Bill. Things changed, however, when I met and married my wife, Carla. Newlyweds couldn't live on a bus driver's salary and the GI Bill. Bob Lee, a college friend who later became a respected attorney, was a police reporter for the *Monroe Morning World* working afternoons and evenings. He wanted to take a day assignment and invited me to take his place on the police beat. That meant I could attend classes during the day and work at night. I went with him on his rounds one night to see if it was something I wanted to do.

At the Monroe Police Department, I met the assistant chief, H.B. "Yankee" Johnson. We began to talk, and before I left, he offered me a job making twenty-five dollars a month more than the newspaper was going to pay me, plus assurances that I could continue my education. In fact, the police chief, James Kelly, had implemented a novel plan that paid police officers more if they had college credits. The scale was $50 extra for the first thirty credit hours, $75 for sixty credit hours, $100 for ninety credit hours, and $150 for patrolmen with degrees. With the basic salary at about $400 a month, this was a substantial incentive to go to college.

Chief Kelly was a tough, innovative, and courageous officer who saw the future of education in law enforcement. He saw the future in other ways too. He confronted the Ku Klux Klan with the same fervor as he did Black Muslims; his attitude was simply that if they violated the law, they had to deal with him. He hired black police officers and, later, female police officers and displayed a farsightedness that was uncommon both then and now in most police executives. His example stayed with me throughout my law enforcement career. In particular, I learned that in an imperfect criminal justice system, the path to justice is not always easy, and that I must not let personal bias influence my professional behavior.

I took the job. After attending the basic police academy in Bunkie, Louisiana, I started out as a patrolman. I was assigned to a more senior patrolman and still recall my first call with him. The dispatcher advised two women were fighting at 1303-1/2 Washington Street. We drove up to the address and walked past the houses bordering the street to a house in the rear. There were two women there who had obviously been in a fight. Their clothes were torn and their hair was sticking out in every direction. An older woman was sitting on a porch swing holding a small child. We learned that one of the combatants had told the other, who was the mother of the child, that the child looked like the white owner of a nearby grocery store.

The officer walked up on the porch, looked at the child, and said, "By God, he does look like old [name of the store owner]." He then warned the women to quit fighting or he would arrest them for disturbing the peace, and we left. Somehow the incident failed to fit the image I held of the noble profession I had entered, but I soon learned that dealing with such issues was a great part of a police officer's life.

For several years I worked nights and went to school in the daytime, then worked days serving warrants and went to school at night. Police officers worked forty-eight hours a week and were not paid for time spent in court. It wasn't unusual for me to work from 10:00 PM to 6:00 AM, go home and change into a coat and tie, then return to Municipal Court for the day. If I had a class scheduled during court, I had to skip the class, make my court appearance, and head home to snatch a few hours of sleep before returning for the night shift.

I was transferred to the detectives, where I investigated burglaries, armed robberies, homicides, and other major offenses. This was when I met the FBI agents assigned to the Monroe Resident Agency. In particular, I had contact with Special Agents Jack Gilbert and Tom Fay, who encouraged me to apply for the FBI after I graduated from Northeast Louisiana University in May 1971. I initially ignored the application they gave me but finally got around to it after they kept badgering me. Carla helped me with the personal references and other paperwork, and eventually I returned the completed application to the agents.

MAY 20, 1973, was a gray, overcast day in Washington that seemed to reflect the mood of the city itself. Watergate was gaining momentum and the future of the Nixon presidency was beginning to be questioned. The Statler Hilton where I stayed was a couple of blocks across Lafayette Square from the White House, and that afternoon I spent time walking around the outer fence of 1600 Pennsylvania Avenue for the first time. There was a tent set up on the South Lawn, though there was no function under way at the time, and the White House had the appearance of being deserted that Sunday afternoon. The mansion itself seemed distant and forbidding.

I did not sleep much that night, as I was apprehensive yet excited about the path my life was about to take. The next morning, laden with luggage, I caught a cab to the Department of Justice to begin a new career. Assistant Director Thomas Jenkins, a large man with a formidable presence, swore us in, and suddenly I was an FBI agent. My career began that day with a president under siege for lying. Little could I have expected then that more than twenty-five years later on July 31, 1998, my retirement would come while another president was under siege for a similar transgression.

I was to have a much closer view of the second than of the first.

CHAPTER 3

BLUE-COLLAR AGENT

"I sold a baby."

FBI informant to I.C. Smith

Members of the New Agents Class (NAC) 13 reported to Quantico, Virginia, the afternoon of May 21, 1973. The facility there, the dream of legendary FBI director J. Edgar Hoover, was already impressive, though still unfinished. If only the training staff had been up to the same standards. I was proud of being a street cop who had made hundreds of arrests and encountered countless dangerous situations in the line of duty and therefore distrustful of career training officers. Theirs was a career apart from actual investigations and experience on the streets.

Some of my classmates were in the same situation. A number were former military personnel, and some had law enforcement experience. But many others brought very little in the way of life's experience to the FBI. I'm convinced that prior military or law enforcement experience brings an extra dimension to an agent's capability; they've been through a winnowing process others haven't.

Years later, when I was assigned to a command post at FBI headquarters during the time of the Oklahoma City bombing, I found myself looking at the FBI command staff with that same thought. Director Louis Freeh, Deputy Director Larry Potts, Criminal Division Director Bill Esposito, and National Security Division Director Bob Bryant were engaged in some discussion. Of the four, only Potts had prior combat military experience—Esposito and Bryant had none, while Freeh had been a reserve officer—and none had law enforcement experience. This is an unhealthy trend that has led to disastrous management decisions. There is something about having been under strict military discipline and personally exposed to danger that has a steadying influence on those who make decisions of life and death and that cannot be duplicated at Quantico.

My training there was a breeze both academically and physically. There was a lot of emphasis on firearms and physical fitness, and while these are absolutely necessary, the truth is most FBI agents never have to pull their weapons and the average FBI agent probably doesn't make a dozen arrests in his or her career. That is particularly true in today's FBI with its overuse of SWAT teams, which are called in for even the most routine of arrests. There's also an increasing tendency of United States attorneys to issue a summons for felony suspects even when there are tactical investigative advantages to arresting them as opposed to allowing them to simply report to the U.S. Marshal's Office.

The power of arrest carries an awesome responsibility, for it is the power to deprive a citizen of fundamental liberties that are the very foundation of our republic. As a police officer who worked in a tough part of Monroe, I knew the potential for abuse that power offered. Most of my classmates had not experienced anything comparable to serving in the military or being on a one-man patrol on the third shift. That was readily evident during discussions both in and out of class.

The FBI I joined back in 1973 had a blue-collar work ethic and took pride in long hours. The agents were, for the most part, first-generation college graduates, and many of them had worked their way through college as I had. I was surprised at how many had been working to get into the FBI for years and can only imagine the personal devastation of those who never made it—or worse, who went to Quantico and failed to make it to a field office. NAC 13 had a number of those.

After graduation, we departed to our respective field offices with little fanfare. We were issued .38-caliber revolvers, a bullet pouch with a half-dozen rounds of standard ammunition, our shiny new badges, and our credentials, and were ushered out the door with a handshake. I was assigned to the St. Louis Division and reported in on August 31, 1973. My wife Carla, our daughter Lara, and I had packed up and left Monroe with a bass boat in tow; little did I know I'd never use it again. We arrived in St. Louis without a place to stay or a friend to help us unpack. Relocation became commonplace over the next quarter of a century, but this first move had a special anxiety and excitement.

Carla got a job teaching in the Hazelwood School District, Lara was enrolled in school, and we settled into a home in Spanish Lake, north of St. Louis near the Mississippi River. I was assigned to Lou Caputo's squad, where Larry Cordell gave me advice that I used my first day. I reported into the office in mid-afternoon, but Cordell told me that if I stayed for 109 minutes past 5:00 PM, I would qualify for overtime right away. In 1973, FBI agents were paid overtime equal to 25 percent of a GS (Government Service)-10's salary, the pay rank for entering FBI agents. Though I reported for duty in the middle of the afternoon on the last day of the month, by staying until 6:49 PM I met the standard of averaging 109 extra minutes every day I worked that month and immediately qualified for overtime pay. I learned a valuable first-day lesson: listen to the senior agents, for their insights yielded important career—and in my case, financial—lessons.

THE SPECIAL AGENT IN CHARGE (SAC) in St. Louis was Robert Kunkel, a former favorite of J. Edgar Hoover who had later gotten crossways with acting director L. Patrick Gray and been banished to the Midwest. Kunkel was miserable there and never even moved his family to join him. Consequently, he sometimes made life miserable for the rest of us. He wore starched white shirts, and I never saw him walking through the office with his suit coat off.

Kunkel held biweekly payday conferences where he discussed various items from FBI headquarters and the field office. One such day, he observed that the office floors had been recently scrubbed and waxed. He insisted that a part of each Friday afternoon be spent cleaning up the office, as did most FBI field offices in those days. The longer he talked about the importance of cleanliness, the redder his face got. After the tirade ended, employees were tiptoeing about their work when I noticed an agent dribbling coffee across the freshly polished floor. Agent Don Jones was exceptionally resourceful but went his own way. In later years I learned someone like that could be a manager's nightmare, but the best thing to do was give them the latitude to use their skills to their best advantage. It was the Don Joneses who made the reputation of the FBI, not the timid souls whose primary goal was to avoid controversy and advance their careers.

Like the FBI in general, the St. Louis office was undergoing a transition. William Ruckelshaus was the acting director following L. Patrick Gray's departure, after which President Nixon did something good for the FBI by appointing Clarence Kelley as permanent director. Some changes were only cosmetic, such as allowing agents to wear colored shirts and even go to offices without a coat and tie. But other changes were substantial and lasting: minorities were recruited, women were joining the ranks, and the FBI was moving to investigate more complex matters thanks to new legislation such as the Racketeering Influenced and Corrupt Organization (RICO) and Interstate Transportation to Aid Racketeering (ITAR) statutes.

My first case as an FBI agent was a little less glamorous, known officially as "Theft of 6 Jackets and 7 Shirts from Southwest Transportation Truck Lines, 9/14-17/73, Theft from Interstate Shipment." When I grumbled that I had worked better cases as a police detective in Monroe, a senior agent named Bob Stewart advised me cases like this were something to keep me busy until the "big one" came along. He was absolutely right. One of the great strengths of the FBI in 1973 and today is its ability to marshal resources quickly to concentrate on a single large and complex investigation. The attacks that occurred on the United States on September 11, 2001, provided ample evidence of the FBI's ability in those areas, even as it fell tragically short in other ways.

While there was little the FBI could teach me about basic investigations, I did have to learn about the paperwork and methodologies unique to the Bureau. Even more important, the time in St. Louis also taught me about the camaraderie within the organization. In fact, I developed a great appreciation for that camaraderie in Mike's Bar. The Court Plaza Bar, somehow known as Mike's Bar, was located about a block from the FBI office and next to a lot where most agents parked their vehicles. Parking there was inexpensive, with payment on something of an honor system, and I always believed it was set up that way to lure us into the bar. If that was the goal, they were quite successful. Any occasion was an excuse to stop in, and it wasn't infrequent that stopping for "just one" lasted until closing time. We used that time to size one another up and see who could be counted on in a crisis, and it was in Mike's Bar that I began to feel that I was part of the FBI.

After a time, the field office opened a resident agency at Lambert-St. Louis International Airport, and I was chosen to staff it along with Peter Symonds and Ed Moreland. Moreland was a senior agent who had been in St. Louis for a long time and seemed to know, and was known by, just about everyone that mattered in the area. Symonds, originally from around Boston, had taught high school before joining the FBI. This was during a time when the FBI was energetically working to combat the large number of aircraft hijackings in the United States. St. Louis was especially tough at its security checkpoints, and we were on constant call to investigate the slightest violation. Calls came invariably on weekends, holidays, and late at night, and the duty agent had to respond to every single incident no matter how insignificant, from carrying a concealed weapon to making some joking reference about a bomb.

I met some interesting people answering these calls. I met St. Louis Cardinal running back Terry Metcalf as he was on the way to the Pro Bowl in January, 1976, after he was reported to have made some joking reference to a bomb in his carry-on luggage. Metcalf later paid a civil fine. I also met Julius Erving, the Hall of Fame basketball player, who had a tape knife in his carry-on luggage, which he used to cut the tape he wrapped around his ankles before games. Erving was quiet, articulate, and cooperative during his interview with me and two other agents. While I did not allow celebrity to influence how I investigated those calls, I must admit I have a photograph of me standing next to Erving in the FBI office at the St. Louis airport.

My tour at the airport also allowed me to meet one of the true gentlemen I have known in my life, Supreme Court Justice Henry Blackmun. Justice Blackmun was a friend of FBI Director William Webster, and on occasion, when Justice Blackmun traveled through St. Louis to change planes between his home in Minneapolis and Washington, I would meet him and visit with him in one of the airport VIP lounges until his next flight. On the several occasions I had conversations with him, I was always surprised at how small and frail Blackmun looked, but I also became aware of a great inner strength and the certainty of his beliefs. But I also had a continuing concern for his safety. After he wrote the Supreme Court's majority opinion in the landmark abortion case, *Roe vs. Wade*, Blackmun had been demonized by those who did not agree with the Court, though Blackmun himself seemed to be mystified by the hatred directed at him by that decision.

I also met Clarence Kelley and instantly liked him. At the time he was named FBI director, his wife was ill and remained in Kansas City. Kelley would periodically fly from Washington to Kansas City, and when he had to change planes in St. Louis, we would be notified at the airport.

On occasion, Kelley would have short layovers and insist that he just remain at the departure gate. Kelley did not travel with an entourage, as did later directors, and usually traveled alone, carrying his firearm as was expected of all agents traveling on airlines. One evening I met him alone, and he kept telling me, "Go home to your wife and girls, I'll be all right." But I demurred, explaining I had been told to stay with him until his flight departed and asking if he wanted me to get in trouble with my SAC. He responded, "I won't tell him, go on home," but I stayed anyway. During this time, Kelley had an operation on his arm for cancer and wore a sling. He was attempting to perform his duties as director of his beloved FBI while looking after his dying wife half a continent away. I still have vivid memories of Kelley boarding a TWA flight, arm in sling, literally pulling himself up the stairs to the plane with the other arm due to fatigue.

I did not know it at the time of course, but years later Kelley and I would have a common interest in the welfare of Eva and Morris Childs and Operation Solo when I worked in Miami and they were hiding nearby. They always spoke fondly, even with some reverence, when Kelley's name was mentioned and were ever grateful for the personal attention he gave to their situation. Kelley's contributions to the country and the FBI have been underappreciated and accolades due him were never given until after his death; even then they were insufficient.

MY GREATEST SATISFACTION in St. Louis came from working with informants, including one career criminal with a long scar running from the upper part of his chest down below his waistline, who seemed to wear shirts open just to expose the hideous mark. I would meet him alone in various dives, usually along the Missouri River, spend hours with him, and sometimes receive information of some value.

He said he was a prison acquaintance of James Earl Ray in the Missouri State Penitentiary and had nothing but disdain for Ray's criminal prowess. He said Ray had bungled most of the jobs he had tried except for his escape from prison. He took issue with the accepted version of the story that Ray hid in a bread box that was loaded into a truck. The informant took a napkin and drew a rough outline of the penitentiary compound, showing a spot that was invisible from the guard posts due to a reduction in the number of guards that the prison did not want to admit had happened. He said Ray simply climbed the wall where he couldn't be seen by the understaffed guard detail and ran away.

I asked him if he thought Ray had killed Dr. Martin Luther King, and he stated he had no personal knowledge of the matter but believed he had done so in order to have some stature in the criminal world. He explained that Ray had been low in the prison pecking order due to his ineptness at being a criminal (for example, the oft-told story of Ray trying to rob a bank in St. Peters, Missouri, and dropping his gun in the lobby), and it was important for Ray to be a big shot in the eyes of the other prisoners. And yes, he was capable of the murder. He regarded Ray as having few emotions.

Sometimes an informant's story revealed unexpected connections. On Sunday, September 12, 1976, an auxiliary police officer named Fred Bergmann was killed during a burglary in downtown St. Charles, Missouri. The St. Charles police were having little luck in solving the murder. The following May I got a phone call, at home, from a St. Charles County deputy sheriff saying a robbery suspect, who was from out of state and wanted in several jurisdictions, was in the St. Charles jail. He thought I might want to talk to him. So on a Sunday afternoon, I decided to pay him a visit.

After he and I spent quite some time getting to know each other and feeling each other out, the prisoner began to cooperate. Among other things, he told me that he and a local resident named Benny Russo had been planning a robbery and Russo was teaching him how to react if the police arrived on the scene. Russo had gone on to describe how he had been in a building recently when a police officer arrived and had reacted by killing the officer. The description was identical to Bergmann's murder. It turned out Russo was the alias of Benjamin Rosado, a New York killer who had entered the Witness Protection Program and, incredibly, been relocated to St. Charles. But even with Rosado's involvement in Bergmann's murder, a New York Strike Force attorney named Mike Carey delayed the prosecution by calling and angrily accusing me of blowing Rosado's cover.

Tom Smith, a St. Louis Drug Enforcement Administration agent familiar with Rosado from a previous assignment in New York, told me Rosado entered the Witness Protection Program after he was to testify against other members of a group who were charged with killing a DEA informant. Smith felt he should have been told that Rosado had been relocated in St. Charles, particularly since he believed Rosado himself had killed the informant. My boss, however, Special Agent in Charge Harlan Phillips, said I was spending too much time on the case. But I continued to help the police anyway and simply neglected to write what I was doing on my "3 card," the card agents filled out every day indicating where they would be, when, and whom they were contacting. Benjamin Rosado was subsequently convicted of Bergmann's murder.

FEW CASES HAVE STAYED with me as personally as one that came to light when I was interviewing a prospective informant about a burglary ring. I thought I had exhausted his knowledge of thefts of horse trailers, farm machinery, expensive horses, and so forth, when he looked at me and stated, "There is something else."

From his tone I thought he was about to tell me about a murder. But I wasn't even close.

"I sold a baby," he said.

He explained he was dealing in stolen heavy equipment with a well-to-do individual in Mississippi and learned that this man and his wife could not have children, though they desperately wanted to. He also had an acquaintance in St. Louis with an infant daughter, born out of wedlock, that she could not care for and did not want. The informant and his brother simply bundled the child up in a blanket and took her to Mississippi. He had been paid a few hundred dollars but said he would have done it for free since the child would have a much better life in Mississippi than she could expect in St. Louis.

I asked him if he had seen the child since, and he told me of driving past a large and expensive house in Mississippi a couple of years later and seeing the child out in the big front yard. She was playing in the grass, wearing nice clothes, and obviously happy and well cared for by the well-to-do adoptive parents.

I returned to the office and, after some thought, decided to have a little fun. I called for Jim Christy, the squad supervisor, who took my call on a speaker phone in the office of Harlan Phillips, the SAC. I told Christy I needed to ask his assistance in determining the recovery value of an item I would have to claim on a statistical sheet we were required to keep. He asked what the item was.

"A baby," I told him.

It got quiet on the other end of the phone. Then Phillips cut off the speaker and got on the phone privately. I agreed to get "more details" before we decided how to handle the matter. That was the last word anybody ever said about it.

AIRLINE EXTORTION THREATS were not uncommon at a busy airport like St. Louis. One day, TWA received a call demanding that a suitcase of money be placed over a storm drain in a certain apartment complex. Bob LaVere and I drew the assignment to set up a stakeout in the drain. We headed straight from the office in our coats and ties, not looking forward to sitting in a storm drain in the damp, cold weather. We discussed the incident with TWA officials, including their security chief, my friend Dick Bennett, a retired Kansas City police detective and a personal favorite of Clarence Kelley. When I explained our lack of enthusiasm for the plan, particularly when this threat had all the earmarks of a harmless prank, Bennett left briefly then returned with several single-serving miniature bottles of scotch and bourbon.

LaVere and I descended into the storm drain, the bottles clinking as I walked down the ladder. Once down in the drain, I advised LaVere what I had in my pockets. It worked out well, since LaVere drank scotch and I drank bourbon. After a couple of bottles, the cold didn't seem to penetrate as badly as before. As the evening wore on, no extortionist showed up, but the SAC would not call off the operation. LaVere and I continued to find warmth in the miniatures. Finally, well into the evening, a couple of agents came to the drain and shouted down through the darkness and chill, "We're calling it off."

"Hell no," we hollered back, "we aren't ready to quit!"

This, of course, was not the response they expected, and it was not until the drain lid was lifted that they saw the miniatures scattered around and the reason we weren't ready to give up.

IN SPITE OF OCCASIONAL HUMOR, the job took its toll. At times I went for days without seeing little Lara and her new baby sister, Amy, when they were awake. I would go home late in the evening and be gone again by daylight. It was an unfair schedule to Carla and the girls and certainly not what I had envisioned when I had long ago looked forward to having my own family.

The FBI can be a demanding and jealous mistress. It's easy to become seduced. There were times when I was clearly in danger of succumbing to the lure of the organization and, in the process, losing sight of the importance of family. Perhaps that was what Clarence Kelley was trying to tell me when he insisted I leave him alone at the airport and go home to my family. But the family and I persevered; I came to treasure the time we had together and never take it for granted.

On February 17, 1978, Roy Klager, the SAC, called me into his office and gave me an envelope. As he handed it to me, he said in his wonderful radio announcer voice that he hoped I was pleased. It was my transfer letter to the Washington field office. I told him that yes, I was, in fact, pleased. The following weeks were a blur. Carla and I made plans to move and decided she and the girls would stay in St. Louis until school was out so she and Lara could finish the school year. On April 8, without my family but with a healthy dose of Bureau esprit de corps that would follow me for the remainder of my career, I took a flight for Washington, first-class upgrade courtesy of TWA.

I didn't realize I was departing St. Louis at a time when it was still possible to have laughter in the FBI, and that those days were coming to an end. There was a great joy then attached to simply doing a good job, a feeling that seemed to diminish ever more rapidly in the years ahead.

CHAPTER 4

CHINESE TAKEOUT

"Spies are the most important element of war."
Sun Tzu in *The Art of War*

I reported to the Washington field office shortly after it had been moved from the old post office on Pennsylvania Avenue to Buzzards Point on the Anacostia River. It was an abysmal location, far off the beaten path, its only redeeming feature being free parking in the muddy areas nearby. Even the building was substandard, with shoddy workmanship that became more obvious over time as equally poor maintenance took its toll. I arrived during the ABSCAM investigation into the activities of elected officials on Capitol Hill, which brought attention and controversy to the FBI. This timely and courageous investigation was conducted out of the dismal confines of Buzzards Point; the running joke was that Congress would probably never let the FBI move as payback for exposing their high jinks.

I found myself working in areas where I had scant experience, but investigations are basically the same regardless of the violation, and I felt confident I could handle the change. The squad supervisor was Elmer Todd, an old-time supervisor with over forty agents assigned to him. After an initial few days spent getting to know my way around, I was assigned a role in a public corruption investigation involving several congressmen and other powerful figures in the Washington area. Due to the success of the ABSCAM case, the Bureau had gained both skills and confidence in conducting that type of investigation. I worked principally with two case managers: Tom Marsh, whose smallness of stature belied a very real strength and commitment to doing the job; and Dan Sullivan, a big, outgoing former state trooper and hospital administrator who was an extraordinarily competent agent.

The investigation had taken off after a Capitol Hill staff member, Stephen Elko, got into a bind and decided to cooperate with the FBI and the strike force at the Department of Justice. He detailed freewheeling corruption, principally within the House of Representatives, that had become a standard way of doing business. This corruption was controlled by a political seniority system that went unchallenged. The principles included such colorful characters as Daniel Flood, a powerful Democratic representative from Pennsylvania and former Shakespearean actor who sported a long flowing cape, handlebar mustache, and silver tipped cane, and Otto Passman, the Democratic congressman from the Louisiana district where I grew up.

The case proceeded under the guidance of the Department of Justice strike force and, in particular, John Dowd, a large, red-faced man who later represented Major League Baseball in its gambling case against Pete Rose. Dowd and his staff gave us full support in conducting aggressive investigations that were ultimately successful—in marked contrast to the investigations I would be engaged in later headed by other DOJ attorneys. Ultimately, Flood and several others were convicted. Passman, who had been indicted on income tax charges among other things, invoked his right to be tried in his home district thanks to an oversight by the Department of Justice. He was acquitted, but his political career was over. After growing up in Louisiana, where we expect our politicians to provide at least a modicum of entertainment, I was sad to see him and his colorful colleagues pass from the scene.

As the corruption investigation was nearing completion, I visited with Ken Schiffer, an old acquaintance who was on the Chinese foreign counterintelligence squad. Schiffer, a former schoolteacher originally from Wyoming, learned Chinese after entering the Bureau. He was an accomplished and innovative agent known as "Cowboy" for his fondness of roping cows and riding his quarter horse, Bill. I told Schiffer I was ready for a change and felt I would like to try foreign counterintelligence work. Schiffer made the introduction to Larry Torrence, a seasoned agent who had handled Soviet Union counterintelligence matters until being promoted to supervisor of the Chinese foreign counterintelligence squad. My request for transfer was approved, and on March 19, 1979, I left the sunshine of criminal investigations for the counterintelligence world of shadows.

I learned more from experienced agents on the squad and my own research than I did in the counterintelligence classroom. I had visited Hong Kong in the Navy and had long been interested in the Far East. I took informative courses at the Department of State and the Department of Defense that gave me a greater awareness of Chinese culture, history, and geography. That led to my introduction to Sun Tzu's *The Art of War*, a book that should be required reading for anyone in command positions, especially those in the military and in intelligence or counterintelligence work.

After Torrence's promotion to FBI headquarters in the fall of 1980, I was selected to replace him, pending successful completion of a management aptitude program course at Quantico. I passed the course without contingencies and was promoted to supervise the squad, though many on the squad were senior to me both in time in the FBI and in counterintelligence experience. It was then that I became engaged in one of the most important espionage cases, and certainly the single most important Chinese spy case, in the history of the FBI.

As I ENTERED Larry Torrence's office at headquarters, after he had called and asked that I drop by, he skipped the customary banter between friends and went directly to the topic at hand. He stressed the need for absolute secrecy, advising me to discuss the matter only with my supervisors and whomever I assigned the case to back at the Washington field office. Torrence handed me a single piece of paper, not even filled halfway, but the brief statement was a blockbuster: the

Central Intelligence Agency reported receiving information that the CIA had been penetrated, an incursion that had been going on for years. The information was sketchy—just a few notes about a government employee suspected of spying and when he had traveled in the past. The only clue to his identity was that he was ethnic Chinese. In violation of past agreements with the Department of Justice and the FBI, the CIA had failed to report the security breach and spent months in a fruitless attempt to find the mole on its own. Moreover, the CIA inferred that the spy had to be an FBI employee since they were confident, based upon their internal investigation, that it wasn't one of theirs. Torrence had given the case the codename "Eagle Claw."

Driving back to Buzzards Point I thought about the nature of the assignment. While our counterintelligence agents had been able to convince many in the FBI and in government of the threat posed by the Chinese, we did not have a significant case to demonstrate their capabilities. If successful, this case would provide a great boost to the Chinese counterintelligence program—ample evidence of the threat posed by what was still a new and strange adversary completely unlike the Soviet Union and its Warsaw Pact allies.

The penetration of an adversary's operation is the ultimate goal in foreign intelligence, and from all indications, the Chinese had succeeded masterfully. The results could be devastating. At the time, it was incomprehensible to me that the CIA could itself be spied upon, though that view changed dramatically in later years. I knew if the source in the CIA was well placed, then lives had certainly been lost due to his betrayal. Sun Tzu had written centuries before the birth of Christ, "What enables the wise sovereign and the good general to strike and conquer, and achieve things beyond the reach of ordinary men is foreknowledge." Further Sun Tzu stated, "Knowledge of the enemy's dispositions can only be obtained from other men," and, "Spies are a most important element of war." I had no doubt that the People's Republic of China would aggressively seek to obtain the "foreknowledge" Sun Tzu advised. I knew almost certainly that they would select ethnic Chinese to do their work, expecting their loyalties would be to China first, not the United States—a blood bond was stronger than politics or citizenship. Chinese Americans would be aggressively targeted with appeals to help the motherland, especially their own village and family.

I assigned Thomas J. Carson, an Alabama native with years of experience in Chinese counterintelligence, as the case agent. He was respected by his peers and had a remarkable ability to mine information from dormant files, analyzing methodically and accurately. The CIA had tried for months without success to make the identity. I doubted they had given us all available information in the sketchy report Torrence handed me. But I felt confident that Carson, aided by other agents in New York and Torrence at FBI headquarters, would be able to succeed where they had failed.

Because of the complexity of the case, the length of time the spy had been at work, and the CIA's reluctance, I expected this to be a slow-moving investigation. Yet within the amazingly short span of four months, Tom Carson put a name to our mysterious interloper: Larry Wu-tai Chin, sixty-one years old, recently retired after more than three decades of U.S. government service, and still on the payroll as a contract employee.

The breakthrough came in a tiny needle of information in the enormous haystack of data that Carson and his team were sifting through. Thanks to an unidentified source providing information from within China, we knew that the spy had traveled to China over a certain period of time, but that there had been flight problems. Our source discovered that in February 1982 the spy went to China, but his original flight schedule was interrupted by a delay or cancellation.

This was where Carson's tenacity and attention to minutiae paid off. Without knowing exactly what he was looking for, he began reviewing contacts with the Chinese embassy in Washington and found an obscure contact with a Chinese official that coincided with the time frame of the spy's original date of departure. The contact with the official was somewhat out of the ordinary, in that private U.S. citizens don't normally call an official from a foreign embassy in the U.S. and ask for advice when their travel plans are interrupted. This simple breach of security provided the first clue to the identity of Chin. Chin's arrival date in China was identical to the date of the spy's arrival; a cross-check of U.S. Customs records for returning passengers revealed Chin's identity.

The CIA officially confirmed that Chin was a former employee who had retired from the Foreign Broadcast Information Service in January 1981 but had been retained on a contract basis since his retirement. As we worked, the full magnitude of Chin's betrayal became apparent.

Chin had originally been employed by the government of the United States in 1944. This was during the time not only of the final push to defeat the Japanese in the Pacific but also of the death struggle in China between Mao Tse-tung's Communist forces and the Kuomintang (KMT) Army of Chiang Kai-shek. Chin had already thrown in his lot with the Communists, even though he was working as a translator for the U.S. Army liaison office in Fuzhou, China, and his American employers were officially supportive of Chiang Kai-shek and the KMT.

In Fuzhou, Chin had roomed with a fellow employee of the Army, Doctor Wang Li. Wang was a committed Communist, though due to the Kuomintang dominance of mainland China, at the time Communism was not openly promoted. In effect, Wang was underground. It was the influence of the mysterious Dr. Wang that convinced Chin to cooperate with the Communists of Mao Tse-tung years before Chiang Kai-shek was forced to flee the mainland for Taiwan, indoctrinating him with the idealistic aims of the Chinese Communist Party. Chin could have bought the Communist line, or he could simply have been hedging his bets. As a respected employee of the U.S. Army, he would have been protected if Mao's armies were defeated; if Mao won though, he would have been one of the many loyal Chinese Communists who secretly aided the revolution.

After the war in China ended in 1948, Chin was transferred to the U.S. consulate in Shanghai as an interpreter. That was where Chin entered into a more formal relationship with the Communists of Mao Tse-tung. Doctor Wang introduced Chin to the Shanghai police and another Mr. Wang, who prevailed upon Chin to work directly for the Communists who had just come to power in the country. Thus the course was set for decades of spying against the very country that had provided him a livelihood far beyond anything he could have expected had he remained in China.

After the Communists pushed Chiang's forces onto the island of Formosa (present-day Taiwan), the U.S. severed relations with the newly formed People's Republic of China. In 1949, Chin was transferred to Hong Kong to serve as a secretary and interpreter, then to Korea, in 1951, during the Korean War to interview Chinese prisoners of war. There, he was in a position to identify not only those who cooperated with United Nations forces but also, more importantly, those who were willing to be inserted into China as American spies. When Chin returned to Hong Kong in early 1952, he passed that information to the agents of the PRC, with the result that those spies were caught and executed. For Chin, life was cheap; he was paid only $2,000 for his act of betrayal, a relatively paltry amount even in those days. Chin very likely also identified the CIA personnel in Hong Kong who were under official (diplomatic) cover, as well as others cooperating with Americans there.

Tragic as the betrayal of Chinese POWs was, that treason pales when compared to the number of American soldiers and other United Nations personnel who died because of Chin's treachery involving the Korean armistice itself. A major negotiating point for China was the issue of forcible repartition. Chin was in the perfect position to provide the Chinese with the U.S. position on that issue, which in turn caused the war to drag on and U.S. military personnel to continue to be killed, wounded, and captured as the Chinese maneuvered for better leverage. Thanks to Chin, the Chinese knew exactly how to take advantage of American interests.

The compromise of sources is a constant worry for the intelligence community, and history teaches us that human failures, not technical, mechanical, or logistical faults, lead to most compromises. That was the case here with those who had been persuaded to return to China to work for America against the Communists: they were betrayed from within the very organization that had recruited them. It became apparent to the CIA during the Korean conflict that spies recruited from among Chinese prisoners were being caught regularly inside the PRC. But no one ever considered the common denominator of Larry Chin, a valued employee who spoke four Chinese dialects and was always eager to help his American employers.

In 1952, Chin was assigned to the Foreign Broadcast Information Service on Okinawa. The FBIS, an arm of the CIA, monitored Chinese radio broadcasts and publications for news and events in which the U.S. might have an interest. One of the great misconceptions about intelligence is that all information of value must come from highly classified sources. Not so. For instance, we didn't have to rely on in-country secret sources to monitor the seismic events of China's Cultural Revolution—what was occurring, who was responsible, who was being purged—yet the expert analysis of such events was just as rewarding as information from clandestine sources.

While the work of monitoring public information is unclassified, it inevitably provides indirect access to classified information. There are always tidbits of information to glean from casual conversations with colleagues, a quick glimpse (or more) of a classified document being mishandled, or even a careless slip or lapse in judgment on the part of someone with access to protected information. In at least one case, an employee handed Chin a classified document and asked him his opinion of it.

Given human nature, it is practically impossible to avoid some compromises if people without official access are working in an area where classified material is circulated. Chin was not yet a U.S. citizen and therefore could not receive a security clearance. But his multiple moves, his past work on intelligence-related matters, and his willingness to be helpful provided him with an aura of loyalty that would have been easy to exploit.

As an employee whose home was still officially in Hong Kong, Chin was allowed to travel back there periodically; the government actually paid for such trips every other year. So Chin had the ability to travel to Hong Kong at U.S. government expense at least four times between 1952 and 1961, when he could meet with representatives of the Chinese intelligence services. It was during those years that Chin began to spend time with his principal handler, Ou Qiming, a name that would be used to the FBI's advantage years later.

In 1961 Chin was transferred by the FBIS to Santa Rosa, California, where he continued to spy. Between 1961 and 1970 he made six trips to Hong Kong, receiving money from Ou on four occasions. By now, Chin had the best of both worlds: he was earning a good wage in a respected and responsible position with the U.S. government, yet he was also a valued spy for his mother country. He had been able to provide essential information to the Chinese without even having a security clearance. But that little inconvenience was about to be addressed.

In 1965 Chin became an American citizen and continued to work with FBIS until 1970, when he was eligible for a security clearance. That process involved both a background investigation—not especially problematic for Chin as there was no way for anyone to conduct a background investigation in China—and a polygraph. Though Chin admitted many of the things that were very likely known to CIA investigators (i.e. that he was a womanizer, gambled, had domestic difficulties, and had traveled frequently to Hong Kong), incredibly, Chin was granted a security clearance. He was given official access to both CIA headquarters and highly classified documents that had, officially at least, so far eluded his grasp.

By the time Chin received his security clearance, he had been a Communist Chinese spy for over a quarter of a century without detection or apparent suspicion. One can imagine the elation in Beijing when Ou Qiming reported that Chin had been granted a security clearance allowing routine access not only to secret documents but also to actual case officers from the CIA's Directorate of Operations. He was then able to review incoming reports on China from well-placed sources around the world, as well as documents from all throughout the U.S. government, including the Department of Defense and the Department of State. Among these documents were National Intelligence Estimates, or NIEs, reports derived from the totality of information from agencies within the intelligence community and issued with great secrecy and little fanfare by the National Foreign Intelligence Board.

Years later, when I represented the FBI on the NFIB and observed firsthand the machinations of that select group, I thought more than once of Chin and his access, and how he had, for all practical purposes, penetrated that highly secretive group itself.

CHAPTER 5

CODENAME EAGLE CLAW

"It was worth it."

Larry Wu-tai Chin

In the summer of 1970, with one single document, Larry Chin repaid the Chinese for everything they had invested in him over the years. If he had never sent them another word, this one coup made a quarter-century of spying worthwhile.

Chin somehow gained access to a document that outlined President Richard Nixon's intentions, terms, and strategies for reaching out to China in an attempt to reestablish diplomatic relations. This information outlined the very thoughts and intentions of the president. Chin had, in essence, penetrated the Oval Office itself.

The faithful spy then took what might seem to be an extreme risk, though in practice it wasn't especially dangerous: he secretly carried the document home, photographed it, then returned it to the office the next day. FBIS employees were not routinely subjected to searches of their packages, much less their person. Chin simply strolled out of the building at the normal time and returned the next morning as usual, while carrying this extraordinary document the same way he very likely carried many others over the years.

Chin's normal means of communication with the Chinese (outside of his occasional trips to the Orient) was to contact them in Hong Kong, then bring undeveloped film of secret documents to a designated shopping mall in Toronto. A Mr. Li met him there, took the film, and carried it back to Hong Kong for developing and analysis. This is classic intelligence agency tradecraft, which the Chinese faithfully follow in their many U.S. spy operations, never to meet a source in the source's home country.

Knowing President Nixon's game plan for Chinese normalization was an absolutely astounding coup for China, and a disaster for the United States. Not only did the Chinese have information in advance of the U.S. overtures, but in subsequent communications that Chin could access, they had information detailing the U.S. negotiating position as the normalization process evolved. Chin made five trips to Canada between 1978 and March 1981, the last one two months after his retirement from the CIA. After each trip, approximately $7,000 (translated into U.S. funds) was deposited in his Hong Kong bank account. Another $5,000 was deposited after he traveled to Hong Kong in the summer of 1981. These were simply paltry amounts for the considerable damage Chin was doing.

When I saw my first photograph of this exceptional spy, he didn't look the part. He was slight of build with thinning hair, wore wire-rimmed glasses, and looked anything but the picture of the super spy who had penetrated the very inner sanctum of the United States' best-known intelligence agency. He would be largely unnoticed in a group. While the popular notion of a spy is more akin to Ian Fleming's James Bond character, the really effective spy is closer to George Smiley, a principal character in John LeCarre's *The Spy Who Came In From the Cold*, who "was short and rather plump. He had glasses and wore odd, expensive clothes; he was a kindly, worried little man and Liz trusted him somehow without knowing why." It is essential that a spy does not bring attention to himself, and Chin had honed that persona to perfection.

As the investigation intensified, the FBI began to watch Chin closely. He had retired abruptly from the CIA in January 1981. I believe he was concerned about his ability to continue eluding the inevitable polygraph test. He told his Chinese handlers his retirement was driven by fear that his wife, Cathy, would expose him, explaining she was trying to catch him having an affair with another woman. Actually that had already occurred. His wife had caught Chin in bed with another woman, and though she confronted them with her discovery, the lovers ignored her and continued their activities. The wife telephoned an acquaintance for advice, who said she should pour a bucket of water on them to cool their ardor. Unfortunately, I didn't learn whether she took her friend's advice, but clearly the reason he gave his handlers for his retirement was not truthful.

Chin waited a year after retirement, as required for former U.S. government employees with secret clearances, to travel to Beijing. In November 1981 Chin met Ou in London to discuss an upcoming trip to the Chinese capital. In February 1982 Chin traveled to Beijing where he again met with his handler and, on this occasion, dignitaries from the Ministry of Public Security as well. There he was feted and praised by a succession of ministers.

But the MPS did more during that trip than just toast him with glasses of the fiery Chinese liquor mou tai, sing his praises, and give him an honorary rank of deputy bureau chief. They also arranged for just under $40,000 to be deposited in his Hong Kong bank account, sort of a golden parachute for a job well done.

THEN CHIN MADE another mistake. The Bureau had information that on a previous trip to Beijing, the spy had stayed in room 533 of the Qianmen Hotel. This little detail was filed away in the memory of FBI Case Agent Tom Carson. Then we learned that Chin was to depart Washington on May 31, 1983, for Hong Kong. FBI agents arranged to search his luggage for documents, but what they found was a key to room 533 of the Qianmen Hotel. We knew that the unidentified spy had stayed in room 533. Now we knew Chin had a key to that room. If there had been any doubts that Chin was the spy, this incident erased them.

By the time Chin took his trip, I had been promoted to FBI headquarters in the Chinese Unit and, for a while, was not directly involved in Eagle Claw, though I was periodically briefed by Torrence. I later resumed work on the case as headquarters manager after Torrence's transfer. By then our goal was to collect enough proof of probable cause to apply for electronic surveillance on Chin. After a lengthy trip through the FBI and Justice Department bureaucracy, our request reached the Foreign Intelligence Surveillance Court, a secretive court of federal judges established in 1978 under the Foreign Intelligence Surveillance Act to consider applications by government agencies, principally the FBI, for wiretaps and search warrants to collect foreign intelligence information.

On the appointed day, I was ushered into the sealed vault where applications to the FISC are heard. There were only four people in the room: the judge, a recorder, an attorney from the department's Internal Security Section, and the *affiant*, meaning the FBI agent who could attest to the accuracy of the affidavit. In other words, me. The judge, a fellow Southerner, listened intently. When I finished, he sat quietly for a moment then said he had no questions and complimented me on the thoroughness of the affidavit and presentation. I had no doubt the request would be approved, as indeed it was. Now we had ears to accompany the eyes already in place as the monitoring of Chin continued.

Though the investigation itself proceeded with dispatch, there were still obstacles to overcome. Simply stated, the CIA didn't want Larry Chin prosecuted, because then the Agency would have to admit it had been penetrated by a hostile intelligence service for decades. I faced an array of attorneys, analysts, and operational personnel, all of whom hoped to sweep Eagle Claw under the rug before it became public knowledge. While I could understand their position, I could not believe their willingness to put Agency image above the rule of law, particularly after the CIA admitted that a polygraph Chin had taken to maintain his security clearance should have sent up warning signals.

On one occasion, I became so exasperated that I exclaimed, "My God, in a time of war, Chin would be executed for treason! He's responsible for the death of your own people!" This seemed to weaken their zeal in defending their position against prosecution, but their resistance, doubtless on orders from their superiors, continued. The CIA finally agreed that prosecution was an option, but one matter we all agreed on was that there would be no public exposure of Eagle Claw until the source who was helping us was safely out of China.

Both the electronic and physical surveillance continued, with occasional surprises that broke the customary somber mood of the case. One such example involved a "niece" in her early twenties that Chin had in New York. Periodically he would contact her, and she would fly to Washington, where they would retire to a hotel for an afternoon of sexual play before she caught a return shuttle to New York. Our interest in the young woman heightened when, in a conversation with Chin, she was instructed to bring the "machine" with her as they made plans for another hotel meeting. Their conversations were in Mandarin Chinese, and the most literal translation for the object was "machine," though we tried without success to determine exactly what was being discussed so urgently. If it were some sort of communication or recording device, it would be a real coup to gain access to it. The FBI secretly searched the young woman's checked luggage, only to discover the machine in question was a battery-powered sexual aid.

For all their sexual escapades, could this "niece" also be part of Chin's escape plan? The best spies always have a prearranged means of disappearing in the event their position is compromised. These plans are well thought out but are totally dependent on immediate execution; minutes make a difference between success and capture, and the contacts must be completely above suspicion. For instance, at the height of the Cold War, a Warsaw Pact nation had a well-placed source who was a professor at a small U.S. college. One day during a lecture, someone not visible to the class called the professor from the classroom. The professor told his students he would be gone just a moment, stepped outside and closed the door, and was never seen again.

Our source reported that Chin's escape contact was a Catholic priest in New York named Father Mark Cheung. Amazing. I was taken aback by the very audacity of the Chinese but at the same time admitted a grudging admiration for their shrewdness. The priest, an ethnic Chinese, had been recruited to work for the Chinese Ministry of Public Security and spent years establishing his cover serving parishes in the South Pacific and Hong Kong. In an emergency, Chin was to meet with Cheung in the confessional of his Transfiguration Church in Chinatown. Cheung later returned to Hong Kong and, after an interview by FBI agents during which he was completely uncooperative, reentered China never to resurface.

As the cased progressed over the months, I became more and more intrigued with our own informant inside China who had done so much to help us tighten the noose on Larry Chin. I had assumed responsibility for handling the increasing amounts of information he sent and had assigned him the codename Planesman. One of the simple pleasures of my position in the FBI bureaucracy then was that I got to assign codenames to important cases. Different agents used different methods to come up with names. I used submarine terminology taken from my service aboard the USS Razorback. The planesmen, who controlled the diving planes (fins) on diesel-electric boats like the Razorback, were responsible for setting the underwater operating level of the sub. Planesman, our secret source, was submerged in a covert role, and his reporting provided the level of buoyancy for the investigation.

Whoever he was, Planesman was exceptionally resourceful and apparently reckless beyond belief. More than once I commented to my CIA contacts that from all appearances, Planesman had a death wish. I was constantly concerned for his safety and wondered whether Chin's eventual arrest (which wouldn't be made while Planesman was still in danger) would occur after Planesman was safely out of China, or after he was dead.

From the time the FBI began monitoring Chin in early 1983 until the fall of 1985, every scrap of information relating to his behavior was observed and catalogued. This information was fed to behavioral scientists who developed a psychological profile of Chin: his strengths, his weaknesses, things that made him happy, and situations he was uncomfortable in handling.

The Larry Chin that emerged was an extraordinary spy and a fascinating study in contrasts. He could be meticulous in sifting through reams of reports for small bits of information that might be of use to his Chinese masters at the Ministry of Public Security, but he absent-mindedly kept the room key to his Beijing hotel room. He was a womanizer who seemed to have an insatiable appetite for sex, yet apparently had little emotional attachment to the women in his life. He gambled lavishly, yet lived frugally. He was a hardworking employee who seemed to immerse himself in his work for the good of the CIA and his adopted country, yet basked in the glory of the awards the MPS gave him that fed his massive ego.

It was this type of information that the Bureau had to consider when planning the interrogation of Chin, an interrogation that would be absolutely essential to any successful prosecution. One of the great difficulties in espionage cases is the problem of handling highly classified information relating to techniques, sources, and methods. Often prosecution has to be dropped in order to protect a source or procedure. The decision has to be made weighing national security against the desire to prosecute and the likelihood of conviction. A successful interrogation— a confession—is the only sure way to avoid having to choose between revealing secrets in an open courtroom and dropping the prosecution. Intelligence case interrogators usually have one shot; they either hit a home run or strike out.

The profile of the suspect also indicates what kind of agent should lead the interrogation. What developed in the Chin case was a departure from the usual practice of allowing the case agent to conduct the critical interview. Based on the advice of those at Quantico analyzing Chin's psychological profile, we decided that Tom Carson, who had so successfully handled the investigation for three years, was not the person to conduct the critical interview. The task was given to three relatively young agents who were outside the inner circle of those immersed in China operations. The oldest of the three, Terry Roth, was chosen due to his maturity relative to his counterparts Rudy Guerin, son of a former high FBI official, and Mark Johnson, Carson's co-case agent.

Guerin and Johnson (especially Johnson) could be brutally direct and even irreverent, displaying none of the deference to age and experience associated with the Chinese culture. They would make Chin uncomfortable, one of the key goals of a confrontational interrogation. The three rehearsed the interview, planning the sequence of questions and anticipating various reactions. Guerin, the lead interrogator, virtually scripted the interview to the point where it was as detailed as a screenplay. When the decision was made to arrest Chin on November 22, 1985, they were ready.

Late that afternoon, after they confirmed that Chin was at home, the three agents knocked on his apartment door on the eleventh floor of the Watergate at Landmark, a sprawling apartment complex in Alexandria, Virginia. Chin himself answered the door. Guerin, Roth, and Johnson identified themselves as FBI agents and asked if they could go in. Concealing his surprise, Chin politely invited them inside. Waiting anxiously in a room nearby was a surveillance team, hanging on every word and devouring Chinese carry-out.

The interview was an exercise in strategic maneuvering. Guerin probed, and Chin parried with denials and failed memories. The breakthrough came with the mention of Ou Qiming, Chin's longtime handler. When Ou's name came up, Chin reacted visibly, and the agents knew they had hit a sensitive chord. I can imagine Chin's dismay. The Chinese had certainly assured him of his safety and security. Then, suddenly, three FBI agents mention the name of the very individual who had made those assurances. Chin confessed. The interview continued successfully with Geurin's script and the FBI psychological profile right on target.

In the agents' opinion, Chin had made sufficient admissions to warrant his immediate arrest. Assistant United States Attorney Joe Aronica was standing by to consider a warrant. Clearly there was the very real probability that if he weren't jailed promptly, Chin, who had refused to surrender his passport, would flee to the safety of the People's Republic of China, and we'd never see him again

From a pay phone in the lobby, Ken Schiffer, then the supervisor of my old squad, briefed Aronica, providing details of the interrogation, but Aronica initially declined to authorize the arrest, preferring to wait for an indictment by a grand jury. At one point, Aronica suggested that perhaps a polygraph would be in order. Finally, after it was made abundantly clear that if Chin escaped, Aronica would be responsible, the attorney authorized Chin's arrest. At about 10:30 PM, Carson, as case agent, was granted the privilege of formally arresting one of the most harmful spies in the history of this country. Though it was nearly midnight by the time the agents got back to the office, they took the time to enjoy a brief champagne celebration, with champagne provided by Van Magers, a native of Mississippi, an attorney, unabashed admirer of William Faulkner, and one of the real stalwarts of the FBI's China counterintelligence program.

IN DECEMBER 1984 I accepted a transfer to the Office of Inspections with mixed feelings. I felt swept along on a career path I had little control over. Later I took a whirlwind tour, conducting the inspection of field offices across the country, a special assignment in New York, and legal attaché offices in Hong Kong and Tokyo. While in Hong Kong, a city I had last visited as a sailor, I rode the Star Ferry across the harbor several times. I couldn't help but wonder how often Larry Chin had taken the same ride and met with his contacts from the MPS and later, the MSS. (The Ministry of State Security had been created in 1983 as part of Deng Xiaopeng's reforms and had assumed control of the Chin case.)

Eagle Claw was never far from my mind, and periodically I received status briefings on it, usually from Van Magers, who had been promoted to unit chief of the Chinese unit and now had management responsibility for the case. It was in good hands. In November 1985 I traveled to New Orleans on business, then flew to Monroe to visit a favorite aunt and uncle, Vivian and Robert Weems, and revisit the place I had grown up. While watching the network news the next morning, I learned Chin had been arrested the day before. I was both exhilarated and depressed. I felt somehow I had earned the right to be involved in the final chapter of Eagle Claw, yet here I was sitting in my boyhood home far removed from the big events in Washington.

My aunt noticed my interest in the news story, and perhaps my somber mood as well, and asked me if I was okay. I could not discuss the case with her and simply replied that "I had a little to do with it." But I was eager to know what had happened to Planesman. Chin's arrest meant that our faithful informant was either safely out of China or dead. It was the following Monday before I could confirm that Planesman was indeed safe and that the arrest and subsequent interrogation of Chin had gone well.

For many involved in Eagle Claw, the trial itself was anticlimatic. The case was heard in federal court in Alexandria, Virginia, February 4–7, 1986. Joe Aronica did a superb job of prosecuting Chin without having to expose national security information, relying almost exclusively on the results of Chin's interrogation and evidence collected by FBI agents during the lengthy investigation. Evidence presented included diaries kept by Chin, the Qianming Hotel room key, evidence of the use of his 35mm camera, passport and customs records, and verification of Chin's travels to China and Hong Kong. Experts in Chinese intelligence operations from the FBI, U.S. Army, and CIA were called to testify, and Aronica continued systematically building an overwhelming case against Chin.

Chin's attorney had little to offer in defense. Chin himself testified, but his testimony did little to refute the government's case. He claimed that his purpose in providing information to the Chinese was to improve U.S.-China relations, a time-honored justification for many who commit espionage but one with little credibility. He also claimed at first to have passed only declassified information to the Chinese to help in reconciling differences between China and the U.S. but then admitted receiving $180,000 from the Chinese for his work.

Late on Friday evening, February 7, the jury filed out of the courtroom to consider the evidence. A little more than three hours later, they found Larry Wu-tai Chin guilty of espionage. Chin showed no remorse and indeed attempted to rationalize what he had done. He commented publicly, "When I think about what I accomplished—the improvement of the livelihood of one billion Chinese people—my imprisonment for life is a very small price to pay. It was worth it." He appeared on *Nightline* and made the same assertions, but events to follow clearly established he did not personally believe what he had stated.

By the time of the trial, I had been promoted to unit chief dealing with East Germany and Bulgaria but received almost daily briefs on the status of Eagle Claw. On February 21, 1986, I learned that Chin had committed suicide in jail. He hid a plastic bag prisoners were given to clean up their cells, placed it over his head, tied it with a shoestring, and suffocated himself. It was an incredibly desperate but disciplined act that effectively closed the book on Eagle Claw. Apparently a life in prison was not worth the good he had claimed he had accomplished.

I was frustrated by Chin's suicide, but only from the standpoint that his death meant we would never learn all the details of his miserable past. I had no compassion for his death from a personal standpoint, since his traitorous actions had caused the deaths of so many others. Espionage is not a clean sport. It is a deadly business that exacts a great human toll.

SOME TIME LATER I had the opportunity to meet Planesman, and while there has been, correctly, no public acknowledgement of either his identity or the role he played in the Chin investigation, there have been tantalizing glimpses of him in the press from time to time. The FBI has a long history of keeping the identity of its sources secret. However, in the years since the Chin case broke upon the scene, more information than ever has come before the public eye. In 1996 former ambassador to South Korea and later China, James R. Lilley, whom I met in China in 1991, testified before the Senate Committee on the roles and capabilities of the United States intelligence community. Lilley insisted that "years and years of work on Soviet targets, surveillance, contact, cultivation, assessment, recruitment, training, use in place, paid off. This paid off in China." (Lilley proceeded to characterize the "payoff." But in the pre-publication review of this manuscript, the CIA has requested that the actual statement made by Lilley be deleted.)

In March 1999, Lilley wrote an article for the *Wall Street Journal* entitled "Blame Clinton, Not China for the Lapse at Los Alamos," in which he again made a specific reference to the Chin case and the CIA. Despite the fact that this is public knowledge since the *Journal* reported it, the FBI still requested that a single sentence quoted from that article be deleted from this manuscript. While Lilly's characterization of Planesman provided some indication of his position in the People's Republic of China, it did not provide any specific identity.

Much has been written about the case over the years, including *The Chinese Secret Service: Kang Sheng and the Shadow Government in Red China* by two French authors, Roger Faligot and Remi Kauffer. This book was translated to English in 1987 and made the following references to the Chin case in a chapter entitled "The 'Son of Kang Sheng' Defects to the West":

A translator at the American consulate in Shanghai, Larry Wu Tai Chin had joined the CIA in 1948. For the Chinese, he was a top-class recruit. An interrogator of Communist prisoners on the Korean front, he began to inform his new masters and compatriots on the results of these interrogations. As time went on, he became one of their best informers on American plans in South-East Asia, particularly during the Vietnam War.

An officer in the CIA's Radiofusion Department at Langley in Virginia, then still very active after his retirement, Larry Wu Tai Chin confessed to the investigators that he had received since 1952 the handsome sum of $140,000 for his good and loyal services. The most "fair-minded" of the CIA men readily admitted that he did not "steal" this money (paid in small amounts in Hong Kong), considering the quality of the information of all kinds that he shamelessly gleaned over thirty-four years' covert and solitary work to the advantage of China.

Why was he caught? Although U.S. counterintelligence refuse to admit it, it was doubtless because of information supplied by the recent defector, Yu Zhensan, Kang Sheng's adoptive son. After all, Yu Zhensan is the cousin of Yu Zusheng, the grandson of Chiang Ching-Kuo and the great-grandson of Chiang Kai-shek. Moreover, secret negotiations immediately began between U.S. emissaries and Taiwan government envoys, anxious to welcome back the prodigal son.

The *Los Angeles Times* of September 5, 1986, was even more specific: "Yu Zhensan, once head of the foreign affairs bureau of China's Ministry of State Security, was spirited to the United States 'within a couple of weeks, one way or the other,' of Chin's arrest Nov. 22, said the official, who refused to be identified."

If one accepts the writings of Faligot and Kauffer, Planesman was not just an ordinary Chinese citizen employed by the MPS. He was one of China's "golden youth," the offspring of China's political elite. I became convinced that the "golden youth" were in a better position to see the hypocrisy of the Communist system under which they lived, even though they benefited from it. Communism was not a pathway to a utopian society; it was a way to retain power in the hands of the political elite by any means necessary. I believe Planesman saw this hypocrisy and at some point determined he would strike back in his own way.

His actions were simply audacious. He strolled around MSS headquarters, routinely photographing documents on desks, pulling files, and making inquiries, and being the son of those with influence, he benefited from special treatment. He even pilfered the desk of his supervisor, whom he referred to as the "Beijing Bitch," where he was able to gain access to the most secret of the information contained within the MSS.

According to Faligot and Kauffer, Yu Zhenshan had the reflected influence of a powerful mentor. Kang Sheng, described by Faligot and Kauffer as Planesman's adoptive father, was the former head of the dreaded and oppressive secret police apparatus that controlled China from within for Mao. A dedicated Communist who was extraordinarily sadistic and who is said to have caused the death of more of his friends than this enemies, Kang had been in Shanghai as a Communist under the Kuomintang, before the Communist takeover in 1949. Described in some reports as an addicted opium smoker who could write calligraphy with both hands, Kang had helped to orchestrate the calamities of the Cultural Revolution before his death in 1975.

Planesman in the flesh was a gregarious, animated individual who spoke in fractured English, but who seemed to have a very real zest for life. When we met at last after Operation Eagle Claw was over, he confirmed my long-held suspicion that he was the ultimate risk taker. I had the impression he would have paid the CIA to allow him to be their spy. We had lunch together and then returned to the parking lot. As he got into his car he turned, smiled broadly, waved, and drove away.

I never saw him again.

CHAPTER 6

THE PRESIDENT AND THE GENERAL

"I would like to have marched with you."

Taiwanese Lieutenant General Gih Sang-Dong

Though the Chin case was a paramount responsibility during my years as head of the Chinese foreign intelligence squad, not everything involved Oriental intrigue. On Monday afternoon, March 30, 1981, I was sitting in my office engaged in the humdrum of paperwork and listening, as usual, to the radio when I heard the news flash that President Ronald Reagan had been shot. Reagan, barely in the third month of his presidency, was hit on the sidewalk near the Hilton Hotel off Connecticut Avenue. I was quite familiar with the area, near the Chinese embassy and home to a number of good ethnic restaurants. I instantly visualized the stone wall that was later so vivid in the news footage.

The special agent in charge, Ted Gardner, was away from the office, and Phil Parker, the assistant special agent in charge for counterintelligence, was the ranking agent present. Parker, a native Virginian with a handlebar moustache, was a respected counterintelligence professional with a deep understanding of the Russian culture and the Soviet intelligence services. But on this occasion, the job requirements were of a different nature: with the world watching, he had to put in place a massive criminal investigation into the attempted assassination of the president of the United States.

Ted Gardner had established a command post system that presaged the large dedicated spaces in many field offices and at FBI headquarters today. A conference room was converted into a command center, though without the vast array of computers, telephones, radios, and maps that is commonplace today. It was a rudimentary yet effective conduit for massive amounts of incoming information, ensuring a coordinated and concentrated investigative effort.

In Gardner's absence, Parker opened the command center, and the office geared up for a massive operation. Telephone calls were already pouring in from the media, politicians, and seemingly everyone of any rank at FBI headquarters. My St. Louis years taught me that large investigations were the FBI's strong suit, and under Gardner's enlightened leadership, the office was prepared to carry out its considerable responsibilities.

There was a brief meeting before I returned to my office, where the radio still played and the paperwork still waited. As a relatively junior supervisor, I did not have a specific role in the command center but stood by to be assigned as needed. Incoming data was not encouraging. The president had been shot with a .22-caliber pistol. I thought of Robert Kennedy and how the .22 rounds from the revolver fired by Sirhan Sirhan had virtually disintegrated after entering the body. I could also recall the deadly impact of .22 rounds in the homicides I had investigated as a detective in Monroe and how devastating that small piece of lead could be if it hit the right spot. If Reagan had sustained a wound to the head, especially at his advanced age of seventy, he could be in serious danger.

Early in the evening Ted Gardner returned and took command of the investigation after determining Parker had done a superb job in his absence. Gardner was a no-nonsense SAC with tremendous leadership skills but was a man of few words. He came into my office and asked how I felt; I said I was fine. He asked if I could stay up all night, saying he needed a night supervisor to run the command post. I, in an attempt at humor during a depressing time, told him I thought my late evenings at the Washington Navy Yard's Officers' Club with Phil Parker and Bob

Wade, a supervisor of a Soviet counterintelligence squad, had been a secret, but yes, I could stay awake all night. We went to the command center where I received briefings and prepared to spend the night along with a small staff. We sent out for food, made more coffee, and went to work. I called Carla and told her not to expect me home.

I learned a valuable lesson from Gardner that night. He had both the courage and foresight to send most of the agents home, with instructions to report early the next morning. Many managers would have kept supervisors and agents standing by just in case something occurred. But Gardner sent the vast majority of the staff home and left the command post in the hands of a relatively inexperienced supervisor from a counterintelligence squad with a skeletal staff. This allowed him to begin the next day with a fresh staff to tackle the long, arduous investigation that had just begun.

I turned my attention to two primary functions. The first and most critical was recovering all the president's personal effects, particularly safeguarding anything related to national security. We had teams at the shooting site and the hospital admitting area, both now designated crime scenes. Every scrap of clothing that had been cut from the president's body was seized as evidence, and this led to a couple of interesting events. Agents could locate only one of the two presidential cufflinks Reagan was wearing. They scoured the area several times and interviewed everyone that had access to the area. They searched the presidential limousine and the area of the shooting where Reagan had been shoved into the car. They looked in trashcans at the hospital emergency room, under equipment, and everywhere they could think of, but the cufflink was never recovered.

Late in the evening I received a telephone call from Jim Werth, an agent at the hospital who was taking custody of Reagan's personal effects. In an inner suit pocket he had found an envelope containing the "Doomsday" codes for use in the event of a nuclear attack on the United States. There was a heated discussion at the hospital regarding the disposition of the codes, with White House staff members insisting the codes be turned over to them. Nobody with the official authority to do so would be making any decision that night, and I wasn't going to bother Gardner at home over the matter. I called FBI headquarters and recommended that the FBI take custody of the codes until the next day, when a formal determination could be made about who should receive them and how they would be transferred. I did not want the FBI to be accused of turning over the codes to some staff member at the White House with no authority to have them, and I knew they would be secure with me in the command center safe.

I told Werth to bring the codes to the Washington field office. There was a solemnity to the occasion as I opened the safe and he gently placed the cards inside. Werth, a stocky agent off a terrorism squad, knew all too well the dangers of the moment due to the sometimes erratic behavior the Soviets and the tensions of the Cold War. He also knew, and expressed to me, his concern for Reagan's chances of recovery, for the clothing and the codes had been taken from a gravely wounded president.

The second responsibility of the evening was to monitor the deluge of teletypes coming in to Washington from FBI field offices virtually all over the United States and from FBI legal attaché offices around the world. Lacking today's computer capabilities, I made a synopsis of pertinent information, both incoming queries and facts about the developing investigation, on 3 x 5 cards for Gardner to review when he returned the following morning. The investigation summary also served to avoid duplication from the multiple agencies that were running around, with jurisdiction or without, trying to play a role in the matter.

One teletype in particular caught my eye. The Dallas field office reported that John Hinckley had purchased .22-caliber ammunition in Lubbock, Texas. The type of ammo was alarming: Devastator rounds, designed to explode upon entering the body. I knew Reagan had not been in surgery yet, however I felt it was imperative to get this information to the surgeons as quickly as possible. I highlighted that information for Gardner and stressed it during the morning briefings of the previous night's events. The president had in fact been shot with Devastator ammunition, but it had not performed as advertised.

Instead of exploding, it had remained intact, very likely saving President Reagan's life.

After being advised by the FBI of the type of bullet, hospital physicians reconsidered a previous decision to let a slug remain in Reagan's body and removed it without incident. Hinckley no doubt purchased that particular type of ammunition hoping for maximum damage. It cost several times more than standard .22 shells, and this troubled man, obsessed with impressing actress Jody Foster, had bought it so as to cause the most possible harm to his target, the president of the United States.

Periodic news reports were cautiously optimistic about Reagan's survival, but the information I was getting directly from the hospital was much more guarded, and at variance with the broadcast reports. I don't believe the general public ever knew how close Reagan came to death that dark day in March 1981.

I went home that morning to sleep, but sleep did not come easily. It wasn't so much all the coffee I had drunk in the command center over the course of a long night as not knowing whether or not the president of the United States would be alive when I woke up.

BY JANUARY 13, 1982, the president had recovered from the assassination attempt, but Washington witnessed a tragedy of a different sort. A snowstorm hit the area with unexpected intensity. As usual, the federal bureaucracy was slow to react, and the snow was blinding before government workers received permission to depart. A large number had simply taken a vacation day and left anyway, but as the squad supervisor over about twenty employees, I could not go until I was confident the agents had all departed with a reasonable expectation of getting home safely. I had already told them to leave, and we would sort out the administrative details later, but because of carpools and the remoteness of Buzzards Point, some could not get away until late in the afternoon.

The listless and dreary day was electrified by reports that an aircraft, Air Florida flight 90, had been seen crashing into the Potomac River.

The first call came from an FBI agent stuck in traffic on the Fourteenth Street bridge traveling toward Virginia who had been narrowly missed by the DC-9 as it crashed into the icy river. The office scrambled with limited resources and limited ability to get around. The streets of Southeast Washington, terrible in the best of times, were virtually impassable due to the snow. Though the rivers had been choked with ice for days, someone authorized use of the FBI's boat to try to get to the crash site and assist with rescue efforts. To reach the scene, the boat would have to go down the Anacostia River, past Buzzards Point, then turn up the Potomac River at Haines Point toward the area of impact.

This was during the height of the Cold War, when there was a myriad of emergency plans for essential personnel in the U.S. government to escape Washington if it appeared nuclear war was imminent. The Bureau kept a boat for getting the FBI director out of harm's way. The plan included placing him on the back of a motor scooter (assuming vehicular traffic would be hopelessly gridlocked) and whisking him through the streets to the Anacostia River. There he would sail down the Anacostia to the Potomac and on to Quantico, Virginia, and the safety of the FBI academy. In retrospect, the plan was simply amusing. Knowing then-Director William Webster and his straight-laced demeanor, I cannot imagine him clinging to a motor scooter buzzing through the streets of Washington.

FBI agents dispatched to the boat found it locked, but since those with keys could not make it to the location, the lock was broken. I stood in the window of my office overlooking the Anacostia as the boat struggled through the ice, its crew standing in the freezing snow in a futile attempt to provide assistance. By the time the boat passed Buzzards Point, news cameras had already caught the incredible scene of the heroic rescue of a few survivors from the wreck.

By the time the remaining squad members were on their way home, the area was completely immobilized. I called Carla later, and we agreed I would not attempt to make the trek to our house in Burke, Virginia, just outside the Beltway. I always kept a change of clothes and toiletries in the office for such occasions—such was the nature of the work for the

FBI. I called a small neighborhood hotel I was familiar with, secured a room, then drove to FBI headquarters well after the traffic had cleared. After parking the car, I rode the Metro to Dupont Circle and walked up Connecticut Avenue, overnight bag in hand.

As the snow began to abate, I realized I had not eaten since that morning and stopped in Timberlakes, a favorite pub on Connecticut Avenue, and found the scene inside almost surreal. The television was turned on, and the stations continued to replay the dramatic scenes of the crash, particularly the scene of Lenny Skutnik jumping into the frozen Potomac to save the life of Prisicilla Tirado, a passenger who had managed to get out of the wreckage before Air Florida flight 90 sank, dragging down more than seventy passengers and crew into the cold and murky waters.

Normally, Timberlakes was a happy place, and a beautiful snow could be cause for a festive occasion. But that evening the laughter was muted, and I was content to sit at the bar alone with my thoughts of how quickly disasters could occur and how such disasters could bring out the very best of mankind.

The weather reminded me of another monster snowstorm almost four years before with far happier memories attached. It was February 19, 1978. Carla was teaching in the Fairfax County School District, where our daughters Lara and Amy were also enrolled. Our neighborhood in Burke, Virginia, was quiet and picturesque. That February morning we awoke to find almost two feet of snow on the ground. It was a beautiful sight through the front window, but it was also cause for concern because Carla and I were expecting our third child any day.

I knew it would be a while before our neighborhood street was plowed, so I grabbed a snow shovel and started the daunting task of digging a path through the neighborhood street to the main road in the unlikely chance that Carla would need to go to the hospital. I was joined by Tom Bloch, an FBI agent who lived in the neighborhood, and another neighbor, Mas Egawa. We worked virtually nonstop, digging a pathway about the width of a car down the street, not finishing up until the late afternoon. I went back into the house, showered, and prepared to relax after a day of strenuous shoveling when Carla told me it was time to go to the hospital. As the contractions came with increasing frequency, we bundled up, drove out our newly shoveled street, then negotiated the roads to the hospital where our third daughter, Leah, was born within a couple hours. Our family was now complete.

AFTER TWO YEARS in the Chinese Unit, where I handled the Larry Wu-tai Chin investigation and other duties involving China's increased presence in the United States, I was transferred to the Office of Inspections, which is responsible for conducting audits of field offices. It is a comprehensive and labor-intensive process designed to ensure field office investigations are conducted within applicable laws, rules, and regulations, and that financial matters, promotion policies, etc., are practiced with strict adherence to written dictates.

My first inspection was in Miami. At the time I had little inkling that within eighteen months it would be my new home. There I had my first exposure to Cuban intelligence matters and the Cuban culture that I came to love and appreciate. I also made inspection trips to such cities as New York, Milwaukee, Omaha, New Orleans, and Sacramento, as well as to legal attaché offices in Tokyo and Hong Kong.

I had last been in Hong Kong many years before when aboard the *USS Bauer*. Yet my love for that city remained. Even after a long day's work in the consulate-general, I felt energized when I walked outside—the sheer energy of the place seemed to absorb that day's fatigue and I wouldn't want to retire to the hotel. I became convinced that the U.S. consulate-general had been penetrated by the Chinese, if not electronically, certainly with personnel—a fact that was reinforced years later when I did a security survey of that post while detailed to the Department of State.

It was in Tokyo though that I encountered another of those memorable personalities I was fortunate to meet during my career. Lieutenant General Gih Sang-Dong was a member of the Taiwanese Army who had fought the Japanese during World War II, then had been part of Chiang Kai-shek's Kuomintang army fighting the Communists of Mao Tse-tung.

After the KMT had been forced off the mainland, General Gih settled in Japan where he married a Japanese woman—a highly unusual choice given the Chinese people's animosity toward the Japanese for their atrocities committed in World War II—and spent the rest of his career in his wife's country. Vince Lugani, the FBI's superb legal attaché who spoke both Japanese and Mandarin Chinese, had made his acquaintance, and helped organize a quiet dinner hosted by General Gih and subordinates of equal rank to those of us on the inspection team.

Dinner started with a tray of food arranged in the shape and color of a bird that looked more like a painting than something edible. Next came a series of courses intermingled with a succession of toasts with Chinese liquors. As the evening grew longer, General Gih's face began to grow redder, and, with the continuous flow of liquor, his eyes became nothing more than slits. It seemed that the general was challenging Bill Wells, head of our Inspection Division, to a drinking marathon. I knew, from past experience, while willing, that Wells would be no match for General Gih. As a means to divert attention from the unspoken challenge, I asked if there was any mou tai to drink.

General Gih's eyes widened, and he issued an immediate order—an aide leapt up and promptly returned with the familiar short and squat white bottle with its red label and ribbon. Mou tai is a clear liquid best drunk in small doses and much loved by the Chinese people. The famous picture of Richard Nixon and Chou En-lai toasting one another with small glasses of clear liquid was almost certainly mou tai. I proposed a toast to General Claire Chennault, a fellow Louisianan much revered for his exploits on behalf of the Chinese people during WWII while commanding the Flying Tigers. The toast was translated by one of the General Gih's aides. He nodded, and we emptied the glasses.

The salutations continued. Just before we left, I stood, raised my glass to General Gih, and proposed a toast to a "free China." The general stood with glass raised, and I noticed a tear trickling down a cheek. We then emptied the glasses one final time. He looked intently at me and spoke something to an aide, who then turned to me and said, "General Gih said, 'I would have liked to have marched with you.'"

I was somewhat taken aback by the compliment and could only respond, "The honor would have been mine." We made our farewells, and as we walked from the restaurant, I felt little influenced by the wine and mou tai. I was much more affected by the wonderment of the compliment I had received from General Gih.

IT WAS ON A TRIP to New Orleans that I learned I had been transferred and promoted to the position of unit chief for the unit concerned with counterintelligence matters involving East Germany, Bulgaria, and Yugoslavia. Neither Bulgaria nor Yugoslavia had much of a political presence in the United States, so the primary emphasis of the unit was East Germany. The East Germans had a superb intelligence service. For the most part the only exposure I had to it was in novels such as John LeCarre's *The Spy Who Came In from the Cold,* but I quickly realized this was no ordinary adversary. The East Germans' Stassi was a tough, disciplined intelligence service which, in their own minds, was superior to the Soviet KGB. In time, I came to agree with them.

In May–June 1986, I spent three weeks in Germany as a guest of the West German Internal Service, the *Bundesamt fur Verfassungsshutz* or Federal Office for Protection of the Constitution, commonly referred to simply as the Bfv. This was an exchange agreement between two allied counterintelligence services with a common foe. My travel to West Germany had been preceded by visitors from both the Bfv and the *Landesamtes fur Verassungsschutz,* the State Offices for the Protection of the Constitution, commonly referred to as the Lfv, to ensure my trip would be a success. When asked about the goals of my trip, I said I hoped to see and get a feel for the environment in which they worked and by which they developed their assessments of both the East German Stassi and the Soviet KGB and GRU.

After arriving in Frankfurt, I caught a train to Bonn, spent the night and the next day registered in the Senats Hotel in Cologne, the home city of the Bfv. Each day was filled with nonstop briefings, breaks for lunch, more briefings, and, finally, dinner. This was during asparagus season, and my hosts insisted on this great delicacy with every meal. Finally I persuaded my hosts to give me a free evening and went to the China Restaurant in Cologne. There I had a wonderful Chinese meal and afterward inquired about the availability of mou tai. The Chinese waitress, who spoke some English, returned with the owner who was carrying a bottle with him and joined me at the table as we shared several glasses of the liquor. With the waitress translating, he told me that patrons seldom asked for mou tai in Germany and he was pleased to share the occasion with me.

Cologne was a beautiful city. I explored it alone between the end of the last briefing session and dinner time and would take walks with my hosts at noon. I toured the Roman Tower, a brick structure with intricate designs that had been built at the time of Christ, and, of course, the cathedral. Its twin spires dominated the skyline, and I was thankful that it had not been hit by Allied bombers during World War II. One of my hosts explained the spires were spared in part because they were a landmark that could be used to locate bridges and other strategic targets.

The briefings continued in Berlin, where I was met by members of the Lfv, as well as my official Bfv hosts. I squeezed in a quick shopping trip to get some gifts for Carla and the girls. I had been in Cologne on Amy's birthday and never liked to miss such occasions with my daughters. I viewed the Brandenburg Gate, where the chariot and horses had been turned around by East Germans to face East Germany when the Berlin Wall was constructed.

I also saw the Reichstaag, a structure so much a part of German history, the dome of which had been destroyed during the war when it was the headquarters of Hitler's Third Reich. The building was practically empty, but the Bfv had arranged for a tour of the interior. We drove to a parking area, walked along the Berlin Wall, the West Berlin side filled with graffiti, and entered the Reichstaag. We went upstairs to a narrow passageway where there was a ladder. I followed my hosts up the ladder and found myself on the roof of the building, overlooking East Berlin.

I could see the East German border guards in their towers, with rifles, watching us through binoculars. Some of them were taking photographs.

I was told it was seldom that anyone was on the roof and there would be an obvious curiosity about the identity of the visitor that sunny day in May 1986. What I found most striking was the difference in activity between East and West Berlin. It was early afternoon, and the West Berlin side was a picture of hustle and bustle. Cars moved up and down the streets, horns blowing, sidewalks filled with pedestrians, all in marked contrast to the East Berlin side. We did not see a single pedestrian, and only a couple of cars were moving along the eerily quiet streets.

As we prepared to leave the roof, I turned to Mr. Hildebrand (not his real name), who had been my primary host and was fast becoming a firm friend, and asked if he thought he would ever see the wall come down. He walked toward the back of the Reichstaag, looked across the roof toward East Germany and its quiet streets, guard towers, and barbed wire, and turned back, sadly and quietly responding, "Never in my lifetime." I was inclined to agree with him, for neither of us realized how rotten the core of Communism was and how swiftly it would crumble within a few years. At the time though, the wall and the guard towers seemed permanent fixtures. That scene on the Reichstaag roof was both profound and indelible, a poetic example of the contrast between freedom and a police state.

A few days later I was escorted aboard a small ship operated by the *BundeGrenzSchutz*, something akin to the U.S. Coast Guard, and we traversed the North Sea along the East German border to Neustadt, being shadowed and photographed by an East German patrol boat. As we neared the dock, the BGS commodore, who hosted my visit, asked if I could tell where the border was along the far shore. The answer was easy. On the West German side the beach extended for several yards above the water line, while on the East German side the grass and shrubbery grew almost to the border and the water's edge. Clearly the people of East Germany were not allowed to use the beach, while the West Germans made full use of the beach and water. The commodore wryly pointed out the West German beach had been designated a topless beach for female bathers just to entice the East German border guards. The stark difference between Communism and the West was glaringly apparent.

I left Germany with a much better picture of the face of Communism and increased respect for the West German security agencies that were at the forefront of the Cold War battle every day. I did not know then that the wheels were already in motion that would lead to new challenges and opportunities for me and an environment for my family unlike anything we had dreamed of.

CHAPTER 7

CHILDS PLAY

". . . any sacrifices we have made are a small price to pay for the privilege of living in this great country."

Morris Childs

A promotion to assistant special agent in charge of the Miami office was one I could not easily decline. The opportunities were significant, yet so were the challenges. Severe management and morale problems remained in the wake of a horrendous shootout on April 11, 1986, the deadliest day in FBI history, when two agents were killed and five wounded in an ill-fated stakeout of area banks after a series of especially vicious bank robberies. While out-numbered, the two robbers, Michael Platt and William Matix, who had already shot several people in previous robberies, simply outgunned the FBI, who tried to respond to automatic weapons fire with small caliber handguns and a shotgun, with devastating results. I had the distinct impression that Bill Wells, the new special agent in charge with whom I had traveled to Hong Kong and Japan the previous year, had been told by Director William Sessions that he would be able to restaff at least part of the senior management of the office as he saw fit.

I went home that evening and discussed the prospect of our moving. Lara was in college, but both Amy and Leah liked the idea of moving to Florida. Unfortunately, it would mean that Carla would have to give up her teaching seniority and start once again at the bottom of the ladder.

But, as a group, we agreed it was a good move. While counterintelligence was not the highest priority in Miami, with its major cocaine networks, violence, and fraud, it was a program that allowed for my contributions and offered the opportunity to become familiar with Cuban counterintelligence.

I was named as assistant special agent in charge (ASAC) and prepared to report to the Miami office in September. The self-styled "America's Casablanca" had held my interest for a number of years. It was a city of contrasts, home to various ethnic groups, each of which possessed its own unique and powerful culture, making conflict inevitable. The blacks had their greatly misnamed Liberty City and the Jews their Miami Beach. The Cubans had their Little Havana and the Haitians their own Little Haiti. Increasingly, whites were retreating from Miami's ethnic cauldron into the suburbs. I doubt more than five percent of the FBI employees there lived in Miami proper—including black and Hispanic employees. Those who came to Miami without a thorough briefing on this most unique of cities were in for a real lesson.

In some ways, our office mirrored the city it served. A few months after I arrived, two agents, a husband and wife, were exiting a swingers club (a club for group sex and spouse swapping) when they were accosted by a robber. A gunfight erupted, the robber was killed, and the female agent was shot in the stomach. Another agent resigned just before being fired for stealing from informant payments. And it was in Miami that one of the first cases of an FBI agent's involvement in drug trafficking was uncovered.

I arrived in Miami in September 1986 and lived temporarily with my boss, who had moved in advance of his attractive and outgoing wife, Linda. In some respects, the fact that Carla and the girls were not with me was a godsend. Those early months were characterized by exceedingly long hours as we tried to come to grips with all the problems in the office and prepare for an inspection in December. I rented a house in Ft. Lauderdale while we were having a home built in Davie, a community then known for its horses and rodeos and relaxed atmosphere. Carla got a job with the Broward County Schools, Amy and Leah enrolled in classes, Lara remained at Radford University in Virginia, and once again we settled into living as a family.

At the office there were important changes to be made. The squad that had been involved in the shootout was in disarray. The desks of the deceased agents, Ben Grogan and Jerry Dove, were still in place, as was the office of the supervisor, Gordon McNeill, who had been severely wounded. The agents' desks were virtual shrines. I told the new supervisor to put his own pictures on the office wall and to remove Grogan and Dove's desks. The first day in the office, Agent Edmundo Mireles paid me a visit. Mireles, a large bulky man with a quick smile, was easy going, always ready for a good time, and obviously found real joy in his work. He had been severely wounded in the left arm during the April shootout, and it was his actions that had captured the imagination of both the FBI and the public. He had emptied his twelve-gauge shotgun at his assailants, racking the rounds into the chamber with one arm while sitting on the ground. As the two killers, Platt and Matix, tried to drive away, he staggered toward their car and emptied his revolver at them, effectively bringing the shootout to an end.

Mireles came into my office with his arm in a sling and, after a few minutes of pleasantries, began to talk about how he could still make a contribution to the FBI, though his handicapped left hand would inhibit his ability to qualify on the firearms range. I had a fondness for Mireles from the time I knew him in Washington and knew his wife Liz as well, an agent who had been on the Cuban counterintelligence squad that I had inspected the previous year. I was determined to do something to help them.

I asked Mireles about the psychological support he had received. He volunteered that the assistance had been fine at first but was short-term. He said psychologists had come to Miami within a few days of the shooting, but left after the wounded agents' survival was assured, even though their counsel was still needed. Mireles related how he had joined a group of agents at the FBI academy who had been wounded by gunfire, and that one agent had immediately taken a photograph of his wounds from his wallet and shown it around. Mireles observed, "We all tick, but some of us tick louder than others." Clearly the FBI's psychological program was ineffective.

I called John Otto, the deputy director of the FBI, who had a great personal interest in the welfare of the agents involved in the shootout. I told him that I thought any of those agents who requested a transfer should be accommodated, both for their own well-being and that of the office. Further, I recommended that Mireles and his wife be transferred to the FBI academy to ensure he received physical therapy. I also thought Mireles could be a point of inspiration for new agents during their initial FBI training. However, some of the staff at the academy resisted taking Mireles on board, stating he did not have the necessary academic credentials—an absolutely obscene stance reflecting their detachment from the reality of the law enforcement they were teaching. Otto, of course, prevailed and both Liz and Ed Mireles joined the staff at the academy, taking a much needed dose of FBI street sense to a group largely prone to wallow in their own academic aura.

As time went by, the squad began regaining its confidence. But an incident of the magnitude of the shootout on April 11, 1986, is not easily forgotten. This became crystal clear to me one month (to the day) after I arrived. The FBI holds annual memorial services for agents slain in the line of duty. October 29 would be the first such service since Grogan and Dove were killed. Bill Wells, as SAC, was expected to moderate the solemn ceremony, but he advised he had something else to do, as had all the ASACs who had been in Miami at the time of the shooting. The afternoon before the service, Wells told me I would preside over it. I was at a loss. Here I was, still learning the names of the employees, almost a stranger in the office, yet being given this most sensitive and emotional task. Still, I had my duty, and the service had to be held.

That morning when I entered the room, many of the employees were already crying. The somber mood was acute and overwhelming, and I felt like I had to push myself through the heavy, tense air just to reach the lectern. I had struggled with what I should say, though I knew it would have to be short, and finally decided to borrow in style from Fleet

Admiral Chester Nimitz's moving statement, made after the surrender of Japan at the ending of World War II.

After a brief opening statement, I said, "Names like Shanahan and Hollis, and now, Grogan and Dove, names that represent a cross-section of the very democracy they took an oath to protect and serve and who now, have made the ultimate sacrifice." With a brief closing line or two, I concluded the meeting. Nearly everyone was openly crying. Long after the ceremony had ended, the employees continued to linger in the room. As I made my way through the group toward my office, several reached out and touched me without saying a word. As the day wore on, some even came by my office just to stick their heads in and say, "Thank you."

ON SUNDAY, OCTOBER 5, 1986, in the remote countryside of Nicaragua, a Southern Air C-123 aircraft was shot down by a Soviet-made surface-to-air missile fired by a Sandinistan soldier. This obscure and nameless soldier certainly had no idea his actions would cause a crisis in the United States that has left questions unanswered even today.

Southern Air was a Miami-based airline that ostensibly handled air cargo for commercial customers. On that day, however, one of its planes was flying over Nicaragua to drop supplies for the Nicaraguan Democratic Front (FDN). These were the anti-Sandinista fighters usually referred to as Contras, literally meaning "against," who were attempting to overthrow the Communist government of Daniel Ortega and his group that had gained power in this impoverished country. There were four members of the crew: a pilot, a copilot, a Contra security guard, and a tall, beefy American, Eugene Hasenfus, who was the "kicker." His job was to push the supplies from the slow-flying aircraft that then parachuted to the Contras on the ground. Hasenfus was the only survivor.

News quickly spread that the aircraft had been shot down, and the Sandinistas paraded Hasenfus around in public as their trophy prisoner of war. The soldiers rifled through the personal belongings of the deceased pilot and copilot and discovered the name "Max Gomez" (the *nom de guerre* of Felix Rodriguez) in an address book. Rodriguez was a storied figure in anti-Communist activities who was present when Che Guevara was captured and executed in Bolivia in October 1967, and who later became a valued and respected friend. His past association with the CIA was no secret, and the ties to the United States gave both the Sandinistas and the U.S. press definitive proof of America's involvement with the Contras.

Since Southern Air was based in Miami and there appeared to have been arms aboard the aircraft, the FBI had jurisdiction under the Neutrality Act and began an investigation that would soon make many uncomfortable. It was discovered that the pilots and Hasenfus had had past dealings with the CIA, and the agents assigned to the investigation were hard pressed to keep ahead of the press. FBI headquarters was initially slow to realize the implications of the incident, then they were frantic in trying to find out what was occurring on an almost hourly basis.

The investigation was first assigned to Paul Philip, a tall, outgoing black supervisor who had formerly been a Washington D.C. police officer and who spoke excellent Spanish. He and his team would provide much of the information leading to an eventual crisis in government for the Reagan administration and propel an obscure Marine Corps lieutenant colonel, Oliver North, to a prominent place in contemporary American history.

After Philip was transferred to Detroit, the investigation passed to Eduardo Sanchez, a large, muscular agent with an extensive military background. He joined the rest of the squad in conducting a thorough investigation, though it was becoming increasingly apparent that United States Attorney Leon Kellner, appointed by Ronald Reagan, had no interest in pursuing the matter. Kellner, known as "Neon Leon" for his flashy dress and love of being in the news, had been in civil practice before he was named as U.S. attorney. Agents distrusted the U.S. attorney's office, especially after they caught a young assistant attorney going through an FBI trash can. He had insisted on knowing source information that was normally contained in the administrative part of a teletype. Agents had torn off that portion of the message before allowing him to read it, and he was caught trying to retrieve the torn off portion from a confidential trash can in the squad area.

On January 8, 1988, Mike Todd, representing the office of special prosecutor Lawrence Walsh in Washington, visited me in Miami and told me the prosecutor would be taking over day-to-day control of the case. I objected strenuously, but to no avail. I told Todd that regardless of any argument I could make, his mind was obviously made up. They were going to assume control, but with no guarantee the investigation would be in better hands. He did not disagree.

My first encounter with special prosecutors, strongly reinforced years afterward during the Whitewater scandal, convinced me that criminal investigations are harmed by removing control from experienced investigators and putting them into the hands of inexperienced attorneys. Walsh's office assumed responsibility for the investigation. It was staffed with personnel who did not have the language skills, investigative experience, or the feel for Latin American investigations demonstrated by the agents in Miami. Many observers remain convinced that political influence stymied a vigorous prosecution and public airing of the whole matter.

I'D HEARD ABOUT OPERATION SOLO during a briefing on Soviet counterintelligence before I took on my new assignment in Miami. Only later did I realize it was arguably the most important spy case of the Cold War. The principal players in this long-running drama, Morris and Eva Childs, lived under cover in the Miami area. Morris Chilovsky and his brother Jack had adopted the surname of Childs in the U.S. after emigrating from the Ukraine in 1911. As prominent members of the Communist Party of the United States of America (CPUSA), they had become intimates to the titans of world Communism. However in the early 1950s, in their advanced years, they began a thirty-year collaboration with the FBI that was perhaps the single most important coup for the Bureau during the Cold War. The depth and breadth of their reporting was simply astounding. As a widower, Morris Childs married Eva

Lieb, and she too became an integral part of the courageous team that penetrated the inner sanctum of Communism.

By 1981 they had made more than fifty missions behind the Iron Curtain where exposure would have meant certain death. But the years of strain were taking their toll. Their health was beginning to fail. There were also indications that their cooperation with the FBI might be exposed any moment. Jack Childs had died, everyone was tired, and abruptly the operation was shut down. By the time I reported into Miami in the fall of 1986, Morris and Eva had literally walked out of their apartment in Miami and disappeared, under the watchful protection of the FBI, to a location in Hallandale, a suburb north of Miami near Ft. Lauderdale.

The agent assigned to look after the Childses was Wes Roberts, tall and slender with a military bearing befitting his Virginia Military Institute and U.S. Army background, who was approaching retirement age. He did not have a counterintelligence background, but did have innate social graces and graciousness that were ideal for his assignment. It was through Roberts that I first arranged to visit the Childs.

I was struck by how small they were. Morris was barely over five feet tall and Eva even shorter, and both were stooped with age. Somehow they did not fit the image of the bold and fearless spies who secreted documents from under the watchful eyes of Communists around the world. They had ferried vast amounts of cash from the Soviets to support the activities of the CPUSA into the United States, where every dollar was counted and serial numbers recorded by the FBI. Further, they had not told even their immediate families of the roles they had played for so many years.

Both were at the door when we arrived at their apartment, a wonderful location in a high-rise overlooking the ocean. They were quite cordial and I was impressed with the affection they displayed toward Roberts. I had stopped en route and picked up a plant to give them, and from their reaction one would have thought I had taken them a prized painting.

I learned quickly that Morris suffered fools badly, but they were kind enough to point our conversations toward subjects I was more familiar with, such as China and Cuba. It was simply exhilarating to sit with the single individual who probably knew intimately more members of the worldwide Communist elite than anyone else on earth. He was personally acquainted with Mao Tse-tung and Chou En-lai of China. He knew Fidel Castro; Nikita Khrushchev, Leonid Brezhnev, and Yuri Andropov of the Soviet Union; and East German leader Erich Honecker. He was also acquainted with Josip Tito of Yugoslavia, Ho Chi Minh of North Vietnam and many others who entrusted their most intimate thoughts to him over the decades he had been a prominent member of the CPUSA.

I was particularly eager to listen to him discuss the personalities of those world leaders. Morris had met Chou En-lai on several occasions and found him to be a charismatic and remarkable individual, though a dedicated revolutionary and Communist. Morris said the Chinese people seemed to genuinely love Chou, but that Mao Tse-tung did not inspire that same feeling. Morris personally loathed Mao and said on one occasion that he found Mao to be "smelly," having "bad breath," "bad manners," and—perhaps the most damning given the breadth of Morris's intellect and love of culture—a "peasant."

He laughed at his own rather inept attempts at politics, though he had openly campaigned for public office in Chicago as a Communist. He avidly followed politics in the United States and read and watched the news voraciously. He once rather humorously compared Castro to the populist politician Huey Long, from my home state of Louisiana, in their ability to sway an audience by the very force of their spoken words and personality.

I tried to keep my visits relatively short, as Morris tired easily, but I also knew he was still hungry to have the intellectual stimulation of good conversations on world events and personalities. And I became convinced that he still had something to offer to the FBI and America because of his decades as an intimate of the leadership of virtually every Communist country on earth.

Working with Bob Wade and his section chief, Don Stukey, and with a personal telephone call to Tom DuHadway, a deputy assistant director for the Intelligence Division, I obtained formal approval to pay the Childs a monthly stipend for the remainder of their natural lives. I made this decision not based on any financial necessity on their part. The relatively small monthly payment was more of a gesture of the FBI's appreciation for their service and acknowledgment that the FBI would always be a part of their lives. It was assumed then that their exploits would not be acknowledged publicly during their lifetimes, and the increasingly smaller number of people in the FBI who knew about Operation Solo were the only people they could discuss their years of service with.

I was determined to establish a formal mechanism to ensure their continued recognition even as those in the FBI who knew about the case retired. I did this after an inspector's aide had questioned the value of continuing to pay them. His comment as reported to me was, "Why are we still paying those old Jews all this money?" Clearly the FBI could have a short memory, and it was apparent that there were those who had no appreciation for all that those old Jews had contributed.

I was incensed not only by the abject anti-Semitism attached but also by the fact that he would be so naïve not to recognize and appreciate all that they had done. They had been paid only expenses over the years and had actually rejected large bonuses and awards. I knew of specific instances where the government had paid individuals literally millions of dollars for doing considerably less than the Childses, whose cooperation with the FBI had often actually cost them money.

I learned there was a plan to award Morris and Jack Childs National Security Medals, though the process had been languishing for a couple of years. I renewed efforts to see that the medals were awarded, relying once more on my contacts at FBI headquarters. News that the awards were coming soon seemed to give Morris renewed energy, though he was visibly fading. He had given a series of oral interviews to FBI personnel about specific events and personalities seen from his unique perspective, as well as Eva's, and this seemed to reassure both that they were not being abandoned. Finally, the medals were approved and Morris was scheduled to receive awards for himself and his deceased brother Jack in Washington. There were the inevitable logistical and administrative problems, such as getting permission for Morris and Eva to fly business class on account of their age and infirmity.

Director Sessions awarded the medals on behalf of President Reagan, ostensibly for security reasons, though, in retrospect, arrangements should have been made for the president to attend. Sessions rose to the occasion and gave obviously heart-felt comments, but it was Morris who stole the show.

The ceremony took place in a small conference room with only a few invited guests. Some there in Morris's family realized for the first time he had been working decades for the FBI and was not the avowed Communist he had portrayed himself to be. When Sessions started to make his comments, Morris insisted on standing up and he was helped to his feet by Eva—supporting him physically as she had supported him so many ways throughout most of Operation Solo. There was this frail and elderly man, leaning on his cane and supported by his elderly wife, virtually standing at attention while the long overdue accolades were bestowed.

Then Morris insisted on speaking. He was gracious toward Sessions and acknowledged many of those present who had been involved in the Solo operation. Then he spoke about how some may question why they could have endured the sacrifices they had and how their work had adversely affected their lives for so long. But he seemed to draw himself even straighter, and in a clear voice emphatically stated that "any sacrifices we have made are a very small price to pay for the privilege of living in this great country." There were misty eyes in the room and I found the moving comments made by Morris to be high drama. Here was a frail old man, in the winter of his life, who stood only with great physical effort, expressing unabashed patriotism and actually thanking the FBI for the privilege of performing such a service for his adopted country.

I often wondered what makes anyone perform such services when the personal toll is so great. In *Kim*, Rudyard Kipling wrote, ". . . what he loved was the game for its own sake—the stealthy prowl through the dark gullies and lanes, the crawl up a water-pipe, the sights and sounds of the women's world on the flat roofs, and the headlong flight from housetop to housetop under cover of the hot dark." Kipling could just as easily have been writing about Jack Childs, for he did his work in part because of the sheer excitement of it; he was the ultimate risk taker, on par with Planesman in the Larry Wu-tai Chin case.

But for Morris there seemed to be something different and more complex at work. One day I asked him why, given the passage of time, he had decided to disregard the idealist utopian view of Communism and cast his lot with the FBI and, in essence, the capitalist society that Communism was intent on destroying.

He said one reason was that the discrimination he had observed in the Soviet Union was worse than that he had experienced in the United States. In time I came to believe that Morris had originally been lured by the idealistic society portrayed by the Communists. But I believed also that he had been pushed toward Communism by the abuses he had suffered at the hands of the Czar's police apparatus in the Ukraine during his youth. This was compounded by the discrimination he experienced as a lowly Jewish immigrant when he arrived in the U.S. at the turn of the century. It was only in later years, when he began to see first hand the hypocrisy of Communism as practiced in the Soviet Union and by Gus Hall, the head of the CPUSA, that he began to waver. It was through the remarkable efforts of agents Carl Freyman and Walter Boyle that he began to work for the FBI against Communism with the same intensity and fervor with which he had embraced the teachings of Marx, Lenin, and Engels.

The FBI has plaques and monuments scattered all over buildings and grounds at FBI headquarters, the FBI academy, and FBI field offices all over the United States and around the world. However there is not a single reference to Operation Solo. There is no conference room named after the Childses, no plaque on a wall, not even a reference to Operation Solo on the FBI's tour route that chronicles much of the Bureau's history. This is an oversight long overdue for correction. Louis Freeh, shortly after becoming director, dedicated a bust to an Italian magistrate and personal acquaintance, who had been killed by the Mafia in Italy.

But there was no interest in recognizing Operation Solo. And with current Director Robert Mueller's apparent disdain for the FBI's past history and those who served before he became director, I have little confidence he will correct this long overdue oversight either.

CHAPTER 8

LA LUCHA

"You are my first American friend."
Cuban General Rafael del Pino

As the ASAC in Miami, I was responsible for all programs except drugs and applicant investigations, which left white-collar crime, organized crime, terrorism, civil rights, property crimes, bank robberies, kidnappings, fugitives, terrorism both domestic and international, and of course, counterintelligence. I was constantly faced with having to change my focus from moment to moment depending upon the telephone call or visitor to the office. But the Cuban issue was at the forefront of my daily agenda. The office carefully monitored the local Cuban community as well as activities of the Cuban intelligence service, the *Direccion General de Inteligencia*, or DGI.

In Joan Didion's book *Miami,* she speaks of *la lucha,* which means "the struggle," which describes the Cuban expatriates' preoccupation with the overthrow of Fidel Castro, particularly those who fled Cuba in the wake of Castro's rise to power. Didion writes, "One man's loose cannon is another's freedom fighter," but I found that for many Cubans the struggle and the appearance of struggle were as important, perhaps even more important, than the actual goal. A group of men would gather in a mangrove thicket armed with weapons and prepare to get underway on a boat theoretically bound for Cuba, when a whispered call would come in to the FBI or the Miami police, who would then stop the insurgents. Often these freedom fighters would not be arrested but simply given summonses. They would then return to the coffee houses on Calle Ocho and boast about how they would have really given Castro a bloody nose, except the FBI and police had stopped them. In their eyes, *la lucha* continued.

While *la lucha* serves to bind many of the original immigrants to Miami in the wake of Castro's rise to power, it is meaningless to the 125,000 *marielitas*, refugees, including a large number with criminal pasts that Castro dumped on an ill-prepared Miami in 1980. And it's also of little significance to the younger generation of Cuban Americans, who have no memory of Cuba before Castro and have no interest in ever living there. For the original immigrants, time is running out and most will never return to the Cuba of their youth, reclaim their property, and resume the lives they once knew.

The DGI and its successor organization, the *Direccion de Inteligencia*, or DI, created after General Arnaldo Ochoa and Colonel Antonio de la Guardia were executed in 1989 and the Ministry of the Interior was purged, have continued to foster a virtual siege mentality. This serves to bolster their ability to operate a police state, to quell dissent, to have neighbor spy on neighbor, all to save their country from both inside and outside forces. It also causes the DI to be willing to take risks, to be unpredictable, and to do anything necessary to protect their homeland from largely imagined threats. The DGI and the DI have been especially resourceful organizations with an uncanny ability to exploit people's weaknesses—gambling, drinking, homosexuality, and much more. Their successes have been legion.

For instance, in 1992, Juan Pablo Roque, a Cuban Air Force MiG-23 pilot, swam across Guantanamo Bay, asked for political asylum, and became a model escapee. He wrote a book critical of Castro and the Cuban military, made broadcasts into Cuba, married a Cuban American, and became a visible opponent of Castro's government. However, on February 24, 1996, Cuban MiGs shot down two planes operated by the Miami-based Brothers of the Rescue, a humanitarian group that attempts to save Cuban rafters trying to float from Cuba to Florida. Four pilots were killed. The next day, Roque appeared in Havana—without his wife—being feted by the Cuban government as a hero. He had been a false defector, an extraordinarily reckless role that very few intelligence services are willing to undertake. Paul Philip, by then the head of the Miami FBI office, admitted in a newspaper interview that the FBI had paid Roque thousands of dollars to act as a criminal informant.

Then there was Mariano Faget, an Immigration and Naturalization Service officer based in Miami who passed information from his office files to the Castro government, including information on such individuals as Norberto Fuentes and human rights activist Ricardo Bofill. Faget was arrested on February 17, 2000, and later convicted of four counts of espionage.

But the single biggest success of the Cuban intelligence apparatus wasn't in Miami; it was at the Pentagon itself. On September 21, 2002, Ann Belen Montes of the Defense Intelligence Agency was arrested by the FBI and charged with spying for the Cubans for sixteen years. She was the DIA's highest-ranking analyst on Cuban matters and had volunteered her services to the DGI. Further, like Larry Wu-tai Chin and Aldrich Ames, Montes had passed a polygraph during her government service. She pled guilty to the espionage charges and in October 2002 was sentenced to twenty-five years in prison. But she was not contrite. At her sentencing she said she felt "morally obligated to help Cuba defend itself from our efforts to impose our values and political system on it."

Even with its considerable successes, Cuban intelligence in Cuba is not nearly as effective as its reputation and these examples might indicate— there has been a steady stream of defectors to the U.S. Best known have been such athletes as Orlando "El Duque" Hernandez, who pitches for the New York Yankees, and artists such as Norberto Fuentes. There have also been many mid-ranking military and diplomatic defectors, but when I arrived in Miami, none had come from Castro's inner circle. Yet.

ON THE AFTERNOON OF MAY 27, 1987, a sunny Thursday, I was at the FBI's new building in North Miami Beach when I got a phone call from

Andre Fortier, the senior resident agent in Key West. He breathlessly notified me that a plane had just landed in Key West piloted by a Cuban air force general, Rafael del Pino Diaz. I told Fortier I would be back in touch shortly, because I knew my immediate action must be to make sure the military kept del Pino away from the news media, who would doubtless learn of the flight in short order. I insisted that the personnel at the naval air station refrain from making any public statements.

I also immediately contacted the CIA in the Miami area. I had excellent working relations with and a great deal of professional respect for the group. I advised my counterpart there of the defection and gave him del Pino's name over an open line, apologizing for the elementary breach in security because the secure phones were difficult to operate, unreliable, and frequently unintelligible.

My counterpart had not heard of the defection, nor was he familiar with del Pino, but he promised to get back to me right away. While I was awaiting the return call, I briefed SAC Bill Wells and called Alex Nogueiras, acting supervisor of FCI-1, the foreign counterintelligence squad that normally handled Cuban matters, to stand by. I also instructed him to be alert for any incoming calls from their own sources that offered any knowledge of the defection.

Within a few minutes, my CIA counterpart returned my call. His first words were, "He's a big one!" He provided me with a brief biography of del Pino, and we agreed to jointly handle del Pino's defection for the next few days. After I got off the phone, I briefed FBI headquarters. They insisted on immediate details, and Fortier and his associates were able to provide the sort of minutiae that bureaucrats thrive on.

At about 1:40 PM, an incoming aircraft had been detected on radar flying both slow and low from the east, the direction of Cuba. The Air Force scrambled two F-16s that quickly picked up a Cessna 402, color red and white, with about ten seats. The aircraft was the property of Aerocaribe, a Cuban government carrier. With del Pino at the controls, and escorted by the Air Force high performance jets, the Cessna continued toward Key West. As he approached the naval station, del Pino contacted the air traffic controllers and told them he intended to land there.

At about 2:00 PM, the aircraft touched down, obviously at the hands of an expert pilot, and taxied to a stop where it was immediately surrounded by Navy personnel.

Five passengers emerged: General del Pino; his young and attractive wife, Laura; a twenty-seven-year-old son and Cuban air force pilot, Rames del Pino Danta; a sixteen-year-old son, Rafael del Pino Lopez; and a two-year-old daughter, also named Laura. Del Pino, wearing his Cuban general's uniform and carrying a .44-caliber magnum revolver, asked for political asylum. The Navy had called Fortier, who in turn called me, within less than thirty minutes of the plane's landing.

It didn't take long for the media to start hounding us, but I refused to make any statements or have direct contact with the press. News of the defection filled the airways of the Spanish-language stations of Miami, and the coffee houses along Calle Ocho buzzed with a new topic of conversation. The Cuban community was galvanized by the news, and my own contacts within that extremely excited group started flooding me with calls.

The first concern was to determine if del Pino had any important military information. Was any type of hostile action imminent that the United States should be aware of? After del Pino insisted there were no such plans, the primary concern then became how to handle him and his family, including his sons by previous marriages. Incredibly, it appeared the members of the family knew nothing of del Pino's intent until just before he landed in Key West. According to Fortier, they seemed to be in a daze.

I had handled a defection in the past—a Chinese one—and thought there were lessons learned that could be applied to this case. Defectors go through mood swings which can be quite wide at the beginning, with wild extremes of exhilaration and depression. Over time, if all goes well, the swings become less pronounced and disappear altogether. It's important to try to control these swings early—it not only simplifies the resettlement process, it also produces better debriefings.

We had formed two teams of agents to handle the defector from China. One team, always dressed in coats and ties, handled the official and administrative matters, including the debriefings. Members of the other team, often dressed more casually, were assigned to have meals with him, drive him around, and in effect be a group he could relax with away from the worrisome formal details of a debriefing. It's important not to mix work and play while handling defectors, especially in the early stages.

I had learned that the fewer practical matters a defector has to worry about, the more he relaxes and the more reliable and useful he becomes. If a defector needs clothing, get him clothing. If he needs medical assistance, get him medical assistance. In the case of the Chinese defector, whom I'll call "Mr. Lau," as both his name and codename are still classified, we found he was overwhelmed with making decisions about what brand of toothpaste to buy or what color of jacket to wear—decisions he was not accustomed to making in a Communist society with few choices. Defectors must also have a complete assurance of safety. And while they must be allowed time alone, somebody should always be nearby unobtrusively to gauge their moods. Failure to do so often results in major problems, even embarrassments—such as the one experienced with Mr. Lau. Unfortunately, we had underestimated the depths of his mood swings. While no one was watching, he impulsively contacted the Chinese embassy from the apartment we had provided him, which was foolishly within the twenty-five-mile radius Chinese diplomatic personnel could travel without State Department notification. The embassy immediately dispatched someone to pick him up. However, after being at the embassy for a few days, where he was watched around the clock as arrangements were being made for his return to China, he realized his mistake. Using considerable guile and appealing to the consumerism of his Chinese holders, he persuaded them to take him shopping with his American money, promising to buy them items as well. While the car was stopped on a crowded Connecticut Avenue, Mr. Lau jumped out, ran down a street, and ducked into a bank where he provided a startled manager with my name and telephone number and begged him to call and ask if I would pick him up. When I got to the bank, he profusely apologized and, after further debriefings, was eventually resettled in the U.S.

Given the importance of del Pino, I was determined to take those previous lessons to heart and not make the same mistake. My first concern was to make certain the family felt safe and secure, so it was decided that the remainder of the day they landed would be spent behind the guards of the naval station in Key West. The family was assigned rooms within the officers' quarters and given food. We made sure to have guards posted just outside. Given the tension of the flight and the suddenness of their freedom, I wanted to allow the family time to sort out their own thoughts. Del Pino had dinner with the base commander—an important gesture, for it demonstrated to del Pino that he was regarded highly enough to be entertained by the highest ranking officer at the base.

I recommended to the CIA head that we use the weekend to take care of del Pino's personal interests and postpone in-depth debriefings until we were satisfied that his emotional state was showing signs of stability. He agreed, and arrangements were made for del Pino and his family to spend the weekend at Homestead Air Force Base, south of Miami. On Friday, about noon, the general and his family were escorted aboard a U.S. Navy Beechcraft C-12 twin-engine plane and departed Key West. But instead of flying to the Washington area, as was reported by the *Washington Post*, the aircraft made the short flight to Homestead. There, awaiting the flight, was a cadre of FBI, CIA, and Air Force personnel, all arranged for the purpose of making the family feel at ease.

One initial problem was clothing. The group had flown without any provisions whatsoever and had only the clothes they wore. I assigned Cecelia Woods, one of my agents, to meet the family and specifically take care of the wife. I reasoned that Woods, who always dressed impeccably, would be a good first impression for del Pino's wife and, given she was also fluent in Spanish, would ease her sense of alienation. I also sent Alex Nogueiras, a very capable Cuban-American agent, and Pedro Martinez, a senior member of the squad whose calm demeanor would aid the settling-down process. It was decided that the Air Force would open the base PX after hours and allow the family to go shopping, with the FBI footing the bill, though at the time, I didn't have permission to make such expenditures. After their shopping expedition, the family had dinner, settled into their comfortable quarters with their guards readily visible, and, unlike the previous night, got some rest.

The next day, I went to visit del Pino—not at all what I expected of a Cuban Air Force general. I met a smiling man, short and stocky in build, with curly, graying hair, who just didn't project the image of a Cuban revolutionary. We settled down, and I spent the first part of our conversation ensuring myself that he was satisfied with the arrangements that had been made on his behalf. Clearly he was. His sixteen-year-old son strolled through wearing fashionable tennis shoes, dressed in typical American teenager apparel. His wife, Laura, was also casually dressed, with Cecelia Woods's handiwork clearly evident. Together, they projected the very image of an American family—a primary goal of the initial stage of defection.

We spent the next several hours alternately talking about various events and doing some degree of debriefings. Much to my surprise, del Pino was ready for the inevitable debriefings and seemed to be eager to start. But given the fact that most of his privileged knowledge involved military matters, I was content to let those experts handle that. I simply wanted to get to know him, to let him get comfortable being surrounded by a group of people that forty-eight hours earlier were the enemy of his country.

I knew the del Pinos would leave Florida on Monday, so I decided we should have a special occasion on Sunday. I asked the squad members to arrange for a picnic in the fenced area behind the guesthouse del Pino had been assigned, which would include grilled steaks, ice cream, and other all-American food. On Sunday morning, I took del Pino a couple of books from my personal library, a copy of Edward Jablonski's *Airwar*, a book filled with aircraft pictures and information, and a book of paintings, *The Aviation Art of Keith Ferris*. I also presented him with a large American flag, a gesture that obviously touched him as he visibly attempted to keep his emotions under control. We passed a delightful afternoon eating American steaks, sitting in a back yard under the waving flag of del Pino's new country.

During those conversations with del Pino, I learned a great deal about his past. The general had actually protested against the corrupt and brutal regime of Fulgencio Batista, the Cuban president and former military leader driven from office in 1959 by Castro's rebels. At one point during his teens in the mid 1950s, del Pino's father had sent him to the Harrison Chilhowee Baptist Academy in Seymour, Tennessee, a small town in the hills near Knoxville. This had occurred after del Pino had been arrested in an anti-Batista demonstration while still a high school student. His father, a Baptist himself, apparently hoped, that the daily exposure to religion and his friendship with students who did not advocate revolution, would have a settling effect. But he underestimated the depth of the anger, especially among the youth of Cuba, at the Batista government, for del Pino did not quit his flirtation with the older firebrand Castro and became instead, upon his return, Castro's confidante and traveling companion even before the success of the revolution. The lure of flying had been ingrained in him since he was a child, and when Castro overthrew the Batista regime, del Pino volunteered for the fledgling Cuban Air Force and soon became an accomplished pilot.

I deduced that del Pino had been a part of the Cuban forces that repelled the Americans during the Bay of Pigs. I asked him about his involvement, and he responded that, as a soldier, he had simply been doing his duty, defending his country during a time when he believed the revolution was for the good of the Cuban people. But this was before Castro proclaimed he was an avowed Communist. Del Pino's exploits were chronicled in Peter Wyden's *The Bay of Pigs: The Untold Story*. As the youngest member of the Cuban Air Force assigned to stop the invaders, del Pino flew an aging T-33 aircraft that was in poor condition. He had already crashed in one such aircraft, and the mechanical condition of the second made him think it might meet a similar fate.

Del Pino knew he would be facing American pilots whose skill he greatly admired. But he took off anyway and soon spotted a B-29 from the invading force. Del Pino got so close to the enemy aircraft before opening fire he could actually see the pilot's helmet. He continued firing until the large World War II vintage bomber crashed into the water. The following day, del Pino was in the air again when he spotted a destroyer from the U.S. Navy. He mistakenly assumed another invasion was underway as there were a number of small craft and debris in the water between the destroyer and the shore. He strafed the boats and sent a message to his superiors that another invasion was under way, when in fact there was no invasion. But he returned a hero and was prominent among those feted for defending against the invading forces.

Still, del Pino did not become an avowed Communist and never became a member of the ruling hierarchy. Perhaps his familial past as a Baptist in Cuba was part of the reason, and he never embraced the tenets of Communism itself. He was, instead, a professional soldier who served his country over the years, which eventually lead to his being assigned to Angola as head of the Cuban forces fighting in that civil war.

Del Pino and I engaged in long discussions about Castro, Cuba, baseball, families, and his career as a pilot. Del Pino's favorite sports team, as it was for most Cubans, was the New York Yankees. While talking to del Pino and baseball, I thought of Ernest Hemingway's magnificent book *The Old Man and the Sea* and the scene where Santiago, the old man was telling the boy, "The Yankees cannot lose."

"But I fear the Indians of Cleveland," the boy worried.

"Have faith in the Yankees my son. Think of the great DiMaggio."

We talked about his being at Homestead Air Force Base, a large facility to the south of Miami itself that could be considered the first line of defense if the Cuban government (or their Soviet allies during the Cold War), were ever foolish enough to launch aircraft toward the U.S. Del Pino stated he was quite familiar with the base. On October 5, 1969, a Cuban Air Force lieutenant defected to the United States flying a Russian-made MiG-17 fighter plane, landing at Homestead. Several days later, it was arranged with the Americans for del Pino and another pilot to fly to the base and return the plane to Cuba. As he approached the base, del Pino pretended to be confused about the runways and circled the base several times. His aircraft had been equipped with cameras, and he photographed the base while circling.

We also talked about Castro, who del Pino confirmed was in excellent health but paranoid about being assassinated by the CIA. Castro had given up scuba diving for fear that a porpoise with explosives attached to its head would be directed by the CIA to crash into him. Castro retained a love for duck hunting but, as the supreme commander, had little patience in waiting for the ducks to fly. His solution was that Cuban pilots were ordered to fly low over the resting, feeding ducks, causing them to take flight and giving Castro a perfect opportunity to shoot. As a longtime associate of Raul Castro, Fidel's younger brother and head of the Cuban military forces, del Pino had a personal and intimate perspective of the heir apparent to Fidel. But del Pino expressed serious doubts whether Raul was up to the task of succeeding his brother. He did not possess Fidel's charisma and, according to del Pino, would fail if ever he ascended to the position.

One trail of conversation I found particularly fascinating concerned Vietnam. At the end of the war, del Pino had headed a group of Cuban military officers that went to Vietnam on a "shopping" trip. Del Pino described his considerable surprise at the amount of military equipment that had been abandoned by the departing American forces and the defeated South Vietnamese. This included weaponry of all kinds and, to del Pino's astonishment, aircraft that had been left entirely intact. One such aircraft was a high performance F-5 fighter jet. Without ever having been in such an aircraft, del Pino climbed into the cockpit, studied the numerous dials and controls, then started the engine, taxied down the runway, and went up for a spin. Amazing. Nothing about this general with his calm demeanor gave any indication of the daredevil pilot who could boldly fly a plane he had never seen before.

Del Pino also spoke of the increasing stress Cuba was facing—how the war in Angola had sapped a great deal of Cuba's vitality. He mentioned that as the numbers of dead grew—estimating the losses at over ten thousand—the Cuban government buried their soldiers in Angola to avoid giving the populace a true picture of how that dirty little war was costing them. Castro had been painting a much more romantic picture of the campaign.

The conversation continued until late in the afternoon, and as dusk approached, it was time for me to depart. The next morning del Pino and his family would be flown from Homestead to another location for debriefings and ultimately to a new life in the United States. I was convinced they would be fine. After taking pictures and bidding farewell to the family, I said a final goodbye to del Pino himself. He grabbed me in a bear hug, thanked me for all that had been done, and said, "You are my first American friend."

I have never seen him again.

The next week I had a visit from a member of the Cuban exile community, a Bay of Pigs veteran who had been imprisoned in Cuba after being captured on the beaches during that ill-fated attempt to overthrow Castro with CIA-trained Cuban freedom fighters. Of course del Pino's defection was a primary topic of conversation, if not the real reason for the visit itself, and at one point he mentioned he would like to meet del Pino. I responded, perhaps inappropriately, that I assumed he would like to meet del Pino in order to kill him, but he smiled and said that was not the case at all. He went on to explain that he had been among the small boats that had been strafed by del Pino, and while del Pino had been making strafing runs from his T-33 aircraft, he had been firing at del Pino's plane. I was blown away. Neither del Pino nor this veteran, one-time mortal enemies, exhibited any real hatred toward the other. I learned that in conversations as prisoners of war, fighters from both sides could almost give a person-to-person account of who was where during the Bay of Pigs engagement. The combatants had been few enough in number that their individual roles had been chronicled, not just the unit and battalion records that are normally recorded. It was that personal.

I did hear from del Pino the following year in the form of a personal letter, written in a neat, flowing hand, which had been forwarded to me in Canberra, Australia, where I had been transferred as legal attaché. He wished me well, then wrote, "All of you helped me a lot, especially in the uncertain moments after the arrival. The courtesy, friendship, and support you gave us I'll never forget and really were decisive at the beginning of our new life." After reading that statement, I knew our tack for handling del Pino had been the right one, though there were many who were irritated that intense debriefings did not start almost instantly.

In his letter, del Pino mentioned he was completing his book, later published with the title *Proa a la Libertad*, literally, "In the Direction of Freedom," and then made a request. He asked that I attempt to have the .44 magnum revolver returned to him, even if it was "deactivated," for he wished to keep it along with his uniform and medals that he had taken with him on that "unforgettable flight to freedom in May the 28th 1987." I notified the Miami office of del Pino's request but never learned if the weapon was returned to him.

Del Pino has not become a vocal part of the extreme anti-Castro element, but on occasion has weighed in on issues with a measured and thoughtful approach. He was a soldier, and as Marcus Aurelius wrote, "I do my duty; other things trouble me not." He did his duty, but he became disenchanted with the direction he saw Cuba had taken, even feeling a sense of betrayal, and finally arrived at the conclusion nothing was going to change in the near future.

He concluded his letter to me with, "God bless you and your family"—certainly not the parting wish of a Communist revolutionary.

CHAPTER 9

THE MEETING THAT NEVER WAS

"Was this Mr. Smith lying to us?"
Fidel Castro

O ne of the great misconceptions Americans have about the relations between the U.S. and Cuba is that the longstanding U.S.
embargo has resulted in virtually no contact between the countries. This
is simply not the case. Cuban Americans can and do travel to Cuba
using third-country flights, at least, before the Bush administration's ill-
advised recently enacted restrictions on such travel. They also communicate by both telephone and rather ingenious codes. For instance,
someone could call a Spanish-language radio station and mention he is
going fishing on Key Biscayne later that day along the pilings of the
bridge, unless a storm comes up unexpectedly. A listener monitoring the
broadcast in Cuba will recognize the caller and the coded message that
signals money being mailed, a trip being planned, or perhaps warning
that a planned escape should not be carried out.

Fernando (which is not his real name, for he must remain anonymous even today) was one such man. He was a member of a prominent
family in Cuba who, it was said, had been imprisoned after Castro had
overthrown Fulgencio Batista and then ransomed for a sizeable sum.
Fernando had made a successful life in the United States, but as most of
those who had been forced out by the Castro regime, still longed for a
return to his Cuban homeland.

Fernando had the ability to travel to Cuba and had even been culti-
vated by Castro in the dictator's attempt to gain influence within the
exile community in Miami. Certainly Castro would have known of, if he
not had been personally acquainted with, Fernando's politically prominent family in pre-revolutionary Cuba, and I always suspected Castro
made overtures to Fernando through relatives that had remained in
Cuba. One day in the late spring of 1987, Fernando told me he was traveling to Havana along with a companion I will refer to as Roberto. He
mentioned he would be visiting Colonel Antonio de la Guardia, a member of Castro's palace guard, as well as the head of the DGI, General
German Barrios. Fernando and Roberto believed that de la Guardia
would like to meet with me. I told them that while I would love to meet
the colonel, I couldn't agree to it without getting clearance through FBI
channels since Bureau policy precluded formal contacts with Cuban
officials. They agreed but were not going to be deterred, far-fetched as
the proposal was. Fernando made it clear to me that he wanted to show
the Cubans he had personal contacts within the U.S. government, and it
was apparent he viewed me as such a prominent contact. So I sent a note
with Fernando, a generic wish-you-well-on-your-trip message on plain
bond paper, that I assumed would be shown to de la Guardia and
Barrios.

De la Guardia, who had been a prominent fixture within the DGI for
years, was known as a confidante of Castro himself. In Tad Szulc's book
Fidel: A Critical Portrait, Szulc writes, "Over the years (José Luis)
Padron (assisted by Tony de la Guardia, another Security colonel at the
palace) had met secretly with senior United States Department of State
officials in Miami, New York, Washington, Atlanta, and Cuernavaca,
Mexico, to explore the possibilities of agreement between the two
countries."

Fernando and Roberto returned from Cuba with a note and a box of
Cohiba cigars from de la Guardia. I didn't ask how they managed to get
the cigars past customs officials. I opened the envelope, which was not
sealed and obviously had been read, if not copied, by Fernando and
Roberto, and found the neatly typewritten note as follows:

Dear Mr. Smith,

I was very pleased to receive your note. It would be very nice to have a meeting and to this aim our common friends [Fernando] and [Roberto] are carrying you a message to make possible this meeting.

My regards, sincerely,
Antonio de la Guardia

Members of Castro's innermost circle wanted to meet with me and had sent a box of rare and expensive (and illegal) cigars as a gesture of friendship. I was required to report all such gifts to FBI headquarters, so I prepared a teletype describing the gift and my awareness of the prohibition against receiving them, and that consequently they were being "burned." I didn't receive a response.

After closely questioning Fernando and Roberto, I determined that this invitation was not being made by de la Guardia alone. In fact, Barrios had been part of the conversation, and the offer was approved by the powerful interior minister General Jose Abrahantes Fernandez, as well as Castro himself. The more I thought about it, the more awestruck I became. In effect, Fidel Castro, through trusted subordinates, was reaching out to establish a dialogue, and I had been chosen to represent our side. I asked Fernando and Roberto why he picked the FBI. They told me Castro didn't trust the CIA or the Department of State but did trust the FBI. This was a curious distinction but likely attributable to the FBI's historically aggressive investigation under the Neutrality Act of exile groups who were attempting armed excursions against Cuba. The big question now was: how could I possibly report the general's invitation for a meeting to FBI headquarters in a way that would give it any hope of approval?

I took my best shot, and the response was both shortsighted and predictable. There would be no meeting.

But I persisted by making telephone calls, stating my position in numerous communications to FBI headquarters. When FBI headquarters would respond with another reason why the meeting should not occur, I would respond with some reason debunking their latest refusal to approve the concept. Finally, the FBI agreed to reevaluate the opportunity. When Fernando and Roberto notified me they were returning to Cuba, and after FBI headquarters had tentatively agreed to consider a meeting in Washington, I proposed that I reciprocate de la Guardia's courtesy by sending gifts to him and Barrios.

I asked the supervisor of the FCI-1 squad, an insightful and intelligent agent named Sherry Frew, to provide me with her best analysis on the advisability of the trip. She agreed there was much to gain by meeting with de la Guardia. With that little bit of encouragement, I requested authority to purchase gifts for de la Guardia and Barrios. I received approval to buy one gift, not two. This made for an awkward situation, since it would be exceedingly difficult for Fernando and Roberto to present a gift to de la Guardia, their principal point of contact, without having one to present to Barrios, his superior, as well. I argued with my point of contact at FBI headquarters to no avail. To avoid embarrassment, Fernando and Roberto had to have two gifts. Fortunately, a local department store had some handsome leather valises on sale so I could buy two for almost the original price of one. At my request, the sales clerk kindly indicated I had bought only one item on the sales receipt— I was determined to be reimbursed.

While Roberto and Fernando were in Havana, my secretary, Kerry Jo Hochheimer, answered the phone, then sat bolt upright, her eyes as big as dinner plates. "Mr. Smith," she said, "you have a call from Cuba." It was General de la Guardia. I picked up the phone and talked directly to the Cuban DGI, not the kind of conversation an FBI agent expects to have. De la Guardia was pleasant and spoke softly in accented, almost musical English, not unlike much of what I heard along Calle Ocho in Little Havana. We tentatively scheduled a meeting in Washington, contingent upon my gaining approval. I told de la Guardia that I hoped we would have the opportunity to meet, exchanged a few pleasantries, and concluded our conversation. The pace of events was quickening.

Fernando and Roberto returned with another note, again neatly typewritten:

Dear Mr. Smith,

First of all I would like to thank you for your nice present.

On relation with our conversation, I am sending you the name of one of the persons that will travel with me, the other name will be sent next week. We will travel from Havana to Canada and from Canada direct to Washington. [Roberto] will travel with us from Havana.

I hope that when we arrive to Washington [Fernando] and members of your staff will be waiting for us.

Signed: Antonio de la Guardia

This information was reported to FBI headquarters. And, of course, they decided there would be no meeting.

The next time I met with Fernando, he mentioned the Cubans were having a difficult time learning anything about me, which was frustrating them. I never talked about my personal or professional past with Fernando or Roberto, and he knew little except that I had served in Washington. In fact, while we were talking I received another phone call from de la Guardia. His first words were, "Ah, Mr. Smith, now I know what you look like." A few days previous I had given an interview to a Spanish-language television station that was largely viewed by the Cuban exile community. Apparently, the signal was monitored in Cuba as well, and de la Guardia got his first glimpse of Agent Smith.

A proposal to meet the Cubans in New York was also soundly rejected, but FBI headquarters did propose a meeting be held in another country in the Western Hemisphere. (The CIA, in its pre-publication review of this book, requested that the specific country be deleted.) I objected to meeting in that country, especially when I found out the authorities there would not even be notified. I knew de la Guardia would be on any country's immigration watch list of known Cuban intelligence officers, and if we were observed together the FBI would be in hot water having to explain why such a meeting took place on the soil of a staunch ally without their being notified.

I had continued to stress to Fernando and Roberto that I could not meet with de la Guardia just for the sake of meeting. There had to be some tangible objective. Of course, I couldn't discuss purely political or intelligence matters due to FBI policy, but perhaps we could cover the area of law enforcement. There were scores of American fugitives in Cuba, and while I didn't expect the Cubans to turn over high-profile figures like JoAnne Chesimard or Robert Vesco to me, I thought there might be some good-faith gesture involving lesser known and politically less sensitive criminals—bank robbers, aircraft hijackers, or the like. Fernando and Roberto relayed this sentiment to de la Guardia and assured me that he understood my point.

The Cubans, at this time, had a certain amount of smug confidence, for once again they had embarrassed the United States. In an extraordinary and unprecedented action, the Cubans televised an eleven-part series entitled *La Guerra De La CIA Contra Cuba,* or *The CIA's War against Cuba.* Under the auspices of the government-controlled Cuban Television Information Service, the Cuban Ministry of Interior showed the world how CIA operations in Cuba had been compromised for well over a decade. In excruciating detail, with surprisingly advanced production values, the Cubans proved the CIA had been outwitted for much of the previous decade, if not longer. There were images of CIA officers, identified with full names and photographs, conducting dead drops, i.e. leaving and picking up packages containing radios, money, and instructions for Cuban agents ostensibly working for the CIA, but in actuality, working on behalf of the Cubans.

The Cubans provided figures revealing the number of CIA officers posted since the opening of the Interest Section in Havana, broken down by duty: 179 officers, 27 lie detector operators, 28 communication technicians, and 18 collaborators. They claimed knowledge of 122 intelligence drops around Cuba and showed in fascinating detail some of the tradecraft associated with such activities. Examples included such tried and trusted techniques as marks on walls and park benches that would indicate if a meet was on as scheduled, if one was being followed, if a meet had been conducted, etc. One Cuban double agent explained how different color shirts provided signals to CIA personnel, who would drive by and see their contact sitting on a bench. There were false CIA rocks that DGI personnel cut open to reveal hollow interiors, which might hold radios or cash.

And some of it was just downright humiliating. There were scenes of a CIA officer searching for a package in tall grass while his wife, sitting in a car, whined in the background for him to hurry up, all captured with state-of-the-art color video and remarkably clear audio equipment. One CIA officer, after locating a package, discovered he had lost his car keys. The film showed him anxiously scouring the ground for his keys. It was obvious the Cubans wanted to show the CIA in the worst possible light, and they exceeded beyond anyone's expectations.

The CIA faced a worst-case scenario, having to consider all operations now compromised and thus all information received from the agents as suspect. In effect, the human intelligence (HUMINT) capability of the CIA and the United States, as far as Cuba was concerned, was suddenly zilch.

The Cuban TV series became the topic of many meetings within the U.S. intelligence community. When Fernando and Roberto were planning a trip to Cuba after the broadcast, I asked them almost as an afterthought if they could get copies of the shows dubbed into English. I didn't expect any real response and became a little concerned when they didn't return as planned. They got back a day late and explained it was because the Cubans had complied with my request and it took an extra day to complete the translation. A few days later at a meeting in the Miami office with FBI and CIA personnel, a CIA representative offered to play the "CIA Tapes," apologizing that they were in Spanish. I interrupted to say I had English copies. When he asked, surprised, where I had gotten them, I simply stated, "I asked them for a set," and walked away without further explanation.

But the fact was that Barrios, certainly with the approval of Abrahantes if not Castro himself, had provided me with the requested copies. This meant they were serious about establishing a dialogue with me. I redoubled my efforts to make the meeting occur.

Finally a meeting was scheduled in Madrid, Spain, for after the first of the year. My persistence had finally worn down their tendency to be risk averse and to adopt the attitude that it was easier to say "No" as opposed to attempting to see the larger potential value in such an operation. It had taken months to even get them to raise the issue with the CIA and the National Security Council. They displayed little imagination, little understanding of the potential benefits of such a meeting, and little willingness to take any risk in any operation, not just that involving de la Guardia. But with the eventual acquiesce of the CIA and the National Security Council, the FBI could no longer legitimately continue to resist the meeting. The CIA, after the debacle with the tapes, wasn't in a position to object and the National Security Council, in the absence of any opposition from the Agency, had no basis for objecting either. The plan called for Fernando and Roberto to travel to Cuba to meet with de la Guardia, then the three would jet over to Spain and await my arrival. At last, everything was set. I hustled to update my passport. As was my habit, I had not provided details of my impending adventure to Carla but simply told her I would be traveling to Spain for a few days for some meetings.

Arrangements had been made for a series of final contacts to confirm my plans, and once again, Fernando and Roberto departed for Cuba. I was to call de la Guardia at telephone number 1-700-460-1000, extension 219812, before departing to ensure him that the trip would indeed take place and discuss any last minute details. On the day that the call was to be made, January 7, 1988, two hours before my scheduled contact with de la Guardia, I received a telephone call from FBI headquarters stating the trip had been cancelled.

To put it simply and politely, I was disgusted. I asked the caller, since the FBI bureaucrats had been so generous and forthcoming in offering advice up to that point, what they proposed I tell de la Guardia. And further, what was the reason for the eleventh hour cancellation of the trip that had the approval of both the CIA and the NSC? I was told the trip had been cancelled because a member of Vice President George Bush's staff on the NSC had found out about the meeting and objected to it. Bush was then beginning his 1988 presidential campaign.

When I questioned the reason for the objection, I was told there was concern that if news of the meeting leaked out—a meeting sanctioned by the Reagan administration itself—the news would hurt Bush's electoral prospects in Florida among the exile community in the upcoming Super Tuesday primary elections. I was both depressed and appalled that a meeting of this sort, designed to provide a conduit of communications between the Cuban and U.S. governments, with incredible potential to head off future misunderstandings and disputes, had been cancelled for blatantly political reasons.

I persisted in pressing the caller. What should I tell de la Guardia when I was to call him in less than two hours? It was apparent they had not given that matter any thought, so I told him I would fall back on diplomatic language, something I was loath to do, and simply tell the colonel it wasn't "convenient" I travel at the time. This was agreed upon by the headquarters caller, who was by then simply anxious to have the matter over with.

At noon I started trying to place the call to Cuba but couldn't get through. I kept calling. No results. I notified agent Sherry Frew, whose advice had been so helpful in cultivating my relationship with the Cubans and who was also dejected by the sudden turn of events. As the afternoon wore along and I was becoming increasingly frustrated, the phone rang. My secretary told me I had a caller from Cuba. It was de la Guardia.

I apologized for not placing the call at the appointed time, explaining the problem with the phone lines. He was polite and understanding, but when I told him it was "not convenient" that I travel to Spain, he got quiet. He said little else as I told him I regretted the last minute cancellation, wished him the best, and hung up. I never heard from de la Guardia again.

The following day Fernando returned from Cuba and came to see me. He too was dejected and provided details of what occurred when the meeting had been cancelled. He said he and Roberto were in a room with de la Guardia, Barrios, Abrahantes, and Castro himself. Barrios had erupted in anger, stating it had all been a plot to embarrass Cuba again. But Castro remained calm. He turned to Fernando and asked, "Was this Mr. Smith lying to us?" Fernando replied, "No, I think he just got caught up in politics." Castro then responded, "I can understand that," and walked out. But this did not end my involvement with de la Guardia.

A short time later I discovered I was being considered for the position of legal attaché in Canberra, Australia. Sean McWeeny, the head of the Office of Liaison and International Affairs, wanted to recommend me in part because he knew I had an interest in international matters, had done inspections of the offices in Hong Kong and Tokyo, and had been of assistance to the legal attaché offices in the Caribbean and Central and South America. The assignment would include my establishing relations with the independent nations of the South Pacific, a first for the FBI. I thought back to my days of reading Michener's *Tales of the South Pacific* immersed in the stories of those great battles during World War II. I was intrigued by the prospect and discussed the matter with my family. The next evening, after I had returned home and was in the swimming pool, Carla came out, stood on the edge of the pool, and said she and the girls thought we should "go for it."

As we waited for word on the Canberra opportunity, I received a telephone call from Richard Held, the SAC in San Francisco, who needed a favor. I had known and liked Held for a number of years and told him of course I would do what I could. He explained there was a group of about a hundred wealthy individuals, principally Californians, who were members of the conservative World Business Council. This group periodically took fact-finding trips and had managed to obtain permission to travel to Cuba for sixteen hours, chartering a Lockheed L-1011 jumbo airliner for the few minutes' trip to Havana from Miami. One of the members, Robert G. Holmes, had asked if someone could provide them with a briefing about Cuba before they went. Held recommended me for the job.

I agreed and on February 5 found myself in front of a well-informed group providing an unclassified briefing of the economic, political, and social situation in Cuba. Among other things I told them not to be surprised if Fidel Castro himself showed up, though he wasn't on the itinerary, for he wouldn't want to miss the opportunity to impress a group of conservative Republicans who had influence in the White House.

After the meeting ended, I was approached by Mr. Holmes, who said he had an acquaintance at the Hungarian embassy in Havana and had tried without success to make arrangements to visit him during the trip. He had been constantly rebuffed and asked if I had any suggestions. I thought for a moment, then told him that he should not ask any questions, but I would try something. I gave him one of my business cards and on the back wrote the name "Colonel Antonio de la Guardia Font." I said he should ask for de la Guardia and show him the business card, explaining we were friends, and see if de la Guardia could be of assistance. Holmes looked at me somewhat incredulously but took the card.

While we were in the car talking, the car phone rang and an obviously agitated Bill Wells notified me I had been selected to go to Canberra. Wells had intervened to try and keep me from being selected and in fact, another individual had initially been chosen; but when Oliver "Buck" Revell, a Bureau classmate of Wells, heard of the selection, he went to Director William Sessions and the selection had been changed. I turned to Holmes and told him that he was the first to know I was being transferred to Canberra. Holmes congratulated me; his enthusiasm was a welcome contrast to Wells's dour conversation.

The next morning the group departed for Havana, and after they returned late that evening I received a call from Holmes. He was obviously elated with the trip. He described how, when passing through customs, he had asked a guard to see Colonel de la Guardia. Holmes said the guard had noticeably stiffened and had quickly talked to a supervisor who had gone to a telephone. A short time later de la Guardia had shown up. Holmes said he showed de la Guardia the business card at which time the colonel asked Holmes if he was with the CIA. Holmes assured him he wasn't, that he was just a businessman who was a friend of mine. De La Guardia responded, "If you are a friend of Mr. Smith's, what can I do for you?" This resulted in Holmes being able to visit with his acquaintance from the Hungarian embassy in Havana.

Holmes then told me how the group had been assembled for a series of briefings and that Castro had indeed appeared. He described how when Castro walked in, the guards and staff members had quickly come to attention, except de la Guardia, who seemed quite at ease in Castro's presence. The colonel continued to lean against a wall and did not stand in rapt attention as did the others during the resultant long speech by Castro, a speech that Holmes laughingly told me, almost convinced him of Castro's view of the world. Holmes said he had found de la Guardia to be rather cosmopolitan, wearing Gucci shoes, an avid sailor with a sense of humor. Of course, as happy as I was for Holmes's success, the call only served to make the disappointment of my cancelled trip more acute.

The Super Tuesday primaries took place on March 8. The race was hotly contested with Senator Bob Dole, Congressman Jack Kemp, and television evangelist Pat Robertson refusing to cede Ronald Reagan's mantle to Vice President Bush. The New Hampshire primary had been especially acrimonious, as Dole had asked Bush to quit lying about Dole's record. The Iran–Contra matter was still unresolved, and Marine Corps Colonel Oliver North had been charged with sixteen criminal counts related to that whole sordid affair. But on Super Tuesday, Bush easily carried Dade County and received the vast majority of the Cuban vote, a vote that was influenced by their belief that Bush was the heir apparent to their hero, Ronald Reagan.

In July 1989, after my transfer to Australia, I received a note from Holmes with a newspaper clipping. The article detailed how General Arnaldo Ochoa, the hero of the Cuban revolution and a compatriot of General Rafael del Pino's in Angola, had been put to death. Also on the list of those who has been put on trial and were to be executed was Colonel Antonio de la Guardia, "who headed the intelligence agency entrusted with circumventing a U.S. economic embargo." This brought an end at last to the de la Guardia story, a missed opportunity on a giant scale, for when Fernando returned from Cuba that last time, I asked what he thought were de la Guardia's motives for initiating the contacts with the FBI and his persistence in view of all the setbacks. Fernando told me he believed de la Guardia was exploring his prospects for defection. De la Guardia was certainly mercenary and would have liked to know what he was worth before leaving the relative security and comfort of Castro's inner circle, though he knew all to well even that position was fraught with danger.

In Castro's Cuba, the sun shines only on Fidel. I am convinced Ochoa's demise was due to his popularity among the troops he had served with in Angola, and among average Cubans on the street, especially when compared with Raul Castro, Fidel's longtime heir apparent. As for de la Guardia, certainly there was a relationship with Ochoa, but there was also a relationship with longtime fugitive financier Robert Vesco. Years later, Vesco would also fall from favor with Castro. Perhaps de la Guardia came under suspicion, and in Castro's Cuba being under suspicion is comparable to being found guilty. If he was in fact plotting to defect, it would have been a remarkable intelligence coup and if not, and his intent was only to establish a medium of communications, then too, that would have been a promising turn of events. Somehow I believe the embarrassment of the defection of General Rafael del Pino played a part in the decision by Castro to eliminate Ochoa and de la Guardia.

On my last day in the Miami office, in a surprise ceremony, I was awarded a plaque by Georgia J. Ayers, director of The Alternative Programs, a program designed to help the youth of the area who are at risk, with the inscription: "You Are One Of A Kind." That remark could more appropriately be applied to Ms. Ayers, a remarkable lady with a great sense of dedication to helping her fellow man. It also could have been applied to Miami itself. A city full of passion and energy. A city that, despite its tendency for violence, I would miss.

I was also surprised by a visit from the CIA, which presented me with a medal. I protested, saying it was the effort of the counterintelligence squad members who were deserving of any accolades. My counterpart, whom I had grown to like and respect, responded, "You set the atmosphere for cooperation."

On April 21, just a few days before I departed, Fernando paid a last visit to my office. When he came in he could barely speak. He had always worn his emotions on his sleeve. We talked briefly, he thanked me, told me I would not be forgotten, embraced me, and with tears rolling down his cheeks, Fernando left my office for the last time.

CHAPTER 10

DOWN UNDER

*"We still live in one of the billabongs of the world,
away from the mainstream."*

Professor Geoffrey Blainey in *The Tyranny of Distance:
How Distance Shaped Australia's History*

D uring World War II, well before the formation of the CIA, the FBI was conducting operations against German operatives in South America. Today's FBI legal attaché is part of an American embassy staff working to build effective relationships with the law enforcement, security, and, to a lesser degree, intelligence agencies of that country and others in the region. In a post–9/11 world, the FBI's overseas role takes on an added, even critical, importance to the nation's security.

Though an assignment as legal attaché could hamper my career advancement potential within the Bureau, I was willing to take the risk for the sheer joy and challenge of working in Canberra, Australia, establishing relations with the law enforcement agencies in the South Pacific. Buck Revell staffed the FBI's legal attaché program principally with agents who had been integral to the Bureau and had full intentions of returning to the FBI with new international skills. But Revell's vision was not shared by everyone in power. Once Revell moved to Dallas and Louis Freeh replaced William Sessions as director, the legal attaché program fell victim to the cronyism and antimanagement attitude that quickly permeated the FBI under Freeh. The program was eventually staffed by many with no prior management experience, no social grace, and none of the essential diplomatic skills or international awareness necessary for representing the U.S. abroad.

The indoctrination started quickly. The week after my family and I arrived in Canberra, outgoing legal attaché Jim Sturgis arranged for an ambitious round of introductions. In Sydney, I met John K. Avery, commissioner of the New South Wales police. A small, dark-haired man with a perpetual five o'clock shadow, Avery was a rarity among Australian policemen in that he had academic degrees and studied in the United States. He was a farsighted law enforcement officer who had responsibility for one of the more demanding law enforcement jobs anywhere. He and I soon became fast friends, or in the Australian vernacular, "mates."

As legal attaché, I became a member of the Country Team consisting of the heads of various embassy staff agencies and departments within the State Department. This advisory group discussed issues surrounding U.S.-Australian relations, providing insight and suggestions to ensure smooth diplomatic cooperation. It was essential that the FBI remain a visible participant in embassy affairs. Even though I represented the FBI and the Department of Justice, I felt sure my actions were subject to the approval of the ambassador.

Carla and I often played host to embassy guests at official functions, just like Foreign Service officers and their spouses did. These events were not for the entertainment and pleasure of the embassy staff. We were expected to take care of official guests and others to improve our relations with them. Carla became a "guide" for the ambassador's residence, learning about its paintings and architecture. In short order we were hosting a steady flow of visitors to Australia as representatives of both the FBI and the embassy staff.

We were visited by Senators Alan Simpson and Jesse Helms, the latter of whom was, at least from the standpoint of the Foreign Service officers, something akin to a pit viper on the loose. The officers consciously avoided him, and so I found myself chatting with him a good part of the time. He told me I sounded like Russell Long, longtime

Louisiana senator and son of Huey Long, the legendary Kingfish. I took it as a compliment. Simpson, the tall, angular, slow-talking senator from Wyoming, was entertaining and just as candid in private as he is publicly. Carla and I ate dinner with him that evening and had a delightful time—he seemed genuinely interested in what we were doing and how we were faring, and thanked us for our work.

Chief Justice William Rehnquist visited on another occasion, and I was assigned to play host to him at the inevitable embassy reception. Rehnquist was somewhat imperial and not especially sociable, but I attributed that to the fact his back was bothering him noticeably. The contrast to the affable and polite Harry Blackmun was apparent, and though I asked that he give Justice Blackmun my regards, I never had any confidence he would do so.

EARLY IN MY ASSIGNMENT I visited Peter McAuley, the commissioner of the Australian Federal Police, at his farm on the outskirts of Canberra. We were walking around the property when McAuley, a tall, grizzled man who had spent his adult life as a police officer, suddenly asked about my relationship with the CIA and whether I was familiar with the Whitlam matter. It was a story the Australians knew well. On November 11, 1975, Labor Party Prime Minister Gough Whitlam was dismissed by Governor General Sir John Kerr in what was termed a "budget crisis." There were comments that the CIA had been involved which, if true, would be a serious violation of the CIA's stated policy of not interfering in the internal affairs of a friend and ally.

In 1986, the Public Broadcasting Network of Australia aired a six-part series that included interviews with former CIA personnel claiming that the CIA was involved in Whitlam's dismissal. Startling information in the series came from Christopher Boyce, who, along with Andrew Daulton Lee, the infamous "Falcon and Snowman" of movie and book fame, had been convicted of espionage for spying for the Soviet Union. Boyce said that while employed by TRW in California he had seen a teletype between CIA representatives in Australia and CIA headquarters in the U.S. indicating the CIA had been involved, aided by the acquiescence of the Australian Secret Intelligence Service and the Australian Security Intelligence Organization. I had my own diplomatically sensitive encounter with the ASIO, which wanted direct contact with the FBI in all counterintelligence matters and not have them filtered through any other entities. But the CIA head in Canberra, a friend of mine, suggested I channel all intelligence and counterintelligence contacts through his office. I told him that was unacceptable, but if he insisted, through the ambassador, I would go directly to FBI Director Sessions with the matter and, further, would suggest all counterintelligence matters be handled through liaison officers in Washington. The matter was not raised again.

Still some did not get the word. In the wake of the Cold War, after I had been reassigned to Washington, a CIA officer approached a foreign police force about confidentially providing information on organized crime to the CIA. (During its pre-publication review of this book, the CIA requested the police force not be identified.) This was during a period when the Agency was scrambling to find a mission in the post–Cold War period. While I had no problem with the CIA collecting such information if organized crime posed a threat to a country's stability, there was no basis for collecting it from an ally whose government wasn't so threatened. It was simply an ill-advised and even stupid act, especially with the memory of alleged CIA activities in that country far from forgotten.

The police officer who had been approached by the CIA officer politely refused the request and promptly reported it to the FBI's legal attaché. Imagine the hew and cry if it had been revealed—and it certainly would have come to light at some point—that the police were providing intelligence information to the CIA on that country's own citizens.

I CONTINUED TO TRAVEL extensively. Among other places, I visited the Cook Islands, Kiribati (formerly the Gilbert Islands), Western Samoa,

Vanuatu (formerly the New Hebrides), Tonga, Fiji, and Papua New Guinea. I grew to appreciate and respect the law enforcement and public safety professionals in those places, even though their lives, training, professional mandates, and personal goals were sometimes far different from mine. I saw Polynesian royalty, spent time at solemn and moving World War II memorials, admired the beautiful people and laid-back lifestyle that so captivated the painter Paul Gauguin, stood at the grave of Robert Louis Stevenson, and collected enough memories to last a lifetime. It was a life I never imagined as a youth in Calhoun, Louisiana, reading James Michener's *Tales of the South Pacific*.

One noteworthy trip was to Bangkok for a National Academy retraining session. One night I ended up with some Australian colleagues in the Patpong bar district so accurately portrayed in the Broadway production *Miss Saigon*. We entered a place where a kickboxing match was just getting started, with one of the boxers getting beaten rather soundly. At the end of a round, I went to his corner and offered some advice. I noticed he was leading with his left leg and getting counterkicked. I gave him a beer, suggested that he fake with his left leg and kick with his right, and waved an Australian twenty-dollar bill as a reward if he won. Properly inspired and refreshed, he returned to the match and soundly beat the other boxer, using his right leg as I had suggested. My companions murmured that I had been in Bangkok only a few hours and had already fixed a fight.

I traveled to Sydney more frequently than anywhere else, and it was there that I gained some degree of notoriety. One morning I received a telephone call from John Avery at my office in Canberra who said, "Mate, I just used your name, and you are probably going to get a telephone call." He explained he had been questioned about a series of four brutal murders of women in their eighties on Sydney's North Shore, across Sydney Harbour from the famous opera house. The press had dubbed them the "Granny Murders."

The New South Wales police were under considerable pressure to do something, and Avery had mentioned he was requesting assistance from the FBI's legal attaché in Canberra. Shortly after we talked, a reporter from the *Sydney Morning Herald* called, and I confirmed that I was providing assistance. That made news, not only in the near daily references in the *Sydney Morning Herald*, but Sydney television stations as well. Numerous requests came into my office for comments, but I continued to refuse to speak to the press. After all, this was an investigation being conducted by the New South Wales police, not the FBI legal attaché's office. I traveled to Sydney and met with the police and suggested how they should put together a comprehensive package that behavioral scientists at the FBI academy could analyze for them at Quantico, including time of the day of the murders, weather, maps of the area, crime scene photos, information about the victims, and other crimes in the area. The idea was not to identify a specific individual, but to take the totality of available information and determine what *type* of individual could be responsible for such a series of crimes. The media learned I was in the police station and staked out the building, so I was secreted out a side door and down a fire escape. But the reporters persisted, and after discussing the matter with Avery, I agreed to an interview with a Sydney television station. When I was asked if there would be more murders, I said that there would very likely be more, a statement that would be replayed for weeks as, indeed, additional murders occurred.

I also agreed to be interviewed by the international edition of *Time* magazine about the FBI's role in the investigation. The article included a photograph of me standing in front of an Australian flag. I received a request from the *Sydney Morning Herald* for something akin to a personal profile. Based on advice from Avery, I overcame my original reluctance and agreed to do it. I met a delightful reporter named Lindsay Simpson in the hotel, and we discussed my background and my assignment in Australia. I posed for photos sitting at a desk, looking out a window, etc., then the photographer asked if I would pose a few more minutes to allow her to use up the last few frames. One photograph, taken somewhat tongue-in-cheek, was of me standing under a light in a corridor of the hotel, holding the reporter's small tape recorder as if it was a walkie-talkie. In the background was a shapely female acquaintance of the reporter with her back to the camera.

Of course the newspaper editor liked that photograph, so the large article, "Agent Smith, The FBI's Man Down Under," appeared in the *Sydney Morning Herald* on December 9, 1989, with the picture of me leaning against the wall as if I was talking into a walkie-talkie and a mysterious woman standing in the background of the darkened corridor. The photograph received more comments than the article. I didn't bother sending a copy to FBI headquarters, but the press people at the embassy in Canberra regarded the whole series of articles and television appearance as a positive image of U.S.-Australian relations. The New South Wales police continued their investigation, eventually making an arrest of a lone individual whose profile was remarkably close to that provided by the FBI's Behavioral Science Unit.

I was not the only member of the Smith family who had contact with the Australian media. Carla was asked by the embassy to appear on a Canberra-based radio station to discuss what Halloween, unknown "down under," meant in the United States. Leah had a brush with the media as well. Vice President Dan Quayle traveled to Australia in April 1989 and conducted a well-received visit that belied his reputation in Australian circles as something of a bumbler. Quayle appeared at the embassy during his trip, and the embassy staff was encouraged to attend a tree-planting ceremony on the grounds. There was a long tradition of distinguished visitors planting trees on the embassy grounds—thus there was the George Bush yellow poplar, the Gerald Ford Michigan white pine, and so forth.

Leah had been at school when Carla picked her up to attend the ceremony. Along the way, she stopped and bought a small bouquet of flowers and, still wearing her green and white Girl's Grammar uniform, stood in the crowd with other children from the embassy staff. After making a few remarks, Quayle started walking along the line of embassy employees and their families. He approached Leah, and as she handed the bouquet of flowers to him, he reached out and touched her hair. An explosion of flash bulbs erupted, and the photograph that appeared in the *Sydney Morning Herald* the next day accompanying the story of Quayle's visit to Australia was none other than Leah holding the bouquet of flowers and the vice president touching her hair. The paper noted, "He told Miss Leah Smith, of Canberra's Girls' Grammar School that her red hair was pretty." I later purchased a copy of the photograph from the paper and by contacting an excellent Secret Service agent, George Sexton who was on Quayle's protection detail, was able to get the photograph autographed for Leah.

ANOTHER BRUSH WITH THE PRESS wasn't as agreeable. Late in 1989 I received a request from Peter Marshall, the New Zealand Police Department liaison officer posted in Canberra, that had to be handled quickly and carefully. I provided an initial response and then asked that the matter be closely held until I could get a response from Washington. In a highly publicized case, Dr. Elizabeth Morgan had gone to jail in March 1987 for refusing to reveal the location of her young daughter, Hilary Foretich, so that her father, Dr. Eric Foretich, could have unsupervised visits. Dr. Morgan had accused her husband of sexually abusing the child, so when the courts ruled that the father could have unsupervised visits, Dr. Morgan secretly arranged for her parents, William and Antonia Morgan, to take the girl to New Zealand. Facing deportation after eighteen months on a visitor's visa, they applied for permanent residency. New Zealand immigration authorities asked the police to conduct a background check on the child and her grandparents through the FBI in Canberra, which revealed their connection with the Morgan case. I knew of the case from daily stateside reports and told Marshall of the sensitivities surrounding the whole matter.

Any extradition from New Zealand would have to be handled carefully, given the nature of the allegations and the sympathy Dr. Morgan had garnered for going to jail rather than revealing her daughter's whereabouts. I put all this in a lengthy teletype and asked the Office of Liaison and International Affairs in Washington to handle the matter quickly. Despite additional requests and phone calls, that didn't happen. Finally, the case broke, receiving wide-ranging publicity—but not because the FBI took up the matter with any dispatch. It was ultimately handled outside the bureaucracy-choked official channels. An Australian Federal Police liaison officer based in Washington was drinking with some Washington metropolitan police officers at the Fraternal Order of Police bar in Washington. The Washington detectives expressed their frustration at not receiving any details on the exact location in New Zealand of the fugitive grandparents and child even though months had passed. The AFP officer volunteered to check with his own agency and communicated directly with his counterpart in Wellington, who in turn went to immigration authorities, who provided the address on the residency application. This resulted in Dr. Foretich flying to Christchurch, New Zealand, amidst much publicity and requesting that a New Zealand court grant him custody of the child.

I received several telephone calls from the media, and with the exception of a conversation with Felicity Barringer of the *Wall Street Journal*, I declined to respond, mainly because I could not explain the delay in handling the request without pointing a finger at the FBI in Washington. The *New York Times* ran the story under the heading of "Clue in Hilary Search Held for Months by U.S. Official," and in the *Richmond Times-Dispatch*: "U.S. said to hold Hilary Foretich clue for months."

The FBI's press office was besieged by inquiries. Someone there decided to offer the lame excuse that they were trying to establish communications between New Zealand and Washington police when the case broke. While this was somewhat accurate, it had occurred after the case broke and was not the cause for the delay. The whole incident strained relations between the New Zealand and Australian Federal Police due to the informal inquiry that had been made. No one at the FBI was willing to step forward and admit that the request had been badly mishandled by OLIA, but they were perfectly willing to let me take the heat for holding the clue to Hilary Foretich's whereabouts for months. Such incidents simply reinforced my distaste for the Washington bureaucracy. On several occasions I found some satisfaction in knowing that when I was standing on the Western Australian shore facing the Indian Ocean, I was as far from Washington as I could be without getting my feet wet.

CHAPTER 11

DIPLOMATIC MISSIONS

"You won't believe whom I just spotted."

Special Agent Bill Cleveland

W hen I reported to FBI headquarters in Washington after my
tour in Canberra, the first thing Ray Mislock said to me was,
"You poor son of a gun." Not the greeting I expected.

I had known Mislock for a number of years. He was a hard worker,
unapologetically ambitious, and after a tour in San Francisco as the
assistant special agent in charge was assigned to the State Department
by Jim Geer, assistant director of the Intelligence Division. This was in
the wake of security lapses in the Soviet Union in particular, involving
such matters as Clayton Lonetree, the Marine security guard who had a
relationship with a Soviet citizen in Moscow; and Felix Bloch, the
Foreign Service officer suspected, but never charged, with being a Soviet
agent. Based on the expected hew and cry from Congress, the State
Department agreed to allow an FBI agent to be in charge of the Office
of Counterintelligence Programs. Mislock got the job. And while he
earned the respect of many of his subordinates, he garnered the disdain
of many of the higher ranking Diplomatic Security personnel.

I wanted to confront this resistance to an FBI employee being in the
midst of the State Department. I made an appointment with Clarke
Dittmer, a deputy assistant secretary of state and former Diplomatic
Security chief of investigations. A slender man of medium height,

Dittmer had an office that was neat and orderly, perhaps too neat and orderly in some respects. It was clear he was not fond of Mislock and did not like the idea of an FBI agent in a position of authority within DS itself. I made it clear that I would simply fulfill my assigned tasks and then leave DS, allowing it to get along without outside assistance. (This was a time when many people—not just Capitol Hill wonks but Foreign Service agents and, surprisingly, DS personnel—believed the FBI should assume responsibility for all Diplomatic Security functions, and it still remained a sensitive issue.) I also made it clear that the FBI had no intention of taking over Diplomatic Security, although after some time I did conclude that they could certainly use our help in matters of security and counterintelligence.

As we talked, I noticed a State Department seal behind his desk. DS personnel told me it had been in the American embassy in Moscow years before and had a microphone installed in it by the Soviets. I saw it less as a monument to Soviet expertise than as another example of the institutional inability of the State Department to maintain adequate security within its own facilities. This historical weakness very likely continues to this date, as evidenced by the embarrassing fact that a Russian microphone was discovered in a conference room near Secretary of State Madeline Albright's office a few years back. In the end, Dittmer and I reached an accommodation of sorts. I told him that while mine was projected to be a two-year assignment, I hoped to reevaluate the position within a year. I liked Dittmer, and while there were points of disagreement between us, I respected his tenacity in looking after what he viewed as the best interests of Diplomatic Security.

One issue facing me was the inadequacy of the DS counterintelligence security survey system for embassies abroad. While I was certain we could improve it, I was less confident that I could get the Foreign Service population of the State Department to pay attention to the findings and recommendations of DS, an entity they generally held in low regard. I was told I would need to visit several posts to test the adequacy of the surveys and to familiarize myself with the particular problems of the individual embassies.

In September 1990 I traveled to Managua, Nicaragua, with DS officer Ed Wood. This was shortly after Daniel Ortega, bowing to considerable external and internal pressure, foolishly allowed popular elections. He lost to Violeta Chamorro, the widow of the murdered Pedro Joaquin Chamorro, editor of *La Prensa*, an opposition paper against the corrupt—but U.S.-supported—regime of Anastasio Somoza Debayle. Ortega, who had been the darling of many in the United States, had nevertheless been an outspoken thorn in the side of the U.S. and had lost some of his support by revealing that, like so many self-styled revolutionaries, he was better at fomenting revolution and demonstrating in the streets than governing.

Inflation was rampant. Moneychangers filled the streets clutching huge rolls of *cordobas* willing to negotiate the exchange rate to obtain U.S. dollars. One thousand *cordoba* bills would have the numbers blacked out and be stamped with *un million de cordobas*. The currency was virtually worthless.

The American embassy was largely staffed with unmarried personnel who had little prospects of a social life. There were no parks, no golf courses, no movie theatres. There was little interaction with diplomatic personnel from other countries and social contact with the local population was also discouraged. The Americans there were surrounded by diplomatic contingents from potentially hostile countries, all interested in compromising American personnel—China, Vietnam, North Korea, and Cuba.

In many respects, the embassy benefited more from the largesse of those in the Nicaraguan government than from their own efforts. Periodically someone would throw over the embassy fence a package containing internal documents and photographs from the *Direccion General de Seguridad de Estado* (DGSE), or General Directorate of State Security—photographs of embassy personnel, an accurate listing of CIA personnel, surveillance logs, and so forth, all of which appeared to be legitimate. While often slightly out of date, they at least proved the capability of the Nicaraguan intelligence services, which were largely influenced by the Cubans.

We interviewed a select number of embassy personnel in an effort to raise their awareness of counterintelligence activity and also to learn what we could from their own observations and experiences. I asked one senior member of the embassy staff if he had any real concerns he wished to discuss with me, making no secret of my affiliation with the FBI. Although it took a little prodding, he finally revealed the activities of a Foreign Service communications officer, one of the most sensitive positions in any embassy, as such an individual had access to virtually all communications to and from the embassy to Washington and other U.S. embassies around the world. Based on what I was told, the communicator was clearly acting in a manner that invited compromise. He was wandering the streets of Managua late at night, driving an American-made four-wheel-drive vehicle with diplomatic license plates, frequenting Lobo Jacks—a rough-and-tumble bar complete with free-flowing whiskey and prostitutes—and having contact with Nicaraguan females in spite of the non-fraternization policy. This had not been reported to the regional security officer, and when I asked why, the staff member responded, "It wouldn't have done any good." That was the view shared by a large number of Foreign Service personnel, and demonstrated the disdain of Diplomatic Security by the diplomats they were charged with protecting.

An investigation revealed that this communicator, who occupied one of the more potentially damaging positions in the embassy, had acted the same way in a previous posting where his actions were also ignored. He was eventually fired.

UPON RETURN TO WASHINGTON, I faced the conditions at the ever-controversial and vulnerable American embassy in Moscow and the consulate in Leningrad. Andy Dillard, the DS officer with counterintelligence responsibility for the Soviet Union, was a small wiry man with a wry and infectious sense of humor and a good dose of common sense. He and I agreed that a visit to the USSR was essential to determine the exact nature of security measures in that most vulnerable of overseas missions.

This was in the wake of the defection of former CIA officer Edward Lee Howard, who had access to CIA operations in Moscow before he eluded FBI personnel at his residence near Santa Fe, New Mexico, prior to his defection. One could assume he had provided his Soviet saviors with details of the CIA operations in Moscow. Dillard and I were briefed by knowledgeable people in the CIA and the FBI, which revealed that the Soviet KGB had not lessened their aggressive activities against American personnel.

When we arrived in Moscow, I saw for the first time the boorishness and inefficiency of the Soviet system. The air terminal was dimly lit, cold, and drafty, and we waited almost an hour for our luggage, though I could see my suitcase on a cart outside surrounded by ramp workers talking and smoking. There was very little traffic on the way to the hotel, and the streetlights were dim and sparse. The Soviet Union was operating at twenty-five watts in a one-hundred-watt world. The Ukrania Hotel, one of the "Seven Ugly Sisters" built at the end of World War II by German army POW slave labor, was simply a monstrosity—dirty, gray, drafty, foreboding in architecture and shoddy in construction. Prostitutes roamed the halls and characters taken from a George Raft Mafia movie lurked in the shadows. It was clear that organized crime coexisted with the KGB in the Soviet Union. This hotel, where the Moscow embassy usually housed its guests, was a threat to our counterintelligence security and, quite frankly, our health as well.

The first sight of the American embassy was appalling. Due to concerns about foreign nationals working on the premises, their movements had been severely restricted, making it impossible for them to sweep floors, pick up trash, or take care of any basic housekeeping. As a result, the place was a dump. Trashcans overflowed. The floors were sticky and dirty and disgusting. It was apparent that State Department employees weren't inclined to clean things up, and no one of authority insisted on it. As I continued my overview, I became convinced the boorishness and inefficiency of the Soviet system had permeated the American embassy itself.

Security violations were rampant. Marine security guards routinely found classified materials left exposed on desks. When such breaches were reported, embassy workers wouldn't change their behavior; they'd just get upset with the Marines for telling on them. But it was the regional security officer's office that was cause for the greatest concern. He had virtually no relationship of consequence with either the CIA officers or the Foreign Service officer contingent. He didn't even have a counterintelligence background—unthinkable given the long history of counterintelligence concerns at Moscow—and had virtually no interaction with embassy personnel. People would tell me openly that they would not report security concerns to the RSO. At least one junior member of the RSO's office, at great personal risk to his career, expressed concern for the conduct of the RSO himself.

For example, during a dinner at the Ukraina Hotel, the RSO and his wife engaged in a loud protracted argument in front of everyone in the dining room. Not only was the whole scene embarrassing, it gave members of the KGB, who were all over the place, ammunition for identifying those to be targeted for compromise. The KGB was arrogant and sloppy and made no pretense of attempting to use any finesse in conducting their duties, duties that were a way of life in the Soviet Union. One morning before leaving my room, I placed a hair across the locks of my luggage. Not only was the hair gone when I returned, but the suitcase was moved and its contents rumpled. There wasn't even an attempt to hide their activities.

Outside the embassy itself, old women sold half rotten vegetables and gristly meat on the cold, gritty sidewalks. I walked past Lenin's Tomb, gazed at St. Basil's Cathedral and its onion domes, strolled down Gorky Street, and learned that though it was difficult to flag a taxi, you could make them fight for your patronage by holding up a pack of Marlboro cigarettes.

There was a large new American embassy building in Moscow that had been completely compromised during construction by Soviets, who implanted listening devices throughout and used the metal beams as antennas. The building was absolutely unusable, and wrangling continued for years over what to do with the unfinished carcass as the steel skeleton stood exposed to the elements, slowly rusting away. It was simply another embarrassment by a naïve State Department who had allowed Soviet construction workers to work without any oversight by embassy security personnel at the height of the Cold War.

Leningrad was far more aesthetically appealing than Moscow, but the security compromises and professionalism of the personnel were as bad or worse. The RSO, for instance, wasn't even a career Diplomatic Security officer with a security background. He was a technician by training. I considered the Leningrad Consulate to have been completely compromised and the city itself under complete control of the police apparatus. One afternoon I took a walk in the snow, but as the snow became heavier I decided to go back to the hotel. Retracing my steps I suddenly encountered a single vehicle on the street, occupied by two men wrapped up against the cold. I was being followed! I continued to retrace my steps toward my hotel, somewhat amused that I had inadvertently stumbled upon those charged with keeping an eye on me. I suspect there are photographs somewhere in Russian archives of me enjoying the sights in Leningrad (and Moscow too, no doubt).

Andy Dillard and I concluded that the actions of the American ambassador in Moscow and consul general in Leningrad presented very real problems for the Marines in charge of security and for the RSO. Ambassador Jack F. Matlock Jr. had a son who was married to a Soviet national and both the son and wife lived in the ambassador's residence. On at least one occasion the ambassador's wife had escorted her in-laws past the Marine Security Guard detachment to the ambassador's office, a clear violation of embassy rules. The situation in Leningrad wasn't much better. The wife of the consul general had insisted that a Soviet Jew, who had become a U.S. citizen then returned to the Soviet Union, be hired without a background investigation.

Dillard and I returned to Washington and began to provide briefings of our findings. The result was somewhat disconcerting. Spencer Brown, head of the Office of Counterintelligence Programs, shared our concern for the RSOs in both Moscow and Leningrad, but when we went to share our findings with Greg Bujac, another deputy assistant secretary of state, it was clear he had no interest in our highlighting of problems, especially in Moscow. We walked out of his office with no confidence that steps would be taken to resolve the Moscow situation, especially when I learned from a DS officer that the RSO and Bujac were longtime close associates and Bujac had been responsible for the RSO's promotion to Moscow. I had the distinct impression that after all that had occurred there was still no commitment to reform within DS.

A WEEK LATER I was off on a similar trip to the People's Republic of China, encouraged by the American embassy in Beijing and the consulate in Shenyang. Due to a dearth of DS personnel with counterintelligence backgrounds, and Chinese counterintelligence experience in particular, I asked the FBI to nominate someone to travel with me and a couple of inexperienced DS officers to China to conduct the surveys. It was decided at FBI headquarters that Bill Cleveland, assigned to the San Francisco FBI office would travel with me. Bill Cleveland was a longtime counterintelligence agent in San Francisco with responsibility for investigating Chinese matters. Generally considered one of the top half dozen experts in his field, he came from an FBI family: his father retired as a well-respected assistant director. Small of stature, always in excellent physical condition, soft spoken, and extremely competent, he was the ideal person to accompany a small team and me and to deal effectively with Foreign Service officers in China.

The ambassador in Beijing, James Lilley, was a retired CIA officer and former ambassador to South Korea as well as the head of the U.S. representation to Taiwan after normalization of relations with the People's Republic of China. He was a realistic diplomat with a hard line toward China. The RSO was a professional who, in marked contrast to Moscow and Leningrad, had good rapport with the embassy family and the confidence of the ambassador as well as the head of the CIA. However, during the course of our survey, I developed concerns about some of the activities of the office of the military attaché. I emphatically expressed those concerns to the defense attaché, Rear Admiral Eric McVadon. While I suppose I derived some personal satisfaction as a former petty officer telling an admiral of my concerns, and the error of their ways, I did not leave the meeting with any confidence that McVadon would address the issues.

One Foreign Service officer was having frequent meetings with Chinese university students and faculty members. When we talked to him about the practice, he expressed little concern for his actions and was disdainful of PRC intelligence and security capabilities. He said he met with students for cultural acclimation, but there was no official reason to hold those meetings. This was only about a year after the Tiananmen Square massacre, which had resulted in students in particular coming under closer scrutiny by the omnipresent police apparatus.

Our survey also revealed, incredibly, approval for obtaining a visa to travel to the U.S. was controlled by Chinese employees of the embassy. That meant only those Chinese approved by the PRC's security apparatus were allowed access to the compound by the Chinese guards, for any Chinese working at the embassy would have done so with the explicit approval of the security apparatus and its implications of complete cooperation with the Chinese authorities for being allowed to work in the relatively comfortable job. Clearly the Chinese went out of their way to make themselves indispensable and had eroded the role of the consular officer to the point where the only function he provided was the final signature of approval. This allowed the Chinese to send their spies to the United States virtually with the official sanction of the U.S. embassy.

Mail was another problem. Embassy employees' personal mail was picked up in Hong Kong by a PRC contractor who transported it to Beijing and other missions in China. The Chinese weren't always subtle about their spying: frequently the envelopes arrived with slits in them where they had been opened before being forwarded to their destination. From a counterintelligence standpoint, knowing the personal lives of potential targets was invaluable.

One bitterly cold day I decided to walk outside the area of the embassy and entered Ritan Park, literally "temple of the sun," located in the vicinity of the foreign mission area. After a while I began to get cold and turned, as I had in Leningrad, and retraced my steps. Suddenly I encountered another pedestrian, the only one I had encountered to that point on such a cold day, whose face disclosed his surprise at seeing me almost upon him. He turned and suddenly became quite interested in a mural nearby. Again, I had unintentionally discovered that I was being followed in a Communist country. After walking away for some distance, I turned and photographed him, still uncomfortably looking at the mural. Around a corner was a black automobile with two Chinese men inside, with the motor running. In China in 1990, an automobile was almost the exclusive domain of officialdom, and it was clear the Ministry of Public Security was watching my every move. I did not press my luck and take a photograph of that vehicle.

After Beijing, Cleveland, Ed McGrath, a young but intensely interested Diplomatic Security officer, and I traveled to Shenyang, a city located near the North Korean border, where one of the most incredible moments in my career took place. After checking into the hotel, McGrath and I were in the lobby sitting at a table in a lounge off to one side, when suddenly I observed Cleveland approaching the table, looking somewhat surprised. Then he leaned over to me and said, "You won't believe whom I just spotted!" He said he had just observed a Mr. Lee, a scientist who had been employed at a sensitive laboratory in the United States and was fired after he came under suspicion in an FBI espionage case. ("Mr. Lee" is not his true name. Though his name has been in numerous publications, as has the codename of the investigation, the FBI disallowed their inclusion in this book. I appealed to Director Robert Mueller in September 2001. Three years later I had not received a response from him or even acknowledgement that he is considering the appeal.)

Bill Cleveland had handled the investigation of Mr. Lee and had interviewed him during the course of that long and intense investigation, though Lee was never prosecuted. Cleveland decided to make certain it was in fact Mr. Lee, who could be seen talking to a couple of other people near the hotel door. So Cleveland strolled past the group; though Mr. Lee had his back to him, his voice could be heard. Cleveland returned to the table somewhat wide-eyed and simply said, "It's him!" We wondered at the odds that Bill Cleveland and Mr. Lee would meet in the Zhongsan Hotel lobby in Shenyang, China, at that particular instant.

As we sat there pondering our next step, the people talking with Mr. Lee departed. We agreed that Cleveland should speak to Mr. Lee. But before he could make his way to him, Lee observed Cleveland. Shock and dismay registered on his face. He began to walk around the lobby, seemingly unsure what he should do. Cleveland finally stationed himself near the hotel elevator and when Lee rounded a corner and found Cleveland standing there alone, he had no choice but to speak. Mr. Lee shook hands and said it was good "to see old friends." When Cleveland commented that he wasn't certain that they could be considered friends, given the circumstance of their acquaintance, Mr. Lee responded, "Anyone from California is a friend."

Though Mr. Lee was clearly uncomfortable and somewhat flustered with the encounter, they discussed how long Mr. Lee would be in Shenyang. He said he was on business and the two of them discovered they were on the same flight returning to Beijing in a couple of days. Cleveland noted that perhaps they would see one another then at the airport. But when we arrived at the airport for our departure, Mr. Lee was nowhere to be found.

I awoke the next morning still marveling at the sheer coincidence of encountering Mr. Lee in Shenyang, China. But I was concerned as well, for I had no doubt that Mr. Lee would report encountering Cleveland and the FBI. Though my diplomatic passport was filled with entry stamps from all over the world, it would not be difficult to learn from diplomatic personnel lists that I was not a Diplomatic Security employee. All of us were also aware that we were in a brutal, totalitarian police state and that a knock on the door could occur at any time.

We left Shenyang for Beijing where I briefed Ambassador Lilley in the "bubble," the only place in the embassy deemed secure from the prying eyes and ears of the Chinese. We had determined that the U.S. embassy in Beijing, as well as the consulate in Shenyang, was completely compromised, both physically and technically, by the Chinese. I told Lilley of my concerns and observations, though he seemed to think the primary focus of the Chinese was on American businessmen. I wasn't certain that was the case and while I doubted the Chinese would attempt to recruit the vast majority of Foreign Service personnel, I had no doubt they were being subjected to scrutiny around the clock. I was convinced that not only the sanctity of the embassy but also the residences of embassy personnel were routinely being violated.

Our next stop was Hong Kong, where the debate continued about how the intelligence community should prepare for and respond to the upcoming transfer of power from Great Britain to the Chinese. Should all CIA personnel be placed under non-official cover, or should they remain posted in the consulate, where their ability to remain undetected was less but where they enjoyed some diplomatic immunity? The FBI was also considering what its response should be, for certainly there could be no counterintelligence discussions by the legal attaché with the Hong Kong authorities after the transfer in 1997. It was our considered conclusion the counterintelligence threat was already high and likely to only get higher. We returned to Washington with thorough security survey reports that showed what everybody already knew: embassy security was a serious problem. Yet to have the results accepted by the entrenched State Department bureaucracy—where there was then, and is today, a disdain for security—was another issue altogether.

A few weeks after we returned, I received a telephone call from Bill Cleveland over an unsecure telephone line. He was clearly uncomfortable with the call, but stated, "They knew we were coming, even before we even left." It was clear to me that "they" were Chinese security personnel. He continued, speaking cryptically, that a source of "J.J.'s" had told the Chinese of the trip before we even departed. I knew "J.J." was J.J. Smith, an FBI agent assigned to the FBI's Los Angeles office who was assigned Chinese counterintelligence matters. We concluded the brief conversation and didn't really speak again for several years. But the call explained why we had been subjected to such scrutiny while in Beijing—we had been followed in a trip to view the Great Wall and I had detected being observed while strolling through a market area near the diplomatic compound as well. And I also began to think the chance encounter with "Mr. Lee" in Shenyang was perhaps not a chance encounter after all. But I also assumed that the source who had told the Chinese of the trip would be closed as a source and would become the object of a counter-intelligence investigation. I was, as events unfolded years later, wrong.

IN APRIL OF 2003, I received a telephone call from an acquaintance in Washington, D.C., who, while not in the government, had good sources among government agencies. He said that I should stand by, for the FBI was going to get ". . . another black eye." He went on to explain that J.J. Smith would be arrested as well as a Chinese-American female who was not only passing classified information to the PRC that had been provided by Smith, but also that Smith had a sexual relationship with her.

I wasn't surprised at the allegations directed at Smith. He was a smug and arrogant agent who showed great disdain for those in authority in Washington. He, for instance, often showed up for work without a tie which was very much a part of an FBI agents "uniform," and exuded a cockiness that was not earned by his investigative exploits. The caller continued that there was a second FBI agent who was also having a sexual affair with the female and while he had not identified the second agent by name, he knew he was employed at the Lawrence Livermore laboratory.

I told him that I knew one agent at Lawrence Livermore, Bill Cleveland, but I could assure him that Cleveland would not be involved in such a fundamental breach of FBI rules and would never have a personal relationship with an FBI source. Again, I was, sadly, wrong. The details have been simply devastating to the FBI. Both Smith and Cleveland have admitted to having longtime sexual relationships with Katrina Leung, whose codename was Parlor Maid, though there is no indication that either Smith or Cleveland knew of the other's relationship with her. It has been determined, based on public indictments and news accounts, that Smith routinely took classified material to meetings with Leung where he would go into another room and not observe her perusing them and presumably, keeping copies of those she wanted. A search warrant at her residence revealed several such documents.

The investigation has been cause for the FBI to be subjected to ridicule on the late-night comedy shows on television, editorial cartoons, and the like. Further, all the information that Leung, whom I was quoted on PBS's *Frontline* program, "From China With Love," as being a "classic dragon lady," in that she would do whatever necessary to accomplish her goals, provided has to be suspect until proven otherwise.

Leung, a large contributor to the Republican Party, had also provided information to the FBI about the campaign finance investigation that was directed at Chinese money being funneled to the Democrat Party. That information too, has to be suspect. But there seems to be an attempt by the Department of Justice for the case to just go away. In May, 2004, in a low-profile announcement, Smith was allowed to plead guilty, incredibly, to simply lying about the long-running sexual affair with Leung, with the expectation that he would cooperate with the government against Leung. I was simply incensed at this turn of events. Here was Smith, who had met with Leung alone, in violation of FBI rules, had taken her to FBI functions, in violation of FBI rules, had taken FBI documents to her, in violation of FBI rules, had withheld information about her relationship with the Chinese, in violation of FBI rules, had a sexual relationship with a confidential source, in violation of FBI rules, had mishandled classified information, in violation of FBI rules, and inexplicitly, he was allowed to plead to a misdemeanor and keep his ill-gotten pension. He had flaunted the rules, very likely compromised sensitive investigations, had caused the FBI—who had paid him well for years, given him awards, given him status in his community—great embarrassment. He had betrayed the trust of both his country and fellow agents, and he paid only a minor price. There is no equity in the Department of Justice's decision in this matter, but given the potential political sensitivities of an aggressive investigation, I am not surprised.

I was contacted by an agent of the Department of Justice in August, 2004, who expected me to travel to Washington, D.C. and sit in a secure room at Justice and be interviewed for several hours about the Leung matter. After giving some thought to the request, I declined. After the Department of Justice's actions in handling this investigation and the unconscionable act of basically giving J.J. Smith a pass for his virtually treasonous activities, I was in no mood to inconvenience myself just so they could say they interviewed me.

HOWEVER, THE STRAIN of my assignment at the State Department was growing. I met with various Foreign Service personnel who visited Washington, and without exception they voiced their delight that I was in the assignment and believed I could bring some credibility to the Office of Counterintelligence Programs. These sentiments were shared by the rank-and-file DS agents as well as the intelligence community. I had taken on the role of advocate for DS and insisted that their officers be treated as equals in FBI investigations involving State Department personnel or facilities. But that notwithstanding, the goal of those in DS was to get rid of the outsider, and by April the acrimony reached the point that I was reassigned to FBI headquarters.

I returned with my head held high, but with a degree of frustration. I felt I had somehow failed the young DS professionals who had worked with me. I wished I'd had the time and authority to improve how they were viewed by the State Department. But, as I eventually discovered, the decks were stacked against me before I ever got there. Still I had personally benefited from the assignment, working with a fine contingent of men and women who seldom receive the credit they deserve for serving in some of the more inhospitable places in the world. I also had an opportunity—rare for an FBI agent—to see Communism's ugly side first-hand in the Soviet Union and the People's Republic of China. I had been followed, had observed (especially in the Soviet Union) a dispirited and surly population, and had seen the incredible inefficiency that resulted from a lack of personal initiative.

While I came back with the decided opinion that Communism's threat had been overstated from economic and perhaps military standpoints, I never suspected that I had seen Communism's last gasp in the Soviet Union and the rise of budding entrepreneurs in the People's Republic of China. The experience was personally enriching, but I was under no illusions that I had made any difference in the operations of Diplomatic Security, or in the way DS officers are viewed overall by the Foreign Service contingent.

CHAPTER 12

A SPY AMONG US

"Nice job, I.C."

Thomas DuHadway, FBI assistant director

My first assignment when I returned to FBI headquarters was the Office of Inspections, then I became section chief of the Analysis, Budget, and Training section of the Intelligence Division. After a few months, an old acquaintance, Tom DuHadway, was named assistant director of the division. DuHadway was a real professional with universal respect from within the U.S. intelligence community and law enforcement agencies, as well as the international community.

On September 10, 1991, as I was on the telephone, Tom opened my office door and said, "Nice job, I.C." When I completed my call, I went to his office, where I learned he had taken leave to play golf. Within a couple of hours he died on the course of a heart attack, surrounded by the street agents he loved and with whom he had such great rapport, which was unusual for someone of his rank. He was forty-nine.

I'm not sure why DuHadway stopped on his way out to tell me I had done a good job. But it was soon clear that his death was a disaster from which FBI counterintelligence still hasn't recovered. DuHadway was followed by a succession of assistant directors who were unschooled in the nuances of counterintelligence. Some were even hostile to it. This led to the de-emphasis and subsequent degrading of counterintelligence within the FBI. Those who had dedicated their careers to that vital area were pushed aside; career prospects for counterintelligence agents evaporated, producing a demoralized and sometimes inept counterintelligence force. The Wen Ho Lee case provides ample evidence of the disintegration of the FBI's once-vaunted counterintelligence program in general and the Chinese program in particular.

In all my years of government service, the entrenched bureaucracy of Capitol Hill was the most insular and petty I ever encountered. To them, it was all about self-survival. Few had any investigative or operational background. They were simply budget nitpickers whose primary focus was to retain their positions on the Hill. The lack of term limits is more a problem for the entrenched bureaucracy on Capitol Hill than it is for the elected officials they purport to serve.

I became the FBI's principal point of contact for dealing with the international community. That was due in part to my having been a legal attaché, and I was the only person in the Intelligence Division at the Senior Executive Service level who had served abroad. So I was usually the first person the Office of Liaison and International Affairs called to brief a foreign visitor, host a group, or attend a diplomatic function. Having played the opposite role in Canberra, Carla and I knew the importance of attending those functions, and we managed to make most of them.

One morning, Tim Caruso, a unit chief responsible for analytical matters involving Russia, came into my office. He was clearly ill at ease. Caruso had the reputation as both a tenacious investigator and having a keen analytical mind. Though at first he appeared to be introverted, he had a wry sense of humor and was a good conversationalist. Caruso said he had been called into a meeting where his superiors Pat Watson and Ray Mislock told him he had to take an assignment about which he could give no details to me, his direct supervisor. When he objected, they told him he had no choice.

This meeting with Tim would in fact be my first contact with the Aldrich Ames spy case. While espionage is only a very small part of counterintelligence, it is the area that stirs the most interest. And no case got more attention than Aldrich Ames.

Listening to Caruso heightened my awareness that there was something afoot within the division, for I had observed the closed doors and Mislock's rush past others with appointments waiting to see Wayne Gilbert, the assistant director. Mislock always thought whatever he was doing was the most important work imaginable and everyone else's paled in comparison. This time he was right.

I WAS IN QUANTICO meeting with a new agents' class when I ran into Les Wiser, case agent for the Aldrich Ames investigation. I didn't know the name of the case then, but concluded from what I had heard that it involved a penetration of the CIA. Wiser seemed dejected. He explained he had been chewed out by Mislock and was considering asking to transfer off the case. Wiser worked at the field office, where investigations were supervised. Under no circumstances should a senior member at headquarters call a field office investigator about one of his cases, least of all to chew him out. Back in Washington I told John Lewis, ASAC at the Washington Metropolitan field office, what Wiser said, but he was not aware of the incident. He agreed Mislock should never contact investigators directly, especially to vent his anger at a junior employee who wasn't even under his command. He immediately went to see his boss, Robert "Bear" Bryant. The next day or so I saw Lewis and Bryant in the hallway at FBI headquarters, both grinning from ear to ear, hinting that they had a break on the case. They had called Pat Watson, deputy assistant director for investigations, to give him the details, and expressly asked that Mislock not be present at the meeting.

I later learned Mislock had been upset over the failure of the Washington field office to keep Ames under surveillance during what appeared to be a critical time in the investigation. Thanks solely to Wiser's initiative in continuing a trash cover on Ames' home, there was absolutely no doubt that Ames was a spy.

Lewis's SAC, "Bear" Bryant, was promoted to assistant director in November 1993, and soon afterward I was called into his office. Both Watson and Mislock were there, looking somewhat downcast. Bryant said he had directed them to brief me into the Ames case. I suppressed a grin and solemnly nodded and walked out. I first had to have a polygraph and arrangements were made promptly to do that. Tim Caruso then provided a detailed briefing, grinning throughout.

He asked me if I knew Aldrich Ames, usually called "Rich." When I told him I did not, he sighed with relief. I was evidently one of the few former counterintelligence supervisors at the Washington office who didn't know him. I learned that the counterintelligence investigation codenamed Courtship, an investigation that I as an inspector had written up as being of marginal value, had been compromised by Ames years before. Courtship had been a joint CIA and FBI investigation that Ames had access to, resulting in its compromise. Somehow I felt vindicated for my findings during the inspection, though at the time I had been the object of considerable ire by Bryant at the Washington field office and Mislock and Watson at FBI headquarters.

When Ames was arrested on February 21, 1994, there was a feeding frenzy about the breach of security within the U.S. intelligence community and the CIA in particular. The FBI began to cooperate with the media to the point where I was concerned about the FBI's almost deliberate attempt to smear the CIA. In a staff meeting chaired by Bryant, I commented that remarks about the case had the effect of continuing to "jab a stick in CIA's eye," and the FBI should not be too smug for there were FBI failings in the case as well. I reminded the group that the FBI had been embarrassed by Richard Miller's spying for the Soviet Union, though I conceded there was little damage in comparison with what Ames had done. Years later, in 1996, the Earl Pitts arrest brought the consequences of that decision home. Again the FBI experienced the embarrassment at having one of its own betray his country. The rush to exploit the misery of the CIA in the Ames case seemed even more unseemly after that. Then, of course, on February 20, 2001, the Robert Hanssen case became public. When I heard the news I was sickened, but again I thought of the way the FBI had mishandled publicity in the Ames case.

To me, a penetration of the FBI was worse than a similar penetration of the CIA. The FBI is a counterintelligence agency specifically assigned to detect spies in our midst, while the CIA is essentially an offensive intelligence agency where counterintelligence is secondary. I also thought of how the FBI had capitalized on the Ames case not only for the self-aggrandizement of a few, but also to humiliate a fellow member of the intelligence community who had offered much to both the FBI and the country. I knew the FBI would pay later for the actions of those involved in the Ames arrest.

After I had made my point that the FBI should not be a party to exploiting the Ames case, I heard that Peter Maas was being given exclusive contact with Bryant, Lewis, Wiser and others to research a book. The selection of Maas was curious, given he had not written on intelligence matters in the past. At one point my section's analytical personnel were even assigned to provide Maas with a synopsis of a number of historical cases, including codenamed cases that were closely held, as they involved the identity of sensitive sources.

I wrote an informal note to Bryant pointing out that this unusual cooperation with Maas was a violation of an executive order; furthermore, the FBI had recently argued against a CIA request to do that very thing. Exposing the identity of past sources seriously hampers an agency's ability to develop other sources in the future. I never heard back from Bryant. However, I later met Maas in the corridor between Bryant and Freeh's offices on the seventh floor of the FBI building and realized the cooperation was continuing. Other writers were interested in the story, of course, based on what I was told by agents, not all authors and reporters were given equal access.

That wasn't surprising. In a June 21, 1994, memorandum to Bob Bucknam, who made a career of looking after Louie Freeh's interests, Maas wrote about his vision for the book. He wanted to avoid a story "filled with anonymous, informed sources attribution." He continued that he wished to "show the FBI in action" and mentioned the fact that "codenames and actual names of three KGB sources developed by the FBI have been widely and authoritatively reported." For his project, Maas "envision[ed] bringing them to life, to make them real persons." This would mean of course, a discussion of the individuals themselves, though it had long been the policy of the FBI to not discuss sources even if they publicly identified themselves.

Finally, Maas wrote, "But (and correct me, if I'm wrong), it seems apparent to me that the Ames investigation went into overdrive after September 1—after Louie became Director. Knowing Louie, I've got to believe he took immediate and decisive action, and I want to be in on it." Reading that, it became clear: Maas was holding out the carrot of lionizing Freeh, though the investigation was progressing nicely before he was named director and would have very likely had the same conclusion. Maas described how Freeh had ". . . mentioned the great work of the young men used in the surveillance and how it was important that I talk to them." This was a reference to the Special Surveillance Group (SSG), a highly trained and clandestine group whose specialty was in conducting counterintelligence surveillances. As a group, their identities were not well known, if known at all, and then only to a small, select group of FBI counterintelligence agents with a specific need to know.

Finally recognizing the perception that Maas was receiving preferential treatment, the FBI held a news conference where select agents were ordered to appear and answer questions. This was the only time the media had access to the story and there certainly was none of the exclusive contact with individual agents that Maas enjoyed.

In his book *Killer Spy: The Inside Story of the FBI's Pursuit and Capture of Aldrich Ames, America's Deadliest Spy*, Maas wrote as follows: "In the shambles that the KGB found itself in after the collapse of Communist rule, someone had finally been found who had access to the files of Directorate K in the First Chief Directorate. He did not know Rick's identity, only his codename 'Kolokol.' 'Kolokol' was in CIA counterintelligence. He had begun providing information in 1985. He had met his controller in Bogota and, in the latter 1980s, in Rome. The source that the FBI had developed was a closely held secret, even from the investigating agents. He was still actively providing information about others who had been in the pay of Russian intelligence."

This was a clear breach of security such as I had warned against. That paragraph alone was filled with warning signs, i.e., "closely held secret, even from investigating agents. He was still actively providing information." One could conclude that Maas was given details about a sensitive source that were being withheld from agents who were conducting investigations based on that source's information.

Killer Spy was published in May 1995, fifteen months after Ames was arrested, and did provide a good account of the investigation. I picked up a copy to browse through the index and found it did not have one, attesting to the speed with which the book had been rushed to print. Scanning the text, I noted Ray Mislock's name was seldom mentioned. Mislock, who had managed the case from FBI headquarters, had made many contributions to the case, and had direct liaison with the CIA almost daily. This omission was not an accident.

After the case was over came the inevitable damage assessment: how much information was compromised? It's usually not direct access, but indirect access that does the most harm—looking at a document on a colleague's desk, talking with someone in an unguarded moment, and so forth. Ames could visit the FBI's Washington field office, speak with acquaintances including members of the Soviet counterintelligence squads, or visit with supervisors. The contacts may have continued over drinks at the Navy Yard or at social gatherings at homes, all of which offer the spy considerable opportunities to collect intelligence information.

When the damage assessment begins, everyone who had a personal acquaintance with the spy should remain outside the process. Any one of them could have provided the indirect access through their own oversight or carelessness but would likely try to cover up evidence of the mistake rather than report it. It is not human nature to admit to such a lapse, and if the spy's friends conduct the assessment, the end result is a nagging feeling that the result is incomplete. I had that feeling with the Ames case.

The case strained relationships among various components of the intelligence community, but there was work to do and we did our best not to dwell on the past. This was evident at the periodic meetings of the National Foreign Intelligence Board (NFIB), where for a time I was the FBI representative. The dynamics of the group were quite interesting. The original director of central intelligence (DCI) who chaired the meetings when I first became a member was James Woolsey, an attorney who was very much engaged in the minutia of the actual wording of National Intelligence Estimates. He ably debated issues with State Department INR Assistant Secretary Toby Gati; Air Force General James R. Clapper, head of the Defense Intelligence Agency; and Notra Trulock, the Department of Energy representative, who usually sat to my immediate right.

Another member of the NFIB was U.S. Navy Admiral Richard Macke, a tall, slender officer who cut a fine figure in his dress uniform, resplendent with rows of ribbons and gold braid. But he was haughty and had an imperial air, and I somehow knew he would never have been accused of being a "sailor's officer." In 1995, after taking command of all U.S. forces in the Pacific, Macke got in hot water after three servicemen were accused of raping an Okinawa school girl by observing publicly that they could have hired a prostitute for the cost of their rental car. After he was forced to retire, he was censured for having engaged in an improper relationship with a junior female Marine officer. Later it was established that he kept an airplane and crew waiting for three days while he had a dalliance with the officer at a hotel. If one is going to be a jerk, then he better live the life of a saint, for those being abused will invariably exact revenge by reporting any improper conduct. When I heard of the problems Macke was encountering, I felt certain one of the subordinates he so routinely abused was delighted to spill the beans.

While Woolsey was intense and thoughtful, he was in complete contrast to his successor, John Deutch. We would assemble for a meeting, the door would fly open, and Deutch would arrive with an entourage of subordinates, including military personnel in dress uniforms. His aides seemed to spend their time gazing fondly upon Deutch, ready to respond at the slightest beck and call. I had to stifle a laugh the first time I observed his grand entrance. He was brusque, imperial, and he seemed more interested in technical issues than in human ones. I was not surprised when he was found to have entered classified information on his personal unclassified computer at his home. His arrogance was that evident.

A MOVE WAS AFOOT that soon spelled doom for the FBI's counterintelligence program. After his appointment as director, Louis Freeh embarked with considerable fanfare upon a program to downsize FBI headquarters by three hundred agents, even though he had never been a manager in the FBI. It was done arbitrarily and without a real assessment of how the action might harm headquarters' ability to perform its essential duties. This was especially true in the FBI laboratory, where Freeh mandated an immediate reduction of FBI agents in examiner positions. They were to be replaced by nonagent personnel. While the plan may have had validity, it takes time to recruit and conduct backgrounds on personnel. It takes even longer for them to be trained and certified as qualified examiners who can provide expert testimony in court. The already unacceptable backlog of cases in the laboratory lengthened to an even more unacceptable level.

For the newly-named National Security Division, developments were even more ominous. Bureaucratic rearranging left fewer agents in important roles and sent people to areas outside their expertise. Counterintelligence became a second priority within the National Security Division after international terrorism became a part of the division's responsibilities. But it got even worse for counterintelligence. Bryant quickly embarked on a campaign to transfer domestic terrorism from the Criminal Division to the National Security Division. His fanciful argument was that there was a relationship between international terrorism groups and domestic terrorism groups. I found it incredulous to think that somehow Middle Eastern terrorists would have any contact with the Aryan Nation. The domestic terrorism program was transferred to the National Security Division, much to the relief of many in the Criminal Division, and immediately became the primary focus of Bryant's attention at considerable expense to both international terrorism and counterintelligence. It was an ill-advised decision justified by faulty logic and driven by empire building.

Sometime after my retirement, at Bryant's behest, the FBI created an Analytical Division combining all FBI analytical resources in a single division: drug analysts, organized crime analysts, counterintelligence analysts, terrorism analysts, etc. The specific reason given was to upgrade the analytical capabilities of the criminal program, but the inevitable result was to diminish the counterintelligence analytical capabilities, which up to that point was the most accomplished analytical area within the FBI. This was an absolutely insane idea. A separate division, headed by an individual with absolutely no analytical background, only placed more administrative barriers between the analysts and the investigators, causing many in the operational areas to not utilize their services.

Terrorism analyses had already become problematical. In 1995, when Ramzi Yousef was captured in Pakistan for his role in masterminding the February 26, 1993, World Trade Center bombing, the FBI obtained several boxes of documents. At the time of the attacks on September 11, 2001, in New York and Washington, according to the *Washington Post*, those boxes had never been reviewed and analyzed. That is precisely the type of information that accomplished analysts can decipher—raw data that could be of value to investigators not only for past crimes but also to predict crimes of the future. Apparently Robert Mueller quickly recognized the folly of Bryant's grand analytical plan that had been approved by Freeh. Three weeks after being named FBI director, in the immediate aftermath of 9/11, he dismantled the relatively new division. But by then, any meaningful effort that would have prevented the events of that terrible day by an analysis of the considerable data that was readily available was lost.

As section chief, I continued to speak frankly, knowing at times that my positions at odds with Bryant would have career repercussions. In one meeting, I opposed Bryan's idea of arming members of the Special Surveillance Group, the extremely accomplished counterintelligence surveillance group consisting of nonagent personnel. He commented that I needed to go along if I expected to have a career future. I responded without thinking, "I would rather be right than an SAC." Bryant just looked at me from the opposite end of the table where we habitually sat during staff meetings and didn't respond. After pondering my comment later, I was comfortable with my position, regardless of any career consequences.

But it did have an effect. The SAC position in Jacksonville, Florida, became vacant. While I had not specifically asked for the position, when one was on the SAC promotion list it was assumed that you should be interested in any vacancy. I had been considered the front runner for the Jacksonville vacancy and had even received some real estate information from agents there who were hoping and expecting that I would receive the assignment.

However, Director Freeh, with Bryant's strong support, selected Mike Kehoe, though it was well known that Kehoe very likely had some exposure for his role in the Ruby Ridge incident. I received two calls from members of the Career Board who commented they had supported me for the position but couldn't overcome the fact I had not received the support of my own assistant director. Bryant, they told me, had said the Bureau needed someone "aggressive" in Jacksonville. Kehoe, who was under an investigative cloud at the time of his transfer, later pled guilty to destroying documents in the Ruby Ridge investigation and served a prison term.

On April 19, 1995, the Alfred P. Murrah Federal Building in Oklahoma City exploded and collapsed in a horrific scene of destruction. The FBI, playing to one of its great strengths, immediately mobilized to conduct a massive investigation. After a couple of days, I was assigned to be in charge of the FBI's command center from 6:00 PM to 6:00 AM. This meant I had to arrive at the center at about 5:00 PM to attend the afternoon briefings with the various field offices, and not depart until after the morning briefing occurred at about 8:00 AM the next day. In an investigation on the scale of Oklahoma City, there is no down time. Agents worked and information poured in around the clock, just as it had years before when I had occupied a similar position after the assassination attempt on President Ronald Reagan.

But the two weeks I spent in that capacity revealed a readily evident flaw in the FBI's decision-making hierarchy. Larry Potts, Bryant, and Bill Esposito in particular had developed the attitude they had to be available at all hours to make decisions and, increasingly, second-guess the decisions made by field commanders. They demanded to know every minute detail in the investigation and after a few days they were literally out on their feet. I was glad there weren't any strategic decisions that would have required clear heads. The career of one of the FBI's brightest SACs was ruined as his "aggressiveness" was questioned, regardless of the fact that both tactically and legally he was right. It was almost as if Potts, Bryant, and Esposito vied to see who could stay up the longest and drink the most cups of coffee. I often thought of the lessons I had learned from Ted Gardner during the Reagan investigation about the value of going home to rest. Though I suggested the same to my superiors, I had little success.

After the end of my assignment in the command center, it was time for me to either move on to a field assignment or simply to retire. I had seen an ugliness at FBI headquarters with which I became increasingly uncomfortable.

BUT I STILL HAD some unfinished business. Upon returning to Washington, I resumed contact with Eva Childs after the death of Morris on June 2, 1991. As Morris and Eva had wished, John Barron had begun to work on a book about their story, drawing not only on his hours of contact with them in years past but also on his encyclopedic knowledge of the Soviet Union and its spy apparatus.

Indeed, Barron's knowledge was so formidable that, as revealed by Vasili Mitrokhin in his book *The Sword and the Shield: The Mitrokhin Archive and the Secret History of the KGB*, the KGB had specifically targeted Barron to discredit him after he had written his exceptional book *KGB: The Secret Work of Soviet Secret Agents*. Though it was published in 1973, the book is still considered the bible for understanding the operations of the former KGB.

With that background I was confident that any book about Operation Solo, the codename for the operation involving the Childses, would be very well done even though the FBI could not officially assist in the book; to acknowledge the fact that Eva, Morris, and Morris's brother Jack Childs had been working for the FBI would conflict with what was then a longstanding tradition of not commenting on sources. However, a problem developed with an agreement between Barron and Eva Childs. Eva had retained Ken Whitaker, a retired SAC in Miami to handle legal matters and he had influenced Eva to consider an alternative writer. I began getting calls from both Whitaker and the writer, who had never written about intelligence matters. I explained to both that I was not in a position to assist in writing a book and my sole interest was to look after the best interests of Eva who was advanced in years, practically alone, and whose health was beginning to deteriorate. But the calls continued, and when I traveled to Miami on unrelated business and stopped by to visit with Eva, I learned Whitaker's phone calls, innocuous as they were, were being billed to her.

I did not wish to interject myself into a decision for which I had no personal or professional basis, but I increasingly believed the author Whitaker chose was simply not the right person to record the definitive account of Operation Solo. Finally, I decided I would have to place a call to Eva. I apologized for intervening in a matter that I could not officially be a part of, but I expressed my personal concern for the ability of the writer to fully appreciate and be able to write the story that would do justice to all concerned. She listened politely and asked what I recommended and I told her I would recommend that she reconsider Barron as the author and perhaps enlist the services of a nephew, Charles Goodbar, who was an attorney in Chicago, in drawing up a contract. She both liked and respected Barron, who had been at FBI headquarters when she and Morris had received their medals from Director Sessions, and who had even interviewed them years before but never revealed their story. She entered into a new contract with Barron and the story began to be written at last.

In December 1994, when I received the usual holiday card and fruit basket from Eva, I decided it was time, with Barron's book nearing publication, to explain the origin of the fruit basket to Carla and the girls. I sat the fruit down on a counter, assembled Carla, Amy, and Leah, and briefly told them the story of Morris and Eva Childs and how Eva came to send all of us the fruit basket. They listened quietly and when I completed my rather inadequate explanation, Amy said wide-eyed, "You mean, we have been getting a fruit basket from a spy?" I told her that, yes, in the purest sense, that was correct. But they were more than just spies. They were remarkable patriots as well, whose contributions to our country were immense. With Barron's book, perhaps the public could be made aware of all that they had done.

One day in June 1995, I received word that Eva had died the previous evening. I was under transfer to Little Rock by that time but had ensured Eva and Barbara Moser, the agent who had assumed Wes Roberts's duties after his mandatory retirement, that I would continue to look after Eva's interests even in Arkansas. Later in the day I got a call from Roberts, who had looked after her so long. He had indulged her passion for chocolates, was available to drop what he was doing at a moment's notice to respond to her needs, and had become, in effect, a part of her extended family.

I decided to make one last contribution to Eva and Operation Solo by sending Roberts and Moser to the funeral, representing the FBI. I had a budget meeting on Capitol Hill that couldn't be ignored, so I couldn't attend myself. But it was entirely fitting that the agents who had been so close to Eva in the final years of her life should be there. Also at the funeral were Barron and Jim Fox, who had so long also looked after the Childs, as well as those retired agents who been involved in Operation Solo over the years, Carl Freyman and Walter Boyle. It was the last time the principals of Operation Solo would ever be together.

The following year, *Operation Solo: The FBI's Man in the Kremlin* was published. I only wish Eva and Morris could have lived long enough to see it.

CHAPTER 13

TRAVAILS WITH
THE TRAVEL OFFICE

*"[William Held] Kennedy advised . . . that the
matter to be discussed was being directed at
the 'highest level' at the White House."*

"An Internal Review of FBI Contacts with the White House as Related
to the Investigation of the White House Travel Office" by I.C. Smith

On July 31, 1995, I reported as FBI special agent in charge for the
state of Arkansas. Because of my family ties to the state—a great
aunt, Stella Boyle Smith in Little Rock, an uncle in North Little Rock, an
uncle in Heber Springs, and my father in Pine Bluff—I was fully aware
of its overheated political climate. Even so, I greatly underestimated the
intensity of the situation and how it would impact my criminal investigations. My first day on the job was also the day I met Ken Starr. He
came to my office and we sat among the unpacked boxes and talked for
two hours. Neither of us could have anticipated the events of the next
three years and what it would do to our lives.

Arkansas is a state with low self-esteem and Little Rock, the state capital, is a city of contradictions and complex relationships that belie its
relatively small size. As my old friend FBI Inspector George Clow once
observed after spending two weeks there, "Now I know why it's not
called Big Rock." The downtown area is largely abandoned after business hours, with the exception of the bars and restaurants of the River

Market area, which is adjacent to the site of the presidential library of the state's most famous son, William Jefferson Clinton.

The informal "Scandal Tour" that the locals are known to show visitors includes such landmarks as the Rose Law Firm; Quawpaw Towers, an apartment complex where Gennifer Flowers resided; Madison Guaranty, once operated by Jim and Susan McDougal; and the State Capitol and the Old State Capitol, which became the backdrop for Clinton's presidential campaign events. For the insiders there are other places as well, such as The Afterthought, a bar that Clinton frequented, especially during the two years he was out of the Governor's Mansion. These are all names and places that have become familiar to a great many people outside of Arkansas since Clinton's presidency. For most of the locals, this attention is both unwanted and resented.

It was in this city of contradictions that I lived and worked for three years, a city that lost its deserved obscurity and became the topic of late-night television jokesters and editorial cartoonists around the world. This was all due to the election of Bill Clinton, and most residents of Little Rock seemed to look forward to the time when he would leave office and their city could slip back into its former state of anonymity.

Arkansas as a state ranks near the bottom in virtually every category: economic growth, education, per capita income—it only ranks high in categories like teen pregnancy. Considerable federal money flows to Arkansas, though even after their native son was in the White House, little of the government largesse seemed to reach the people who needed it most.

The Great Seal of the state of Arkansas carries the motto, "The People Rule." Lofty and idealistic as it is, I found it to be a motto without foundation. The people of Arkansas do not rule by any stretch of the imagination. The state is ruled by a social and economic elite who consider their positions a birthright to greater riches and stature within that small and wonderful state. Ken Starr and I were faced with the state political machine that had produced the president of the United States. Though we went our separate ways, many times our investigative paths were parallel and involved Arkansas' political ruling class.

I ALREADY KNEW, from an experience when I was still in Washington, that Arkansas was a world apart. Joe Johnson, a longtime friend and deputy assistant director of the Inspection Division, called to ask if I could take a special assignment, a potential "hot potato" that had to be done quickly. Intrigued, I accepted. When I arrived for a 5:00 PM meeting in Deputy Director Floyd Clarke's office on May 25, 1993, I could tell by the assembled group that this was not a routine matter. Besides Clarke, the group included Weldon Kennedy, an associate deputy director; Joseph R. Davis, the assistant director of the Legal Counsel Division; Johnson from Inspections; Fred Verinder, another old friend who was a deputy assistant director of the Criminal Investigative Division; and Larry Torrence, a special assistant to Clarke. After the usual pleasantries and joking among longtime associates who are also friends, Clarke got down to business.

He asked me to drop everything for the next few days and concentrate on a top-priority project. Apparently the FBI had been manipulated by the White House Travel Office in the matter the media had already labeled "Travelgate." Of course I'd read the press accounts and just assumed the Clinton staff was having the same problem I had personally observed during the early stages of the Jimmy Carter administration: the new staff simply wasn't up to the task of governing. I also had the advantage of following Clinton's career in Arkansas and overhearing discussions between my aunt Stella and her friends. They affirmed that Hillary was the tougher of the two Clintons and managed to intervene in virtually everything that happened in the governor's office, while her husband didn't seem to want to be bothered by non-political issues.

Clarke gave me a deadline of June 1 to have a completed report to the attorney general's office and explained that the assignment was twofold: I was to establish a chronology of contacts by the White House with the FBI, then ascertain if the FBI violated any existing rules, policies, or regulations as a result. Essentially, my narrowly-defined job was to find out what happened without worrying about why. When I asked why I got the assignment, I was told I had a reputation for being able to write quickly under pressure, was outside the Criminal Division where the White House contacts had occurred, and was known for my complete candor. I laughingly added that apparently I was also completely expendable.

I quickly determined that the prime point of contact at the White House had been William Held Kennedy III, a native of Pine Bluff, Arkansas, whose father was a respected banker and past president of the American Bankers Association. Young Kennedy had gone to law school and then been hired by the Rose Law Firm as an underling to the triumvirate of Hillary Clinton, Vince Foster, and Webb Hubbell—the acknowledged "royalty" of the firm. Kennedy, burdened by his esteemed heritage, never lived up to his father's standing in Arkansas circles. But he tried desperately. He bought a house at 2 Edgehill Drive in Little Rock, arguably the most expensive residential real estate in the city, yet was reportedly unable to modernize or even maintain it.

Kennedy had been in touch with the FBI prior to the Travel Office matter because his position at the White House involved monitoring the progress of special inquiry background investigations. These are required for political appointments, which naturally occur in great numbers during the change of administration. The numbers were even larger than usual early in the Clinton administration, which appeared loath to retain anyone from the Bush ranks. Kennedy's main FBI contact for these investigations was Jim Bourke, a unit chief of the Special Inquiry and Backgrounds Investigative Unit. Kennedy had initially contacted Bourke with the Travel Office matter simply because he didn't know anyone else at the FBI.

His first call came on the afternoon of May 12, 1993. Kennedy advised Bourke that he wanted guidance and possibly assistance in a confidential matter possibly involving an embezzlement of funds. Bourke told Kennedy that he would find out who his FBI contact should be and get back to him. The next morning Bourke discussed the call with Richard Wade, the unit chief for the Governmental Fraud Unit, but decided they didn't have enough details to determine who should handle the inquiry. Bourke called Kennedy again for further details. But, as Bourke later told me, Kennedy remained vague on the details and insisted the matter had to be handled immediately—something like "fifteen minutes"—or else he would refer the investigation to the Internal Revenue Service.

Kennedy was then contacted by Howard Apple, the unit chief of the Interstate Theft/Government Reservations Crime Unit. Kennedy demanded they meet personally, and Apple told Kennedy he would arrange for an agent from the Washington Metropolitan field office to meet with Kennedy, noting that the field agents, not agents at headquarters, were the ones who conducted criminal investigations. Kennedy insisted on meeting with someone at FBI headquarters, saying the matter was being directed at the "highest level" of the White House. Of course, based on past history in Arkansas, it was clear to me that this meant that although the president may not be involved, certainly the first lady was. (In my final report, I wasn't given the latitude to make such suppositions, and so I simply stated, "Kennedy advised . . . that the matter to be discussed was being directed at the 'highest level' at the White House." This line was replayed over and again during the course of the investigation, though Kennedy never admitted who the "highest levels" included. But there was no question that Kennedy was marching to the orders of Hillary Clinton in the White House, just as he had at the Rose Law Firm.)

Apple met with Danny Coulson, and it was agreed that Apple and Pat Foran, another experienced unit chief, would meet with Kennedy. At that meeting, Kennedy was clearly stressed, repeating again and again that this matter was being directed by the "highest level" at the White House. He then proceeded to outline evident financial inconsistencies in the White House Travel and Telegraph Office, discussing the employees' tendencies to live beyond their salaries, the lack of competitive bidding for services, the fact that a new employee was "shunned" by office personnel, etc. Kennedy said that his only three options were to fire all seven employees, send them home and conduct an audit, or send half home and use the remainder to assist in an audit. Apple and Foran told Kennedy that if there was evidence of a crime, then the FBI would have jurisdiction. If there actually was an embezzlement case at the bottom of all this, the Bureau determined that Rich Wade's Governmental Fraud Unit would have responsibility for such a matter, so Wade and agent Tom Carl returned to the White House on May 13.

They met with Kennedy, who said he had gotten his information from Catherine Cornelius, a recent employee of the Travel Office, omitting the fact that Cornelius was a distant cousin of the president. Kennedy tried to impress upon Wade and Carl the urgency of the matter and introduced them to Vincent Foster, deputy counsel to the president. Foster also impressed upon Wade and Carl the importance of the matter, that quick action was paramount before the whole thing became public knowledge.

There was an unusual urgency attached to what seemed a rather routine criminal case, even if it did involve the White House. As Apple and Foran were telling me of their meeting, it was apparent that whoever the "highest level" was, it was someone Kennedy and Foster were very much afraid of. Professionals with their pedigrees and positions don't usually beg for action involving such relatively innocuous matters. It was clear to me that the single individual both Kennedy and Foster feared was Hillary Clinton, their old boss at the Rose Law Firm, who was solely responsible for the two of them being in Washington. Foster and Kennedy were told that the FBI would conduct an investigation only if there was sufficient predication. Wade and Carl then met with Cornelius, who repeated what Kennedy had already said about the wrongdoing she had seen in the Travel Office. However, she added a bit of new information, claiming that Billy Dale, the head of the Travel Office, was demanding a five-percent kickback for contracts from a Miami-based airline. (Cornelius did not, of course, tell the agents that she had an expressed interest in assuming control of the Travel Office and was pushing to be placed in that position. Nor did she advise of her kinship with Clinton.)

Given that new information, Wade advised Foster and Kennedy that while an alleged kickback demand was sufficient cause for an investigation, it would have to be discussed with the Department of Justice.

Foster said he was going to initiate a "performance review," and initial arrangements were made for FBI personnel to monitor it. As an example of Kennedy's lack of understanding of Washington and its myriad of independent agencies, he discussed getting assistance from the Central Intelligence Agency, the Resolution Trust Corporation, or the Federal Deposit Insurance Corporation to conduct the audit of the Travel Office books. These were incredibly naïve musings, clearly showing how far out of his element Kennedy was. Later, Vincent Foster called Wade to say that FBI agents would not be allowed to be present at the review. When I expressed concern for such a refusal given his past insistence that the FBI become involved immediately, Wade said Foster declined to explain his position.

On Saturday, May 15, Carl met with Kennedy and Patsy Thomasson at the White House, as well as auditors from Peat, Marwick. Their audit, conducted over the previous twenty-four hours, showed that the Travel Office did not meet standards that would ensure an adequate account-ability of funds and business was conducted in an atmosphere that could lend itself to abuse. Even so, they had not uncovered any specific criminal act.

THE CRIMINAL DIVISION had given me a chronology of its White House contacts, but John Collingwood, head of the FBI's Office of Public and Congressional Affairs, had failed to do so, though I had made repeated calls to his office. Given the brief deadline I had to complete the report, I arranged to interview Collingwood in person and found him uneasy and anything but forthcoming with his responses. I later learned why he was so uncomfortable. On May 19, Collingwood had issued a press release stating, "We understand that the results of the audit of the White House Travel Office will be referred to the FBI for our review." A routine copy of the release was forwarded to both the White House and the Department of Justice, but there was no reaction from either.

Subsequently the White House advised the press that the FBI had been to the White House, prompting the FBI to issue a press response.

For the FBI as well as other agencies in the federal government, a press *release* is just that, information that is released to the press. A press *response* is a statement made in response to a specific question on a particular subject. The press response of May 20 stated, "At the request of the White House, the FBI has had preliminary contact with the White House and the auditors brought in to audit the White House Travel Office. We anticipate receiving the final report of the auditors soon and will analyze their findings and conduct appropriate investigation. Beyond that, we are not in a position to comment." As with all such responses and releases, the copy was approved by Director Sessions and Clarke and provided to the Department of Justice and the White House.

Later that day, the response was modified by Collingwood without the customary formal approval and forwarded to the White House and the Justice Department. Instead of saying "findings and conduct appropriate investigation," the modified version was altered to read, "findings to determine the next steps in the investigation." Collingwood said he made the change to more accurately reflect what was being stated by the White House. It was later learned that the change had been made at the behest of Dee Dee Myers, the White House press spokesperson.

On May 21, while eating lunch at the Old Ebbitts Grill, Collingwood was paged and summoned to the White House by the director of communications, George Stephanopoulos. Without notifying anyone at FBI headquarters, Collingwood went to the White House, where Stephanopoulos was waiting for him. Later, when I interviewed Collingwood and specifically asked who was present, he recalled seeing Dee Dee Myers, White House staff member Dave Levy, and several others in what he described as a crowded room. I later learned that Bernard Nussbaum, Vincent Foster, and Bill Kennedy were there, among others. After the meeting, Collingwood returned to FBI headquarters and made another modification to the original press response, adding, "The contact produced sufficient information for the FBI to determine that additional criminal investigation is warranted." That modification was also not approved by anyone above Collingwood and was provided to the White House and the Justice Department.

The White House then took the audacious step of releasing the FBI press response as a press release without any consultation with the FBI. In doing this, the White House released an FBI document that was meant for "guidance" in responding to press inquiries about the Travel Office affair with no regard for the problems it might cause the FBI. That same day, IRS investigators showed up at the offices of Ultrair, a small Nashville, Tennessee, charter airline the White House Travel Office had used. The investigators arrived with subpoenas for company records, without ever explaining why they had decided to conduct such a review. I didn't think then, and don't think now, that this was a coincidence and am reminded of Kennedy's warning that if the FBI didn't conduct a criminal investigation of the White House Travel Office immediately, he would refer the matter to the IRS.

Though incomplete in my view, my report was submitted to the Office of the Attorney General on time. I had concluded that the FBI had acted appropriately with its White House contacts as far as the criminal investigation was concerned. But I did not comment on the inappropriateness of Collingwood's reaction to White House pressure by modifying press releases and responses and attending a meeting at the White House without advising anyone at FBI headquarters until well after the fact.

The Department of Justice promptly sent a copy of my report to the White House without telling the FBI they had done so, an early indication of the growing politicization of the department. At the same time, the White House announced it was conducting its own review. In effect, the Department of Justice gave the White House a guide to follow that would avoid glaring contradictions with the FBI. Indeed, John Podesta's final "Management Review" contains excerpts, virtually verbatim, from my report.

With much fanfare, Podesta had been assigned to conduct the in-house review of the actions of White House personnel involved in the Travel Office matter. On June 30, shortly after I arrived at work, I received a telephone call from Joe Davis who assigned us to review Podesta's report by mid-morning, supplying comments to the department for a noon release. We made the deadline, but by then the White

House had already released Podesta's report without our having had the chance to check its accuracy.

The pressure didn't stop there. The White House, through the Justice Department, asked the FBI to submit a letter stating it was in agreement with the facts in Podesta's report. I told Davis I thought it was inappropriate for the FBI to write such a letter, regardless of the fact the report was substantially correct. Although no such letter was written by the FBI, the Department of Justice did issue a letter complying with the White House request.

IN OCTOBER 1995, just over two months after I had transferred to Little Rock as SAC, Collingwood notified me I was to testify before the House Committee on Government Reform and Oversight chaired by Congressman William F. Clinger. I prepared an opening statement for approval by the Justice Department, as requested, including references to the fact the department had sent my report to the White House, and that the White House released Podesta's report before the FBI had reviewed it for accuracy. Those references were, of course, excised by the Department of Justice and were not in the official version that went to Capitol Hill.

I traveled to Washington to testify before the committee. The panel included John Podesta, Michael Shaheen from the Department of Justice's Office of Professional Responsibility, Nancy Kingsbury of the General Accounting Office, Gary Bell of the Internal Revenue Service, and me. Sitting behind the panel were several former Travel Office employees. Podesta was the target of most of the committee's questions, and I found him intense and combative as he attempted to defend what was in many respects indefensible. On more than one occasion he pointed out that not a single fact of his report had been repudiated. I sat next to him knowing that was possible, in part, because the department had provided him with a copy of my report, ensuring that there would be no contradiction.

He ably defended his report, but the committee continued to hammer away at the actions of the White House during the early days of the administration. They kept returning to the fact that Harry Thomason, a Hollywood producer, had virtually unrestricted access to the White House but for all practical purposes did not have to comply with ethics rules and financial disclosure requirements for government employees. Darnell Martens was a partner with Thomason in TRM, Incorporated, an executive jet consulting service that had provided services for the Clinton presidential campaign. He had proposed a $499,000 study to look for ways to cut government waste in aircraft costs, a proposal that would have likely been awarded if the Travel Office matter had not erupted in the media.

But Podesta had difficulty in justifying the fact that Bernard Nussbaum had kept Vincent Foster's personal diary for a year, even though it had been covered by a subpoena from Independent Counsel Robert Fiske Jr., Kenneth Starr's Whitewater predecessor. Shaheen, from DOJ, noted Foster was "a compulsive note taker and had maintained a daily log, which would have been very helpful," and that there was "no way of mistaking that his [Fiske's] subpoena specifically requested precisely those documents . . . that had never been tendered to me or to Mr. Fiske." Podesta even voiced his "surprise" when he learned of the diary and could do little to justify Nussbaum's actions.

A great deal of the testimony also centered about the IRS audit of Ultrair in Tennessee. Bell, the IRS panelist, repeatedly cited rule Section 6103 of the Internal Revenue Code of prohibiting the disclosure of any information regarding taxpayers as reason to avoid responding to pointed questions about that audit. I could not avoid thinking how easy it is for a government agency to hide its actions behind some regulation. During a break, I visited with Kingsbury and voiced my disbelief that it was just a coincidence, mentioning Kennedy's comment that if the FBI didn't help him he would go to the IRS. I asked Kingsbury if she believed the Ultrair investigation was a coincidence. She responded, "No way! We just didn't have time to prove it."

But it was Michael Shaheen who delivered the most forceful and damning testimony. He testified that the lack of cooperation by the White House was "unprecedented" and the worst he had encountered in his years of government service. When asked to put the level of White House cooperation on a scale of one to ten, with ten being the highest, he opined that the White House cooperated at about a level of four. Shaheen's considerable candor sent a clear message to the White House and the Department of Justice that he would not be a part of the politicization of the department, a fact that I believe led eventually to his premature retirement.

Meanwhile, Podesta stated that Hillary Clinton's involvement in the whole affair was "rather limited." An absurd assertion. It was Hillary Clinton's former Rose Law Firm partners, Vince Foster and Bill Kennedy, who were obviously feeling the pressure to resolve the issue. Combine that with the appearance of longtime Hillary Clinton confidantes Bernard Nussbaum and Patsy Thomasson on the scene, and it was clear to me that Hillary was the one applying the pressure so evident in the urgency, even desperation, of those trying to resolve the Travel Office matter. Of all the great issues facing a new administration, including health care, foreign affairs, vacant positions to fill and more, there were a group of Hillary Clinton sycophants—Nussbaum, Foster, Thomasson, Kennedy, and others, all with responsible positions— totally preoccupied over a relatively minor issue for nearly a week. The allegations of misconduct by loyal, longtime employees was of the White House's making and was ultimately unsubstantiated.

The White House Travel Office matter sent a clear message to the Congress as well as independent counsels that this White House would be different. Lying, withholding evidence, and considering—even expecting—underlings to be expendable so the Clintons could avoid accountability for their actions would become the norm. It was an early lesson that was not well remembered by many engaged in future investigations, but it was a lesson I remembered when I got involved in the CAMPCON case, another situation involving friends of the Clintons engaged in unethical and criminal conduct.

Billy Dale, head of the White House Travel Office, was indicted, a puzzling and unfortunate course of action. Sloppy record-keeping is not a crime, and even if a crime was committed, sloppy record-keeping can be as much a defense tool as it can evidence for the prosecution. After a highly publicized trial held in the District of Columbia, with its very favorable view of the Clintons, a jury took only a short while to find Dale not guilty.

After I returned to Little Rock from my appearance before Congressman Clinger's committee, I wrote Podesta a brief note at the Georgetown Law Center where he was teaching. Somewhat tongue in cheek, I thanked him for fielding most of the committee's questions and allowing the rest of us to sit idly by. I told him it was nice to have made his acquaintance. I liked Podesta but didn't envy the job he had then, or later, when he returned to the White House. I have always written such notes when I meet someone for the first time. Perhaps it's a Southern thing.

I didn't receive a reply.

CHAPTER 14

ARKANSAS BOUND

"[It is] not the duplicitousness . . . that concerns
so much as the polished ease, the almost habitual,
casual, articulate way he bobs and weaves. He
has mastered the art of equivocation."

Paul Greenberg, *Arkansas Democrat-Gazette*

When I arrived in Little Rock as special agent in charge in the summer of 1995, the imposing political figure of William Jefferson Clinton still cast a shadow over Arkansas. And as time passed, more and more Arkansans were uncomfortable with that shadow, which, as his presidency continued, became a dark cloud that brought little economic benefit or self-esteem to a state in dire need of both. Most hoped he would just go away and let them get on with their lives.

The single greatest political campaign ever conducted in Arkansas was not actually conducted by an Arkansan. That distinction goes to Huey Long of Louisiana. In 1932, Long traveled to Arkansas and barnstormed for Hattie Caraway, the first woman ever elected to the United States Senate. She had been elected to complete the year remaining on her deceased husband's term, but powerful Arkansas politicians, while willing to concede that small term to her, had decided that they would not support her election for a full six-year term. They did not count on Huey Long. He invaded Arkansas with campaign literature, sound trucks, and record players, appearing with Caraway at several stops a day timed with military precision. Arkansas had never seen anything like it and hasn't since. The campaign lasted only seven days but included almost forty speeches crisscrossing two thousand miles. His efforts cleared the way for a Caraway landslide.

While stories of the Kingfish are infinitely amusing, they also reveal an unsettling cynicism toward the Arkansas electorate and the assumption that they're easy marks. Yet Long's cynicism came nowhere close to that of the Clinton campaign. Perhaps no one revealed this more succinctly than George Stephanopoulos when he admitted the Clinton campaign had "kept all the promises we intended to keep." As I came to know and understand Bill Clinton's Arkansas, I discovered that statement to be a vivid description of Clinton the politician, much to the detriment of the state itself.

While Clinton claimed Arkansas as his home, Arkansas is not Bill Clinton. It's much better than that and undeserving of the ridicule Clinton's presidency brought on it. As I traveled throughout the state, giving about a hundred speeches during my tenure there, I became convinced that Clinton's electoral prospects had diminished considerably by the time he went against his promise to complete his final term as governor and ran for the presidency in 1992. Clinton is a high maintenance public figure: there was a very real "Clinton fatigue" in Arkansas well before those became buzzwords to describe the condition many Americans felt when he was president. On more than one occasion, Arkansans told me that the only way to get rid of Clinton was "to send him to Washington."

Deborah Mathis wrote an interesting column in the May 16, 1997, issue of the *Arkansas Times*, commenting on how Clinton always lived for the next campaign and had been on an Arkansas ballot every two years since 1974. She viewed Clinton as "bored" without the "energizing fire in his belly," observing that for him "[g]overning had been the unavoidable consequence of winning." Mathis was certainly onto something. After a change in the state constitution that gave the governor four-year terms instead of two, Clinton faced four years without the urgency of an impending campaign. He realized 1992 was going to be his last chance to run for the presidency as an incumbent elected official. According to observers, his Republican opponent in the 1990 governor's race, Sheffield Nelson, had displayed Clinton's vulnerabilities such that only a last-minute strategy had allowed him to avoid losing by an embarrassingly small margin. Governing seemed more difficult than campaigning for Clinton, a hallmark characteristic of most successful revolutionaries throughout history.

Unquestionably, Clinton the politician benefited from Arkansas, since during all but his last uncompleted term in office he ran in an election every two years. In effect, he ran a perpetual campaign. After losing the governor's race in 1980, Clinton's political ideology became that of getting reelected, not standing for anything of any consequence that might risk political capital. This resulted in the rise of a more powerful state legislature and gave roots to the corruption I encountered when I arrived in Arkansas in 1995.

I am not so naïve as to think Arkansas was devoid of corruption before Clinton became governor, but his tenure, during which he literally ceded behind-the-scenes legislative power to a few state senators and representatives, almost insured that corruption would increase. These legislators were content to allow him to retain the electoral spotlight and fly around the United States in pursuit of his higher political ambitions with an apparent disregard for what was—or rather wasn't—being accomplished in his home state. Power was consolidated and compromises were reached so that Clinton could return to office while Arkansas continued to lag behind almost every other state in economic progress, quality of education (the Achilles heel for Arkansas), and confidence in government.

In Arkansas, Clinton has a well-established reputation as one who compromised for personal political gain. After he had drawn number 311 in the lottery, virtually ensuring that he would not be drafted and not have to honor his commitment to enter the ROTC, he wrote a letter to Colonel Eugene Holmes that said in part, "I decided to accept the draft in spite of my beliefs for one reason: to maintain my political viability within the system." Even in those days he had no principles that were above being compromised for his "political viability."

Early in his ascendancy, Clinton managed to eliminate his chief future political competition in one fell swoop. During the Senate race of 1977 when he was state attorney general, Clinton had to decide whether to run for the Senate or seek some other alternative for his political ambitions. David Pryor, the incumbent governor, decided to contest the Senate race. His principal opponent was the political star-in-waiting Jim Guy Tucker. When Clinton decided to run for governor, he watched the tightening Senate race where Tucker was clearly in a position to beat the older Pryor. A close acquaintance of Clinton's explained to me how Clinton threw his support to Pryor.

Clinton, according to some, was part of a whisper campaign against Tucker and with his already formidable statewide network of supporters in place, was able to help get Pryor elected while politically destroying Tucker. According to the close Clinton acquaintance, this accomplished two things. It got Pryor out of Arkansas, but with him being entirely indebted to Clinton; and it removed Tucker as a political rival. With Dale Bumpers already in Washington occupying the other Senate seat, Clinton was left without a political rival of note for the remainder of his time in Arkansas.

Firsthand observers say that Bill, and even more so Hillary, would not tolerate any political challenger. The spotlight was to shine on them and them alone. Consequently, when Clinton left office and was followed by a still politically wounded (and future felon) Jim Guy Tucker, there was no Democratic Party heir apparent for the governor's office. That continues even today. This situation resulted in a Republican political novice, Mike Huckabee, being elected lieutenant governor when Tucker was elevated to the governor's office, and later easily winning election as governor after he assumed the office when Tucker resigned under pressure following his own conviction on two felony counts.

When there wasn't a real issue to wave in front of the voters, Clinton supplied one. During his run for reelection as governor in 1984, the bogeymen were schoolteachers. On the surface at least, Governor Clinton took on the powerful Arkansas Education Association by advocating what was regarded by the teachers union as almost heresy: requiring that teachers be tested to retain certification. For a short while this cost him the support of the AEA, but it was a popular move with the public, and he easily won reelection.

The proposal had racial overtones, particularly in the Delta region where there were a high number of black teachers. Poor white families who couldn't afford to send their children to private schools saw this as an opportunity to get rid of what they regarded as underachieving black teachers and allow them, the white families, to take back control of their public schools. After Clinton's '84 reelection, the program was implemented with great fanfare and essentially removed any local control from the local school districts. In my conversations with elected county officials, every one of them considered the program an unmitigated disaster, with increased demands for reports and paperwork but with few actual improvements.

On the basis of student test scores, the program was a miserable failure. In school year 1992–93, the Little Rock School District average score on the American College Test (ACT) was 19.7 out of a possible 36 points. In school year 1996–97, the average was 19.3. Some didn't fare that well. In the Alpena School District in the northwest corner of the state, 1992–93 ACT scores were 21.4 and in 1996–97 had fallen to 18.9. The statewide average remained unchanged between the two periods at 20.3, ranking it in the bottom quarter nationally.

As I traveled around Arkansas, I also became aware of the burgeoning problem of teen pregnancy. I saw teenage mothers with their infant children shopping in the small-town grocery stores where I would stop to buy a soft drink, or walking along the highways and the streets. In 1985, Arkansas ranked nineteenth out of the fifty states and the District of Columbia with a teen pregnancy rate of 111 births, miscarriages, and abortions out of every 1000 females ages fifteen to nineteen. In 1996, Arkansas ranked seventh. If sex education is being taught in Arkansas schools with any urgency, it isn't working.

On May 2, 1996, I was visiting with a county judge who was a self-described "yellow dog Democrat," a dyed-in-the-wool Democrat who would vote for a yellow dog before he'd vote Republican. When I asked him how there could be support for Clinton given the poor record Arkansas had achieved in academics on his watch, the judge somewhat wryly responded, "If it hadn't been for Bill, maybe we would be ranked fiftieth."

This judge was a lifelong member of the Arkansas Democratic Party, active in politics, and a longtime supporter of Clinton, but even he had grown disillusioned by the constant flow of revelations that brought embarrassment to the people of his home state. He even declined to wear an Arkansas lapel pin when he traveled. He talked of Clinton's notoriety as the "fastest zipper in Arkansas" and his blatant philandering when he was away from Little Rock. The judge said it was a constant worry to his supporters and seemed almost as if Clinton wanted to be caught.

DURING A LATE-NIGHT CHAT with a well-known former official who had held a responsible position in government, he told me that when he campaigned with Clinton in the early years, Clinton expected entertainment every night they were away from Little Rock and Hillary. At the end of the day, Clinton would ask this former official what he had been able to line up for the evening and he would respond, "Do you remember in Fordyce there was a little blonde on the front row . . . well, that's what I lined up for tonight."

This same former official described in explicit detail a tryst Clinton had with a cabaret singer at The Afterthought, a small piano bar in the Heights area of Little Rock, after the bar had closed and a few regulars stayed inside to drink and talk. While I doubted the explicit details initially, this individual said he was in the bar that evening and at least one other person had been the recipient of the same story. As time passed and I heard on separate occasions from two people who knew the singer that she openly discussed her dalliances with the governor, I decided the story was entirely plausible.

Clinton was said to be having an affair with the owner of a boutique in the Heights and was known to drop by the shop unannounced. The owner would retire to the back office with Clinton for awhile, then he would exit, returning to the state police car. One day Clinton came in and was fidgeting about while the owner waited on a customer when he suddenly spied one of Hillary's friends enter the store. He quickly grabbed a purse and loudly told a sales clerk, "I think Hillary will like this one." She rang up the purchase, and Clinton discovered he had just bought a $400 purse. My source related the story with great mirth, claiming to have been an eyewitness.

NOT ALL THE STORIES were so amusing. On January 28, 1998, during the Monica Lewinsky matter, I received a call from an individual whom I trusted without question. This person said President Clinton had had a sexual relationship with an extremely attractive young girl from a politically prominent family in Arkansas, meaning the Democratic Party. Though the girl later denied the relationship, she did confirm that she thought Clinton had tried to have a relationship with her. She admitted that when she was enrolled at the University of Arkansas at Fayetteville, Clinton had called and suggested that they meet in a local hotel. He also suggested she pick up a six-pack of Heineken en route. She agreed to meet with him, noting she had met him on numerous occasions and her family were longtime political supporters. She said she assumed he wanted to talk about an upcoming election.

At the hotel, a state trooper escorted her to a room where Clinton was alone. After some initial small talk, they discovered the beer did not come with twist off caps, so Clinton called room service for a bottle opener. When the room service waiter knocked at the door she said she would answer it, but Clinton quickly went to the door, barely cracked it open and reached his arm around the door without revealing himself and took the bottle opener. At that point, she recalled, she began to feel uncomfortable. Clinton then sat on a sofa and asked her to join him. As she was trying to figure out how she was going to extricate herself from the situation she found herself embroiled in, there was another knock on the door.

This time it was the state trooper who reported that there had been a shooting or some type of hostage situation in Clinton's hometown of Hot Springs and he was needed. Clinton had to leave the girl behind to wonder what had just occurred. She later related the incident to members of her family who berated her for being so naïve considering his reputation as a womanizer. I found the resemblance to the story told by Paula Jones eerily similar—the escort by the state trooper, the hotel room, the invitation to sit on the couch. You get the picture. I also learned that a national television network had the same story, that the now grown woman was willing to talk about the incident, but the network brass refused to run the story.

On April 15, 1998, I had lunch with an attractive, confident, and articulate African-American female at Loca Luna's, a restaurant between the Heights and downtown Little Rock. We sat outside on the patio on a sunny spring day ahead of the stifling summer heat that would drive us all inside to the air conditioning in a few weeks. This was near the high point of the Monica Lewinsky media blitz and the president wagging his finger at television cameras intoning, "I did not have sexual relations with that woman." My luncheon companion, an unabashed admirer and supporter of Hillary Clinton, said she did not believe Clinton's denial and shared an experience she herself had had years before.

She had been sitting on stage at some outdoor political function; as it happened the governor was sitting on one side of her and Hillary on the other. Throughout the function, Governor Clinton had constantly leaned over and chatted with her, asking who certain people were in the audience, and so forth. It became obvious to her that his real purpose was to find some excuse to chat with her and she began to feel uneasy with his attentions on stage in front of his wife and the audience.

She told me that after the function concluded, she made a passing reference to Clinton about him and Hillary attending a reception later and Clinton said Hillary wouldn't be joining them, but he would drop by. She went to the reception, which Clinton did attend. She first noticed him as he grasped her elbow and spoke to her as she was talking to others. She greeted him, then moved away. He followed her, continued to grasp her arm and make small talk. After a while she noticed other guests watching them and, feeling uncomfortable, she moved away from him again, said goodbye to the hosts, and hurriedly left the reception.

As she was getting in her car, she heard Clinton trotting up behind her and realized he had followed her outside, undoubtedly observed by those still at the reception. He then got in her car on the passenger side and continued to try to talk to her. She had to start the car and put it in gear before he finally got out. The next day she had to deal with the impression that she had left the reception with the governor and all the resulting implications and innuendoes. Based on her own personal experience, combined with what she had heard and seen over the years in Little Rock, she believed he had an affair with Lewinsky, and had believed it well before his forced admission that he had lied to the American people. Most everyone in Arkansas who had known Clinton over the years seemed to share her opinion.

There were plenty of other stories. I got the impression that this was a frequent topic of conversation in Little Rock. What I found puzzling was that many who told these stories were staunch supporters, even defenders, of Clinton. Yet they were the first to be at their churches' doorsteps on Sunday morning to hear sermons of family values, fidelity, morality, and the Ten Commandments. Somehow they were able to divorce the teachings of their faith from the antics of their governor. To questions or challenges about their ex-governor being a liar, the response in one way or another was (and is) often, "Aw, that's just Bill!"

In time, I came to believe that Arkansas politicians regarded Clinton like a new puppy. The puppy makes muddy foot prints across the clean floor, gnaws your favorite deck shoes, and even soils the carpet, but you can't stay mad at him because he's so darned cute. I think many Arkansans found Clinton so "cute" that it was hard to stay mad at him, though they knew he would just keep on making messes that someone else would have to clean up. But as time passed, I got the distinct impression that Arkansans got tired of cleaning up after Clinton, and, as if the puppy had grown into a full-sized, slobbering dog, they were ready to banish him to the backyard of political oblivion.

Not all of Clinton's antics were considered to be cute, especially if you were on the receiving end of one of his temper tantrums or asked to do something that bordered on impropriety, if not illegality. I was told by one person, a longtime Clinton supporter who was personally acquainted with Clinton and who had witnessed many of Clinton's tantrums, that somehow he believed his victims were supposed to forget how he had just savaged them and continue to like him and to be of service to him. One example involved a state vehicle, an elegant Lincoln with center-opening rear doors hinged at the back. After being driven up to the Governor's Mansion, Clinton had gotten out of the car and kicked the rear door so hard it came off at the hinges. The state police were then confronted with having the relatively new vehicle repaired without daring to explain what happened.

Clinton came to expect everyone around him to act on his every whim, a trait shared by Hillary. One fine state trooper told me how he had wanted to serve on the governor's detail as it would give him the opportunity to serve in a different way from the traditional role of working traffic and conducting criminal investigations. He took the assignment and though he had heard reports of the conduct of the Arkansas first couple, he was not prepared for the manner in which he was treated—by Hillary in particular. He described her language as anything but "ladylike," profane arguments that occurred regardless of who was present or the occasion, and the imperial manner in which she treated the staff. Finally, disillusioned with what he had witnessed, he asked for and received a transfer from the detail.

The Clintons were not above using the state services for their personal use. According to what I was told by acquaintances of the couple, both were embittered when Clinton failed to win reelection after his first term as governor, but while Bill was more inclined to self-pity, Hillary was defiant, angry, and out for revenge. It was Hillary that took all the food and beverages from the Governor's Mansion to their private residence. I was told that not only did they empty the mansion cupboards, but completely depleted the funds appropriated for entertaining, leaving incoming Governor Frank White with no money for that purpose.

MANY CONSIDERED FRIENDSHIP with Clinton a one-way street. Shortly after I arrived in Arkansas, I spoke with a disillusioned Clinton supporter who told me how Clinton had "screwed Bill Bowen." William H. Bowen should be considered a very real Arkansas hero, but he has quietly gone about his business with little fanfare and self-promotion. He grew up poor in Altheimer, Arkansas, a small farming community about fifty miles southeast of Little Rock in the Arkansas Delta. Bowen was a World War II U.S. Navy carrier pilot whose brother died in combat in the Aleutian Islands. He graduated from the Stonier School of Banking at Rutgers University and served as an attorney at the U.S. Tax Court and at the Department of Justice in the early 1950s. He returned to Arkansas, made a fortune in business, and had come to head the First Commercial Bank in its rivalry with Worthern Bank, once headed by investment banker Jack Stephens and later the Riady family from Indonesia. It was generally considered that he had bested Worthern in virtually every category of competition.

In 1990, after his fortune had been made, he felt the lure of public service and agreed to serve as the chief of staff for the much younger and undisciplined governor, Bill Clinton. In effect, he served as the chief executive of the state after Clinton immediately broke his promise to serve the full four-year term and began the marathon run for the presidency. Bowen kept the government running because the Clintons were not about to give Lieutenant Governor Tucker a significant role that could launch his political revival.

I was told that after Clinton left for Washington following the 1992 election, Clinton offered a position to Bowen but never followed through. Eventually Bowen became dean of the law school at the University of Arkansas at Little Rock, the position he occupied when I arrived in the state. I developed an instant liking and respect for the man. He was tall, slender, and erect, immaculately groomed with courtly manners and the very picture of confidence and success, but one who had never forgotten he had come from Altheimer. We would meet for lunch occasionally and I found him completely devoted to the future success of Arkansas. Though he had been disappointed in Clinton, he never betrayed anything but good thoughts about the president.

During those conversations I never mentioned what I had heard about Bowen being "screwed" until after I read a column by Robert Novak in the *Washington Post* on October 31, 1996. Novak's column alluded to the matter of Clinton disappointing his longtime friend and father figure. On April 28 of the following year, I had lunch with Bowen at the Little Rock Club, a private restaurant with a panoramic view of downtown Little Rock and the Arkansas River. As we were chatting, I mentioned the Novak article. Bowen told me Clinton had asked him what job he would like in his new administration, and he had stated he would like to be head of the Federal Depository Insurance Cooperation (FDIC). Clinton had agreed. As time passed, Bowen recalled, the Riady group, his old banking rivals, had opposed the nomination and in fact, John Huang himself had told Bowen that they were opposing the nomination. I asked Bowen if he had felt any sense of satisfaction since Huang's problems had surfaced in the press and he responded, "It's crossed my mind." He didn't elaborate.

Bill Bowen wasn't the only Arkansan Bill Clinton let down. When Clinton became governor in 1980, the median income for a family of four in Arkansas was $15,068. This placed Arkansas 49th of the 50 states and the District of Columbia, ahead of Maine and Mississippi. In 1992, when Clinton left office, Arkansas still ranked 49th ahead of New Mexico and West Virginia. In 2000, after Clinton had been in the White House for eight years, Arkansas ranked 51st with a median income 72 percent of the national median and the only median figure under $40,000. Clearly, neither Clinton as governor nor Clinton as president had an economic benefit for Arkansas.

During the 1996 presidential election, fewer than 50 percent of Arkansans voted, even though their favorite son was running for re-election. As election day approached, I found little discussion of politics in places like Forrest City, Mayflower, Malvern, Ozark, and Beebe. The talk was about the then-dismal performance of the Arkansas Razorbacks, work, hunting, and the weather. I asked an acquaintance who was an avid hunter if politics was ever discussed as they sat around the fire after a day in the duck blind or deer stand. He responded, "Only if there is nothing else to talk about."

Bill Clinton represents the highest evolution of the professional politician, surpassing even Lyndon Johnson. This is something the Founding Fathers never would have envisioned—that is, political leaders who have never made even a cursory pretense of holding a job and whose primary income is derived from politics and the largesse of others.

Paul Greenberg—the courageous and articulate columnist who won the Pulitzer Prize for writing about integration for the *Pine Bluff Commercial*—wrote a remarkable column that I think even today best describes Clinton. On October 28, 1992, the *Arkansas Democrat-Gazette* failed to support Clinton's bid for the presidency. That day Greenberg wrote a column that was simply farsighted in painting a picture of Clinton that has come to be so well-known throughout the world.

Greenberg spoke of how Clinton was "a fighter who never gives up where his career is concerned," a truth later affirmed in the Monica Lewinsky impeachment matter, but also evident in his compromising on such issues as gays in the military. Greenberg didn't get it all right, for he also wrote that, "His triumph . . . would not only boost this long underestimated state's pride, but doubtless provide some welcome patronage." That didn't occur. Greenberg also observed that Arkansas has progressed, "but not nearly as much as it would have if Bill Clinton had been the Bill Clinton of the campaign ads."

Greenberg continued: "But it is not the duplicitousness in his politics that concerns so much as the polished ease, the almost habitual, casual, articulate way he bobs and weaves. He has mastered the art of equivocation. There is something almost inhuman in his smoother responses that sends a shiver up the spine. It is not the compromises he has made that troubles so much as the unavoidable suspicion that he has no great principles to compromise."

I had reservations about a Clinton presidency from the beginning, but those reservations centered about my belief that being a governor of a small Southern state did not adequately prepare one to be president of the United States. I was willing to attribute the blunders on such issues as gays in the military, the obsessive secrecy of Hillary's failed health-care plan, and the White House Travel Office debacle to simply getting his bearings on a Washington fast track he obviously wasn't prepared to handle. But no turnaround took place, and indeed the benefits a Clinton presidency was expected to offer never materialized.

Even Clinton's friends and supporters grew disillusioned. I received a telephone call one evening after I retired from Gene Lyons, who famously proposed on *Meet the Press* that Clinton's relationship with Monica Lewinsky could have been, "a totally innocent relationship in which the president was, in a sense, the victim of someone rather like the woman who followed David Letterman around." I asked Lyons how he felt after it became apparent that Clinton had lied. Lyons said it had been easier for him to forgive Clinton than it had been for his wife, who had taken Clinton's picture off the wall in their house. "I'm not sure she will ever hang it up again."

CHAPTER 15

BIG TROUBLE IN LITTLE ROCK

"I taste nice, too. You ought to try me."
Independence County Sheriff Ron Webb

Though Bill Clinton was the most famous character in Arkansas politics, he was, by no means, the only politician who betrayed the public trust of those who had elected them to high office.

When I arrived in Arkansas, one group I hoped to get to know quickly was the Arkansas Sheriff's Association. As I began making the rounds of their offices statewide, sheriffs told me in many cases that it was the first time an FBI special agent in charge had ever dropped by their office. I had an instant like and respect for the group as a whole that increased over time. A few stand out, including one of the most colorful—and most corrupt—sheriffs I ever encountered.

I met Sheriff Ron Webb of Independence County at the first Sheriff's Association meeting I attended in North Little Rock. He was a huge man, probably 6'4" and over 350 pounds, red-faced with long silver hair and a huge stomach. Unlike most of his fellow sheriffs, Webb had attended college, but his exposure to academic endeavors wasn't readily evident. While I'd had reports that something was amiss at the Independence County Sheriff's Department, I continued to treat Webb with the same respect I did other officers.

But as rumors persisted, I assigned two bright young agents to look into Webb's activities. One of the agents, Mike Lowe, was actually from northwest Arkansas and had played college basketball at Arkansas Tech. He was joined by Troy Chenevert, a young agent from Lafayette, Louisiana, who in contrast to the serious demeanor of Lowe, exuded all the outgoing fun of his Cajun ancestors. They were a good team, and though they lacked experience, they had tremendous energy and a blue-collar work ethic.

It didn't take long for them to find someone who not only had been abused by Webb but also had the courage to help us develop a prosecutable case against him. In June 1997, a surgical assistant named Vickie Hawkins had gone to Webb's office in Batesville because she was worried her husband would be shielded from domestic abuse charges against him on account of his relationship with a local judge. After listening to her for a few minutes, Webb suggested they make a date to get a motel room and "get naked." Hawkins described how nervous she was with him standing around her but had at one point said that he "smelled nice." Sheriff Webb answered, "I taste nice, too. You ought to try me." She rebuffed his advances and left his office. Lowe and Chenevert were absolutely convinced she was telling the truth. At the FBI's request, Vickie bravely agreed to wear a body recorder and pay Webb another visit.

I gave my approval and signed the necessary forms. At this point I also added a female agent, Carrie Land, to the team to rig the recorder, and also just in case Hawkins felt more comfortable discussing any aspect of the case with a woman.

On July 30, 1997, Hawkins returned to Sheriff Webb's office wearing the recorder. It didn't take long for Webb to make his move. He got up from behind his desk and closed the door, then, as described by Hawkins, walked up behind her and placed his hands first on her shoulders, then down her blouse and began rubbing her breasts. She started squirming around, telling him to behave himself, but Webb then walked around in front of her, unzipped his pants and exposed himself. He placed her hand on his penis, asking for oral sex. When she refused and started getting upset and pulling away, he zipped up his trousers, walked back to his desk and said that she was acting like "some kind of kid." She got up and ran out of the office.

The three agents were chastened by what happened. Moreover, the tape was of poor quality and Hawkins had been so upset that she had said little to indicate what was happening, i.e. "Sheriff, don't unzip your pants here," or "Sheriff, don't put your hands on my breasts." But we felt we had enough for an indictment.

While we were targeting Webb, we also wanted the prosecuting attorney for the area, T.J. Hively. In October, as we discussed our investigative strategy, I received a telephone call from Webb. The rumors were flying in Batesville that he was under investigation and he wanted to know what was going on. I asked my secretary, Sandy Finch, to tell him I wasn't in but would get back to him as soon as I returned. Calling Lowe and Chenevert into the office as witnesses, I returned the call to Webb. We talked for a few minutes, but he never asked about any investigation and I never mentioned it.

We wanted to give him an opportunity to help himself. So I called Webb back and suggested that if he was ever in Little Rock perhaps he could stop by to discuss something. He volunteered to come the very next day and I told him that agents Lowe and Chenevert would be waiting for him. When Webb arrived, the agents took him to a conference room and played the recording Hawkins had made. He denied knowing who Hawkins was and said he couldn't identify the voice on the tape. Though at one point he started crying, he insisted he hadn't done anything wrong and refused the offer to help himself. When the agents told me what happened, I told them to proceed with the indictment.

Webb was indicted in December 1998 for a civil rights violation. Of course he denied the charge and told the *Batesville Daily Guard*, "I have spent my whole adult life trying to help people." In a later interview with *Arkansas Democrat-Gazette* reporter Sandy Davis, he commented, "I've heard about 10 or 15 seconds of the tape. And I'm not even sure who the woman is. I think I know, but I'm not sure." In March 1999, he was indicted on a second charge of sexually assaulting and soliciting sexual favors from the woman. He was tried before the late U.S. District Court Judge Henry Woods, a former FBI agent and close friend of Hillary Clinton. During the trial, Hawkins continued to provide sound testimony and with the tape recording as evidence, a jury found Webb guilty of the July 30 incident, but innocent of the earlier encounter.

On July 20, 1999, Woods sentenced Webb to five months in prison and five months home detention for a misdemeanor conviction of violating Hawkins's civil rights. Woods expressed his distaste for federal sentencing guidelines and imposed the minimum time he could and a minimum fine of $2,000. He also made his feelings known when he said from the bench, "I don't think an appeal would be frivolous in this case." He indicated that he was troubled by the facts of the case, declaring there were "elements of entrapment." He rejected consideration of a sentencing enhancement for committing the civil rights violation while using force. This was in spite of testimony that included not only Webb placing the woman's hand on his penis but also using his more than 350 pounds to force the woman down on a couch. Woods said he considered the notion that Webb used force or violence as "weak."

Taking Judge Woods's advice, Webb's attorneys appealed the sentence to the Eighth U.S. Circuit Court of Appeals, which upheld the verdict and sent the case back to Woods suggesting a longer sentence. The judge's reaction amazed even longtime court observers. Red-faced, the judge almost stood up behind the bench and literally shouted, "It ain't the crime of the century! It ain't even a felony!" Another time he pointedly stated he was "thumbing my nose at them," referring to the Eighth Circuit, which had previously removed him from the highly publicized trials of Governor Jim Guy Tucker on corruption charges and Jim and Susan McDougal in the Whitewater affair.

Hawkins also filed a sexual harassment suit against Webb, who assured her she wouldn't "get a nickel." Obviously the courts didn't agree, for on May 24, 2001, Judge Jerry Cavanaugh awarded Hawkins $60,000 and an additional $15,000 for her attorney. He also required Webb to call Hawkins and apologize. Thanks to Judge Woods, the sheriff didn't have to start serving his sentence until his term as sheriff expired in 2001. He ran for reelection, but finished third in a field of six.

ANOTHER MEMORABLE CASE began one morning when I opened the *Arkansas Democrat-Gazette* and noted an article about the difficulties State Representative Ben McGee was having with back taxes. I was surprised to see that McGee was black, something I hadn't known when an investigation into his activities had been discussed earlier. Somehow I knew then that if there ever was a successful investigation against McGee, he would accuse the authorities of being racially motivated. As it developed, I was correct. There was every indication that McGee was a crooked politician using his position for self-enrichment. He was the most powerful black member of the Arkansas legislature, Democrat or Republican, and had a reputation as a crook even among his peers. McGee was a target of an FBI corruption investigation because of his alleged activities, not because of the color of his skin. Yet there were certain sensitivities we would have to be mindful of. He and his supporters would play the race card at the first opportunity.

McGee was from Marion, in Crittenden County, part of the Mississippi Delta of east Arkansas. With its black soil and traditionally black field hands, it is among the poorest land in the South. I often drove through the area and was always depressed with the poverty and the lack of hope. The only stores that weren't boarded up seemed to be liquor stores, jobs were few and far between, schools were falling apart, and yet in the middle of it all was Southland Greyhound Park, Ben McGee's former employer and the point of origin for a variety of questionable activities. The greyhound racetrack was in the midst of the misery of West Memphis, Arkansas, providing easy access for Tennesseans who wanted to gamble, but also convenient for those from the Delta towns of Arkansas whose financial condition would have made it difficult for them to feed a greyhound, much less bet on one. The allegations against McGee concerned mainly his relationship with Southland Racing Corporation, operator of the track.

It didn't take long for news of the investigation to become public knowledge. On December 14, 1995, the *Arkansas Democrat-Gazette* headlined a front-page article, "Dog track bill sics FBI on McGee." It was mentioned that I "refused to confirm the investigation," but I knew from past experience that once a public corruption case becomes public knowledge there's a considerable loss of control of the situation.

As the investigation gathered momentum, FBI Agent Greg Hall determined it was time to interview employees of the track. He made an unannounced visit to the track offices where he contacted Barry Baldwin, the general manager, to say he intended to interview some employees and gave a very general description of his reasons for doing so. Baldwin, somewhat surprised, said he would have to check with his corporate offices in New York. Hall gave Baldwin a business card along with his address in West Memphis. Hall soon received a call from a security officer with Delaware North Corporation, parent company of Southland, who said he was calling from Australia and wanted to know whether the track was being investigated as a subject or as a victim. Hall replied, "Should I be looking at the racetrack as a subject?" He did not receive a response.

The next morning at about 8:00 AM, Hall contacted my colleague Bill Hardin in Little Rock to advise him of the call. However, Hardin had already heard from a retired FBI SAC named Edward Foley, also calling on behalf of Delaware North Corporation to determine some details of the investigation. This was inappropriate. Foley was trying to use his former position to influence Hardin in providing details of an ongoing investigation, which Hardin found repellent. My initial reaction was to call Foley directly and remind him that under no circumstances would he have approved of a former SAC soliciting information from a street agent under his supervision, and that standard still prevailed. Instead, I asked Hardin to refer Foley to me if he called again. He never did.

But Delaware didn't give up. A few days later Hall took a call from another Delaware North employee who identified himself as a member of the corporate counsel's office and, incidentally, was a former United States attorney from Buffalo. He was cordial until he realized he wasn't going to get any information, then abruptly asked for the name of the assistant United States attorney who was handling the investigation. That was the last time Delaware North called the FBI in Little Rock.

But the investigation continued and the evidence was damning. One bit of information regarded a lobbyist from Delaware North Corporation giving McGee a company credit card before the legislature broke for the weekend. This was a tactic that allowed companies to pay off legislators without leaving a paper trail. A lobbyist gave a legislator a corporate credit card, making it hard to connect a name, bank, or account number with that legislator. When the card reached its authorized limit, the lobbyist simply gave the legislator another one. The Bureau got information on this scheme from Bill McCuen, a former Arkansas secretary of state then serving a prison sentence. Hall had recalled the McCuen conversation when he began to conduct more overt interviews. About the third or fourth interview, a witness confirmed that McGee had received a credit card for personal use while the legislature was in session. Delaware North was taken aback when they learned that the FBI knew they had given McGee a credit card.

In time, the investigation enveloped McGee's son, Benjamin Lelon McGee II. We thought this would be valuable leverage against the older McGee, but he refused to consider pleading to charges in exchange for his son not being caught up in the expanding investigation. By then, U.S. Attorney Paula Casey had assigned Pat Harris, an aggressive and experienced assistant United States attorney, to the investigation. We all liked and respected Harris, particularly his no-nonsense approach to prosecutions. On January 14, 1998, McGee was indicted on five counts.

Count one centered around McGee's accepting monies from Southland Racing Corporation in exchange for introducing favorable legislation. Count two concerned McGee's receiving money from the Arkansas Greyhound Association for influencing the same legislation. Count three involved McGee's failing to file income tax returns for five years beginning in 1984. According to the IRS, McGee owed $511,177.30 in back taxes, part of which included the proceeds of a $137,000 settlement from Ford Motor Company for a discrimination lawsuit he had filed. Count four pertained to McGee's attempt to evade back taxes already under collection by hiding assets. Count five involved McGee's obtaining property from an individual who had been charged with drug violations, with the promise he would use part of the money to pay off a state prosecutor.

Despite the overwhelming evidence, McGee continued to proclaim his innocence. So on February 26, 1998, McGee's son was indicted for perjury after lying to a grand jury about establishing a bank account in Memphis, Tennessee, in an effort to help his father hide money from the IRS. McGee's response was just what I expected: he publicly stated the investigation was racially based. But it didn't seem to stir up the commotion he had hoped. The indictment had removed McGee's image of invulnerability and his support in the legislature began to erode. In the words of one observer, the Arkansas Democratic Party "threw him overboard." He was left to fend for himself and increasingly found that even the constituents in Crittenden County failed to rally behind him. On September 4, 1998, McGee pled guilty to two felony charges and the charges against his son were dropped. Defiant to the end, McGee still refused to accept responsibility for his actions, stating, "The burden of trusting my son's future to twelve strangers was too great to bear."

McGee could have been sentenced to up to twenty years in prison with a fine up to $250,000. Based on federal guidelines, Harris recommended that McGee receive a jail sentence of two years for the extortion charge alone. However, U.S. District Court Judge Bill Wilson, a staunch Democrat and Bill Clinton appointee, had other ideas. He sentenced McGee to eighteen months in prison and added that he must return the $2,000 the Arkansas Greyhound Association had given him. The *Arkansas Democrat-Gazette* editorialized, "An invitation to cynicism, the sentencing of Ben McGee," observing that, "McGee did more than disgrace himself when he took money to influence legislation and evaded his income taxes. He betrayed his own proud past and the heroes he once marched with." McGee resigned—which others had not done—from the legislature. Though I had retired by this time, I received a telephone call from Greg Hall to make certain I was aware of that latest development and to thank me as SAC for my support during the investigation. I was glad someone remembered.

OCCASIONAL INTERESTING CASES led away from Little Rock, in one instance, all the way to Alaska. On April 8, 1993, Thomas Lavy was stopped by customs officials as he entered Beaver Creek, in the Canadian Yukon, from Alaska. He declared a shotgun, two .22-caliber rifles, and a muzzle-loading rifle, a large amount of ammunition, a belt buckle that hid a knife blade, and about $98,000 in cash. Lavy also had a plastic bag containing a white powder. As the customs inspectors picked up the bag, Lavy warned them to be careful because the substance was a poison named ricin, and that to even get it in a cut on their hands would be fatal. Lavy explained that he kept the ricin next to his money as protection. He believed a would-be robber would think it was cocaine and would ingest some of it, killing him.

Lavy was fined $750 for trying to enter Canada with the weapons and told to report to the United States Customs Office in Alcan, Alaska, to declare the currency. Lavy reported as instructed and declared $22,500 in U.S. currency, giving his address as P.O. Box 1297, Valdez, Alaska. However, when he entered the lower United States on April 12 at Portal, North Dakota, he gave his address as Box 894, HC 73, Onia, Arkansas.

Lavy's actions set in motion a series of events that led to one of the two or three bad days I had as special agent in charge of the FBI in Arkansas, days that raised very real concerns in my mind about the direction the FBI was taking in its domestic terrorism program.

I had learned about the toxin ricin, *ricinus communis,* in counterintelligence. In 1978, a Bulgarian dissident named Georgi Markov was approaching the subway in London when he felt a sharp pain in the back of a leg. When he turned around, he observed a man holding an umbrella and walking quickly away. Thinking it had been an accidental bumping, Markov continued walking. Within days he was dead. Markov suffered a painful and horrible end before doctors discovered a small capsule no larger than a pinhead in the back of his leg. The capsule, containing ricin, had been injected into his body by the umbrella in James Bond fashion. I learned that ricin is considered the third most toxic poison known to mankind, after plutonium and the botulism virus.

Canadian customs inspectors put Lavy's powder in an evidence locker and forgot about it. However, in April 1995, about two years later, Special Agent Tom Lynch from the Anchorage, Alaska FBI office, who had at one time been assigned to the FBI laboratory, received information through word of mouth of the incident, which became the focus of great interest by the FBI. The powder had tested positive for ricin. Lavy had been both honest and forthright when he had warned the inspectors away from it. There is absolutely no legitimate purpose for an individual to possess ricin. It is an incredibly efficient killing substance that can be made by anyone with the recipe, which is readily available. One particle of ricin the size of a grain of salt can kill someone and there is no known antidote. Why would Thomas Lavy have something like that?

Because of Lavy's Arkansas address, the investigation was forwarded to the Little Rock FBI Office, where it was assigned to Special Agent Roy Christopher in Jonesboro. According to the FBI in Anchorage, Lavy was believed to be living in Onia, Arkansas, in Stone County, about midway between Little Rock and Jonesboro. Christopher learned that Lavy appeared to live alone and had no arrest record, not even a driving violation. He was not atypical of the area and there was certainly nothing to suggest he was part of any larger group of would-be terrorists. Christopher prepared a tactical plan to arrest Lavy and search the premises. I arranged for both day and night aerial photographs to be taken using the FBI's Nightstalker aircraft. Nothing had developed to change my opinion that Lavy was simply a recluse who, for some unknown reason, had decided to make an especially dangerous poison. Neither making nor possessing ricin was against the law.

At first I had planned to stay in Little Rock during Lavy's arrest to handle communications with Washington, as it was exceedingly difficult to communicate from remote Stone County by either radio or cell phone. If the atmospherics didn't cooperate, it was virtually impossible to place a call without a hard-line telephone, which was unavailable anywhere near Lavy's residence. However, I was advised that Attorney General Janet Reno was monitoring the investigation due to it being hyped at FBI headquarters, so I decided that I would be on the scene. Increasingly, I had a feeling of foreboding about the whole operation.

Another concern was the growing size of the contingent to handle the arrest and search. In addition to FBI agents from Arkansas and Alaska, there were members of the FBI's Hostage Rescue Team, the FBI laboratory, the U.S. Army Tech Escort Unit, and the Naval Medical Research Institute, about fifty people in all. I began to feel a loss of control as it became apparent that FBI headquarters was going to turn the Lavy arrest and search into a media event.

There was the laughable expectation of secrecy. The plan was to hold a meeting in Little Rock for all those involved, then travel the three hours to Mountain View to stay in motels for the night before the arrest and search the next morning. I tried to explain that it would be impossible to keep the presence of fifty strangers in Mountain View, Arkansas, a secret the week before Christmas, but to no avail.

When we arrived in the area, we had cautioned the fifty participants to spread out and try to not be noticeable, hoping that they would be viewed by the locals as hunters. That didn't last through dinner. They returned from their meal talking about the inevitable questions from the waitresses: where they were from, what brought them to Mountain View, how long they were going to be in town, etc. At one place, a waitress asked whether the group was going to be around the next day; if so they needed to call in extra staff as they were operating at a reduced level since is was only a week before Christmas.

I had also insisted, over the objections of the Terrorism Section at FBIHQ, on briefing the local sheriff, Fred Black, since we were arresting a citizen of his county. Black had an excellent reputation and I considered his knowledge of the local situation essential. Black knew Lavy, as I had expected he would, but had nothing negative to add to what little information we already collected. He described him as one quietly going about his business, making few contacts with others in the area, but who was a member of the local American Legion post. I explained that our plan was to place SWAT personnel in the woods around Lavy's cabin well before daybreak and wait for him to leave the cabin, then arrest him. I wanted to avoid a protracted stand-off that would attract media attention. I invited Black to join me in a command post in the motor home the FBI was setting up in a cemetery near Lavy's residence. He agreed to come.

The morning of December 20 was below freezing, with ice on the ground. I got up at about 4:30 AM and met with the SWAT team members before they began their cold surveillance. By shortly after 6:00 AM, I was in the command post waiting for something to happen. I still had an uneasy feeling about the whole operation. Shortly after 8:30 AM, there was a flurry of activity that wasn't fully discernible over the poor radio communications, but I got the impression Lavy had exited the residence and was approaching the woods. I heard radio voices exclaiming, "FBI, FBI!" and there was a moment of silence. Then there was a breathless communication that Lavy was in custody.

A few minutes later, Lavy was transported to the command post to be interviewed. I knew immediately that we had badly overreacted to the situation. However, a simple, low-key arrest would not have accomplished headquarters's goal of having a terrorist incident to hype on the network news. We gave Lavy a cup of coffee and he was completely cooperative. He told the agents that yes, he did have castor beans (the source of ricin) in a fruit cake tin on a shelf, but no, he did not have any ricin. He told them of the location of several weapons in the cabin, where books detailing how ricin could be made were located, and that he had a large amount of cash in a canister under the cabin. He said he had not made any more ricin and that no one else was in the cabin. The subsequent search determined that Lavy had been completely truthful. About mid-morning, Lavy accompanied the agents to the cabin to point out the location of weapons, the stash of money, books, castor beans, and so forth. He seemed to be overwhelmed by the large number of personnel involved with his arrest, all wearing fatigues and military uniforms.

It was only later that I learned what had happened when the arrest was made. As the cold but clear morning began to brighten, agents lying on the frozen ground noticed lights in the house and Lavy, seemingly ill at ease, had appeared at the door more than once but had not left the house. Finally, as the agents were growing stiff and cold with waiting, Lavy suddenly walked out of the cabin and, brandishing a shotgun, walked directly toward Special Agent Mark Jessie's position at the edge of the yard.

Jessie, a large and quiet man, rose to face the armed and menacing Thomas Lavy. As Lavy grew nearer, other agents stood up, identified themselves as FBI agents, and ordered Lavy to put down his weapon. They were, of course, dressed in fatigues with no noticeable FBI identification, and Lavy was apparently (and justifiably) uncertain of their claims. He continued to walk toward Jessie pointing his shotgun while Jessie, showing both great courage and restraint, stood his ground all the while identifying himself as an FBI agent. Finally, after what appeared to be an interminable delay, Lavy slowly placed the shotgun on the ground and was quickly handcuffed by the agents.

I felt relieved and even lucky that the situation had not deteriorated into another Ruby Ridge. To have shot Lavy would have been disastrous. He did not know the large men with fatigues and rifles were FBI agents, he had not committed a crime as far as he knew, and he was certainly not thinking about the incident with ricin at Canadian customs more than two years before. He did have the large sum of money hidden under the cabin and could have easily feared that he was about to be robbed and was simply protecting his property.

The search had revealed that Lavy had placed various weapons in strategic locations in the house. There was no place in the cabin that he could not stand and literally have a weapon at arms length. After being shown the location by Lavy, agents found over $18,000 in cash and gold krugerrands in a safe under the cabin floor.

I immediately made the decision that no weapons were to be seized except for the shotgun Lavy was carrying unless they were found to be illegal in some manner. Different militant groups were constantly accusing the federal government of seizing weapons from innocent people and I was determined not to give them an example of armed agents overpowering a lone man protecting his own property and carrying off his weapons. Arrangements were made, with Lavy's consent and assistance, to place the nearly twenty weapons and money in the custody of an acquaintance who Lavy had called for assistance after the search had been concluded.

By noon, the exercise was over. I officially released the Hostage Rescue Team. The team leader seemed almost embarrassed to have been there and his anxiety to return to Quantico was due to more than just it being the holiday season. In the early afternoon I returned to Little Rock and called Paula Casey to brief her on the events. She told me the United States attorney in Alaska, Robert Bundy, opposed allowing Lavy to post bail and insisted he return to Anchorage to face the charges he had been arrested on. Both of us were uncomfortable with that decision given all that had occurred—and equally important, what had not occurred—but this was a decision by her counterpart in Alaska that had to be honored.

Lavy made it clear he did not want to return to Alaska. But when he arrived in Little Rock in custody, he was turned over to U.S. marshals. Lavy retained the services of Sam Heuer to defend him. I was told that Heuer's fee was the $18,000 Lavy had hidden in the floor safe of his cabin. On December 22, a Little Rock magistrate denied Lavy's bail request, citing "clear and convincing evidence that Defendant poses a serious risk of danger to the community and that there are no conditions which the Court could impose that would reasonably assure the safety of the community." This was in spite of Mountain View residents testifying on Lavy's behalf. The government had introduced the testimony of Tom Lynch, the canister of castor beans, and the books seized from Lavy's residence, *The Poison Handbook*, *Silent Death*, and *Get Even: Complete Book of Dirty Tricks*. Heuer countered with the defense that Lavy had originally made the ricin to protect his chickens from coyotes. U.S. Magistrate Jerry Cavaneau ordered Lavy held and that he be transported to Alaska.

On Saturday morning, December 23, I was at home in Little Rock trying to get into the spirit of the holiday season when I received a telephone call from Bill Temple, my assistant special agent in charge. Lavy had been found dead in his cell at the Pulaski County jail earlier that morning. He had apparently hanged himself with a shirt by tying it around the bars, then his neck, then sitting down until he suffocated. His wasn't a quick death. I couldn't help but think of how Larry Wu-tai Chin had suffocated himself years before and wondered how someone could have the will to commit such an act.

I called Paula Casey, apologizing for interrupting her on a Saturday morning, and advised her of Lavy's death. She didn't say anything for a few moments, then quietly commented, "This is a tough business, isn't it?" I had to agree.

I have often thought of the Lavy investigation, and regardless of which angle I approach it, the inescapable conclusion is that Lavy would be alive today if he had been handled differently. The unnecessary use of overwhelming force, the denial of bail, and the insistence on his returning to Alaska all combined to put him in a position that he thought he had no alternative but to end his life. I only briefly met Thomas Lavy that cold morning in a cemetery in Stone County. True, he was a strange man, a recluse who had inexcusably made a horrific poison. But Lavy had served in the military and had been honorably discharged, was an active member of the American Legion, a good neighbor, and before his arrest on December 20, he had never been arrested in Arkansas, not even for double-parking.

He didn't deserve to die as he did.

CHAPTER 16

UNPARDONABLE

*"We don't have a democracy,
we have a federal bureaucracy out of control."*

Prosecuting Attorney Dan Harmon

J ust down Interstate 30 from Little Rock in neighboring Saline County, the activities of longtime prosecuting attorney Daniel H. Harmon Jr. were an embarrassment to the criminal justice system. Even so, he continued to be reelected and had defiantly continued his corrupt practices. I decided, once I had declared public corruption the highest priority for the FBI in Arkansas, he would be the first target of my corruption initiative.

In March 1995, not long before my arrival, the office had initiated a Racketeering Enterprise Investigation (REI) to see if there were federal violations worth pursuing. This investigation revealed that the Seventh Judicial District Drug Task Force had been making many drug-related arrests but with few prosecutions. Dan Harmon had been managing the Seventh DTF since 1991. He was a small man with a volcanic temper whose public spats with various wives and girlfriends were legendary. He was also an accomplished prosecutor who could mesmerize audiences and juries and his defiance of the federal government had made him something of a folk hero. The DTF itself was headed by a Harmon crony, Roger Walls, who wasn't even a certified police officer.

According to the REI, the Seventh DTF sat alongside I-30 and stopped

Hispanic and African-American males with out-of-state license plates—
the worst of racial profiling. The driver's vehicle would be searched, drugs
or cash confiscated, and the individual placed in jail. Invariably, one of a
small group of Benton, Arkansas, lawyers was called to represent the
offender. They would "negotiate" with Harmon to establish an appropriate payment that would allow the offender to avoid trial or incarceration.
This fine, which went into DTF coffers, was calculated on the basis of the
supposed offender's ability to pay and could include cash, vehicles, jewelry, or simply their forfeiting a large bond and never returning to trial.

Bill Hardin, the experienced White Collar Crimes Squad supervisor,
along with the case agent, Cheryl Schaller, began to brief me on their
findings almost as soon as I arrived in Little Rock. We decided to try to
elicit the cooperation of those who had been arrested but not prosecuted by the DTF. This meant we had to be willing to offer grants of
immunity for any offense suspects may have committed at the time they
were arrested. Schaller and her team found fifty individuals with a
record of contact with the DTF but without court dispositions or criminal histories in the National Crime Information Center (NCIC).

We also needed help from someone inside the Saline County criminal justice system, and that person was Sheriff Judy Pridgen, the only
female sheriff in Arkansas. Pridgen had stood up to Harmon in the past,
and consequently had been accused of all sorts of personal and professional misconduct. She knew all too well that if she cooperated and
Harmon beat the federal government again, it would mean her political
death. But she never wavered.

Using letters of immunity from the U.S. attorney, field offices around
the country began hunting for Harmon's victims. Some were in jail,
others refused to cooperate, some were not located at all, but a sizeable
number agreed to help us. Theirs was a chilling tale of law enforcement
abuse. Typically, they had been stopped on I-30. After a search of their
vehicle, whether by consent or not, they were charged with possession
of narcotics and taken to the DTF office, not the Saline County Jail as
was the norm. A "bond" would be established, though a bond is normally set by a judge, and payment had to be cash. If they could not reach

an agreement in a relatively short time, the offender was sent to jail. After languishing in jail, sometimes for weeks, without seeing a judge, the individual would gain his freedom by paying a percentage of the proposed bond, or they would sign over titles to vehicles, etc. Then they were driven to the bus stop and given enough money for a one-way ticket home. They were told if they stayed out of Arkansas they wouldn't be prosecuted.

Schaller quickly accumulated sufficient evidence to obtain search warrants. I was hoping the searches, slated for December 7, 1995, would be a "Pearl Harbor" for Harmon's long run of corrupt practices. It was a timely moment for a search because about a month earlier Holly Harmon, Dan's young wife, had been arrested with cocaine pilfered from the DTF drug evidence locker. We were concerned that this highly publicized arrest would prompt the DTF to make sure their records gave no hint of the missing drugs. We arrested Holly Harmon hoping we could convince her to cooperate. However, First Assistant U.S. Attorney Michael Johnson, who was out of town at the time of her arrest, did not agree with the strategy and accused those making the arrest with "going behind my back," regardless of the fact that Paula Casey, Johnson's boss, had agreed with the decision. That incident, seemingly unimportant at the time, provided the basis for conflict in the future.

Paula Casey, Michael Johnson, and I met with the strike team the afternoon of December 6 to make final preparations. I stressed the need to project a professional appearance at all times and that agents were to wear coats and ties and not the blue windbreakers with the large FBI logo on the back. There was no need to advertise our presence. We discussed each of the eleven locations where search warrants were to be served and what was to be seized, then the meeting broke up. Later that evening, Johnson called me to say no searches were to be conducted of the various attorneys' offices, though he admitted when asked that there was still sufficient probable cause to include them. Further, he wanted Sheriff Pridgen to sign a consent document to have the offices searched and not use the remaining search warrants, an incredible turn of events that had not even been hinted at just a few hours previous.

A meeting with Attorney General Ed Meese on April 19, 1986, before departing for Canberra, Australia, as legal attaché.

The last meeting I had with FBI Director Louis Freeh on July 16, 1998, when he traveled to Little Rock.

Director William S. Sessions in Australia, November 25, 1988.

Taken in Australia's outback in the Northern Territory, in front of a giant ant hill on June 25, 1989.

The big one that didn't get away . . . taken on June 12, 1990, in the Northern Territory of Australia.

The Cook Islands
before a ceremony
by the South
Pacific Police
Chief's Association,
August 1, 1988.

Entertaining members of the South Pacific Police Chief's Association
in our backyard in Canberra, Australia, November 8, 1989.

Standing in front of the
Ukraina Hotel in Moscow,
November 15, 1990.

Standing in front of the
Soviet cruiser *Aurora*
November 17, 1990. The
Aurora is the ship that fired
the first shots of what was to
be the Bolshevik Revolution.

Standing on the Great Wall
of China December 2, 1990,
where we were followed by
the Chinese security service.

In Ritan Park in Beijing, China, November 28, 1990. The individual in the photo had been following me, and when I re-traced my steps, he was quite surprised and suddenly took great interest in the mural.

Aboard a *BundeGrenzSchutz* (West German) patrol boat on May 28, 1986, along the West German-East German border on the North Sea.

On the roof of the Reichstaag, East Berlin, on May 26, 1986, overlooking East Germany.

Dear Mr. Smith

I was very pleased to receive your note.
It would be very nice to have a meeting
and to this aim our common friends ██████
██████████████ and ████████████████ are
carring you a message to make possible
this meeting.

My regards, sincerelly

Antonio de la Guardia

Copy of letter from Antonia de la Guardia . . .
with names of intermediaries deleted.

Dear Mr. Smith

First of all I would like to thank you for your nice present.

On relation with our conversation I'am sending you the name of one of the persons that will travel with me, the other name will be send next week.

We will travel from Havana to Canada and from Canada direct to Washington, ██████████████ will travel with us from Havana.

I hope that when we arrive to Washington ██████ ██████ and members of your staff will be waiting for us.

Yours Trully

[signature]

Another letter from de la Guardia,
also with names deleted.

Cuban Air Force General
Rafael del Pino and his
wife Laura, taken
May 30, 1987.

Photograph of my wife Carla and me along the Virginia sea shore.

After a short discussion I could see that Johnson was not going to change his mind. I then told him, "I will call Washington and advise them that once again, your office had demonstrated a lack of commitment to working corruption cases." Further, I was going to take some action the next day, search warrants or not, and his office could be involved or not. Johnson got quiet and the conversation quickly concluded. We weren't sure what we were going to do, but we had pulled in agents from all over the state to conduct the early morning raids and I wasn't about to send them home without doing something.

Within a few minutes Paula Casey called. She was obviously unhappy with my position and told me, "Like it or not, you have to work with Michael." I told her I had no problem working with Johnson but I did have a problem with an eleventh-hour decision to not search the offices of the lawyers, a decision we had discussed for days prior to the final preparation of the warrants. Finally we agreed that searches would be conducted on the offices of the DTF, Harmon's office, and the Saline County Circuit Court. The number of searches had gone from eleven to three. Casey did promise that further search warrants would be issued for the attorneys' offices at a later date. We in the FBI found that hilarious, since any attorneys who thought they may have exposure would scarcely leave incriminating files lying around after the first round of searches. Of course the remaining eight search warrants were never served. It was only later that I was told Johnson had once said he hated to see attorneys indicted, for they were held in such low esteem by the public that they couldn't get a fair trial. Somehow I didn't view that as an FBI problem.

The searches were made with much fanfare. The press quickly picked up on the story and news cameras and reporters were everywhere. At one point, Roger Walls came into the FBI office declaring his innocence and saying he would "take a lie detector test." We quickly took him up on his offer. The test results indicated he was lying. Walls continued to proclaim his innocence and left the office.

In the days, then weeks, then months that followed, I was besieged with phone calls from the media wanting to know the status of the investigation, when Harmon was going to be arrested, and what was taking so long. Harmon was defiant as usual, stating the FBI couldn't touch him. Even the police chief in Benton, who had been aware of much of Harmon's activities and had looked the other way, told a friend of his, with obvious satisfaction, that Harmon had beaten the federal government again.

I received several calls a week from Rodney Bowers, a resourceful and tenacious reporter from the *Arkansas Democrat-Gazette* who covered Saline County. He invariably asked about the status of the investigation and finally, in a fit of some frustration, I told Bowers that the case was in the hands of the United States attorney, which it was. This resulted in another problem with Casey, who used it as a basis to make a formal complaint against me months later. A full year after the original search, no action had been taken, and for the DTF, it was business as usual.

Finally, one afternoon, Casey called and said she wanted to discuss the Harmon prosecution but could only do it on a Sunday afternoon. I was incredulous, but told her we would be there. So on March 9, 1997, I went to her office along with Cheryl Schaller and a senior agent and attorney, Floyd Hays, who had attended high school with Bill Clinton. Joining Casey was a seasoned assistant named Dan Stripling.

It was a cold and rainy afternoon, made even more miserable by Stripling's morose attitude. We were pushing for an indictment under the Racketeering Influenced and Corrupt Organization, or RICO, statute, but with a twist. The principal source of funding for the DTF was federal funds, so we were proposing that a federally funded entity was being operated as a corrupt organization. The discussion continued, with Stripling resisting the plan and increasingly looking at his watch, as he had tickets to a recital that afternoon. Finally he sputtered, "I don't know why I'm arguing against a RICO indictment when I don't know anything about the RICO law anyway!" (I resisted the impulse to agree with him.) He then added that he had hoped he could "complete my career without getting involved in a RICO case." Finally, Casey agreed that a RICO indictment was the course to take and the meeting adjourned.

On April 11, 1997, Harmon, Walls, and William A. Murphy, another Task Force member, were indicted for racketeering. The law required three specific criminal acts that fit the RICO statute; we listed eleven. One example involved a woman from Indiana who came to Arkansas with $10,000 in cash to post bond for her husband who had been charged with marijuana possession, a charge that both denied. However, upon arrival, she learned she would have to produce more money or agree to have sex with Harmon. She refused to do so and finally her husband was released for the $10,000, but only after signing a statement saying her husband had been arrested with the money in his possession and that they had no claim to it.

Harmon, of course, denied any charges and observed, as quoted in the *Arkansas Democrat-Gazette,* "If they can stick some garbage like this on me, then every American ought to be afraid. We don't have a democracy, we have a federal bureaucracy that's out of control."

The trial was in many respects anticlimatic. Harmon, who had initially stated he would defend himself, declared himself indigent and got a court-appointed attorney. I found it somewhat ironic that Harmon, with his long history of abusing females, was defended by a female attorney. Lea Ellen Fowler was a tall, slender attorney who towered over Harmon, and while Harmon had to have been a difficult client, she ably defended him. Even so, in the face of overwhelming evidence, Harmon was found guilty.

Harmon was allowed to remain out on bond until sentencing despite RICO, extortion, and drug convictions, all of which carried lengthy mandatory jail sentences. In October, Schaller received information from another female acquaintance of Harmon's that he was violating the restrictions of his release by continuing to use drugs. He had also physically abused a girlfriend he had had since Holly divorced him. We planned to intercept him with a search warrant when he was scheduled to appear at the girlfriend's apartment for another afternoon of drugs.

The agents were in place when Harmon showed up on schedule. But Harmon spotted them and ran, diving headfirst into a pond full of dirty water at the rear of the complex. Schaller, surrounded by the other agents, stood on the bank and ordered him out, but for a while he sat crouched down in the water, shaking his hands vigorously under water before finally wading out and laying down on the bank, face down, with his hands behind his back. Schaller seized Harmon's clothing and found a Bic pen in his pocket wrapped in foil with a residue of methamphetamine, still there despite his attempts to shake it out of his pants and into the muddy water. On June 11, 1997, after Harmon was convicted in federal court for using his office as a criminal enterprise and a means to engage in the extortion of drugs and cash, the career of Dan Harmon effectively ended.

On April 15, after the Harmon indictment, the *Wall Street Journal* editorialized under the caption, "Big News From Arkansas," reporting on "the FBI's new top man in Little Rock, Special Agent I.C. Smith. A storied figure in the Bureau, Mr. Smith was sent to Little Rock in August, 1995 by Director Louis Freeh. The Harmon indictment is part of a new interest in public corruption by investigators under Mr. Smith and Ms. (Paula) Casey." On June 13, the *Journal* again editorialized, "Casey brought the case against Mr. Harmon together with a reinvigorated Little Rock FBI office under Special Agent I.C. Smith." I felt that the first shot had been fired across corruption's bow in Arkansas and I was impatient to move on to other investigations.

The Harmon case sent a clear message that the FBI and the United States Attorney's Office were now in the business of investigating and prosecuting corruption cases in Arkansas. However, there was a matter that I had inherited when I arrived in Little Rock that had to be taken care of if we were to gain any momentum in our efforts.

EXCEPT FOR A SINGLE SIX-YEAR HIATUS, Lloyd Reid George had been a member of the state legislature of Arkansas since 1963. He was one of the most powerful politicians in the state. In August 1993, Supervisory Special Agent Stephen Irons, later the primary supervisor for the Whitewater investigation, met with Arkansas State Police Director Tommy Goodwin to discuss both George and Arvie L. Lockhart, the director of the Arkansas Department of Corrections. Goodwin believed an investigation was warranted into the sale of outdated irrigation equipment by George to the Arkansas Department of Corrections at an inflated price.

Goodwin told Irons that he believed Mark Stodola, a longtime prosecuting attorney and failed congressional candidate, had deliberately "rigged" the grand jury and had no interest in seeing Lockhart prosecuted. Irons presented the case to the new United States attorney, Paula Casey, after she had time to settle in her job and after she had named Michael Johnson as her first assistant. They agreed the case had merit and assigned it to Assistant United States Attorney Brent Bumpers.

Bumpers was the son of Senator Dale Bumpers, but had not inherited either his father's outgoing personality or work ethic. He had struggled to pass the bar exam and seemed to consider his position in the U.S. attorney's office as a sideline to his business of baking cookies and operating a Backyard Burgers restaurant. In December 1993, Bumpers advised the FBI that he saw no apparent federal violation and told them not to conduct any further investigation until he had reviewed the case, a demand that was clearly outside his authority. Bumpers even said that one incident in a twenty-five-year career was not something to go after; according to Bumpers, it's evidently okay to be corrupt as long as you don't do it too often.

Bumpers continued to delay the investigation for months, repeatedly claiming that he was "reviewing" it. Then in mid-1994, he advised the agent that if no progress was being made in the investigation, Casey and Johnson were not interested in pursuing the matter any further. He did not, of course, add that he had been the principal reason the investigation was bogged down. I had no preconceived opinions of Bumpers, but after reviewing the file on the George investigation following my arrival in Little Rock, I concluded that at best he had been incompetent and at worst, had deliberately frustrated the investigative efforts of the FBI.

We were beginning to encounter a statute of limitations problem, and George had retained counsel. His attorney Jack Lassiter was a well-known defense attorney in Little Rock who seemed to enjoy unusual influence in the United States Attorney's Office. In particular, he seemed to be close to Johnson. But we continued the pressure and shortly before the statue of limitations expired, on April 11, 1996, George was finally indicted. Included in the indictment were Arvie Lockhart and Doug Vess, the owner of an equipment company in Dardanelle, Arkansas. Lockhart was charged with aiding and abetting the sale of the irrigation equipment for a price exceeding its value "even though the irrigation system was neither designed for nor appropriate for the needs of the Arkansas Department of Corrections." Vess was charged with being a party to the transaction for recording in his company records that he had sold the equipment to the ADC after receiving it from George as trade-in for new farm equipment.

The indictment was simple and direct and I did not anticipate any further obstacles to a successful prosecution. My assumption proved to be wrong.

ONE MORNING THE CASE AGENT, Ed Jernigan, told me that Paula Casey said she had been told a few months earlier by Martha Perry, the head of Senator Bumpers's Little Rock office, that George had been in her office attempting to meet with Bumpers about our investigation, something Casey should have immediately advised my office about. I knew that Perry and Casey were close friends. I had met Perry and found her to be a delightful and especially efficient person with the same engaging personality as the senator himself. I directed Jernigan to interview Perry and she verified Casey's story but added that she wasn't sure the conversation with Bumpers had ever taken place.

I then instructed Jernigan to set up an interview for me with Senator Bumpers, as I knew him, found him forthright and likeable, had corresponded with him on several occasions in responding to constituent matters, and had even sent him a get-well card when he had been ill. He would be coming into Little Rock from Washington in a few days, and I got an appointment to see him then. However, I had to get permission from FBI headquarters to conduct the interview. I assumed the request would be somewhat perfunctory as it had been noted that I was personally acquainted with Bumpers, and the interview would be low-key and nonconfrontational. But I was mistaken. Though Hardin had several conversations with a headquarters supervisor over several days, the supervisor called about two hours before the scheduled interview and denied permission to proceed, saying the decision had been made by Neil Gallagher, the deputy assistant director of the Criminal Division. Gallagher's reason for denying the interview that it was an "election year."

I was incensed. I had been a Bureau classmate of Gallagher's, but I knew he had little feel for the informality of Southern relationships. I thought he would at least have had the courtesy to call me and discuss the interview directly. I also knew the eleventh-hour timing was no coincidence. It deliberately limited my ability to get the decision overturned in time. The decision was even further far-fetched considering that Bumpers wasn't running for reelection.

I called Martha Perry and told her I had to cancel the appointment with Bumpers. She asked if she could tell "Dale" the reason for the cancellation. I suppose I could have made a lame excuse but I told her the truth, that I had been denied permission by FBI headquarters. Perry responded with, "That's crazy!" She said the senator had been looking forward to seeing me and mentioned his appreciation for the get-well card I had sent. I asked that she give him both my best wishes and an apology for any inconvenience.

I then sent a teletype to the personal attention of Gallagher, advising the appointment had been cancelled and included Perry's comments. Of course, I never received a response. The incident was a portent of later investigations when it became clear that Gallagher's first priority was to avoid any chance of controversy that might impede his career. The best way to do that was to do as little as possible when politics were involved.

Problems continued. We learned that Johnson and Lassiter had gone to the Department of Corrections to "review" the irrigation equipment without advising our office. On another occasion, Johnson had sat in on an interview but had instructed the case agent not to include his name on the FD-302, the form the FBI uses to record the results of interviews that may be testimony. That was in clear violation of the rules of the FBI and the Department of Justice.

In January 1997, with the trial date for George little more than two weeks away, Hardin came to my office with a look of dejection and disbelief on his face. He had called Johnson to discuss some minor aspect of the case and learned that Johnson had been so upset he couldn't report to work. Hardin called Johnson at home and Johnson, obviously upset, had told him he wasn't going to prosecute the case. He said this was all a plot by the "master" to get Bill Clinton by making Johnson and Casey look bad by losing the case. Hardin replied that I was fully supportive of his prosecuting the case. Johnson then responded, "I'm not talking about I.C. Smith, I'm talking about Kenneth Starr." He insisted that we were all part of a conspiracy with Starr and taking our orders from him. By this time I thought I had reached the point where I could not be surprised by anything in pursuing corruption investigations in Arkansas. But once again, I was wrong.

I had taken great steps to ensure that Starr's office and the Whitewater investigation were viewed as separate and distinct from my own responsibilities. I tried to be optimistic, but deep down I felt the prospects of George going to trial had diminished to almost zero. That failure would send a message to others that there were still some Arkansas politicians who were immune from accountability. Later, I was advised by a member of the United States attorney's staff that Casey had asked various assistants to take the case to prosecution. They all refused, stating they weren't going to take responsibility for prosecuting a case seventeen days before the trial and then be blamed for losing it.

However, good fortune smiled on the FBI, for a key witness for the prosecution had a heart attack, resulting in a continuance. I meanwhile continued to implore Casey to convince Johnson to handle the prosecution. At one point she discussed dismissing the indictment, then assigned the prosecution to an attorney who handled primarily civil matters. He became ill and couldn't prepare the case on such a short deadline. I later learned she had even contacted the Public Integrity

Section of the Department of Justice about assuming responsibility for the case. Clearly there was no real interest on the part of Casey and Johnson in pursuing the investigation. Their continued emphasis was on how to avoid prosecution, not how to overcome obstacles. But I was determined to not allow the case to slip away at that late juncture.

Finally, Casey and I discussed the prospect of allowing Vess to enter into pre-trial diversion in exchange for his cooperation. Then I received a call from Casey who raised the issue of Lockhart's being allowed to enter into a pre-trial agreement too. I certainly had mixed feelings about giving Lockhart a break. There was an odor of corruption about him that I found particularly objectionable. But I also discussed with Casey the belief that elected officials were even more accountable for their misdeeds. With considerable reluctance, I agreed to reduced charges against Lockhart if it would assure a successful prosecution of George.

It worked. On September 2, 1997, almost seventeen months after his indictment, George entered a plea of guilty and thus avoided a public trial that would have received considerable attention. At first George insisted he wasn't going to resign from the Arkansas legislature, but after considerable public debate and pressure from the *Arkansas Democrat-Gazette* and other newspapers, he finally agreed to step down. He left the legislature, where he had been a fixture for decades, in disgrace. I never did learn what reaction Brent Bumpers had to George's guilty plea.

The Saturday following George's plea, I went for breakfast at the Bards Restaurant in the Heights in Little Rock. I was a frequent patron, not only for the food, but because it was a favorite gathering place for many of the movers and shakers of Little Rock. I usually sat in a far back corner alone and read the paper. Nearby was a group of tables that were pushed together where an informal group met practically every morning where they discussed everything from Razorback football to turkeys. That day, I heard George's name mentioned. Without looking up from the paper, I heard one of the group observe, "If they can get old Lloyd, they can get anybody!" The George conviction had its desired effect.

However, that was not the end of the story. On January 19, 2001, about two hours before he left office, President Bill Clinton included

George among those to whom he granted pardons. I was not surprised. In an article dated February 24, 2001, the *New York Times* provided details in an article entitled, "Access Proved Vital in Last-Minute Race for Clinton Pardons." The story related how Clinton had mentioned, in his January 17, 2001 speech before the Arkansas Legislature, his amazement at the last minute deluge of pardon requests at the White House. After the speech, he had visited his former office in the state capitol where several legislators had cornered Clinton to make a pitch for George's pardon. On January 20, George was included among the 176 individuals who received pardons or commutations of sentences in the two hours before Clinton left office. He was also among the forty or so who received pardons without being processed through normal procedures. Access did indeed count.

I found it ironic that Clinton, who by then had been disbarred in his home state through the determination of attorney Marie Miller and the Arkansas Bar Association, and who had agreed to a fine of $25,000, still had the power to pardon. But the pardon did not change a salient fact. Lloyd George had betrayed the sacred trust of those people who elected him. And a pardon did not remove the fact he is a thief—a thief in name as assuredly as one who steals in the dead of night.

CHAPTER 17

ABSOLUTE CORRUPTION

"If you open this door, you know you can't close it."

I.C. Smith to United States Attorney Paula Casey

T he more I learned about the political dynamics in Arkansas the more I realized the power of the state legislature. And within the legislature, the name of Nick Wilson always seemed to bubble to the surface when the discussion turned to what was wrong with the system. He was an attorney who had served in the Arkansas Senate since 1971, developing a well-deserved reputation for being vicious and unethical, yet he was a power that had to be reckoned with. He was an equal-opportunity abuser who seemed to take particular delight in attacking fellow legislators on the floor. He frequently smoked cigars and, with his dark hair and visage, could be an intimidating presence in any room.

With the help of Bill Hardin, supervisor of the White Collar Crimes Squad, I began to formulate a plan to go after Wilson. I was reasonably confident that Paula Casey would have no reservations about pursuing Wilson, if for no other reason than that her close friend and current congressman, Vic Snyder, then a state senator, had been savaged by Wilson for threatening a pet project of his, the Science Information Liaison Office (SILO), a personal Wilson fiefdom paid for, of course, with state money.

Wilson had a close relationship with Lee Colwell, former deputy director of the FBI who was head of the Criminal Justice Institute at the

University of Little Rock. As I became more familiar with Wilson's activities, I became increasingly wary of the relationship between him and the CJI. Colwell had retired from the Bureau in 1985 and returned to Little Rock to start the CJI under then-Governor Clinton. There he began a push to establish a training program for rural law enforcement personnel throughout the United States—with him in charge, of course. I initially considered the project worthwhile, and after my arrival as SAC recommended to Director Louis Freeh that an additional round of funding to help launch the Institute be granted by the FBI. But as time passed, I became concerned for not only the cost of the training but also the relatively small number of trainees. The cost per student seemed too high, and I thought choosing such places as Kennebunkport, Maine, for training sessions was not setting an example of fiscal austerity.

The second year, I advised the FBI not to provide any further funding. I pointed out that the kind of money being granted to Colwell was not being offered to other criminal justice programs, and I admitted being uncomfortable with the hundreds of thousands of dollars the FBI was giving to one of its own retired senior executives. This position was shared by the FBI's Contract Review Committee, who recommended that the "contract" with the CJI not be renewed. However, then-Deputy Director Weldon Kennedy overruled the committee and me and awarded Colwell an additional amount. By this time, I was well into an investigation of Wilson's activities.

We had information that representatives of a major national restaurant corporation were told they had to pay Wilson a kickback to get a liquor license. The company declined to pay the bribe, but we learned of the bribe attempt and put together an undercover operation. An FBI agent from out of town pretended to represent this restaurant company as a "troubleshooter" who had come to Little Rock to work out the details of securing the liquor license. But unexpectedly, the company, which had been so enthusiastically providing its support, changed its mind and advised they would no longer participate in the operation.

With several other members of the team, I traveled to the company's corporate headquarters to make my case that they should continue helping us. I believed it was important that the corporate officers meet the FBI personnel involved in order to have confidence in them. Over several hours we described our intentions in full detail, noting that they had been the victim of a blatant bribe attempt and that I thought they should view that as a personal affront. We were completely frank and responded to all questions.

A few days later Hardin came to my office, obviously elated, and said the company had decided to provide full support for the undercover operation. I felt we had a chance, once again, to pursue Wilson. Our undercover agent met with Wilson, and while he did not openly ask for a bribe, Wilson made it clear that a liquor license could be obtained only if he endorsed the idea. The agent then returned to his room at the Excelsior Hotel in downtown Little Rock. It was only a few minutes before there was a knock on the door.

When he opened the door, he was met by two plainclothes police officers from the North Little Rock Police Department, obviously well out of their jurisdiction. The officers said they had reports that the agent was involved with narcotics and wanted to search the room. The agent showed them his false identification, which they readily accepted, and told them they would have to get a search warrant. They tried to pressure him with veiled threats, but he stood his ground and finally the policemen left. But it was clear that Wilson had played a hand in their being there.

Just as it seemed the investigation was gaining altitude, the company again decided to pull its support. I discussed the turn of events with U.S. Attorney Paula Casey and we agreed at that point we could probably make the case by conducting tough interviews and using the grand jury to lock in testimony from individuals who would likely be reluctant witnesses.

On August 13, 1997, I made an appointment to meet Governor Mike Huckabee, the former lieutenant governor who had assumed office after Governor Jim Guy Tucker was convicted of felony offenses in the Whitewater investigation. I was personally acquainted with Huckabee and had met with him eleven days after he assumed office. I had told him then, without elaboration, that there were ongoing corruption investigations underway and asked if he intended to change any department heads, as that could impact what we were doing. He responded that he had no plans to make any wholesale changes until after he ran for election to a full term. By the time of the August 13 meeting, he had in fact, been elected to a full term as governor.

Though I was there to see the governor on other official business, I spoke in general terms of a corruption investigation and mentioned that the company that had been helping with it had pulled its support. His reaction was immediate and intense. He said that corruption investigations were important to the state of Arkansas and he was willing to "get on a plane and fly to wherever I need to go" to talk to whomever he needed to talk with to convince them their support was important. I asked him if I could convey his sentiments to that company, without mentioning the company by name, the use of the undercover technique, or even the target of the investigation. Governor Huckabee said that absolutely I could use his name in trying to reenlist their support.

I returned to the field office and wrote a lengthy letter to the company conveying Governor Huckabee's thoughts and asked that they reconsider their position. The company said the change of heart was because, in light of a downturn in their business, they had decided not to open a restaurant in Little Rock after all. My letter failed to change their position.

One Friday afternoon, Paula Casey and Michael Johnson dropped by my office, and during the course of the conversation, they asked about the undercover operation. I told them that, coincidentally, I was trying to get the operation back on track and that Governor Huckabee had strongly endorsed the operation. I saw Casey and Johnson glance at one another, but they didn't ask any questions and I didn't think much of it. In retrospect, I should have.

Casey and Johnson later used my conversation with Huckabee as the basis to file an official complaint against me with the Department of Justice for compromising an undercover operation. I learned of this when FBI Inspector Bernie Tolbert advised me Casey had made the official complaint. It was apparent that there was a conscious effort to take a shot at me behind my back. I asked Tolbert what the department's attitude was about the complaint. He told me they weren't overly concerned, given the source, and neither was anyone at FBI headquarters.

Casey added, as related by Tolbert, that I had been suspicious of her and her motives when I arrived in Arkansas and that I had arrived wanting to "clean up the town." Johnson was even more vitriolic, falsely adding that I had, "cursed (him) out," that I had stated he "didn't know what the hell he was doing," and for him to "get off his ass and do his job." I later asked others who were present for the conversation (it was on a speaker phone) about the accuracy of Johnson's statements, which were made during our disagreement over the Harmon investigation search warrants, and both found them laughable.

When Tolbert advised Casey that he would have to discuss their allegations with me, she asked him not to. This alone was an indication that Casey and Johnson had tried to discredit me and paint the worse possible picture. I wasn't overly concerned. The inspectors talked with well over eighty people in the community about me, and the only critical comments were made by Casey and Johnson. There wasn't a single employee who had criticized my management in an anonymous survey, a result the inspector had his staff recalculate because thought there must be a mistake. Indeed, one of the inspectors intimated that there was concern within their ranks that they would be accused of giving me a "kiss" when they reported their findings to FBI headquarters. I viewed their results as proof I was simply doing my job.

A short while later, while I was in Washington in part to discuss the inspection findings, Bob Buckman, Director Freeh's right-hand man, congratulated me on the fine inspection and Freeh himself, who normally discussed inspection findings with SAC's, told the inspectors that given the positive results, it wasn't necessary that he meet with me.

MEANWHILE THE INVESTIGATION moved on. In September 1997, the *Arkansas Times* ran a remarkably accurate story on a bill passed by the legislature that was personally benefiting some of the legislators and their cronies. This was arguably the single most important article that appeared in an Arkansas newspaper during my tenure as SAC, and started a chain of events that would propel our corruption investigation forward. One Thursday afternoon an article by Doug Smith got my attention with its first line: "A new state program approved by the legislature, supposedly intended to help children in divorce and custody cases, actually gives $3 million worth of grants to three lawyers, one of them a legislator himself." This was classic corruption in Arkansas: create an entity designed to help the disadvantaged, then loot it for all it was worth.

The names in the article were familiar. There was State Senator Mike Todd, and Neal Turner, a former aide to Governor Jim Guy Tucker, and his wife, Elizabeth. There was State Representative Wayne Wagner and of course, Nick Wilson. Smith had mentioned another attorney I didn't know, Mona Mizell. A quick call determined she was a crony to many of the influential members of the legislature. All were part of the political elite who viewed government as a means for self enrichment, not for going about the business of taking care of the people who had elected them or were paying their salaries through their tax dollars.

This was an *ad litem* program, literally "a friend of the court," in which the state paid attorneys to represent children in divorce and custody cases. The theory was that children needed their own legal representation, as often times parents would enter into these proceedings without the children's best interests in mind. A judge could now appoint a lawyer to represent a child and the lawyer would be paid under the terms of the newly passed legislation, approved with neither good intentions nor expectations of any oversight. It was free money for a select group of lawyers.

Soon afterward I received word from a Little Rock acquaintance who seemed to have his finger on the pulse of events as they occurred, that Neal and Elizabeth Turner were frightened and looking for a way to get "ahead of the curve" in what they assumed was an almost certain federal investigation. I asked the caller if this meant the Turners were ready to cooperate. My contact said that seemed to be the impression. Later that same afternoon, as I was mulling over my next step, Paula Casey told me that an attorney representing Elizabeth Turner had called and wanted to work out a deal. I was elated. Casey and I discussed the potential impact of the Turners' cooperation, and at one point I told her, "If you open this door, you know you can't close it." She quietly and somewhat gravely acknowledged that was the case.

The next afternoon, Elizabeth Turner entered a hotel meeting room where we had arranged to talk obviously distraught, followed by her husband, who seemed every bit the political hack of his reputation. She was dressed neatly, of slender build with obviously dyed blond hair. He was in jeans and cowboy boots and from the look of his bulky build, had been living quite well. We were there to establish the ground rules. Casey agreed to not prosecute the Turners for anything that they offered that afternoon in the event an agreement could not be reached, but their cooperation had to be absolute. Everyone from the FBI and Casey's staff agreed that there was sufficient information to warrant a grant of immunity.

The meetings continued the next day. Elizabeth Turner's reticence from the previous day had disappeared and she was fully cooperative. She and her husband were interviewed in separate rooms. I joined those interviewing Neal and raised the issue of his contract with the Criminal Justice Institute. According to Turner, a few days before Jim Guy Tucker was to resign as governor, Lee Colwell visited him at the governor's office. When Colwell emerged from the meeting he told Turner, "When this is over, come to see me." Turner said he took that to mean Colwell had some sort of job offer to discuss.

Within a few days of Tucker's resignation, Colwell offered Turner a contract with the Criminal Justice Institute for $75,000 a year, renewable for a second year at the same level. I asked Turner if there was any connection between the $150,000 in discretionary funds authorized by Governor Tucker for the CJI as he was leaving office and after Colwell's visit and the $150,000 total being offered to him. He stated no one had ever told him there was a connection and he hadn't given it any thought at the time.

The contract required him to evaluate locations for a distant learning project at the CJI. But, he added, the contract was a subterfuge. His real purpose was to quietly lobby the legislature to approve moving control of the CJI from the University of Arkansas at Little Rock (UALR) to the University of Arkansas system. This move had Nick Wilson's support and was being done without informing UALR. The contract was in the name of NAE Enterprises Incorporated, (Neal And Elizabeth), a corporation that Turner formed at the advice of Nick Wilson to avoid associating the Turner name with any contract work from the state. This tactic had failed, for the form incorporating the name required a social security number and that led to the public disclosure of the connection between Turner and the CJI.

According to the news media, Turner had been awarded similar contracts from numerous other state agencies and programs that Tucker had recently awarded grants to, including Arkansas State University and the University of Arkansas Poultry Center, all in addition to lucrative lobbying deals with Southwestern Bell, Alltell, and other companies. Turner had also billed the CJI for $62,000 which included 87 days at $500 per day and 12 days at $250 per day; an assistant at $120 per day for 100 days; plus another $12,492.75 for other expenses, for a total of $74, 492.75 for the first year's contract. Knowing how the CJI seemed to always be looking for money from the FBI, I was absolutely appalled at this news.

After my initial conversation with Neal Tuner, I sat alone in the living room of our hotel suite and digested what I had heard. I was dismayed that I would have to conduct an investigation of Lee Colwell, a former colleague who had contributed so much to law enforcement, but I also knew I didn't have a choice.

THE SCHEME THAT ELIZABETH TURNER explained and her husband verified in part was brazen even by Arkansas standards. It started with State Senator Mike Todd, who was in the legislature with only a two-year absence from 1987 until term limits kept him from reelection. He moved to Little Rock, got engaged, and planned to build a large home in Saline County. He needed funds to pay for this change of lifestyle and, according to the Turners, concocted the *ad litem* scheme to get the money. However, he didn't want his name on any contract, so he had gotten the Turners to help: Elizabeth would receive the "program" that would be sub-contracted to him, and Neal would help get it through the legislature.

Of course they needed Nick Wilson's blessing, and that was forthcoming—for a fee. They began to build the legislation, but as word got out, State Senator Mike Bearden and others began to hear of the scheme and also wanted a "program." Each program was worth $250,000, and what started out to be a scheme to benefit Todd, Turner, and, according to Turner, Senator Steve Bell (who was later acquitted), grew to a $3 million enterprise. The final plan included billing the state for work through Nick Wilson's Multi Services Inc.—established with a convicted felon, Mack Harbour, who was later pardoned by then-Governor Bill Clinton—with Wilson receiving kickbacks.

Thus began the investigation that I believed would make a very real difference in Arkansas, a state I had come to love.

Paula Casey proposed, and I readily agreed, that we should meet weekly to discuss the investigation. Johnny Van Horn of the IRS Criminal Investigations Division joined the effort. Colonel John Bailey of the Arkansas state police had been part of the investigation for a while. He was determined to rid the state police of its largely unwarranted national reputation as procurers of women for former Governor Clinton. These meetings were a joy. Someone usually brought cookies, coffee was plentiful, and it was with pleasure that I observed the infectious enthusiasm of the investigators, from the youthful Carrie Land to Van Horn, who was entering the twilight of a long career.

However, this cooperation and sense of harmony did not extend to FBI headquarters. I had kept Charles "Chuck" Owens, a section chief, apprised of developments, but he didn't seem to care about the impact that the investigation of Wilson and his cronies could have on Arkansas. All questions revolved around the investigation of the CJI.

I had telephone conversations with Owens fairly frequently and with my Bureau classmate Neil Gallagher at FBI headquarters. It became clear that Gallagher—well-known for being conservative in conducting investigations, especially those that were politically sensitive and potentially career threatening—had no stomach for the investigation. In fact, I had the distinct impression he was looking for a means to close it down.

In early November 1997 he directed me to justify the investigation. I prepared several pages outlining our concerns and the Turners' information. I pointed out that the United States attorney had already determined an investigation was warranted. I also highlighted the appearance of impropriety of the FBI providing sole-source funding to the CJI. In a subsequent call, Gallagher seemed to think I was trying to investigate the contract review process at FBI headquarters. Finally, in exasperation, I asked Gallagher if he was suggesting that I not investigate the CJI, even though there were indications of criminality. He warned me to watch myself; by his tone it was clear he was reminding me that he was a deputy assistant director and I was only a special agent in charge. A real leader never has to pull rank to prove his point. So much for Bureau classmate camaraderie!

Finally, it occurred to me that there may be an explanation behind the protective attitude Gallagher had toward the CJI and Colwell. Gallagher had been an administrative assistant to Colwell when Colwell was the executive assistant director at FBI headquarters several years previous, an administrative role without any daily personnel management or investigative responsibilities, and one that usually led to career fast tracks due to the influence of their senior bosses. Gallagher was anything but an objective player in the whole matter.

On October 29, I discussed the Wilson and CJI investigations with Freeh during the SAC conference at the International Association of Chiefs of Police convention. He gave no indication that I should do anything but continue to pursue all corruption investigations underway in Arkansas. I didn't mention the continuing problem with Gallagher, though in retrospect I should have.

A search was scheduled for November 5, 1997, in several locations, to include Wilson's offices in Pocahontas and Little Rock, other locations, and the office of T.J. Hively, the prosecuting attorney for the Sixteenth Judicial District. Hively was already a target of a separate corruption investigation involving a former business partner in the bail-bonding business, Gary Edwards, who made land deals with Edwards and avoided prosecution for the crimes for which they were originally charged. One of those crimes involved an eighty-five-year-old man, Willie Clark, who had married a twenty-eight-year-old woman, Kathy Sampson. Included in the marriage arrangement was an agreement that Sampson could continue to live with Roy Fulbright, her lover and the father of two of her three children. Clark had married Sampson ostensibly to allow her to collect insurance benefits and his retirement once he died, but apparently the marriage had been conducted without Fulbright's knowledge.

Fulbright became physically abusive toward Clark. Eventually Clark, tired of being beaten up, killed Fulbright with a shotgun. Edwards posted bond for Clark and persuaded Clark to sign a quitclaim deed to his 5,000-square-foot house over to him, and to sign over control of his personal finances.

Another case involved John Northrop, who had been charged with multiple counts of rape, child pornography, and sexual abuse of a minor. He admitted performing oral sex on two juvenile males after deputies found nude photographs of young boys and sexual related devices. He was charged with multiple counts of sex-related crimes and bail was set at $250,000. Edwards showed up, and within a few days, Northrop had deeded three mobile homes and 2.5 acres on a resort lake to Edwards. Interestingly enough, one of the mobile homes was later used by Edwards to stash Willie Clark after his arrest, though he was charging Clark $350 per month to stay there, funds that he withheld from Clark's monthly stipend.

The series of raids on November 5, 1997, were not without comic effect. Hively was being interviewed by two *Arkansas Democrat-Gazette* reporters, Sandy Davis and Jeff Porter, and as he was denying being the target of an investigation by the FBI, the conversation was interrupted by FBI agents arriving with search warrants in hand. The warrants were productive beyond anything we had anticipated; again we were overwhelmed by the scope of the corruption and the new avenues that were revealed.

Eventually the federal grand jury returned a 133-count indictment against Wilson and Arkansas State Senators Mike Bearden, Steve Bell, Mike Todd, and several others. I knew there were even more people engaged in the scheme who had also betrayed the public trust. But by that time I had no confidence that they would be pursued with any vigor. Several of those indicted pled to charges and Wilson himself was allowed to plead guilty to a single count of racketeering of the original 129 counts on which he was indicted. But it was reported (I had retired by this time but was still living in Little Rock) that he was to fully cooperate in the ongoing investigations.

Incredibly, during the series of trials that followed, Nick Wilson was never called as a witness. The only testimony he ever provided was in the sanctity of a grand jury and has thus far paid only $42,000 of the $1.3 million in fines he was assessed. His wife purchased a $480,000 home—with cash—and his attorney, John Everett, filed a motion to halve his seventy-month sentence for tax evasion and racketeering.

ON SEPTEMBER, 13, 2000, more than two years after my retirement from the Bureau, I received a telephone call from an FBI agent in Little Rock. The news was simply that T.J. Hively, Wesley "Butch" Ketz Jr., and Gary Edwards were indicted on RICO charges. It had been almost four years since the investigation of Hively began, and the impact that a swift and hard-hitting indictment would have had while he was still in office was lost. On March 23, 2001, Mike Todd was sentenced to forty-six months in prison for his role in the *ad litem* matter.

Finally, in March, 2002, T.J. Hively was tried in Little Rock. He was defended by Sam Perroni, while the prosecution was handled by Bob Govar of the United States Attorney's Office. U.S. District Court Judge Bill Moody, who had married Vince Foster's widow, Lisa, presided over the case. It simply turned into a debacle for the government in general and the USA's office in particular.

Starting with over sixty counts to the indictment, Perroni began to whittle away, outperforming the government in all aspects of the case.

Nevertheless, with so many individual counts, I still felt confident that a jury would find Hively guilty of something. But poor health forced Govar to hand the prosecution over to Angela Jegley and Pat Harris. Judge Moody continued to dismiss counts and Perroni, at the top of his form, continued to neutralize the government's witnesses. By the time the case went to the jury there were less than twenty counts remaining, an extraordinarily high number of counts to be dismissed. I began to feel uneasy about the outcome of the case. That uneasiness was well founded, for the jury found Hively not guilty on virtually all the counts, and voted not guilty by a margin of 11–1 on others.

But the investigation was not over. As indicative of the incestuous nature of politics in Arkansas, news surfaced that years before in private practice Judge Moody had represented Hively in a legal matter. The new United States attorney, Bud Cummins, appointed by President George W. Bush to succeed Paula Casey, was determined to proceed with a new trial. In February and March of 2004, Hively was retried and found guilty. It had been more than six years since FBI agents thundered up the steps to Hively's office as he was proclaiming his innocence to reporters from the *Arkansas Democrat-Gazette*.

Ken Starr and Paula Casey, while diametrically opposed in most ways, must share one common fact: both failed to capitalize on the much-vaunted cooperation they received from high-profile defendants such as Webb Hubbell and Nick Wilson. Nothing came from their cooperation, though both were given exceedingly generous sweetheart deals. For all practical purposes, the corruption initiatives were over long before the final Hively trial.

My successor, Charles Prouty, had no stomach for the potentially career-damaging foray into political corruption cases, and Paula Casey was increasingly looking toward retirement. Indeed, after years of the virtually daily turmoil of the Clinton White House and the constant revelations of the misdeeds of its own elected officials, Arkansas itself was simply tired. The initiative against the systematic corruption of the Arkansas legislature, that held so much promise when it began, languished, and no one seemed to care.

CHAPTER 18

HANGING FROM A TRIE

"I was embarrassed to be in the same room
during the . . . grand jury interview."
Special Agent Kevin Sheridan

I originally became involved in the CAMPCON campaign finance investigation after the FBI established a Task Force in conjunction with the department's Public Integrity Section, headed by Lee Radek, in early December 1996. This investigation, located in Los Angeles, Washington, D.C., and Little Rock, centered around allegations that the Chinese government was illegally funneling funds into the campaign coffers of the Democratic Party. The role for those of us in Arkansas was to investigate the activities of Yah Lin "Charlie" Trie, a longtime acquaintance of Bill Clinton from when Trie ran a small Chinese restaurant, the Fu Lin, near the State Capitol in Little Rock. Clinton was known to rush into the restaurant, sometimes with others in tow, wolf down large amounts of food and depart without even making a pretense of paying for it. Trie accommodated Clinton because he liked the attention Clinton gave him, but as one observer noted, had he insisted that Clinton pay for his kung pao chicken, he would have quickly found that he was no longer a valued friend.

Little Rock was also to investigate other current and past Arkansas residents, including Mark Middleton, a former Arkansas political wunderkind and White House aide to Thomas "Mack" McLarty, Clinton's first chief of staff. By this time, Middleton was considered politically radio-active by many Arkansas Democrats though he was raising money for the renovation of Clinton's boyhood home—brief as it was—in Hope.

There were others: prominent contributors to the Democratic National Committee such as Joseph Giroir Jr., formerly of the Rose Law Firm, where he had supposedly been forced out by the threesome of Hillary Clinton, Webb Hubbell, and Vince Foster (a blessing in dis-guise); Mark Grobmyer, a Little Rock attorney; and James Woods, man-aging director of the American Institute for Taiwan, the unofficial U.S. government agency tasked with maintaining relations with Taiwan after normalization of relations with the People's Republic of China.

On February 27, 1997, the CAMPCON investigation team assembled at FBI headquarters to meet with Deputy Assistant Director Neil Gallagher, my Bureau classmate, who reported to Assistant Director Robert Bryant, head of the Criminal Division. Our task was to deter-mine the strategy for quickly resolving the issues surrounding the 1996 presidential campaign.

Gallagher assigned Jeffrey Lampinski to head the Task Force. Lampinski was a slender, well-dressed, youthful agent who was bur-dened by being viewed as Gallagher's personal representative on the Task Force. I, and others, believed he was chosen more for his loyalty to Gallagher than for his expertise in campaign finance investigations. Gallagher was an excellent briefer when he had time to prepare a script but was uncomfortable answering unexpected questions. He was not viewed as an "agent's SAC" by either street agents or his peers and was prone to dwell on the negatives, as opposed to the positives. In effect, he had become a bureaucrat.

The honest truth is that Lampinski's role should have been assigned to someone with more seniority, perhaps someone eligible to retire and not someone with aspirations of being a senior executive in the FBI. Lampinski was ambitious, and it is the rare individual who will jeopard-ize his career to run against the grain of the opinion of those more sen-ior. Our decision-making flow chart was a mess. Information was filtered through a myriad of individuals before it got to the people who needed it. Case agents reported to Laura Laughlin, a pudgy, ambitious, and talkative supervisory special agent whose considerable self-confidence was not justified by either past experience or ongoing performance. From there, information went to Lampinski, then to Gallagher, who was loath to admit to Bryant—certainly no fan of Gallagher's—that he was unable to handle any aspect of the operation.

It quickly became apparent that the Task Force leadership did not appreciate the challenge before them. One member opined we would be finished in about six months. Had anyone been reading the papers the previous few years? If so, they should know that in any issue that might touch on the White House, nothing was handled with expediency. I was also bothered by Freeh's absence; if he thought this was a big case he should have made at least a token appearance. At one point during the discussion, Bryant yawned, got up, wandered out, and did not return.

I said the Task Force would have to move quickly, for if the attorney general used past standards as a guide, an independent counsel was inevitable; I even suggested that Freeh make such a recommendation to Reno. Gallagher opposed the idea, though I later learned that Freeh instructed him to prepare a memorandum justifying that very action. Certainly my opinion about the independent counsel was wrong. The Independent Counsel Act required that the attorney general seek an outside prosecutor upon the receipt of credible information that the president, vice president, or other senior officials of the executive branch *may* have violated the law, not that there was evidence they had definitely done so. Further, the statute could be triggered when Justice Department involvement might result in conflicts of interest. But Reno consistently viewed the different aspects of the allegations as separate and distinct. Using that standard, it was doubtful that conspiracy charges of any sort would be filed and likely that all prosecutions would be pigeon-holed into separate small investigations—a classic example of not seeing the forest for the trees.

I returned to Little Rock with lowered expectations for success. It was clear to me that neither the FBI nor the DOJ had a true first team assigned to investigate CAMPCON.

I had past contact with Lee Radek who had been at the Department of Justice for well over twenty-five years. Though he had spent a large part of his career in the Public Integrity Section, he hadn't been in a courtroom in almost two decades and had evolved into a consummate bureaucrat. According to an acquaintance who left the department in disgust, Radek "looked good, but has no balls." I later learned that description was accurate.

I did not know Laura Ingersoll, the principal attorney for the Task Force, but based on her limited experience, considered her in over her head like Jeff Lampinski.

The Task Force became consumed with compiling a comprehensive "Operational Plan," a huge waste of time that could have been put to better use by getting cracking on an aggressive investigation. But it was a bureaucrat's answer to doing something when they did not have the stomach to conduct a hard-hitting investigation. While the plan was being prepared, witnesses were disappearing overseas or being coached to ensure their stories were consistent, evidence was being destroyed and investigative initiative was being lost. Operational plans are for short-term matters that have well defined goals, not long-term multi-faceted investigations that might lead anywhere. With modern data-bases and instantaneous communication, such plans are almost always a waste of time and resources.

Early on it became apparent that team members, timid and hesitant as their efforts were anyway, would be further hampered by constant inter-ruptions to make some report to Freeh or Reno or the media. There had to be coordination among agencies and participants, since everything tied back to the White House and the Office of the Vice President, but I did expect to be able to conduct an aggressive investigation in Little Rock without bureaucratic interference and second-guessing.

I may have been the only Task Force member who had heard of Charlie Trie or John Huang before the investigation. I had talked with personal acquaintances of Mark Middleton well before the Task Force was formed and had the advantage of not only personal experience with the Chinese culture, but also having handled the White House Travel

Office matter. Perhaps even most important, I had firsthand knowledge of the Arkansas political environment. I believed I had a better feel of what to expect and felt confident that the investigation in Little Rock could be conducted with very little oversight from less-informed bureaucrats in Washington. Furthermore, communication with the Task Force was difficult, with interminable meetings and a lag of days before phone calls were returned.

The week of June 16, 1997, surveillance was established at 1407 South Cleveland in Little Rock, the residence of Charlie Trie. This was a small brown frame house, obviously not the residence a wealthy political contributor. Charlie Trie had a "secretary" of sorts named Maria Mapili, who spent virtually all day, every day, at Trie's residence. It became apparent that Trie's wife, Weng Mei Trie, was not home. Trie was reported to be hiding in Shanghai, but I believed there was very likely communication between Mapili and Trie. Based on FBI observations, a trash cover for Trie's residence was established. (A trash cover is just what it sounds like—authority is granted to retrieve trash and examine the contents for evidence of a crime.)

The cover was productive far beyond what I imagined. We discovered that Mapili had been systematically destroying Trie's business, financial, and travel records dating back to the 1980s. This included documents relating to the Daihatsu International Trading Company, a Trie company that figured into the illegal campaign contribution investigation. Some of these documents were torn or cut into small pieces. Clearly there was an ongoing attempt to selectively destroy documents—not a course of action Mapili would undertake on her own.

A Federal Express envelope from Charlie Trie's trash had an address label from the White House indicating a two-pound package had been sent from there to Trie on May 5, 1997, and delivered the following day. There was a similar package from Delta Airlines delivered to the Trie residence on May 19, handwritten notes regarding a hotel in Seattle, and the name Wang Qing; other related documents indicated a meeting had been set for June 27 at that location. (We learned later that Wang Qing was an airline flight attendant.) There were other handwritten notes as well. One notation said, "10,000, Mike (or Mark) 501 5700324, Larry M, Mark M" (this was probably reference to Mark and Larry Middleton, the latter an investment banker with Stephens Incorporated), various bank account numbers, reference to a "Mr. Lu", "Rm 872", "20,000," and other such notations. Another trash cover was initiated on Mapili's own residence, which yielded further important evidence.

When the Task Force requested a search warrant quickly before more documents were destroyed, the warrant was refused and a subpoena was issued instead. No doubt valuable evidence was destroyed as a result.

At the request of the FBI in Little Rock, the telephone company had worked overtime to place pen registers in place before the target date of Friday, June 27. A pen register is a device that records incoming and out-going telephone calls from a particular number. However, we didn't receive the authorizing documents from FBI headquarters until Monday, June 30. Further, they had been addressed to "Ms. Daniel J. Wehr" and had ended up at the offices of the Whitewater independent counsel where Agent Wehr's wife, Una "Sissy" Stanton, was assigned. Wehr was looking all over the office for the documents that would have author-ized the pen register to no avail, after determining they had been for-warded from Washington, albeit late.

Wehr came to see me, obviously upset. He had been ordered to serve the subpoena on Mapili that day without fail. The Task Force knew the documents authorizing the pen register were still missing and Wehr had asked to delay serving the subpoena until the pen register was operative. This was absolutely essential. With the pen register in place, we could monitor Mapili's reaction when the subpoena was served, i.e. whom she contacted and, just as important, who contacted her. Our pleas were in vain. After all the investigative delays caused by Task Force attorneys, I couldn't understand why, in this critical moment, they demonstrated a complete change of tact and demanded expediency when it was both contrary to their past actions and harmful to the investigation.

I called the Task Force myself and, as usual, found it near impossible to locate anyone in authority. Finally, I talked to someone who made it clear that the decision had been made by the departmental attorneys to serve the subpoena immediately without regard for the advantage of having the pen register in place. I turned in my chair and sat looking out my office window for a long time, wondering if the department really wanted to know who would be in contact with Mapili. My doubts about the Task Force grew.

The subpoena was served on June 27, 1997, and on June 29, an attorney from Fayetteville, Arkansas, W.H. Taylor, drove up to Mapili's residence, where the two of them were seen carrying boxes from the house to his Lexus. On July 1, the trash cover revealed Mapili was still destroying relevant evidence. However, our request to retrieve the documents from Taylor was denied by Task Force attorneys. I appealed the decision to Laura Laughlin, the agent supervisor of the Trie case at the Task Force. I explained the situation and asked her to reconsider allowing the search of Taylor's vehicle. She answered that "everyone had the right to have an attorney."

She didn't get it, and at that juncture, never would. I tried to explain the "wiring diagram" involved and the logistics of any attorney traveling to Little Rock from Fayetteville to represent a client with such modest means, much less W.H. Taylor, personal attorney to Tyson's Foods multimillionaire Don Tyson. Laughlin was unmoved, and Taylor was allowed to leave the residence under the watchful eyes of increasingly frustrated surveillance agents.

The agents finally convinced the Task Force there was sufficient probable cause to search Mapili and Trie's residence, and a search warrant was planned for July 3. However, Laura Ingersoll withdrew permission to search the residences, and I was told it was due in part to Mapili having legal representation—a reason that has no basis in constitutional law and is certainly contrary to the practice of conducting responsible investigations. I found myself surrounded by dispirited agents who were simply trying to do their jobs.

I FIRST MET DWIGHT LINKOUS on May 12 after asking Dan Wehr to make arrangements for a meeting near Linkous's home in Cleburne

County. Linkous evidently had information pertinent to the CAMPCON investigation, but equally important from my standpoint, he had insights to the political environment in Arkansas. I was always on the lookout for someone to just discuss politics and political relationships with that may assist my understanding of separate ongoing investigations.

Linkous had made a lot of money and had friends in high places, but over the past ten years or so his life had started to crumble. In 1989, his wife of twenty-seven years asked for a divorce. He was devastated and began to neglect his business, drink heavily, and at one point attempted suicide. He lost his home in Little Rock, his lake home on Greers Ferry, and his business. To avoid bankruptcy, he liquidated all his assets to pay off more than $1 million in debt, a source of some pride for him. When I met Linkous he was living in a small rented house, drove an old high-mileage Cadillac, and was still battling his drinking problems. He was fragile both physically and emotionally, but he was alert, spoke with confidence, and displayed a great awareness of politics and personalities in Arkansas. I liked him immediately but was determined to not show him any sympathy and not to dwell on his past, rather to emphasize the future for him personally and how he could assist in the investigation.

Linkous related three incidents that I found interesting. The first involved his initial meeting with Charlie Trie, who had asked Linkous to represent him in purchasing an old hotel, the Camelot, in Little Rock, promising him $100,000 if the deal were successful. One of the other investors was Ng Lap Seng, referred to as "Mr. Wu," who had a company called San Chung Hing Property Investment, Limited; another was Mana Han Xiao, usually referred to as "Maria" or Mana Han, whose business was China Overseas Trade Shenzhen Company. Maria also reportedly owned the Haili Restaurant in the Capitol Hotel in Beijing.

I recognized there wasn't anything necessarily sinister by Ng Lap Seng using the name "Mr. Wu." Wu was the Mandarin form of the Cantonese name Ng, one of those bits of information I wasn't certain the members of the Task Force understood. Further, I knew that if Maria had a restaurant in Beijing as claimed, she was herself well-connected with the government of the PRC. One does not own prestigious restaurants in

Beijing and do business overseas without having reached some accommodation with powerful interests in China, which are invariably closely aligned with the Communist government.

Linkous met Mr. Wu through Trie in the spring of 1994 at the Excelsior Hotel in Little Rock. Most of the meeting was conducted in Chinese, but at one point it appeared the discussion centered around Trie's need for expense money. When that occurred, Mr. Wu opened a brief case and removed what Linkous thought was $20,000 in cash. After about thirty minutes the meeting ended, but the visits by Trie subsequently continued, and this led to a second interesting revelation.

During another meeting, Trie stated he had made a $100,000 contribution and that he would be dining with Clinton, along with eight other Chinese associates, at what Linkous recalled was a hotel in Washington D.C. Linkous also said that either Trie or Webb had observed that the occasion would have an impact on the attempt to have China receive a most-favored-nation trade status. (This meeting was later confirmed to have happened.) I immediately saw the importance of this information: it would appear that foreign funds were being funneled to the president of the United States and that he was supporting a Chinese bid to receive a long sought most-favored-nation status. While it would obviously be difficult to state with certainty that there was a direct connection, the implication was compelling enough that it should receive immediate attention.

The night after the meeting, Trie did in fact have dinner with President Clinton at a DNC presidential gala at the Washington Hilton. Trie sat with the president and was joined by the mysterious "Mr. Wu," Ng Lap Seng, Wu's wife, Pun Nun Ho, Jude Kearney, a deputy assistant secretary at the Department of Commerce, and Anita Middleton, the mother of Mark and Larry Middleton. Also sitting at the head table were presidential confidante Vernon Jordan and DNC Chairman David Wilhelm.

It is astounding that a person of modest means such as Trie could contribute over $100,000 to dine with the president of the United States along with a foreign individual who, if not directly aligned with the

Chinese Communist government, was certainly indirectly aligned with it, and yet no one's suspicions were aroused! Didn't anyone look over the guest list, as is done with all such lists where the president is in attendance, and ask who is this Ng Lap Seng and Pun Nun Ho—who didn't even speak English? Wasn't anyone curious at the presence of these foreign nationals at a DNC political fundraising event? They could not have gone unnoticed sitting at the head table with the president of the United States.

Trie had not embellished in his bragging about his contributions; and he wasn't just trying to impress Mr. Wu. He had invited Mark Middleton's mother to the affair, noting that Middleton worked for Thomas "Mac" McLarty in the White House. This was a classic example of the Chinese concept of *quanxi*, where one builds on relationships and one's status is directly attributed to those relationships, or the appearance of relationships.

The attempt to arrange the purchase of the Camelot Hotel continued for the next several months. An obstacle was proper documentation that Mr. Wu and Maria had the financial resources to purchase the hotel. Trie flew to Hong Kong and, due to the tight deadline, agreed to meet Linkous and Lorin Fleming, another partner in the deal, in San Francisco, where he would turn over the needed documents. During the flight, Linkous recalled he had made mention of the briefcase filled with cash that he had observed at the Excelsior Hotel and Fleming related how he had carried "duffel bags" of cash for Trie through airports and the uneasiness he felt in having done so. This was another revelation that I found important from the standpoint of the CAMP-CON investigation.

In the spring of 1997, Linkous started receiving calls from the *New York Times* and NBC News and had been reluctant to return them. But he did contact Lorin Fleming and determined that the media had also been trying to call Fleming. Fleming advised Linkous that Trie had fled the country for China. Linkous mentioned the conversation with Trie where Trie had said he paid $100,000 to have dinner with the president and Fleming expressed surprise that Trie had told that story to Linkous.

On July 2, Linkous was to testify before a grand jury in Washington D.C. His fragile condition had been relayed to the Task Force, and it was made clear that while Linkous had a story to tell, he would have to be handled carefully and that there was mistrust on his part that anything would come from the whole CAMPCON investigation.

Early on July 3, well before 8:00 AM, Wehr came into my office with fatigue mixed with indignation apparent in his expression. He had picked up Linkous late the previous evening after his flight back to Little Rock from Washington, finally getting home himself in the wee hours of the morning. But it wasn't the late hours that had him upset; rather it was Linkous's description of his appearance before the grand jury. Linkous had returned from Washington convinced that there was no real attempt by the Department of Justice to fully investigate the whole issue of campaign finance violations. It was apparent that William Corcoran, the senior Justice Department attorney who asked the pertinent questions in front of the jury, had not even read the FD-302, the official written report of Linkous's interview. Corcoran's lack of preparation was observed by Special Agent Kevin Sheridan as well. During his testimony before the Senate Committee on September 22, 1999, Sheridan stated, "I was embarrassed to be in the room during the . . . grand jury interview," and "when Mr. Corcoran came into the conference room, he was clearly not prepared for the prep."

Far worse than poor preparation, there seemed to be a conscious effort to make Linkous look bad. He was never asked about the comment by Trie about contributing $100,000 to have dinner with Clinton; never asked about the briefcase filled with cash at the meeting with Mr. Wu; nor was he asked about the conversation with Larry Middleton or the comment by Fleming about duffel bags full of cash.

But Corcoran did point out Linkous having failed in business, his alcoholism, his divorce, and his having been a theology student. At one point Linkous attempted to testify about what he considered pertinent items that had been expressly omitted in his testimony. In response, Corcoran asked the jury foreman to admonish Linkous to respond only to the questions asked. Linkous left the grand jury room completely demoralized, and the grand jurors undoubtedly had no clue as to why he had testified. I viewed the whole sorry procedure, then and today, as either sheer incompetence or a deliberate attempt to devalue Linkous as a witness and to avoid getting into any issues that were potentially harmful to the president. It was clear that Corcoran, had succeeded in ensuring that no information that might further the investigation would be forthcoming, thus saving the president and the Democratic Party from further embarrassments, if not criminal liability.

Corcoran and Jonathan Biran appeared in the office on July 3. They sat quietly while I berated them for a lack of aggressiveness and the mishandling of Linkous. By that time I had learned that there was even more reason to be upset with the department: the rescinded approval to search Maria Mapili's residence. Biran had produced an affidavit with sufficient probable cause for a search, but incredibly, Corcoran had traveled to Little Rock to meet with Mapili's attorney, W.H. Taylor, but had overslept and missed the meeting, while Taylor departed Little Rock with boxes of materials from Mapili's house. Normally I would have been pleased for Biran to be in Little Rock, but the miserable grand jury report coupled with Corcoran's failure to meet Taylor left me completely dismayed.

In his single statement to the press on July 10, Linkous declared he had been prevented from telling a federal grand jury all that he knew about the campaign finance scandal and mentioned writing a letter to Attorney General Reno. Linkous refused to make any further statements and has reassumed the life of a virtual recluse in rural Cleburne County, far removed from the status and power he once enjoyed in Little Rock.

I regard the dates of July 2–3 as absolute disasters for CAMPCON. A key search warrant was approved then rescinded, a witness was mistreated, and evidence was lost because the department failed to allow its seizure. I came to question both determination and the ability of the department to conduct an aggressive and credible investigation. This feeling only intensified as further events unfolded.

The trash cover of Mapili's residence continued to be productive. Agents found photocopies of checks from six different individuals with Chinese names in the Little Rock area, each payable to the "Presidential

Legal Expenses (sic) Trust" for $1000 and dated between March 26 and April 3, 1996. The copies were torn into many pieces, but Wehr was able to reconstruct them. I was told Ingersoll had decided not to investigate that aspect of the matter since contributions to Clinton's legal expense fund were not part of CAMPCON. Further, I was told, she stated she had no obligation to notify the Senate of the systematic destruction of records that were clearly under the parameters of a Committee on Governmental Affairs subpoena. I pushed for permission to interview each person who wrote a check to learn the circumstances of their "contribution," but I was not allowed to do that either.

Ingersoll stated she needed "probable cause to convict" before she would authorize a search warrant, a legal standard far beyond what was needed. Hearing that convinced me that the CAMPCON investigation was both being delayed by the imposition of a higher legal standard than was required and that there was no real interest in conducting a quick, hard-hitting, and thorough investigation. Another example was Wehr's request, on April 23, 1997, to interview Lorin Fleming and serve him with a grand jury subpoena on account of his claim that he had carried "duffel bags full of cash" through airports for Trie. The request languished until July, by which time all hope of surprise was lost, though an FBI agent assigned to the Senate Committee, Jerry Campagne, wasn't stymied by departmental bureaucrats. In July, he interviewed Fleming as well as others in the Little Rock area while Radek and Ingersoll continued to withhold permission to conduct the interviews and Gallagher did nothing to move the case along.

On July 31, I met with Wehr and Roberta Parker in my office and was struck by their demoralized state. Parker, an attractive and accomplished FBI agent from Baltimore assigned to the investigation, had traveled to Little Rock to review documents finally obtained under subpoena from W.H. Taylor. They had obviously been tampered with, though it wasn't certain whether it happened before or after Taylor took them from Mapili's residence. After listening to their frustrations and their inability to conduct a sound investigation, I announced that I would call Louis Freeh.

I was not a confidante of Freeh's, but ours was a sound relationship. I viewed my position as an SAC as one where I was to handle every problem I could and call him strictly as a last resort. On July 31, I made the only phone call I made to Freeh during my three years as SAC. When he returned my call the next day, I gave him three or four specific examples of departmental interference with the investigation. At one point he asked to put me on hold while, ironically, he took a call from the attorney general, then returned to our discussion. It became clear that he hadn't been fully apprised of the frustrations among the Task Force investigators, which I had suspected. Finally, he asked me to send a memorandum to his personal attention outlining the incidents I had described, thanked me for the call, and we hung up.

I knew anything I wrote would very likely end up at the Department of Justice, but the frustration of those directly engaged in the investigation was such that I felt it was the proper and responsible thing to do. The greatest responsibility I had as a senior manager was to look after the welfare of my subordinates, and in this case, clearly, no one else was doing that. My memorandum, which ultimately appeared in the press, outlined not only the specific events I had discussed with Freeh, but also my concern "driven by an increasing amount of frustration by the working street agents engaged in this matter, where very elementary investigative steps are being ignored," and mentioned the Fleming interview. I noted that I had advised both Parker and Wehr to keep a record for "future historians" of all the disagreements between them and the department over the issuance of search warrants, etc. and the basis for the disagreements.

I added that while I was well aware of the concept of "prosecutive discretion," I was nevertheless "convinced the team at DOJ leading this investigation is, at best, simply not up to the task." I said I based that conclusion not only on the CAMPCON matter, but also on other investigations I had been engaged in that the Public Integrity Section had handled due to recusals by U.S. Attorneys Paula Casey and P.K. Holmes III. I wrote, "The impression left is the emphasis is on how not to prosecute matters, not how to aggressively conduct investigations leading to prosecutions."

I also used the opportunity to express my concern for the trend that placed FBI personnel in secondary roles in investigations such as CAMPCON and Whitewater. I explained that "attorneys without prior investigative or prosecutive experience should not 'lead' such investigations. Investigators should be allowed to fulfill traditional investigative roles, and prosecutors serve in that capacity alone."

The first response came from Neil Gallagher, who called and questioned why I had communicated with Freeh. I asked if he was suggesting that I couldn't communicate with the director. He then changed his tack and said that I should have advised him of my intentions. I responded that I wished to ensure that Freeh received my views unfiltered. Gallagher then asked if I would send him a copy of my memorandum, a request I took to mean that Freeh had not shared it with him. I did as requested. I had already heard that my memorandum had caused quite a stir at the CAMPCON Task Force and was quietly applauded by the agents.

I did not hear from Freeh directly, but was advised later that my memorandum had been the basis for Freeh making the argument to Attorney General Reno that a new team was needed. Amidst much fanfare, it was soon announced that a new team was assigned to head the CAMPCON investigation. James DeSarno would lead the new FBI team. I had been on a squad with DeSarno years before at the Washington field office. He was close to Bob Bryant, who had been named deputy director, and this, in my view, was the best part of his heading the operation. DeSarno, unlike Lampinski, would not report through Gallagher and would have direct access to Bryant and perhaps—just perhaps—be able to obtain greater front-office interest in the matter.

I did not know Charles LaBella, but I was familiar with him from his handling the prosecution of Ferdinand and Imelda Marcos. When I met him later I instantly liked him and trusted his instincts. Unlike most DOJ attorneys, who become something akin to academics, he was a seasoned prosecutor with the instincts of a street fighter. But I wasn't confident that LaBella would be free to conduct an unfettered investigation. In fact, the press release stated that Lee Radek was left in charge of the Task Force. That meant LaBella would probably continue getting resistance from powerful Washington bureaucrats. The influence of the political appointees in the department—Jamie Gorelick, Bob Litt, etc.—were real and detrimental to the effort.

BUT THE CAMPCON INVESTIGATION continued. Finally, in late October 1997, Parker had the opportunity to interrogate Maria Mapili, who admitted Charlie Trie had instructed her to destroy documents, as the trash covers had so clearly revealed. Belatedly, a search warrant was executed which proved that Mapili had not only continued to hide and destroy documents, she had even hidden them from her own attorney. One can only imagine what documents would have been recovered had the search been conducted in July, as the probable cause dictated.

On January 29, 1998, in an action I found somewhat surprising and even premature, Trie was indicted by a federal grand jury. I later learned that CAMPCON principals at the department had wanted an even earlier indictment. According to DeSarno, the chief impetus behind the timing was to allow the department, in the face of counting criticism for its mishandling of CAMPCON, to show they were doing something in an attempt to quiet the calls for an independent counsel.

The indictment, in some respects laughable, alleged that Trie had defrauded the Democratic National Committee. The indictment portrayed the DNC as innocent victims of Charlie Trie's zeal to buy access and influence. Once again, a friend of the president's was expected to, in paraphrasing David Watkin's comment about the Travel Office matter, "fall on his sword."

The trial was held in Little Rock in May 1998. Trie, represented by Reid Weingarten from Washington D.C., put up a vigorous defense and by some accounts was winning critical points during his cross-examination of Maria Mapili. It was obvious that Mapili, though a government witness (based on a grant of immunity from what I thought were sound obstruction of justice charges due to her systematic destruction of documents) was still loyal to Trie. On the second day, the government called Agent Roberta Parker, the case agent in Washington D.C.

I was later advised by some in the courtroom, including a respected member of the media, that her testimony was simply masterful and so compelling that at the end of the day, before she was to complete her testimony the next day, Trie agreed to plead guilty. I felt a little vindicated by the plea, but wasn't confident his admission of guilt would result in his full cooperation, as promised, and suspected he would join others with White House connections such as Webb Hubbell and Jim Guy Tucker whose commitments of cooperation were long on promise and short on delivery.

CHAPTER 19

STARR CROSSED

"I.C. Smith . . . really chewed my ass out."
Bill Mullenax as quoted in *USA Today*

I first saw the White River in northern Arkansas in early fall of 1995. On October 4, I had traveled to Bull Shoals, a delightful fishing and golfing community near the Missouri border, where I had met with the local police chief and given a speech at the Rotary Club. On the way home in the late afternoon, I stopped on Highway 62 overlooking the White River, and as the sun reflected off the water, it looked like crystals sparkling in the distance. It is a beautiful place, and somehow it seems inappropriate that such a clear and pristine river has given name to one of the more muddled episodes in American history.

When I met Ken Starr for the first time in my Little Rock office on July 31, 1995, I liked him immediately. I knew of Starr from his time as solicitor general and from later newspaper articles about him, before he was named to head the Office of the Independent Counsel. He was considered a legal purist and a man with integrity; nothing has ever altered that impression in my mind.

Starr is unfailingly polite and has a rare courtesy that is both real and sincere. He was always considerate of me and of how his operations affected mine in Arkansas, and was invariably gracious to the employees in my office. But early in our professional relationship, I became aware that Starr had very little feel for the rough-and-tumble world of the criminal courtroom. While the Whitewater investigation was a white-collar crime, it turned out to be just as nasty as any investigation associated with more typical career criminals charged with organized crime or a narcotics violations.

The Ken Starr I met in 1995 would also never ever imagined that individuals would lie under oath, that lawyers would dissemble, witnesses would embellish, or certainly that the president of the United States would engage in fellatio in the Oval Office with an intern.

Starr held the office of the presidency in considerable awe. His was an idealistic view that the occupants of that high office would always be men of the highest moral character. Intellectually, Starr holds the Constitution and our government with reverence, but the Whitewater investigation was not a constitutionally intellectual exercise. It was a dirty and mean-spirited investigation driven by desperation on the part of the Clinton White House. Being in awe of one's target does not allow for tough and uncompromising investigations.

As I became more familiar with the moods and feelings of Arkansans while the Whitewater investigation unfolded, it was clear that many of them, if not quietly cheering Starr on, were willing to take a wait-and-see attitude. The expectation that there would be results and that they would occur with some expediency began with the trial of Jim Guy Tucker and Jim and Susan McDougal in the spring of 1996.

It was a media circus for Arkansas. The local media were largely pushed aside by national and international reporters who flocked in to cover a story the local press had missed for years. Tucker arrived every day at the courthouse in a state car driven by a state trooper, accompanied by his wife, Betty. He always wore the official red Arkansas lapel pin and smiled for the cameras, though in time the smile became more of a grimace as the length of the trial began to tax his physical strength.

Susan McDougal was there too, daily proclaiming her innocence, smiling for the cameras as she helped the hobbling but still defiant Jim McDougal across the street from the Legacy Hotel. Jim McDougal was the unquestioned star attraction. He quoted Shakespeare, denounced the Office of the Independent Counsel, ate dinner with any reporter who would pay for the meal, and in a dreary trial provided the only comic relief to an increasingly sad situation.

The subsequent convictions of Governor Jim Guy Tucker and Jim and Susan McDougal gave the impression that Starr's office meant business. The Clintons' hardcore supporters were despondent at the prospects of further successes, even if they didn't seem to care much for the fate of those just convicted.

Tucker was still something of a political pariah, though he had been elected governor in his own right in 1994. He never developed the deep emotional support from the electorate his predecessor did, and while generally viewed as more workmanlike than Clinton, did not inspire the great feelings of loyalty Clinton did.

Jim McDougal was regarded with some amusement by political observers in the state. He extolled the elaborate manners of a previous century and was always polite, especially when females were involved. I came to regard his courtliness and exaggerated politeness to be similar to Ken Starr's, though Starr did not affect McDougal's level of dramatic flair. Susan McDougal was mainly remembered for her role years earlier in an advertising campaign, perched on a white horse, wearing white hot pants and leaving little to the imagination, though many couldn't recall exactly what she had been selling. It was a case of the commercial's contents overshadowing the message.

The McDougal convictions were the high-water-mark of Starr's effort as far as the people in Arkansas were concerned. Those court victories were followed by the trial of Herbie Branscum and Robert Hill the summer of 1996. Branscum was almost a caricature of the small-time Southern politician. He was known as "Boss Hog" after the character on the old *Dukes of Hazard* television show, and was the self-styled boss of rural Perry County. An attorney, he was also a director of the Perry County Bank, as was his co-defendant, former IRS agent Robert Hill.

The bank handled the "Clinton for Governor" campaign account during Clinton's 1990 gubernatorial reelection effort. It was the manner in which the funds were mishandled that led to the indictment of Branscum and Hill, though their shenanigans had prompted Clinton, after his reelection, to name Branscum a commissioner to the State Highway Commission (probably the most coveted appointed position in state government), and Hill as a commissioner to the State Banking Commission.

On August 1, shortly before a speech I had scheduled at the Optimist Club in Batesville, it was announced that the Branscum and Hill charges had resulted in a hung jury. After the formal meeting I sat around for another hour or so and talked with various members of the club and a local reporter, Frank Wallis. The Branscum and Hill verdict, or lack of one, was a topic of conversation, but what I found interesting was the take they seemed to have on the trial itself. No one suggested the defendants were innocent, but in their view, they were "too small a fish" for Starr to fry. They thought the Office of the Independent Counsel was too powerful to waste its resources and prestige on such small-time players.

According to courthouse observers and attorneys, there was a strong case made against Branscum and Hill, and one of the weakest links in their defense was the testimony of Bruce Lindsey. He was variously described as "warm and funny" and "cold" and a "weird duck," but to a person, listeners regarded his testimony as unbelievable. In particular, he testified to using funds to "get out the vote," a euphemism for the time-honored practice of funneling funds to black preachers to support a particular candidate, a tactic not extended to white preachers and congregations. Several local attorneys thought it was a tactical mistake not to have indicted him too. I agree.

I learned that the failure to convict Branscum and Hill was due primarily to a single juror who voted to not convict them on any count and that the juror had been joined by a second juror on a few of the counts. The jurors had voted 11–1 and 10–2 to convict Branscum and Hill on the more than the dozen counts of the indictment. I assumed that Starr would shortly announce his intent to retry the two defendants. But that was not forthcoming. I was surprised when there was an announcement that there would not be a retrial and later learned that Starr had been counseled by Hickman Ewing, his lead attorney on the case. For all practical purposes, Whitewater was over. By not retrying Branscum and

Hill the opposition to Starr was emboldened and over the next two years he lost the public relations war that doomed what had been considerable prospects for further successes.

I never suspected, nor do I think Starr suspected, that he would be the object of a well-orchestrated attempt at character assassination. It was a tactic unprecedented in the annals of the criminal justice system: an officer of the court was the object of a conscious effort to be destroyed for political purposes. Further, President Clinton sat idly by, if indeed he didn't encourage the tactic to continue, and never once voiced his concern for the methods being employed. It is clear that Clinton had no sympathy with Starr's plight, even though Clinton had been the attorney general for the state of Arkansas, based on comments made in his book, *My Life,* where he savages Starr at every opportunity.

The most visible practitioner of the personal smear tactic was a fellow Louisianan, James Carville, who had been nothing more than an unsuccessful political hack until he joined the Clinton team before the 1992 election. One of his timeless gems that revealed how completely he and his cohorts had lost touch with the promise of their election was his comment relating to Clinton's romantic interest Paula Jones that, "If you drag a hundred-dollar bill through a trailer park, you never know what you will catch." That was a slap at every poor person who ever lived in a mobile home! Further, Clinton had been the beneficiary of campaign contributions from mobile home makers including Johnny Allison, owner of a large manufacturing plant in Conway, Arkansas, who gave thousands of dollars to his presidential campaign.

The viciousness didn't stop there. One of the oddest incidents occurred one day in October 1996. FBI Agent Jack Frost (not his real name; he has requested his identity not be revealed) was a longtime FBI agent, for whom I had developed a fondness personally as well as holding him in high professional regard. He came into my office and advised me of an incident that had occurred the night before. Frost, who was divorced, was dating the daughter of a wealthy Arkansas businessman. They were a visible and delightful couple in Little Rock with plans to marry in the future. But on the previous evening, Frost had seen two people taking photographs outside her house from a car, and he had confronted them with his shotgun. He was justifiably concerned that the clandestine photos may have been part of a kidnapping plan, since her wealth was common knowledge.

Frost learned that one of the two was Bill Mullenax, a controversial former Arkansas state trooper who had been assigned to the Capitol during Clinton's tenure as governor and who was working as a private investigator with Tommy Goodwin, the former head of the Arkansas state police under Clinton. Frost told me that once Mullenax and his companion had been confronted, they had hastily departed the area.

As I was mulling the incident over, wondering why someone would want to take photographs of Frost and his fiancé since they made no attempt to hide their relationship, Frost provided additional details. He said he was told by a Fayetteville acquaintance who had a private investigating business that someone had tried to hire him to catch Ken Starr and Frost's fiancé in an illicit relationship. This rumor was absolutely preposterous. I was one of the few in Arkansas who knew both Starr and Frost's fiancé and could attest to the utter absurdity of such a notion. So I decided to deal with the matter directly. I placed a call to Tommy Goodwin.

Goodwin ran the Mid-South Safety Council, though his main interest seemed to be representing gambling interests pushing for legalized gambling in the state. I asked Goodwin why, if he had a problem with Frost, he hadn't called me directly and told him I resented him conducting a surveillance on an FBI agent under my supervision. Goodwin quickly told me he had nothing to do with the incident and that the contract had been worked by Bill Mullenax. When I countered that surely Mullenax worked for him, he denied having anything to do with Mullenax's business and insisted he just provided management support. He quickly put Mullenax on the phone.

I repeated my questions. Mullenax denied conducting a surveillance on Frost and said he had been hired to take photos of wealthy people for something like *The Lives of the Rich and Famous*. Under continued questioning, Mullenax told me he had been hired by the Matrix Group, address 1208 Butterworth, S.W. in Grand Rapids, Michigan, telephone 800-955-1317, and that his contact was a Greg Crays. He said more than once during the conversation that he wished he had never taken the contract. I never mentioned Starr but was aware that the other private investigator in Fayetteville had specifically mentioned a connection between Starr and Frost's fiancé.

I later learned that the Matrix Group had been short-lived and its personnel had some past Secret Service connections. The incident with Frost remained quiet until February 1998, when Starr issued a wide range of subpoenas in an attempt to determine if the White House had orchestrated a smear campaign against Starr and the staff of the OIC. Among those who received subpoenas were Goodwin and Mullenax. In an article in *USA Today*, Ed Pound, a tough and resourceful Washington-area reporter, wrote of making contact with Goodwin and Mullenax regarding the incident and subpoenas. Mullenax denied conducting a surveillance on Starr and recalled that "I.C. Smith . . . really chewed my ass out." I was contacted by Pound for a comment and told him, upon reflection, I couldn't very well take issue with the accuracy of Mullenax's recollection of our conversation.

However, Starr did not follow through with the matter, and Goodwin and Mullenax did not have to appear before a grand jury. This too caused Starr's toughness to be questioned by many I talked with in Arkansas. I am convinced the whole episode was an attempt to smear Starr, and to my knowledge the matter has never been pursued by the Department of Justice or the OIC.

It was during the period after the Branscum and Hill trial, and the OIC's refusal to retry them, that the way Arkansans viewed Starr began to turn. As I talked with people, I began to sense that there had been some expectations, perhaps unreasonable, that the OIC investigation was going to follow up on its successes with Tucker and the McDougals with further indictments and prosecutions. But this did not occur.

While Starr's office began to lose its support among the people of Arkansas, it was a continuing issue for me in dealing with both United States attorneys, Paula Casey in the Eastern District of Arkansas in

Little Rock, and P.K. Holmes III in the Western District of Arkansas in Fort Smith.

I had developed a personal regard for both—regardless of Casey's attempts to discredit me with the FBI inspectors and the Department of Justice after my conversation with Governor Huckabee touching on (but not naming) the Nick Wilson kickback investigation—but was aware that both were fiercely partisan politically and routinely made derogatory comments about Starr's investigation. On several occasions, Casey had made comments that I was close to Starr, comments that made their way back to me. The dislike for Starr was especially apparent with her, due in part to her office having greater contact with the OIC. An incident early in my tenure served to provide me with a lesson in just how deeply she disliked Starr.

In October 1995, Starr's office had filed a legal brief after Judge Henry Woods had thrown out indictments against Jim Guy Tucker and two co-defendants, John Haley and Richard Marks. In his brief, Starr stated the ruling by Woods was "unprecedented and wrong" and had appealed the decision to the Eighth U.S. Circuit Court of Appeals.

Woods, then well past seventy-five years of age, was a formidable and intimidating presence on the federal bench in Little Rock, where he was also an unabashed Democrat and friend of the Clintons. He frequently made mention of his former association with the FBI. He had served with the FBI in the years 1941–46, which happened to coincide with the time of World War II, when employment with the FBI offered an exemption from military service. Like others, including former California Congressman Don Edwards, Woods found that his commitment to a career with the FBI abated once the shooting stopped.

After the war he entered private practice and became a staunch member of the political establishment, though he did break with that establishment when, in 1957, he took a public and principled stance opposing Governor Orville Faubus and the governor's use of Arkansas National Guard troops to keep nine black students from integrating Central High School in Little Rock.

On March 15, 1996, I was entering the building in west Little Rock that housed both the FBI offices and the OIC when I encountered Debbie Gershman, the press person for the OIC, who was carrying a large stack of documents. I asked if I could give her a hand, and she commented she had copies of the ruling that the Eighth Circuit had just released that not only reinstated the indictments against Tucker, Haley, and Marks, but had removed Judge Woods from the case. When I mentioned I would be interested in reading the Eighth Circuit's reasoning, she handed me a copy as I continued upstairs to my office.

After browsing through the opinion, it occurred to me that given the unusual nature of the ruling, perhaps P.K. Holmes and Paula Casey would be interested in reviewing the ruling too—especially Casey, since she had been a law professor before being appointed U.S. attorney.

I called Holmes and he was quite pleased at the offer to forward him a copy, but the call to Casey was decidedly different. When I mentioned what I had and the results of the ruling, she grew cold and testy.

In a conversation with Casey some months later, when I discussed how the OIC complicated the relationship between our offices, I mentioned her reaction to the call regarding the Eighth Circuit's ruling and how that incident caused me to realize the depth of her discomfort with the OIC. She admitted she had been "frosty" and had thought I was calling to "take a shot" at her. This gave me pause and made me realize I would have to be more conscious of the depth of her feelings toward the OIC in future conversations.

The situation had gotten to the point she would not have any direct conversations with the OIC, though there was every reason for some contact—scheduling grand jury time and various other common interests—once we had begun to emphasize corruption investigations. Nevertheless, she insisted that all communications between the two offices use the Department of Justice's Public Integrity Section as a conduit. So when the OIC wanted to send a message to Casey's office, they would call the department, who would call Casey, whose response would be channeled back to the OIC. I found the whole matter both childish and unprofessional, but it was something I had to live with virtually every day.

In a conversation with Starr, I mentioned my hope that any referrals from his office would be passed to me on a timely basis and not held until his office was shutting down and then dumped on us at once. He agreed to ensure that such information was referred quickly, and in fact it was. But this created another problem, for I didn't want to have to wait for referrals to go through the Department of Justice. So I raised the issue with Casey and her first assistant, Michael Johnson. I asked how she wished to handle such referrals. Before she had a chance to respond, Johnson spoke up and suggested that all such information be channeled to him and he would decide what Casey should and should not see. I didn't respond to that suggestion and the conversation continued in other areas.

Later that day, I received a telephone call from Casey saying she did not agree with Johnson. I responded that I viewed her as the U.S. attorney and I wouldn't have agreed to such an arrangement anyway. The matter was never really resolved and indeed, I did resort to channeling such information to FBI headquarters to be discussed with Public Integrity. I am confident that there were investigations that should have been conducted but were never initiated due to that arrangement.

I continued trying to walk the tightrope between Starr's office and both Casey and Holmes and to ensure that I had adequate resources to meet my own escalating investigative needs. I asked Deputy Director Weldon Kennedy to overstaff my office in March 1996, as there were eleven agents from my complement assigned to the Office of the Independent Counsel. This represented almost twenty percent of the total complement for the Little Rock office. While Kennedy did agree to overstaff the office for a period of time, by the end of 1998, with retirements and transfers, the under-staffing situation continued, even as we were accelerating the investigation of corruption cases of our own, which certainly caused fewer indictments to come out of the Little Rock office.

I publicly made note of that fact after my retirement, when asked by a reporter from the *Arkansas Democrat-Gazette* about the impact Whitewater had on Arkansas. Somehow it was reported that I said if the agents in Starr's office had been able to function as normal in investigations, it would have produced more Whitewater indictments. I wasn't in a position to make that judgment but could make that evaluation from the standpoint of the Little Rock office where there were cases unassigned due to the lack of personnel.

While I thought I would not personally be involved in any aspect of the Whitewater matter beyond administrative matters, I was rudely proven wrong on the evening of March 14, 1998. I received a telephone call from Frank Hartmann, a retired Fort Smith police officer who had been hired to work evenings in the Little Rock FBI office handling complaints, etc. after hours. Hartmann, who had a good sense of when a caller needed immediate attention, advised me that a journalist, Murray Waas, and former Senator David Pryor had both called and expressed concern for the safety of a witness who had information involving the Whitewater matter.

I had previously met Pryor in Washington just after I had spent well over an hour with Senator Dale Bumpers, and was struck by the contrast of the two. While Bumpers had his suit coat off and his sleeves rolled up and was perfectly relaxed, Pryor sat in a straight chair, very formal and correct, wearing his jacket and seeming ill at ease throughout the conversation. When I arrived in Arkansas, there was frequent mention of Pryor being the "most loved politician" in Arkansas, an accolade I increasingly felt was inaccurate as I observed Pryor in public, especially in contrast to the more informal Bumpers.

Pryor had also committed an act that was virtually unprecedented in its rashness and inappropriateness. On December 23, 1997, he had visited with U.S. District Court Judge Susan Webber-Wright to raise the issue of Susan McDougal. Judge Wright had sent McDougal to jail for civil contempt for refusing to answer questions before a federal grand jury such as, "Where were you born?" and "Are you employed?" Pryor was not the attorney of record for McDougal, and as a former senator who had supported Judge Wright's nomination to the bench, he had no business interjecting himself into the matter. The *Arkansas Democrat-Gazette* strongly condemned Pryor's action, noting he "owes a number of apologies in the matter—to the judge, to the law, to the public, and to the students he teaches at the University of Arkansas." That action was just an indication of the rabid and increasingly incoherent defense he made of Clinton the next year in the Monica Lewinsky affair, and it certainly influenced how I reacted to Hartmann's call.

But I decided to call Pryor and, after brief pleasantries, got to my purpose. Pryor stated that Murray Waas, whom he considered "very, very, reliable," had called him regarding a witness in the Whitewater matter being in a life-threatening situation. Pryor admitted he had no firsthand knowledge of the matter, but thought it was important enough to call the FBI. I told Pryor I would check into the situation and be back in touch.

I then contacted Murray Waas in a Bentonville, Arkansas, hotel. I was familiar with Waas from his reporting on the Iran–Contra matter years before. I advised Waas that I had seen an article in the *New York Observer* a few weeks earlier that made reference to an "Arkansas Project." The article alleged that funds had been funneled from Richard Mellon-Scaife to David Hale to ensure he would commit perjury regarding his knowledge that Clinton had applied pressure to ensure Susan McDougal received a $300,000 loan, a matter later confirmed by Jim McDougal.

Waas said he had been involved in the *Observer* article but the story he was working on was for the Internet on-line magazine *Salon*. He was convinced that the witness, Caryn Mann, and her son, Josh, had information relating to Hale receiving payments through Parker Dozhier, a Hot Springs area bait shop owner who had frequently been visited by Hale while under the protection of FBI agents when he was in hiding. I then talked to Mann, who said she had observed Hale receiving money from Dozhier during the several years she lived with him, and that Dozhier had a violent temper and she thought he could be dangerous. But, she added, she had not seen Dozhier in over two years. In my mind, this removed some of the urgency from the matter. But I was still not certain how Waas had gotten this information in the first place.

I contacted Wayne Edenfield, the senior agent in Fayetteville, who was an excellent investigator with great common sense. Though it was nearly midnight by then, I asked him to contact Mann at the hotel and personally determine if she was in danger. The next morning Edenfield reported that Mann did not feel she was in any immediate danger and just wished to go home. He escorted her home, gave her his telephone number, and asked the local police to patrol by her place with frequency. I contacted Pryor again the next morning, advising him of what had occurred and, ever gracious, he thanked me for handling the matter.

The next day Edenfield interviewed Mann in great depth and the mystery of how Waas knew of the matter became clear. On the advice of acquaintances, she had contacted an attorney, David Matthews, with the information about Dozhier and Hale after she had heard Hillary Clinton make reference to the "vast right-wing conspiracy" that was trying to bring down her husband in the wake of the initial Monica Lewinsky allegations. According to Mann, Matthews had put her in contact with the journalists Waas and John Browder.

I knew then that I had to handle the matter carefully. It was clear that instead of contacting me or P.K. Holmes with information about a possible crime, Matthews had chosen to try to extract some political mileage from the incident. But I also knew I had to move quickly. I did not want to have to respond to accusations that a witness had been in danger and my office had not responded with expediency, since the witness was in a position to hurt Starr and one of those who had contacted me was a former senator.

I called Bill Cromwell, the first assistant United States attorney in the Western District, since Holmes was skiing in Colorado. I had great confidence in Cromwell, arguably the best career federal prosecutor in Arkansas. He had been the first choice for United States attorney in the Western District but had refused the job due to the conditions imposed that included his firing a former United States attorney, Mike Fitzhugh, who was still on the staff as an assistant. Holmes, on the other hand, had agreed to take the appointment with those conditions, and Cromwell remained a very able first assistant.

I advised Cromwell of the previous evening's events and the course of action I had taken. He agreed that Mann and her son should be interviewed quickly and also agreed that Matthews's actions were unprofessional.

After the interview by Edenfield, it was less clear that Mann had seen payments being made to Hale that originated with Mellon-Scaife. She may well have seen Dozhier give Hale money, but this wasn't unusual considering the financial straits Hale found himself in. Dozhier admitted he had been on a retainer from the *American Spectator* magazine, but that wasn't proof that the money Dozhier gave Hale was sent to him for that purpose by Mellon-Scaife, a supporter of the *Spectator*. I knew the matter needed to be investigated and was prepared, even eager, to get to work. However, this could be done only on authority from FBI headquarters. My feeling was simple. If Hale had been paid to perjure himself, then he and those who paid him should be prosecuted, regardless of how that adversely impacted Starr's office.

The following Monday I sent a lengthy priority communication to FBI headquarters detailing the incident, and after more than a week finally received a telephone call from Neil Gallagher, the deputy assistant director in the Criminal Division, saying we should not conduct any additional investigation. Given the length of time that had elapsed, I didn't want to be a part of any such investigation anyway, and neither did Holmes. There was little prospect of a successful investigation then, since witnesses could have been coached, made to disappear, documents destroyed, etc. as the bureaucracy ground on at headquarters.

By the time I was dealing with Caryn Mann and Parker Dozhier, Whitewater had taken a back seat to the Monica Lewinsky affair. The primary attentions of the OIC, along with the rest of the country, were on that matter, and Whitewater was pushed aside except for a brief interruption in the summer of 1998 for the trial of Susan McDougal. McDougal had been convicted in May 1996, and she was finally indicted for criminal contempt of court on May 4, 1998. That unnecessary two-year hiatus proved disastrous to the OIC and turned Susan McDougal from a convicted felon of multiple counts into something of a sympathetic figure.

After her conviction in May 1996, her attorneys, Jennifer Horan, an energetic public defender from Little Rock, and Bobby McDaniel, an attorney from Jonesboro and a strong Clinton supporter, were advised by the OIC that they intended to subpoena McDougal before a federal grand jury. While Horan advised McDougal to cooperate with the OIC, McDaniel's first reaction was to call the White House, even before he advised his client of the OIC's intentions, and to advise her not to cooperate. It was clear to me when I heard this just who McDaniel considered his primary client to be—and it wasn't Susan McDougal.

CHAPTER 20

SAD STATE OF AFFAIRS

*"It's a good story, as large and
misunderstood as the state of Arkansas."*

Jim McDougal in *Arkansas Mischief*

By the time Susan McDougal appeared before the federal grand jury on September 4, 1996, she had been interviewed by Diane Sawyer of ABC News, during an unannounced trip to New York. Part of that conversation was later reported by Chris Vlasto of ABC News, but I also learned there were interesting things omitted.

Vlasto originally reported that McDougal promised to reveal all before the television cameras the following day. But her brother, Bill Henley, and longtime boyfriend, Pat Harris (who can now be seen at the side of attorney Mark Geragos when Geragos makes his frequent trips before cameras when representing various high-profile clients), arrived in New York in the early morning and convinced her to not talk with the candor she had promised. Oddly enough, it was Harris himself who contributed to McDougal being sentenced to jail. As a character witness, Harris had testified that he and Susan had begun their affair well before her divorce from Jim McDougal and detailed illicit meetings at fine hotels at McDougal's expense. This did not sit well with the diminutive and moral Judge George Howard, who has been known to quote scripture from the bench. Some observers believed Harris's testimony led to the judge imposing jail time for

McDougal instead of granting the leniency afforded Jim Guy Tucker due to his illness.

While Harris and Henley could be heard off-camera coaching Susan McDougal in her conversation with Sawyer about a $300,000 loan and Clinton's having allegedly influenced the deal, she was also asked about her personal relationship with Clinton. She refused to directly respond, remaining coy to the point that after a while Sawyer became exasperated and asked for McDougal to just say "yes or no" to having had an affair with Clinton. She still refused to give a direct answer.

After her May 1998 indictment, another trial in Little Rock brought the national press back to town. It was another tiresome spectacle for the locals that this time involved McDougal's obnoxious and abrasive—but occasionally effective—California lawyer, Mark Geragos. Condemning Starr before every TV camera he could find, Geragos proclaimed McDougal's innocence and, finally, said that the FBI's claim that Richard Mellon-Scaife had funneled money to David Hale was part of the vast right-wing conspiracy Hillary Clinton had touted. I advised John Collingwood, head of the Office of Public and Congressional Affairs at FBI headquarters, that while I did not intend to call the media, I was going to take issue with Geragos if they called me. He agreed that we could not let such false claims go unchallenged.

The question was too obvious, and I knew eventually I would be asked for a response (though, not surprisingly, the question did not come from the local media). I was asked about Geragos's comments by Julian Barnes of *U.S. News & World Report,* whom I had known when he had worked for the *Arkansas Democrat-Gazette.* I was correctly quoted in a May issue of *U.S. News* when I simply answered: "There is no information in FBI files of payoffs to David Hale."

I would have liked to have said more, for Geragos's claims were blatantly false. That was evident by his not issuing a subpoena for FBI files as he had been crowing he would do. If nothing else, Whitewater brought out the worst in lawyers, who already lack credibility with the public; lawyers like Mark Geragos, who make false claims to sway public attention and divert attention from their clients' own problems, just add to that perception.

Susan McDougal's trial concluded with another hung jury, but not before she testified that she and Clinton had never had a personal relationship. This was in marked contrast to the Diane Sawyer interview where she had refused to make a definitive statement, much to the mirth of the observers around the courthouse. It was generally believed that some of the jurors thought the time McDougal had already spent in jail for civil contempt—about eighteen months—was punishment enough, regardless of their feelings about the veracity of McDougal's testimony and the defense offered by Geragos. Starr's office decided to not retry McDougal, compounding the earlier mistake of not retrying Branscum and Hill.

Of course Geragos touted the mistrial as a victory, but the hung jury was not a verdict of innocent as he wanted the world to believe. A hung jury is a victory only for the guilty. A truly innocent person would want to be completely absolved of the charges against them, which only a verdict of not guilty can do.

Starr had managed to obtain a guilty plea from Jim Guy Tucker on the second indictment with a promise of full cooperation, reminiscent of a similar arrangement with Webb Hubbell. If that cooperation resulted in any information of significance, it wasn't evident in the referrals to my office or in any renewed investigative vigor. I suspect neither Hubbell nor Tucker lived up to their bargains.

For all practical purposes Whitewater was over.

FUNDAMENTALLY, I BELIEVE Starr made three mistakes in handling Whitewater. The first was deciding not to take a leave of absence from his law firm to devote his time solely to the appointed position of independent counsel. While some argue that his continuing abbreviated legal and speaking schedule did not delay the investigation, I disagree. Even if a decision was delayed for an hour, the cumulative effect of many such decisions was clearly detrimental. This is especially true when there was a tendency to manage by consensus, which is seldom achieved in a roomful of lawyers with divergent backgrounds and experiences, as was the case with Starr's staff.

By maintaining ties with his law firm and making speeches before clearly partisan groups, Starr played right into the hands of the Carvilles and Paul Begalas who were at the forefront of the political effort to turn public support away from him. At times, he gave the impression that he viewed his OIC appointment as something akin to being appointed to a commission that met occasionally and wasn't a real drain on his time. I heard this more than once in audiences I was speaking before. They mentioned that Starr was working for the tobacco growers and giving speeches instead of taking care of business with the Office of the Independent Counsel.

A second error was the two-year delay between the failure to retry Branscum and Hill and the indictment of Susan McDougal. This gave credence to the rantings of Carville and his cohorts that Starr had a political agenda and that it was "four years and forty million dollars" wasted in a political vendetta. They succeeded in making a criminal investigation into a partisan political issue, swaying public opinion to the point that Starr was on the defensive. Seldom are corruption investigations helped by delay. As I know from my own experience, CAMPCON for instance, that once an investigation is in the public domain there is a loss of control. Investigators spend time responding to media reports and squelching rumors and misinformation that would be better spent on the investigation. Public corruption investigations must be moved quickly and quietly. Starr did not move quickly, and the White House was skilled in ensuring that the lack of demonstrable progress stayed in the news with the mantra of "four years."

Then finally, there is the issue of how FBI personnel were involved. There is a traditional and time-honored line between the roles of prosecutors and investigators, but the tendency of the recent past is for the prosecutors to attempt to play both roles. This occurred in the CAMPCON investigation as well as Whitewater and other independent counsel investigations.

On June 17, 1996, I met with the agents assigned to the Whitewater investigation in Little Rock at their request. I heard a litany of complaints, some of which centered around their supervisor, Steve Irons, whom they viewed as not being supportive of their positions and of trying to curry favor with Starr and the lawyers on his staff. But the overwhelming concern was their inability to function in traditional agent roles. Because the investigation was not moving with any urgency, they frequently had nothing to do as they waited for decisions to be made and strategies developed by consensus. Junior prosecutors with little criminal prosecutive background and certainly no investigative background were leading interviews of potential witnesses. Appointment to a special prosecution team doesn't automatically endow someone with the skills of a seasoned investigator. Furthermore, no one can both collect testimony and prosecute the case. Once testimony is elicited, the questioner becomes a witness.

The agents also complained of a lack of input and the "lawyers only" meetings that evolved around investigative strategy. This destructive practice continued throughout the investigation. In retrospect, I did those agents a disservice by not raising the issue with Louis Freeh.

THERE ARE COLLATERAL ISSUES attached to such failure to properly utilize FBI agents, and one good example occurred in Whitewater. In June 1998 I attended a meeting of the American Society of Industrial Engineers (ASIE) in Little Rock, where I met Buddy Young, the former head of Clinton's state police protection detail. Young had been rewarded for his loyalty with a highly paid job at the Federal Emergency Management Administration (FEMA). I didn't think much about the encounter beyond the fact that his speech clearly demonstrated he was not qualified for his FEMA appointment—neither in background, principally as a security guard for a governor, and certainly not in credibility, beyond being exceedingly loyal to Clinton when many of those whom he had worked with had gone public with tales of Clinton's serial philandering.

A few days later, several state troopers went public with the news that they had been interviewed by Starr's office about Clinton's sexual history. Of course this created a media firestorm. I thought then, and think now, that it wasn't just a coincidence Young happened to be in Little

Rock a few days before his former colleagues and subordinates went public with the details of their interviews. I found it ironic that they expressed indignation over the tone of the interviews when they themselves had first brought Clinton's philandering to the public eye, sold their stories, and talked to anyone who would buy them a beer.

But when confronted with the news by reporters in Washington, Starr's office denied any knowledge of what had occurred in those interviews, saying they had been conducted by the FBI and his office wasn't always aware what the FBI was doing. That response was both false and laughable. I talked to some of the agents on the Task Force, made a couple of inquiries with the troopers themselves, and determined that the lead questions were being asked by lawyers in Starr's office and, in effect, the agents were along as note takers. I called Steve Irons at Starr's office in Washington, telling him I was prepared to go public with the truth about the way the interviews were conducted. Further, I would recommend to Freeh that he withdraw FBI personnel from the OIC if that impression were allowed to go uncorrected. Irons called back later in the day to say he had conveyed my sentiments, they had gotten the message, and the wording of the press response had been revised. It was later, though, that I learned there was no conscious effort on the part of Starr's office to correct the already public impression, they simply revised the script in the event that they received any additional calls.

But again, the timing of the interviews on presidential philandering gave ammunition to those wishing to discredit Starr. I have no problem with the interviews, but they should have been conducted months if not years earlier, and by FBI personnel alone. This would have diluted any complaint about Starr's office being interested in Clinton's sexual exploits simply to embarrass him, and confirmed Whitewater as a legitimate criminal investigation rather than a political exercise.

If FBI agents are asked to sit in on an interview that is not going to be made a matter of record and not include such things as date, time, place, and more important, the identities of all present, they should decline to participate and leave the room. No testimony of value must be left out, even if it doesn't specifically fall within the parameters of the interview.

If the prosecutor disagrees and wants the agent present, it must be done with the approval of the special agent in charge. I never gave that authority; though I wasn't directly engaged in the investigation, I was responsible for administrative issues surrounding agents' assignments.

I am convinced that the Whitewater investigation was delayed by the lack of the agents being permitted to conduct hard and fast investigations following their own investigative instincts that years of experience had honed. Investigations have rhythms of their own, and the success of an investigation is dependent upon being able to conduct those investigations with that rhythm in mind—conducting an interview at the time to gain maximum advantage, the sequence and tone of those interviews, where and how they are done. This is especially true with corruption investigations which must be conducted sharply, quietly, and expertly, and not be held hostage to decision making by consensus from inexperienced lawyers who had never conducted any investigations of any kind, much less politically charged corruption investigations. This impediment may have ultimately contributed to the staggering finish of a once-promising investigation.

In his book *Arkansas Mischief: The Birth of a National Scandal,* Jim McDougal observed that when talking about Whitewater there was no need to exaggerate: "It's a good story, as large and misunderstood as the state of Arkansas." I think McDougal got it right, for it is a good story that doesn't need embellishing, but I'm not certain the final version has been told yet.

I believe the impact of Whitewater on Arkansas has been mixed overall. Certainly the unrelenting spotlight, usually in a negative vein, did nothing to help the Arkansas view of itself. Where perhaps some in Arkansas hoped Clinton's election would bring respect and much-needed revenue for the state, it really resulted in the state wishing that electoral victory never occurred and looking for any distraction to avoid the inevitable ridicule, a ridicule I began to resent as fervently as any native.

To a large degree, Whitewater was about corruption and, combined with the investigations started by my office, had given cause for the average Arkansan to think even less of himself and the perception the world has of their state. The OIC needed to have maintained a narrow focus, completed its business as soon as possible, and simply quit the state. The fact that an individual is considered morally repugnant does not provide a basis for a criminal investigation.

A FEELING OF PARANOIA surrounded the OIC, a siege mentality. On one occasion Steve Irons, who came into my office once or twice virtually every day while he was assigned to Starr's office, asked to come by my house. When he arrived there, he asked if I thought his phone might be tapped. He was hearing his telephone briefly ring at about the same time each evening, as did mine, without anyone being on the line. I explained I had called the telephone company and they said it was a natural occurrence caused by power surges or something of the like. But it concerned me that an agent assigned to the OIC had gotten to the point he thought someone from the White House was tapping his telephone. In the Whitewater investigation it was the hunters who were in the bunkers and the hunted who walked around in the spotlight—a complete role reversal.

There are consequences for the continued systemic corruption that was evident in Arkansas: cynicism toward the political process and a mistrust of public officials. The feeling of disenfranchisement evolves into hopelessness. The corruption investigations of my office, as well as those of the Office of the Independent Counsel, gave some hope to those looking forward to a better day. Most politicians and public servants are hard-working, decent people who simply wish to make life better for those who are less able to care for themselves. And many in Arkansas appreciated there being an FBI and an OIC to ensure that the corrupt few were not allowed to continue their ways with impunity.

I received telephone calls thanking me for taking on corruption, and audiences I spoke before said they were glad the FBI was looking after the interests of the people of Arkansas. The people appreciated Ken Starr as well. One night Starr arrived in Little Rock on a late flight. Seated near the back, as was his practice, he was one of the last passengers to exit, but when he got off the plane he found a large number of the passengers waiting for him, applauding him as he walked through their midst. Clearly, Starr was not the reviled figure his opponents characterized him to be.

Since retirement, I have visited with Starr once, while he was still at the OIC. Later, I wrote him a brief note when I read an article about his teaching in an inner-city school in Washington. I was teaching a class at a local high school in Virginia, and I invited him to visit with my students. Another time I called his law office in Washington and left a message, as I had just returned from Arkansas and had some news that I thought would interest him. It seems that the independent counsel's office was returning original documents seized during the Whitewater investigation to their owners, but with the lawyers' notes, observations, and comments still attached. I did not know Starr's successor, Robert Ray, but decided to call Starr so he could advise his old office to clean up documents before they were returned. However, neither the note nor the phone call was answered or even acknowledged. It must have been something I said.

In March of 2002, Independent Counsel Robert Ray issued two final reports that brought a much-needed sense of closure to the whole Whitewater affair. On March 6, he issued a report on the Monica Lewinsky matter, followed by the final Whitewater report on March 20. Both reports reflected the prosecutorial timidity that characterized the whole Whitewater investigation. Ray claimed to have had enough information to indict Clinton for perjury and obstruction of justice and obtain a conviction in the Lewinsky matter but declined to do so, noting that Clinton had finally told the truth about the affair. He concluded that Clinton had been punished in other ways, citing the $850,000 paid to settle the Paula Jones sexual harassment lawsuit, his contempt of court citation, the fine of $25,000, and $90,000 in attorney fees he had to reimburse in that case. Further, he cited the final fine of $25,000 and suspension of Clinton's law license in Arkansas. He may have cited those as examples of how Clinton had been punished, but if there was any punishment, it wasn't thanks to the independent counsel.

It's interesting that the most significant punishment in the whole saga was meted out by two female natives of Arkansas. It was Judge Susan Webber-Wright who imposed the fines in the Paula Jones case, and it was Marie Miller, acting on behalf of the Arkansas Bar Association, that caused Clinton to pay the final $25,000 and lose his law license. It was not Ray who imposed the conditions that led to Clinton accepting those sanctions, but Marie Miller, who stood up to David Kendall, Clinton's Washington-based lawyer, and laid down the marker that Clinton would accept those conditions or have the case presented to the Arkansas Bar with a parade of witnesses that would once again serve to remind all of Clinton's past misbehavior. Ray, who was exploring a run for a Senate seat in New Jersey even as he was completing the final reports, should be ashamed to claim credit for causing Clinton to lose his law license.

Then the final Whitewater report was released. Ray claimed that both Bill and Hillary Clinton made "factually inaccurate" statements during the Whitewater investigation, but that there was insufficient evidence to indict them. The lack of resolve by the prosecution was glaringly apparent. Indeed, his report is almost contradictory at times. He noted that, "Although there was sufficient evidence to establish that some of the statements given by both the president and the first lady during official investigations were factually inaccurate, there was insufficient available evidence to establish beyond a reasonable doubt that the president and Mrs. Clinton knowingly gave false statements, committed perjury or otherwise obstructed investigations."

I'm not sure a signed confession by both Clintons would have provided Ray with sufficient backbone to proceed with a prosecution.

The response, tepid as it was (the *Washington Post*, which had trumpeted the whole Whitewater affair years before with front-page stories, placed the story of the Ray report on page five), was predictable. James Carville, in a letter to the *Post*, accused the paper of showing deference to Kenneth Starr, noting that "it was Mr. Starr's written opinion for the D.C. Circuit Court in 1987 [that] overturned a million-dollar libel verdict against the *Post*."

"Apparently, we are to believe that the ruling on behalf of the *Post* has nothing to do with the newspaper's eagerness to agree," Carville wrote, and added, "Though loyalty is a wonderful virtue, it should have its limits—especially when it collides with other ethical obligations." That advice Carville is willing to ignore in his blind loyalty to Clinton over the course of the Whitewater matter.

But Whitewater was, mercifully, over at last. The final report on the Clinton presidency is yet to be written, as new revelations continue to seep into the public domain. There were only losers as far as those directly involved in the investigation, but there were some winners here and there. The media fed off Whitewater for years, writers wrote books, pundits pontificated, and new careers began based on participants' proximity to the Clinton White House or degree of opposition to the president and his escapades. Whitewater joined Watergate in the lexicon of political history, but, like Watergate, it was much more of an issue inside the Beltway than it ever was in Hannibal, Missouri, or Calhoun, Louisiana. After all the years, after all the money, after all the acrimony, Whitewater died with barely a whimper.

CHAPTER 21

INTO THE FIRE

". . . replete with inaccuracies . . ."
I.C. Smith, in a memorandum to the
FBI's Office of Professional Responsibility describing a
signed statement prepared by an agent of that office

This is a chapter I never intended to write in a book I had never intended to write at the time of my retirement. However, after having given a great deal of thought to the whole matter, I decided I had no choice for two reasons. First, I had undertaken to recount my career with absolute candor. Not to include this chapter would not be true to that goal, even if the candor reflected unfavorably on me. Further, I knew that there were people who would probably attempt to discredit me for my candor; indeed, it started within weeks after I retired.

Though I was reluctant to have any ceremony to mark my retirement on July 31, 1998, I was persuaded that I should have a retirement dinner. So on August 28 about 175 people assembled for the festivities, including a cross-section of the community. I received awards from law enforcement agencies, the Arkansas Martin Luther King Jr. Commission, personal acquaintances, and so forth, that all in all made for a delightful evening.

As is tradition with the FBI, there was also frivolity and parody. Just because I was retiring as the head of the FBI in Arkansas did not exempt me from my share of barbs, thrown principally by the master of ceremonies, Brian Marshall, an excellent FBI employee and a valued friend even today. At one point he noted that Louie Freeh would visit a field office and if the SAC was taller than he was, the SAC was gone. Retired agent Tom Ross theorized that Freeh was recreating the FBI in his own image . . . short! There was speculation about my retirement, including a passing reference to vouchers, "letters" written by Dan Harmon and Bill Clinton and in general, a typical, wonderfully irreverent evening.

A few days later I received a call from Doug Smith of the *Arkansas Times*. I had never met Smith but had read his columns and admired some of his work. He stated he had received information that my retirement had been forced and asked if I had a comment. When I asked for the source of his information, he said it came from someone who said he had heard a conversation at my retirement party saying my departure involved "financial malfeasance."

I denied the allegation vehemently, but he persisted and stated he had been told it involved my expense account. I told Smith I'd never had an expense account and that my vouchers received the same scrutiny at both the field office and at FBI headquarters as everybody else's. If I invited someone to lunch, which was quite often, I paid for it myself. I also told him that there had been no suggestion by Freeh or anyone else that I should retire; to the contrary, the director had expressed complete satisfaction with my administration of the office.

Smith was not satisfied and filed a Freedom of Information Act request. FBI headquarters responded that the conversations between Freeh and me were privileged and not subject to FOIA. Smith called again, asking that I sign a waiver allowing him access to my personnel file. I commented that he was, in effect, asking me to provide the knife to stab me with. He admitted that was the case. I told him I would sign the waiver if he would tell me the source of his information. He declined and I never heard from him again.

That conversation reminded me of a comment made by Ephram Zimbalist Jr. when he was asked to comment on all the scurrilous statements about J. Edgar Hoover made in the wake of his death. Zimbalist observed, "When the lion is dead, the rats come out." While I certainly did not consider myself a lion in the same league as Hoover, it was interesting that such attacks were occurring in the short time after I retired.

THIS TROUBLING YET TRUTHFUL STORY began one Saturday late in 1995 with a call at home from Charlie Smith, an assistant U.S. attorney in Ft. Smith and a prosecutor for whom I had high personal and professional regard. He is one of those rare individuals who is born to be a prosecutor and his hard-nosed approach was very much in line with my own views. Smith apologized for calling me on a Saturday but wanted to tell me about a call he'd gotten from an acquaintance who practiced law in Saline County, just outside Little Rock. This attorney said he had a client who had information about a plot to kill an FBI agent. I immediately called Agent Dan Wehr at the office, who assigned another agent to contact the attorney and his client. For the purposes of this story, I will simply refer to this other agent as "Agent Jones." I had been in the Little Rock office for only a few months then and didn't know Agent Jones well, but he had a reputation as an experienced, hard-working agent who specialized in fugitive and bank robbery investigations.

Jones called later in the day and said he wasn't going to pursue the matter any further because he did not like the individual who was the source of the information. I told Jones to meet me at the office. There Agent Jones told me he had met with the source, Ronnie Tyler, but didn't like Tyler and therefore wasn't going to proceed with his inquiry. I was flabbergasted. When somebody threatens to kill an FBI agent, I take it personally. I told Agent Jones that "we are going to kiss Tyler's ass if necessary" until we were able to learn whether or not we had a legitimate threat.

Jones had discovered that the targets of the plot were Special Agent Eddie Young in the Memphis office and an informant who worked for Young. Further, the plot involved a Shelby County, Tennessee, deputy sheriff, Billy Talley, who was being investigated by Young. I instructed Agent Jones to schedule a visit for me with Ronnie Tyler the following morning and to get a technical agent to accompany us just in case Tyler agreed to work with us. I hoped that Tyler would record conversations between himself and Talley that would incriminate Talley in the conspiracy.

The next morning Jones, the technical agent, and I drove to Tyler's residence on a back road outside of Benton in Saline County. There were eight or so pit bulls staked out around the perimeter of the house so that their circles of movement overlapped. There was no way to get to the house without going through an area accessible by at least two snarling dogs. But Tyler came out and led us through the guard dogs into the neatly kept house.

Ronnie Tyler was a large man, perhaps 6'4" tall and easily weighing 300 pounds. He had a bandanna around his head and was wearing jeans and heavy boots. He was gregarious, charismatic, and quite talkative. He had earned more than $60,000 as an informant for the Bureau of Alcohol, Tobacco, and Firearms in Memphis against a motorcycle gang, had entered the Witness Protection Program, then voluntarily exited the program. His mother had been killed and a daughter wounded in Garland, Texas, after he had left the program, presumably by those he had testified against. No one has ever been charged with those crimes.

He also told me about stealing the body of Elvis Presley. I later determined that Tyler had truly been involved in the theft of Presley's body. Tyler said he had been approached by Deputy Talley in the days after Presley's death about a scheme to steal the body. He said the Presley family wanted to bury Presley at Graceland but there was no city ordnance allowing for burials at private residences. So the family hatched a scheme to have the body stolen from its crypt in an unsecured cemetery, then have Talley swoop down on the culprits and save the body. This would demonstrate the vulnerability of the body and pressure Memphis into allowing the burial at Graceland. While I couldn't verify the entire plot, I did verify that Tyler had been in the midst of stealing the body. He had been "arrested" by Talley and the city had passed an ordinance that allowed the Presley family to remove the body from the cemetery and bury it at Graceland. Tyler received a nominal sentence of eight months for the attempted theft of a *corpus delicti*, a misdemeanor.

I was successful in persuading Tyler to cooperate with the FBI in exposing the plot to kill an agent. In return, I promised to try to have him readmitted to the Witness Protection Program, though I warned him I was not especially optimistic of success. He agreed to wear a recorder and the technical agent left the necessary equipment and instructions for operating it. Tyler and I executed the proper authorizations, and I left feeling that at least we had a chance to find out for sure if there was a plot to kill Agent Young. As we were leaving the house, Tyler "embraced" me but in reality, used the occasion to shake me down to see if I was wearing any recording devices. I wasn't.

Initial results were successful in incriminating Talley, who wanted Tyler to kill Agent Young for him. A problem for us was that to make the case in court, we wanted Tyler to turn over the weapon he was supposed to use to kill Young. But as a convicted felon, Tyler couldn't possess a weapon. So I briefed Paula Casey and Michael Johnson in the U.S. attorney's office and discussed what approvals were necessary for Tyler to transport a gun to Tennessee to prove Talley's guilt.

On February 8, 1996, Talley was arrested for his involvement in the plot to kill Young, followed by an indictment on February 20. I was pleased at how quickly the AUSA in Memphis, Fred Godwin, had moved on the investigation and the obvious personal interest he had in the welfare of Eddie Young. On April 15, Agent Jones told me that the ATF had a search warrant for Tyler's residence and that he had been asked to accompany the search party. I was taken aback by the news, though it was a poorly kept secret that Tyler was being investigated by the ATF. Bill Buford, the resident agent for ATF in Little Rock, knew Tyler was cooperating with the FBI in investigating a plot to kill an FBI agent, and I was disappointed that he would take steps that could jeopardize any future prosecution. How eager would our star witness be to help us if other law enforcement agencies were arresting him?

After consulting with Dan Wehr, the acting supervisor; John Kelley, the chief counsel for the office; and Temple, I concluded that we would "play it straight" and not intervene. If Tyler was caught with weapons, we'd have to overcome that problem in a trial. At least we had the recordings. I didn't want to give even the appearance that the FBI would intervene in an ATF investigation, despite the fact that the way they were going about it could destroy our credibility with our witness. I told Agent Jones to accompany the search team to Tyler's house and report back to me.

It was only later I learned that Jones, who was also aware of the ATF investigation of Tyler, had already asked to accompany the search team if and when it went. Both Agent Jones and I had repeatedly asked Tyler to "stay out of trouble" and I felt certain he, too, was aware of the ATF investigation, as was everybody else in the neighborhood.

Later in the morning, Jones reported back to me that the search team had found a single pistol in Tyler's residence, but that Tyler claimed it belonged to his wife, Sherry. I assumed Tyler would be charged with possessing a weapon, though given the past violence directed at his family I thought he could make a pretty good case that his family needed it for their protection.

On August 21, 1996, I hosted a meeting between Godwin, the AUSA in Memphis, and Tyler's attorney, Mark Hampton. Hampton had a reputation as a strong advocate for his clients but had not engaged in personal attacks on law enforcement personnel as was increasingly becoming an accepted tactic with criminal defense attorneys.

The two arrived in my office in mid-afternoon with Tyler in tow to negotiate the terms of Tyler's testimony in Talley's trial. But Tyler continued to interrupt the conversation, so I took him into my office while Hampton and Godwin continued their negotiations. Once in my office, Tyler and I resumed our talk. At one point he commented that he would not have cooperated if I had not intervened that Sunday morning. He also provided further details of the death of his mother—shot in cold blood in her own house—and the wounding of his daughter in Garland, Texas, and noted there was little progress being made in the investigation. He said the Garland police were having difficulty since it appeared the suspects were from out of state. I told him I would see what I could do.

After the meeting, I called the case detective at the Garland Police Department. He admitted there were out of-state leads that needed to be investigated but the Garland police did not have the resources. I sensed some reluctance on his part to get the FBI involved, so I raised the possibility that the FBI could assist him with assurances that they would not take over the case. Then I called the Dallas FBI office, explained the matter to an assistant special agent in charge, and asked them to help the Garland police without taking over the operation. They readily agreed and a joint investigative effort commenced.

In December 1996, Talley's trial began in Memphis. Tyler's recordings made him a compelling witness; Tally was convicted and sentenced to a term of fourteen years. I felt a measure of relief, but I had also been pushing for the indictment of Mark Saripkin, Talley's attorney at the time Tyler made his covert recordings. Saripkin was certainly aware of the plot to kill Young, if not directly involved, and had not reported the threat to anyone.

In December of that year I learned that Ronnie Tyler had other criminal interests, one of which, through a strange and disappointing chain of events, led to a direct and unprecedented assault on my integrity.

Bill Hardin, who supervised the White Collar Crimes Squad, notified me that a private investigator and retired agent, Ray Sorrows, was working an insurance fraud case and had been told that the FBI was covering up for the person under investigation. I immediately arranged a meeting with Sorrows. He explained that the investigation involved Ronnie Tyler, a Saline County attorney, Tyler's wife, and "Jenny Johnson" (not her true name) who had been living with the Tylers' son at their residence.

When I assured Sorrows that I was not protecting anyone, he insisted that he had been told by Bill Buford of the ATF that the FBI, specifically Agent Jones, had warned Tyler in advance of the search warrant that had been served months before. I was surprised that Buford would resort to such unprofessional conduct. I had fully cooperated with him, referred investigations to him, volunteered FBI personnel to assist him in a charitable golf tournament for a slain ATF agent, and made every effort to treat him as an equal, though he was nowhere near the same rank I was.

But I also knew Buford harbored resentments toward the FBI for taking over the Waco investigation, where he had been wounded, and for that reason I had tread lightly when dealing with his office. I told Sorrows I did not believe the FBI had tipped off Tyler about the ATF warrant and that the FBI would fully investigate potential fraud by wire violations. I immediately gave instructions to initiate such an investigation and pursued it aggressively, despite Tyler's help to the FBI in the Eddie Young matter. Some preliminary work was done on the case, but due to the press of business on the White Collar Crimes Squad, and the paucity of personnel to conduct investigations because of the Whitewater drain and the holidays, no actual interviews were conducted until after the first of the year.

On January 15, 1997, the FBI's Office of Professional Responsibility notified me that Agent Jones was the object of an OPR inquiry for having compromised the ATF search warrant against Ronnie Tyler. I was not to notify Agent Jones of the inquiry. I was not told if the inquiry was criminal or administrative, but learned that it was being led by the Department of Justice's Public Integrity Section. After three weeks without any action, I contacted OPR and expressed my personal interest in a prompt investigation, especially given the serious nature of the charges. On February 3 an OPR investigator advised he would be in Little Rock the next day to conduct interviews with the ATF and the ATF informant, Jenny Johnson. When the investigator arrived, I was struck by the hostility of his questions and had the uneasy feeling that I was the object of his investigation. But I dismissed that as simply a matter of personality (or the absence of personality) and told the investigator that I would do anything I could to ensure a prompt and thorough investigation.

I was then allowed to advise Agent Jones that he was the object of a criminal inquiry. He consulted an attorney but maintained that he had not compromised the investigation. I believed him. But I also began to accumulate further facts. I learned that the ATF had made their complaint to Michael Johnson, who then told Paula Casey of the allegations.

He recommended the information be referred to the Department of Justice. Johnson, who had considerable sway with Casey, got his way. I was also told that Johnson had also personally contacted the Public Integrity Section of DOJ and written the referral. I assumed he had called the head of Public Integrity, Lee Radek. Also, he had told the OPR investigator that in his opinion Agent Jones would not have compromised the investigation without the approval of "someone higher up." Clearly this meant me. There was no squad supervisor in place at the time of the search and with my assistant, Bill Temple, not directly involved, I was the only "higher up" left.

I found Johnson's opinion appalling. This was a criminal investigation where information must be restricted to sound facts, not speculation and opinion. I thought of the confrontation I had with Johnson the previous December about the Dan Harmon case where at the last moment he had refused to issue search warrants for attorneys in Saline County. I knew he still held a grudge against me for questioning his decision. (This was verified the next year when he raised the incident with inspectors in the office.)

I told Agent Jones that he should not, under any circumstances, discuss the fact he was the object of an ongoing investigation with anyone and that I was determined to support him with all my effort. I specifically advised him to not discuss the matter with the U.S. attorney's office and Michael Johnson in particular, since Johnson had made the formal complaint against him. However, I later learned that he had discussed the matter with Johnson anyway. My first impulse was to take administrative action as he had deliberately ignored a direct order, but noting the distress he appeared to be under, I didn't take any action that would appear to be piling on. This was another case where I should have followed my basic instincts.

I also learned that the search warrant had been signed by a U.S. magistrate on Friday, April 12, though it wasn't served until about three days later. This led to the conclusion that the ATF did not want to work on Friday afternoons or weekends. I could not imagine sitting on a search warrant that long without compelling investigative reasons. Weekends are in fact advantageous times to execute search warrants. Criminals know that federal law enforcement agencies have significantly reduced staffs on weekends and the element of surprise is greatly enhanced by weekend operations.

On February 17, the owner of a pawn shop in Saline County was interviewed about Tyler's insurance fraud scheme. He provided an extensive overview of Tyler and his family, admitting he knew about the allegations of accidents being staged in order to make false insurance claims. He related how in early 1995 Jenny Johnson said she had been involved in a staged accident in exchange for some of the insurance settlement but had never been paid. He described her as a "piece of sh—."

There was more. The pawn shop owner said he was in Memphis when Tyler and someone else had committed a murder. He also told how he had finally discussed Tyler with the police chief in Benton, Carthel Watters, after he had decided to evict Tyler from a rental house the pawn shop owner owned. Watters had told him to not evict Tyler as they were attempting to "get" Tyler.

While in Washington on February 27, 1997, I provided a sworn statement to the OPR agent and was again struck by his hostility. I attempted to answer all his questions as plainly as possible, but it became obvious to me that he was not interested in conducting an interview so much as an interrogation. He accused me of opening the insurance fraud investigation in order to discredit and "get back" at Jenny Johnson for reporting that Agent Jones had compromised the ATF search warrant. I explained that the investigation had been opened before I even knew the identity of the ATF informant, and cited specific documents and conversations that supported my recollection.

But he persisted along his accusatory lines until finally the deputy assistant director of OPR, David Reis, told him I had explained the sequence of events several times and he was satisfied with my answers. The interview finally concluded with the promise of having the statement to me in Little Rock the next few days for review and approval. In the FBI's system of conducting signed statements, the interviewing agents draft statements for those being interviewed and then submit them for corrections. I had always considered the statement, when I gave them, as "mine," not theirs, and had told anyone I had taken signed statements from that they should exercise complete editing rights when approving them.

By the next week no statement had arrived for my review. Finally, on March 17, after I made several inquiries, I received a fax of the draft copy. I was appalled at what I read. It was filled with inaccuracies, some of which even changed the meaning of the statements, i.e. ". . . learned of a plan to murder a LRD (Little Rock Division) FBI agent . . . ," and by omission of facts, failed to convey the true sense of what I had said. I got out my red pen, made numerous corrections, deletions, and additions and faxed the statement back the following morning, having increased concern for both the competency and objectivity of the OPR agent.

Meanwhile, the investigation continued into the insurance fraud allegations. On March 4, an inmate at a federal prison provided information on the activities of Tyler and his family. He claimed to know of two staged accidents, the role of an attorney in the area, and the part Jenny Johnson played in the scheme. He said Johnson was "no good" and that he had heard she was telling things to the police and "everybody." I thought it somewhat strange that even an inmate had knowledge of Johnson's cooperation with law enforcement.

Jenny Johnson was interviewed by an FBI agent on March 12, with an ATF agent accompanying them for part of the time (he left before the interview was over). Johnson painted a picture of a dominating Ronnie Tyler who ruled his family with threats, intimidation, and physical acts. But she admitted she had participated in an insurance fraud scheme, though she claimed she was pressured into it. She also said she had been promised half of the insurance settlement but had not been given any of it. She further claimed to have seen guns in the house and described the large safe where Tyler routinely kept numerous guns.

Other issues relating to the investigation continued roiling along. On March 10, attorney Mark Hampton advised me he had been contacted by the OPR agent who had not been honest with him. The agent, knowing Hampton had represented Ronnie Tyler in the past, asked if he could interview Tyler. He said he needed to talk to Tyler regarding allegations that an FBI agent had done something improper in an unrelated case involving a search warrant in Oklahoma City. However, Tyler told Hampton the OPR agent had interviewed him about the ATF search warrant at his house in Arkansas, and even asked him to take a polygraph about it.

Hampton recontacted the OPR agent and told him that he had misrepresented his purpose for talking to Tyler. Tyler also commented that he thought Agent Jones was the "straightest" agent he had encountered. The OPR agent replied that he had independent information indicating wrongdoing by Agent Jones. He insisted that "obviously" Tyler had more weapons in his house than had been found, and even opined that Agent Jones had told Tyler to leave one gun in the house to make the search look good. Hampton told me he felt the OPR agent had misled him in two areas: the purpose of the interview and the fact it was a criminal inquiry, not administrative. When I later raised the issue with the OPR agent, he told me he saw nothing wrong in not telling Hampton of his true intentions. I wondered whatever happened to the personal and professional integrity I had always expected of FBI personnel. By this time, I had developed a very real uneasiness about both the personality and character of the OPR agent, an uneasiness, as facts later determined, that was well-founded.

The facts about the OPR agent's obvious bias and reprehensible behavior were promptly provided to Reis in OPR on March 18 but, of course, the agent was not removed from the investigation. The next day I also forwarded copies of several interviews conducted by FBI personnel along with other information that indicated, according to the ATF agent who sat in on part of the Johnson interview, that the ATF Task Force itself had compromised the search. He said the Task Force had been observed by a member of Tyler's family videotaping the residence in the days leading up to the search. I added that Jenny Johnson's cooperation with the ATF was well known—even by federal prisoners—and that since Johnson didn't have a telephone, the ATF had to use a third party's telephone to contact her. That was an arrangement that virtually guaranteed her relationship with the ATF would be revealed.

I also pointed out that on March 18 Paula Casey had said she and Michael supported Agent Jones and she did not believe he had provided advance knowledge of the search. But she also expressed concern that the insurance fraud investigation would appear to be retaliation against Johnson for giving information to the ATF. I responded (again!) that the investigation had been opened before the FBI knew Jenny Johnson was the ATF informant. The target of the insurance investigation was not Johnson but the attorney and a doctor who may have been involved. I also added that Johnson had admitted her involvement and would testify against the attorney.

But after further discussions with Michael Johnson, I agreed to transfer the investigation to the postal inspectors, gave them copies of all investigation that had been conducted, and personally requested that the matter be investigated aggressively, regardless of where it led. I can't speak to the nature of the investigation, or even if it was investigated at all, but I can state that the investigation has never been pursued by the USA's office. In retrospect, I am not surprised.

The rumors about Agent Jones continued. A police chief in another area of Arkansas called me to say that Chief Watters and an ATF agent claimed, to him, the FBI was covering up for Tyler, who had just moved to the area, and specifically mentioned Agent Jones. I assured the chief that wasn't the case and that he knew it wasn't in my character. I filled him in about Tyler, from the death of his mother to the theft of Elvis, and promised him I was at his service if he needed help investigating Tyler. But once again, I was distressed at the continuing lack of professionalism being displayed by the ATF and Watters, who was a career law enforcement officer and graduate of the FBI's National Academy; his lack of conviction to enforcing the law had been displayed when he ignored the activities of Dan Harmon in his own area.

In the months after Talley's conviction in Memphis, I had approved the recommendation of a cash bonus for Agent Jones for his work on the investigation. I had mixed feelings about cash awards to employees for simply doing their jobs, especially for the Senior Executive Service of which I was a member, but had gone along with the practice. During an all-employees conference I presented Jones with a substantial cash award and made laudatory remarks for his work.

But the investigation continued to drag along through the spring and summer and into the fall. Then I received word from OPR that Agent Jones would have to take a polygraph. On October 22, I forwarded a comprehensive memorandum to OPR reminding them that their initial communication in January had not indicated that the inquiry was a criminal inquiry, or that the DOJ's Public Integrity Section was heading the investigation. I described how my statement provided by the OPR agent had been ". . . replete with inaccuracies . . ." and the delay in providing the statement for my review was ". . . indicative of how this investigation has been handled." I reviewed the matter of the OPR agent having misled Mark Hampton. I outlined how, at the request of OPR, copies of all telephone calls from the Little Rock FBI office for the period of April 1–20 had been provided to OPR to ascertain if there were any calls to Tyler's residence. There were none.

I observed that a polygraph couldn't be used in a criminal prosecution. Agent Jones had originally agreed to take a polygraph, but once he had learned that his was a criminal investigation, he declined on the advice of counsel. I related how, when discussing the issue with the OPR agent, he admitted that Public Integrity had to give permission to polygraph Agent Jones but he wasn't allowed to provide them with the results. I found that laughable. I noted that the OPR agent had admitted that Public Integrity had refused to close the criminal investigation though, in the words of the OPR agent, there was "insufficient evidence" to proceed. Such decisions would have been made by Lee Radek, the head of Public Integrity.

When interviewed by the OPR agent, Ronnie Tyler denied that anyone tipped him off and presumably he had testified to that when he was subpoenaed before the grand jury. I make that assumption based on the fact there have been no criminal indictments in the matter.

Agent Jones took a polygraph and returned to the office saying he had been told he had shown deception. Somehow I wasn't surprised. He was in a state of high stress and preoccupied with the prospect of losing his job. I told him that he couldn't be fired for telling the truth and that I would continue to support him. He took a second polygraph and again returned to Little Rock stating they claimed he had shown deception when asked if he had compromised the ATF search warrant. But the investigation continued to linger with no prospects of it being resolved as we went into 1998.

I had however, begun to view the role of Public Integrity in the investigation with increased concern. I had written the critical memorandum regarding the CAMPCON investigation to Freeh on August 4, 1997, with full expectations that its contents, if not the actual memorandum itself, would be made available to Radek. I had initially thought perhaps the unwillingness of Public Integrity to simply close the investigation of Agent Jones, given the lack of a credible basis to continue the effort, was simply another example of the well-documented inertia that characterized decision-making in Public Integrity.

I KNEW THAT THE Department of Justice didn't treat allegations of misconduct against FBI personnel the same way as allegations against members of the United States attorneys' offices. It increasingly became evident to many of us that it was "payback" time as far as the DOJ was concerned—payback for the years of independence the FBI had enjoyed from an increasingly politicized department. But in recent years, the FBI, due in part to its own making, had lost control of its ability to investigate and discipline its own personnel without DOJ interference. I based my observation of inequity between the way allegations of misconduct were pursued between FBI and USA personnel on my own personal experience.

In latter January 1997 an FBI agent who had been at the USA's office in Little Rock said one of the assistant United States attorneys wanted to discuss something with me. I called this attorney and offered to come to his office, but he insisted on meeting in private at the FBI. This was no surprise; other AUSAs had told me Paula Casey and Michael Johnson did not like them to talk to me outside their presence and made their displeasure known to those who did. We made plans for a meeting to take place on Tuesday, January 30.

That morning the AUSA came into my office and I closed the door to ensure the conversation was private. In the next few minutes this person, not once, not twice, but three times made specific and detailed allegations of misconduct against a senior member of the USA's office. If accurate, they were serious allegations that went to the very heart of the credibility of the criminal justice system. In this case, the defendant was a prominent fixture in the Little Rock area who directly benefited from the misconduct.

The AUSA indicated that there was no confidence in raising the issue with Casey. The attorney also commented that there were several other members of the USA's office who were willing to discuss their concerns with the conduct of the office in Little Rock, but only if they were asked. I thanked the AUSA for his confidence in me and assured him the matter would be handled confidentially. I was all too aware that Johnson, in particular, could be vindictive toward subordinates.

I was on the spot. A serious allegation had been made against a Department of Justice employee by a credible person and the allegation was against someone outside the FBI. I did not want the AUSA to be able to say later that he had brought information to the head of the FBI in Arkansas and it hadn't been acted upon. So I decided to call Howard Shapiro, the head of the FBI's Office of General Counsel, for advice.

When I explained what I'd just been told, Shapiro immediately recognized the importance of the situation and stated he would get back to me shortly. And he did. Later that morning he called to say he had discussed the matter with David Margolis at the Department of Justice. Based upon that conversation, I was instructed to prepare a memorandum to Shapiro's personal attention that he would provide to Margolis. I sent the memorandum to Shapiro the following day. I told Shapiro that I was prepared to discuss the information with Paula Casey, if that was the decision, but when he called back he said the decision had been made by Margolis that I should not discuss the information with Casey. That made me uncomfortable. While I knew such a conversation with Casey would be decidedly unpleasant, I did not wish to appear to have gone behind her back with allegations of misconduct by one of her employees.

However, based upon what I was told by members of the USA's office, the matter was never pursued. I was never contacted by anyone and could only take slight solace in the fact that I had done what I was supposed to do. Once again, the Department of Justice revealed itself to be a less-than-shining example of integrity. Their famous symbol of a blindfolded lady holding the scales of justice was just that, a symbol without any real meaning, especially when it came to investigating its own.

On October 3, Bill Buford from the ATF came to see me in my office. I had juggled him in between a conference call about the CAMPCON investigation and a scheduled meeting with Neal and Elizabeth Turner to further discuss the information they were providing about corruption in Arkansas. After we visited for a short time, Buford finally said he regretted ever talking to Michael Johnson about the allegations against Agent Jones and that he should have come directly to me. I agreed and appreciated his candor in coming forward. We shook hands and I hurried out of the office.

On July 2, 1998, I was in Virginia Beach for the birth of our first grandson, Ivan Hammje. Carla and I were joined by Leah, and with Amy and her husband, Jonathan Bennett, joining us, it was very much a family affair. With proud parents Lara and Eric on hand, ours was an enjoyable, albeit brief, visit where we had the whole family together at once, the first such gathering in some time. I realized how much I missed such occasions and increasingly, at that stage of my life and career, realized I should consider reordering my priorities.

CHAPTER 22

THE TEST

"To every thing there is a season,
and a time to every purpose under the heaven."
Ecclesiastes

In mid-June 1998 the director's office contacted me about scheduling a trip to Little Rock, the first such trip Louie Freeh had scheduled in the almost three years I had been in that assignment. When I had mentioned his not visiting my office to other SACs, they advised me to leave well enough alone; his aides told me he didn't think there were any management issues in Little Rock that needed his attention. Freeh had developed a reputation, not entirely deserved, that his arrival usually meant the departure of the SAC.

I told Freeh's office that the director was welcome any time, though on July 2 I intended to be in Virginia for the birth of my grandson. The caller laughed and said Freeh would certainly understand. We scheduled the visit for July 16. Before I left for Virginia, Agent Jones came to see me. The meeting also included the ASAC, Bill Temple, and Agent Jones's supervisor, Brent Mosher. Jones told us the Office of Professional Responsibility had ordered him to submit to a third interview and polygraph, and had literally threatened him with being fired. He pleaded for me to intervene and try to keep OPR from making him undergo a third interrogation and was concerned that he would lose his job. He was in the worst state of distress that I had seen him in the eighteen long months the investigation had been going on.

I told him I didn't think I could keep him from having to submit to a third interview, but that he should just continue to tell the truth that he had not tipped off Ronnie Tyler about the search warrant. Then Agent Jones made an admission. He said he might have unintentionally told Tyler of the impending search warrant.

I was momentarily speechless. I thought of all the times, literally hours, Agent Jones and I had been alone discussing the OPR investigation and conducting other business. He had never indicated that he may have inadvertently compromised the investigation. He had consistently said he didn't know about the search warrant until the day it was executed. Now, without further elaboration, Agent Jones admitted he had known about the warrant earlier. He pleaded with me to do something to keep him from taking a third polygraph. After a moment I finally responded, "I can't help you." After the meeting I sat looking out the window and felt betrayed. Agent Jones was at the mercy of the OPR investigators and I could only watch and wait. At least, I thought, his new version of the story would finally bring the investigation to an end. I was wrong.

On vacation, I spent a couple of days driving around Virginia's Northern Neck and Middle Peninsula. I was looking for a place to retire. Before departing for Virginia Beach, I had called the FBI retirement office and asked about advantageous dates to retire (dates at the end of pay periods, which simplified the paperwork), and also asked for a printout of my financial benefits should I retire in the next few months. While looking around Kinsale, Lottsburg, Tappahannock, White Stone, Urbanna, and Wicomico Church, I thought long about my future and decided that retirement sooner, as opposed to later, was in my best interest. I did not want my grandson and future grandchildren to grow up without Carla and me around them. The recent deaths and illnesses of several friends near my age had reminded me that life is quite fragile and I didn't want to work so long that I didn't have the opportunity to enjoy the family and pursue other interests. I had to decide the time.

Along with many of my colleagues, I had come to believe that the position of SAC offered great possibilities but was also fraught with danger. It seemed like there was a virtual open season on SACs, and if an SAC was accused of anything, there was little expectation of any support from headquarters. I had seen several of my friends retire embittered, and I was determined that it wasn't going to happen to me. I knew that in some respects I had been controversial in Arkansas, but there was no indication that Freeh was unhappy with my performance. Yet I also had long believed that controversy had its limits and that an SAC should have limitations on how long he remained in place, especially one that was an engine for change as I had been. I knew I had pushed my luck as I neared my three-year anniversary in Arkansas. I also knew that for the first time in my quarter-century career, I was beginning to lose the eagerness I had always felt when going to work. That change in attitude wasn't fair to the office or to me.

I had begun thinking seriously about retirement in June of that year after receiving an absolutely aggravating and inappropriate communication from the Terrorism Section. It had been authored by a petty junior bureaucrat, but approved by senior executive-level bureaucrats who had not been in a field office for ages. They were willing to embellish the threat posed by domestic terrorism groups for their own attempts at empire building. I had taken personal umbrage at the characterization of Arkansas as a hotbed of terrorist activity when at least three crime surveys did not support such a position. That communication demanded that I divert resources from public corruption, drugs, civil rights, and other programs into nonexistent domestic terrorism investigations just to justify paying for domestic terrorism resources that had been budgeted without field office input. I increasingly had the feeling there was no place in the FBI for me. I was simply tired.

When I returned from leave in Virginia, I got a call from John O'Connor, the deputy assistant director of OPR. He asked if I was willing to take a polygraph regarding the statement I had given in February 1997, more than eighteen months previous. This was concerning the ATF search warrant served on Ronnie Tyler and the insurance fraud investigation the OPR agent accused me of opening to "get back" at a suspect who had accused Agent Jones of compromising the ATF operation. I said I would if it would help to finally bring the whole matter to an end. O'Connor insisted that I come to Washington for a polygraph immediately, even after I told him that I was expecting Director Freeh in a couple days. I told him I wasn't traveling until after Freeh's visit, and that if he had a problem with that he was welcome to raise the matter with Freeh himself, something I knew he wouldn't do. But clearly he was unhappy. I wondered at the sudden urgency, given the protracted time the OPR investigation had been underway, but we finally agreed to my being in Washington on July 21.

Freeh arrived on July 16 as scheduled, and I met him at the airport. On the drive to the office, I discussed the ambitious schedule I had arranged for his visit, including his usual meeting with the street agents and office personnel without supervisors present, meetings with both United States attorneys, various law enforcement officials, and finally in late afternoon, travel back to the airport for a return flight to Washington.

My plans to tell Freeh I was contemplating retirement during our drive back to the airport went awry when he placed a call to his office en route to the airport and asked, "Do I still have a job?" I then learned that the *New York Times* had just published an article that detailed Freeh's disagreement with Attorney General Janet Reno in naming an independent counsel to handle the CAMPCON investigation. I shared Freeh's position on the issue and admired his willingness to take the stance he had taken, even though I knew there were those at FBI head-quarters that had not endorsed the idea early on and were likely still resisting the effort. Freeh essentially stayed on the telephone until he walked on board the aircraft. I never had the chance to tell him of my plans.

I ARRIVED AT O'CONNOR'S OFFICE the next Tuesday morning just before my 9:30 appointment. I had known O'Connor for several years. He had been an inspector and I had worked with him on an ASAC eval-uation project, though he had not completed his part of the assignment on time. He had been named as SAC for the Pittsburgh office, which was his hometown. That was a rare accomplishment for an employee to be able to return to his home area. But O'Connor had not been comfortable with the demands of field office decision-making and at the first opportunity had returned to headquarters as the deputy assistant director in the National Security Division, responsible for all terrorism investigations. It was a curious assignment given O'Connor's minimal background handling terrorism investigations, but he was among the very few SACs who were eager for a transfer to FBI headquarters. Most of us consciously avoided the place.

I had opposed him in at least two areas in the previous months. In the wake of the Oklahoma City bombing, some of the FBI hierarchy had argued for a lessening of the probable cause needed to conduct domestic terrorism investigations. O'Connor became a strong advocate of that position, though I knew he was only parroting the position of those above him. I was opposed, especially if a change in standards involved any impact on civil liberties.

I had also taken issue with O'Connor regarding the utilization of resources. In a conscious effort to try to prove that budgeted domestic terrorism resources were being fully used, field offices were increasingly being pressed to divert resources from other programs and spend money on terrorism. This was especially acute in Little Rock, where some agents were still being diverted to the Whitewater investigation. As badly as I needed more resources to handle the exploding demands of corruption investigations, I could not in good faith divert resources to train the sheriff of Chicot County, Arkansas, about biological warfare just because somebody had gotten the money approved and would look foolish if it didn't get spent. The whole ruse was inherently dishonest and, for me as a manager, irresponsible. O'Connor was not pleased by the stances I had taken.

But his performance as deputy assistant director for terrorism was apparently not satisfactory, for he was removed from that position and, incredibly, placed in the Office of Performance Review, where he was the deputy to Mike Defoe, who oversaw disciplinary matters involving FBI personnel.

When I arrived at O'Connor's office, it was as if I wasn't expected. I sat around in a waiting room until finally an OPR agent showed up and escorted me into the office. Then no one seemed to know where to find a form I had to sign before being polygraphed. As the agent left the room to look for the form, I made some attempts at small talk with O'Connor who seemed considerably ill at ease. Finally, a different OPR agent returned, I signed the form, and we walked over to another building to take the polygraph.

When we arrived at that building shortly before 10:00 AM, again it was as if my showing up was a surprise. After several minutes the OPR agent and the polygrapher came to the door and escorted me inside. I was surprised at the choice of a polygrapher. He had been my subordinate years before when I was ASAC in Miami, where he had been part of the entrenched palace guard that I believe caused many of the management problems there. He had a good reputation as a polygrapher but did nothing else in the office even though there were days, even weeks, when he would not personally conduct tests. During those days, the Miami office was being practically inundated with investigations of Colombian drug cartels, white-collar crime was rampant, bank robberies were increasing, and organized crime was on the rise. I had proposed that all the coordinators, those agents who were not assigned investigations, be assigned investigations to work when they weren't fulfilling their coordinator duties. That proposal met with considerable resistance. But by this time I wasn't thinking about the fact that the polygrapher might have a personal score to settle with me. I just wanted to get the thing done quickly so I would have time to go by the retirement office before the end of the day, then perhaps catch a late-night flight to Little Rock.

I took my first polygraph when I applied for a job with the Monroe Police Department and had taken several since, most recently when I gained access to the Aldrich Ames investigation. But I had increasing doubts about their usefulness. Reports during the Cold War claimed adversarial intelligence had some success in training their personnel to beat polygraphs. Drew Richards, a remarkable scientist and FBI agent with little regard for the polygraph, conducted research into electronic brain impulses as a possible replacement for the polygraph. And I knew there was a degree of operator subjectivity in the process. At least one FBI polygrapher had a well-deserved reputation for being extremely abusive and assuming anyone he polygraphed was guilty. By the time he was finally removed from those duties, he had done considerable damage to various reputations and careers.

The subjectivity of the polygraph was vividly demonstrated in the Wen Ho Lee case in December 1998. Lee was polygraphed by a polygrapher from Wackenhut, a contractor to the Department of Energy, and was asked about his involvement in espionage against the United States. According to the polygrapher, Lee's responses "disclosed sufficient physiological criteria to opine Mr. Lee was not deceptive." However, when the FBI reviewed the test, it was their opinion that Lee's responses indicated deception. Regardless of which one is correct, it is clear that the results are subject to interpretation. Regardless of my concerns about the polygraph, I knew I hadn't done anything wrong and just wanted to get the test and the interminable investigation over with.

The polygrapher had me sit in a hard, straight chair, a routine tactic as it is a goal of any interrogation, including polygraphs, to make the interviewee as uncomfortable as possible. As the session began, I realized the polygrapher was not well versed on the case. He read from the reports of the interview of Agent Jones as if it was the first time he had read them. Of course, I was not allowed to read them, though they contained allegations against me. The polygrapher told me that Agent Jones had told the OPR agents that he had called me the weekend before the search and I had told him to tip off Tyler. By this time, I was no longer surprised at anything. I asked the polygrapher if Agent Jones had passed a polygraph after making those statements. I was told he hadn't been polygraphed.

I knew then that I had been had. O'Connor had not been up front with me and I felt I had been set up. I said something to the effect, "Let me get this straight. You have an agent who has been under investigation for more than eighteen months for an incident that happened more than two years ago. He has been threatened with his job and failed two previous polygraphs. But when he finally makes a statement that someone wanted to hear—that I told him to tip off Tyler—it's accepted as the truth? He isn't polygraphed but yet I'm dragged in here to be put through this?" Basically the polygrapher admitted as such.

I was seething inwardly, not only at the polygrapher because of the callous manner I had been treated, but at myself as well because I had not given O'Connor's call sufficient thought, distracted as I was by other matters.

Then the interview began, though the machine was still off. As it turned out, the polygrapher admitted that Agent Jones had not actually said I had directed him to tip off Tyler. He had taken something I had said, something to the effect that I had instructed him to "do whatever you think is right" as meaning I wanted him to tell Tyler of the impending polygraph. I not only didn't remember making the statement, I didn't even recall the conversation. I told the polygrapher I had no recollection of receiving a telephone call but I could state emphatically that I never told Agent Jones to tell Tyler about the search.

The polygrapher persisted. He said, "Surely you would remember getting a call from Agent Jones, as that was the most important case in the office." That statement was laughable, if only to show how uninformed the polygrapher was about what was going on in Arkansas. I tried to explain that the alleged phone call took place more than two years before, and that Agent Jones called me at home rather frequently on matters of bank robberies, fugitives, terrorism, church fires, and other crimes that were investigated on weekends or after hours. I described Agent Jones as one who seemed uncomfortable around senior management and when talking to him, it wasn't always easy to follow his line of thought. Further, I pointed out that though it was an important case, there were a myriad of other investigations that required my attention and if judged by importance to the Little Rock Division, the ATF matter wasn't among the most important.

He kept insisting I should remember a conversation that Jones claimed had occurred years before. I told him I didn't recall it. Again I emphatically denied that I had instructed Agent Jones to tip off Tyler, but conceded that I couldn't attest to Agent Jones reading some meaning into something I had said. But I still questioned how "doing whatever you think is right" could be interpreted as me telling Jones to call Tyler about the search warrant.

I also told the polygrapher that my original written statement was correct, but he attempted to get me to state I had "forgotten" about Jones's phone call and all I had to do was to admit it and change the statement. I told him I was not going to admit to something that hadn't happened. As he continued his pathetic attempts to get me to admit something that was not the truth, I began to question how he managed to have such a good reputation as a polygrapher.

Finally the polygrapher said he couldn't conduct a polygraph if I said I "do not recall." This vein of conversation continued until early afternoon when, in exasperation, I finally said that if we could proceed, I would say that "Agent Jones did not call me." This satisfied the polygrapher and at long last we were ready to proceed.

By this time I was tired, I was hungry, I had to urinate, my throat was dry and irritated from sinus drainage—at one point I had asked for some water but the polygrapher had not responded and no water was forthcoming—and was, inwardly at least, absolutely seething. During the lengthy interview, I made up my mind that I just wanted to get the whole thing over with and that the July 31 date the retirement office had identified as a good time to retire was going to be the date I would use.

The polygrapher began to prepare me for the polygraph. After getting the apparatus hooked up, he pumped air into the straps similar to a blood pressure machine. But the device wouldn't work and while I remained strapped into the machine, he left the room to look for another one. After a few minutes he returned, installed the new part and proceeded with the polygraph. But the problems didn't end there. After a while the paper in the machine jammed, so again, while I stayed strapped into the chair, the polygrapher worked on the machine before we could start anew. I was becoming, if possible, even more incensed.

I was asked a series of test questions relating to my time in the FBI, etc., that were easy to answer and would provide a baseline for comparison with the questions of real interest. Then curiously, he asked me if I had ever falsified any FBI paperwork before the signed statement we were discussing. Then he asked about my receiving a telephone call from Agent Jones and my statement that Jones had taken to mean he had my authority tip off Tyler. At one point he cautioned me to remain still. I had been looking at my watch and trying to mentally calculate if I would have enough time to check out of the hotel and catch a flight to Little Rock that evening. Finally, the polygraph concluded.

I was unhooked from the apparatus and again sat in the hard straight chair I had been in for about three hours before the polygraph began. Then the polygrapher told me I had shown deception about those questions relating to the phone call from Agent Jones. But he said I had passed on those questions about having never falsified FBI paperwork during my career. I was simply incredulous at the whole process and of his claimed results.

I told him I couldn't explain the results even as he started to once again to tell how all I had to do was to say I had "made a mistake" or had "forgotten" about the call from Agent Jones. I told him again and again that I wasn't going to state something that had not occurred. I pointed out how incredulous it appeared the polygraph had indicated that in more than twenty-five years I had never falsified FBI paperwork, but showed deception on those matters involving Agent Jones. At one point he commented that when he had been told about the case, "I had hoped that you would pass the polygraph but deep down I knew you wouldn't." I found that statement indicative of not only his bias but the bias of the whole investigation. It was 3:00 PM by this time and as he walked me to the door, he said he was sorry it didn't work out. "No, you aren't sorry," I shot back, "for you can brag about getting a scalp. And as for me, my career is over." He didn't say anything further.

I walked outside and past the J. Edgar Hoover Building with no desire to enter it ever again. I had been issued a badge that morning that allowed me access to the building but I decided to return it from Little

Rock. It was too late to get a flight home that evening, and so I prepared for another night alone while in the employ of the FBI. But unlike all the previous, I knew it would be the last.

In his wonderful narration of the *Victory at Sea* series, Alexander Scourby quoted Ecclesiastes from the Bible: "To every thing there is a season, and a time to every purpose under the heaven." I had often wondered how and when I would know when I should retire. That evening, sitting alone in a hotel room in Washington D.C., I knew that it was the season. It was the time to go. I called Carla and told her what had happened. She was supportive, as usual.

I knew that I could fight the polygraph issue and win. But I didn't want to be further embittered and I knew that to be accused of failing a polygraph wasn't career-ending. Oliver "Buck" Revell in his memoir, *A G-Man's Journal,* talked about having been accused of failing a polygraph years before he retired, and I knew of at least one deputy assistant director in the National Security Division who had been promoted several times after he too had failed a polygraph. I also personally knew a street agent who was said to have failed a polygraph and had a distinguished career in the aftermath of that accusation.

But I also knew that to fight the accusations effectively I would have to destroy Agent Jones. And I wasn't willing to do that. I never received a single telephone call stating, or even inferring, that I should retire, a call that would have likely caused me to forego concern for Agent Jones and do battle with those who had accused me of wrongdoing. I viewed the whole episode as simply providing the incentive I needed to push me to retirement.

I was also convinced that there had been an inherent bias in the investigation from its inception and that Jones was never really the object of the OPR's interest. I thought the hostility of the OPR agent indicated the hostility that was increasingly evident for anyone of senior rank being interviewed. This was clearly demonstrated when three current and former OPR agents, all of whom worked with the agent responsible for the Agent Jones investigation, publicly complained about senior managers getting preferential treatment. Their complaint centered around disagreement with a decision made by Mike Defoe relating to disciplinary action against senior management personnel, including Louis Freeh, concerning the Ruby Ridge investigation. We have all had those above us make decisions we did not agree with—decision-making is not a democratic process. But short of criminality or unethical conduct, we have a responsibility to accept the decisions and not use them as a basis for airing personal prejudices.

The concerns I had during the ATF investigation came back to the forefront on August 23, 2002, in an article in the *Washington Post* concerning the Foreign Intelligence Surveillance Court and how the Department of Justice, under Attorney General John Ashcroft, had attempted to keep an unclassified opinion from being released to the public. After Ashcroft refused repeated requests signed by all seven members of the court to release the opinion, the court, in an unprecedented move and rebuke of Ashcroft himself, released it anyway.

I read the article with increasing amazement, which cited where the FBI had "supplied erroneous information to the court in more than 75 applications for search warrants and wiretaps, including one signed by then-FBI Director Louis J. Freeh." As I continued reading with both concern and dismay for the conduct of the FBI, I was even more amazed with what followed. The article noted that, "In one case, the FISA judges were so angered by inaccuracies in affidavits submitted by an FBI agent (OPR agent) that they barred him from ever appearing before the court."

After reading the article again, I thought back to how that same OPR agent had conducted himself in the inquiry involving Agent Jones and me. But I also thought back to how I had specifically advised the OPR agent's superiors of his conduct, not only for lying to Little Rock attorney Mark Hampton but further, how the signed statement he had prepared for me was "replete with inaccuracies." I reviewed the opinion itself, as released by the FISC, and, "One FBI agent was barred from appearing before the Court as a FISA affiant." Forbidding an FBI agent to appear before any court was unprecedented. The anger I had felt at the manner with which the OPR agent had handled my investigation returned, along with anger toward the FBI's Office of Professional Responsibility. I had specifically drawn their attention to the agent's deceit. Not only did the OPR ignore my complaints, they transferred the agent to another sensitive position within the FBI, where he himself was to be the object of an investigation by the Department of Justice. I hope he is investigated with a greater sense of fairness and accuracy than he used on others.

When I returned to Little Rock the next morning, Carla met me at the airport where we talked some more. Then I went into the office, dead tired, and called Bill Temple and later, Sandy Finch, my secretary, into my office and advised them of my decision. I then called an all-office conference and announced my retirement to everyone. I was not ready for the response. One employee ran from the meeting crying and others had tears in their eyes. Attempts on my part to offer a little levity into the meeting met with failure.

I called P.K. Holmes and Paula Casey. Casey showed up at the office with bottles of wine later that afternoon. I also placed calls to heads of other agencies and talked about retirement and all that we had accomplished. We had been a good and strong law enforcement team.

I had heard Freeh mention that he was going to be out of town that week so I didn't bother to advise him by telephone as was protocol. I sent a one-line letter to him, with a copy forwarded by facsimile, that has been said to be the shortest such retirement letter on record. It simply said, "I am retiring on July 31, 1998." There was nothing else that needed to be said. I also issued a one-line press release that essentially said the same thing. Then I went about conducting the duties of the office. By that time I was anxious for it to end. Suddenly I felt rejuvenated and thought of all the things I wished to do with my life, things that had long been placed on a back burner due to the demands of the job with the FBI.

I could look back on that quarter-century career with satisfaction. I had for the most part refused to compromise my personal beliefs and had been driven by a sense of doing the right thing regardless of the consequences. I knew I had been lucky to have been an SAC, a position

I had never really fought for. I thought a lot of the path I had taken from growing up with my grandparents in rural Louisiana to the great capitals of the world, having occupied positions of great trust and confidence along the way.

I also spent a lot of time talking and thinking about my time in Arkansas, where in many respect the lessons I had learned as a youth had been put to their severest test. I had no regrets for making corruption the highest priority and taking on the political elite in that beaten-down state. I had long considered corruption on par with espionage, but it wasn't the stealing of secrets and selling them for money or politicians using their positions to line their pockets that I considered the greatest crime. To me the greater crime was the betrayal of the public trust. This is perhaps something of an idealistic view, but one that had been instilled in me by grandparents who would have never imagined I would have the great experiences that I have. Someone needed to take on corruption in Arkansas and I landed there when it was the right season, the right time, to do so. But I also knew that I had left much undone. And from all reports, it remains undone. Since I retired, there hasn't been a single indictment of a public corruption case in Arkansas based on an investigation started after my retirement date.

Even as I made my decision to retire, the investigation that precipitated that decision continued. On July 5, Mark Saripkin, attorney for the convicted Sheriff Billy Talley, was finally charged with his role in the conspiracy to kill Eddie Young. I personally had a heated conversation with Fred Godwin, the AUSA in Memphis, about the failure to pursue the case in court and had begun to believe it was just as difficult to prosecute crooked lawyers in Tennessee as it was in Arkansas. In January 1999, Saripkin was convicted of obstruction of justice and once again, Ronnie Tyler provided testimony for the prosecution.

But incredibly, U.S. District Court Judge Julie Gibbons overturned the conviction. Saripkin finally received two years probation for lying to an FBI agent. In a later conversation, Godwin told me I had displayed more interest in investigating the plot to kill Agent Eddie Young than Young's own SAC. I could not imagine doing anything less than I had done.

On July 28, I traveled to Fayetteville to attend the Arkansas Sheriff's Association meeting. When I arrived, I was surprised to see Rob Daniels, an agent assigned to the Fayetteville Resident Agency. Daniels was an experienced agent who, along with being an attorney, had also been trained as a counselor for the FBI's Employee Assistance Program. This program offered counseling for employees who, because of any number of reasons, may be in need of counseling to ease them through a personal or professional crisis.

Daniels told me he was aware of what had happened in Washington and if I desired, was willing to offer the assistance of the EAP. I asked him how he had learned about the details of my polygraph, but he demurred. I didn't press the issue but I wasn't surprised, given the past history of the whole case, that such normally private information would be known to a wide range of people. I told him that while I appreciated his concerns, I didn't need EAP counseling. I explained that I had intended to retire anyway and the whole incident just gave me the impetus to do it. I did mention that I thought Agent Jones was very likely in need of assistance as he was obviously distressed and that I hoped he would reach out to him.

A retired FBI agent and valued friend who was aware of what had happened to me in Washington asked if I wished I had never gotten involved in the case involving Ronnie Tyler and the plot to kill Eddie Young. He said he thought I had probably saved Young's life. I told him I was not willing to claim credit for that. But I did think my intervention resulted in an individual being arrested and convicted who was fully determined and capable of killing Young. I added, "If I had to be cuffed around because of what I did, it was worth it."

On occasion I saw Agent Jones in the office. He usually turned away and would only mumble a greeting, if he said anything at all. I thought about calling him into the office to talk about the whole incident but decided to wait and see if he would come to see me. He never showed up. I felt sorry for him.

The ten days passed swiftly as I prepared to enter civilian life. When it was time to turn in my property—my revolver (I had steadfastly remained loyal to the revolver while most in the FBI had embraced automatics), credentials, and badge—it was the badge, that ancient symbol of authority and responsibility that I had carried for more than thirty years, that I found most difficult to turn loose. At last the final couple of days were upon me and I was receiving a steady flow of telephone calls from friends, both old and new, more than a hundred total, as the hours dwindled away.

On the last afternoon, as people in the office made their final good-byes and the telephone calls increased, I had little time to reflect on my career of the past and of the prospects for the future. As the hours slipped to minutes, I received telephone calls from two longtime friends, Ken Schiffer and Larry Torrence. While we were talking as it neared 5:00 PM, I kept seeing Dan Wehr and Jill Hill, two agents that I had great personal regard for, looking around my door then walking away when they saw me on the telephone. I thought it was rather thoughtful of them to stay around and walk me to the door on my last day in the office. Carla had made reservations at the venerable old Arlington Hotel in Hot Springs; we had planned to depart the office at 5:00 PM and by that time, it was several minutes past.

Finally, the last call was received and the last conversation ended. I was gathering my things one last time when Wehr and Hill showed up at the door again. It wasn't that they had remained behind to wish me well after all. They needed one last authorization that only I could handle. So I placed my signature on one last FBI document, they thanked me, wished me well again, and walked out. Suddenly I was alone in an empty office. I had turned in my revolver and a single bullet to the firearms instructor, there was no badge, no credentials, an empty in-box, and no more phone calls. There was nothing else to do but leave. I walked down the hall to the door, alone, let myself out, and walked out of the building as an FBI agent for the last time.

Carla was waiting.

CHAPTER 23

CAMPCON FALLOUT

*"The reason given to me was that
is the way the American political process works
and I was scandalized by that answer."*
Special Agent Daniel Wehr

I n mid July 1999, while standing among numerous boxes and in the
throes of a severe allergy attack, I got a phone call from Fred Ansell,
chief counsel for the Senate Committee on Governmental Affairs chaired
by Tennessee Senator Fred Thompson. Carla and I had just completed
our post-retirement move to Virginia, where mountains of still-packed
belongings and renovation plans for our turn-of-the-century farmhouse
had us feeling a little overwhelmed.

When I asked Ansell how he had located me since I'd had my new
phone less than a week, he said the FBI told him where I was. I hadn't
known the FBI was keeping up with my whereabouts. He wanted to talk
about my association with the CAMPCON investigation, particularly a
memorandum I had written to FBI Director Louis Freeh in August 1997.
I agreed to talk with Ansell with the understanding that I had no records
beyond personal calendars and any information would be based solely
on recollection of events I had seldom thought of since my retirement.

Before departing Little Rock, I'd heard that this particular memorandum had been obtained by congressional committees. My successor as
SAC in Little Rock, Charlie Prouty, had told me I could expect a call

from a committee member. I had written the memo to express my concern over the way the Department of Justice had mishandled the investigation of the campaign finance investigation, and that the FBI's efforts were constantly stymied by departmental attorneys.

The next call I received in Virginia was from Barbara Comstock, whom I knew from her work on the infamous White House Travel Office matter to be a tough, thorough, and fair interviewer. We talked for quite some time, and I tried to be as responsive as possible but was hampered by my lack of reference documents. She had a copy of my memorandum, though I got the impression it had been redacted, and my recollection of a memorandum written nearly two years before was somewhat vague.

I also received a call from Special Agent Jack Eckenrode of the CAMPCON Task Force, who asked for a telephone interview with DOJ attorneys. I made it clear to Eckenrode that the department should not expect me to provide any solace if they were seeking justification for their actions—actions I found deplorable. I also made it clear that I disagreed with Attorney General Janet Reno's handling of the investigation and opined that I increasingly found her an embarrassment to law enforcement. This was a decision I had arrived at after seeing how she had changed her own standard for the appointment of an independent counsel, her preoccupation with deadbeat dads when the FBI was increasingly faced with very real crimes, how she had tried to make random church burning's into a national conspiracy, etc. Eckenrode stated he did not think he would relay those sentiments to Michael Horowitz, the deputy assistant attorney general, who was a strong supporter of Reno and who had directed him to locate me. But we agreed to set the interview for June 17, 1999.

The call that day came from Jeff Lampinski, the FBI agent who had been assigned at first to head the Task Force, then demoted, then apparently reassumed the leadership role. He put me on a speaker phone and introduced various people including Horowitz, departmental attorney Julie Fagan, Eckenrode, and two or three others presumably from the department. I did not like the whole arrangement and the speaker phone was obviously to allow Horowitz to have multiple witnesses. I began to wish I had at least one witness or had placed a recorder on the phone.

I did my best to answer their questions as frankly and good-naturedly as possible, though I made it clear from the beginning that I was working on memory alone. At one point Horowitz somewhat innocently asked if I had any documents relating to the CAMPCON matter. I had to stifle a laugh. I'd already said I had no such records; if I'd said yes, I felt confident the CAMPCON Task Force would have moved with unusual efficiency to serve me with a subpoena, if not a search warrant. The question was an insult, asked not for information about the documents, but as a fishing expedition to try and discredit me by showing I had kept documents in violation of governmental rules. I didn't even have a copy of the memorandum.

Horowitz assured me that he was simply looking for the truth. I resisted the urge to say that if that was the case, it was a departure from the past. The questions were narrowly specific about the contents of the memorandum, and after a rather lengthy conversation, we concluded the interview.

Later I was contacted again by Ansell and asked if I would testify before the committee chaired by Senator Thompson. Three agents still with the FBI had also received subpoenas: Dan Wehr, who had worked for me in Little Rock, and Roberta Parker and Kevin Sheridan, who had been assigned to the investigation in Washington. I knew all three of the agents and respected their investigative talents. The CAMPCON investigation had only served to enhance their reputations in my view. I agreed to travel to Washington at my own expense to testify on events that I thought were well in my past.

On September 22, 1999, I drove to Fredericksburg and caught a commuter train into Washington with mixed feelings. I was enjoying my newfound anonymity, but I also determined that I would be completely truthful and candid, regardless of the fact that some of what I had to say would most assuredly be painful. I had no desire to publicly criticize either the FBI or the Justice Department.

When I entered the hearing room of the Senate Committee on Governmental Affairs, I noted there were not nearly as many spectators as there had been for the House Committee on Government Reform and Oversight when I testified about the Travel Office matter. A callousness had developed over the years of unending incidents by the administration and the ability for the public to be shocked, or even titillated by the White House had virtually disappeared. I had reviewed a heavily redacted version of my memorandum and had refrained from contacting Wehr, Parker, or Sheridan before the hearing. An FBI attorney attempted to warn me about my testimony. When I asked him if he was trying to censure my remarks, he hastily backed down and mumbled some statement about grand jury testimony. I didn't appreciate his attempt to control whatever I was going to say.

There were two surprising points to the testimony. First, Roberta Parker, one of the agents in Washington, testified about twenty-seven pages that were missing from a spiral notebook she had kept detailing conversations with different people over the course of the investigation (something only the most dedicated and disciplined agents did). I was simply astounded at the testimony. I had seen the notebook, which was omnipresent wherever she went. I had even wondered if, or what, she had written about me. But I also knew Parker was vulnerable and was saddened that she felt compelled to attend the hearing with a personal attorney. I felt absolutely confident that she was telling the truth and wondered at the sheer arrogance of someone removing critical pages from the notebook.

Then there was testimony I found more personal in nature. Senator Fred Thompson, whose presence both physically and intellectually filled the hearing room, began to discuss the results of staff interviews. He testified that Lee Radek of the Department of Justice Public Integrity Section, "apparently said that the problem here is that the FBI was always pushing the envelope and forcing the Department of Justice to restrain them so that the FBI could complain to higher authorities about Ms. Ingersoll." Laura Ingersoll was the principal DOJ attorney on the investigative Task Force.

"In other words, you were trying to set Ms. Ingersoll up." Thompson was looking squarely at me as he made the comments. He continued,

"Radek also said the Department of Justice allowed the FBI CAMPCON team to be more aggressive than normal precisely in order to appease them." Thompson further testified that Radek had stated, when "talking about the lack of action with regard to these destroyed documents [meaning the Trie documents] . . . Radek said he felt that the FBI was going off 'half-baked' and that there was 'no destruction that required immediate action.' I guess it was obstruction that didn't require immediate action.

"And that no important documents were being destroyed, and that he believed the agents investigating merely 'wanted to break down doors.'

"You just wanted to break down doors, you were trying to basically set things up so you can complain against Ms. Ingersoll. And he actually gave you more leeway than ordinary just because you were so rambunctious.

"Mr. Smith, what do you think of that?"

The transcript of the hearing does not indicate the pause in the proceedings that occurred. The audience, the senators, the media, all were awaiting my response. Again, I was taken aback at the sheer audacity of what I had heard. Finally I responded.

"To suggest that there was a nefarious plot on the part of the FBI to cause problems for Ms. Ingersoll is absolutely absurd. As far as the other, I would hate to think that anyone trying to investigate a complicated matter had more restraints than this one did. I just can't imagine trying to investigate a matter in that environment.

"If this was one where we really got a lot of leeway because we were making a lot of noise, I would hate to try to investigate one with less flexibility."

But my thoughts were primarily on the original statement by Thompson that the FBI conspired to make Ms. Ingersoll look bad. I returned to that matter. "But the first suggestion that you made is absolutely absurd, and frankly, I find it patently offensive."

It was only later that I learned that Radek and Ingersoll were sitting directly behind me in the audience. I had talked with Radek on several occasions but had never personally met him, nor talked with or met

Ingersoll. Had I known he was in the room, I would have addressed him directly with my comments.

Comments such as those attributed to Radek are the worst kind one can make. They weren't made directly to the accused and were a conscious effort to discredit someone he was unwilling to face directly. They were the words of a coward.

I was prepared to tell the committee of a conversation between Radek and me during the investigation that indicated the level of his personal courage.

One day he asked me to call United States Attorney Paula Casey and advise her that she would be recused on a couple of cases. I asked, "Why me?" and he responded, "I don't want her hollering at me!"

I called Casey and indeed, she "hollered" until I told her that I was just a messenger and that Radek had instructed me to make the call. She settled down after a while, made an uncomplimentary comment about Radek, and we terminated the call. I called Radek back to say I had delivered the message and placed a memorandum to a file recording the whole incident.

I began to view Radek's refusal to face Casey as an indication of his personal fortitude, and as I sat in the witness chair I could see why the CAMPCON investigation had not been pursued with a zeal deserving of the allegations. If he didn't have the courage to make a telephone call to a United States attorney, albeit one from the president's home state, how could he face up to the political appointees in key positions in the department itself?

Radek's comments to Senate staff members are simply irresponsible if not slanderous. If he thought he had sufficient information of a conspiracy by FBI personnel to make Laura Ingersoll look bad, he should have referred the matter to the Office of Professional Responsibility for a thorough review. But of course he didn't do that. Instead he attempted to engage in character assassination against those he did not have the courage to confront directly, tactics that had become very much a part of the Clinton administration.

Those of us that were testifying were asked by Senator Joseph

Lieberman "whether you have any evidence to present or whether anything was ever said by anybody at Justice to lead you to the conclusion that some of the judgments made here, on the applications for the search warrant, etc., were based on political considerations?"

I responded simply, "None."

Lieberman turned to Wehr, whose response was likely unexpected. He said "Well, I had discussions with Laura Laughlin [Wehr subsequently corrected his reference to "Laughlin" as meaning "Ingersoll"] at the campaign finance Task Force headquarters during the course of one of our joint meetings and I believe it was in May 1997, and I was concerned about the appearance of, based on information that had been presented, people were exchanging evidence, there was reason to believe that solicitations were made for campaign funds in the White House in the presence of the president and these were made by foreign contributors. And to me, that appeared to be a violation of several laws.

"And I was told by Laura Laughlin [Ingersoll] that we would not pursue any matter relating to the solicitation or payment of funds for access to the presidency."

Senator Lieberman then inquired, "Were reasons given?"

Wehr responded, "The reason given to me was that that is the way the American political process works and I was scandalized by that answer."

Lieberman, with that wonderfully mobile face, then responded, quietly, somewhat sadly and almost as if he were talking to himself, "Well, so were a lot of us."

A few other senators asked questions during the hearing. I found Senator Carl Levin's questions to be somewhat curious. He asked if Freeh had met with the agents assigned to the Task Force as I suggested, a valid question that I could not respond to directly, though Parker and Sheridan stated they had not met with Freeh, much to my disappointment. Then he entered into another area by quoting from my memorandum. Levin read, "But I am convinced that the team at the Department of Justice leading this investigation is, at best, simply not up to the task. Frankly"—here Levin interjected, "This is what I am interested in asking you about"—"I base this conclusion not only on the

CAMPCON matter, but other investigations Public Integrity has handled from their office due to recusals from the U.S. attorneys. The impression left is the emphasis is on how not to prosecute matters, not how to aggressively conduct investigations leading to prosecutions."

Levin continued. "So that before this particular set of events which we are describing and looking into, you had your own beliefs that the Department of Justice Public Integrity Section was not acting aggressively, is that fair?"

My response was, "And that would be based on specific examples, yes, sir."

Senator Levin asked, "Previous examples to these events?"

"Yes, sir."

"Were there a couple, two, three, four, five?"

"Yes, I would suspect somewhere around that number, the latter."

He persisted. "So, four or five examples? Give us an estimate. I am not trying to pin down a number precisely."

I answered, "I don't recall exactly how many cases that the department was handling because the U.S. attorney's tendency was to recuse virtually anything. . . . I recall a couple of investigations that this was occurring where I thought that the department seemed to be looking for ways to not investigate the matter as opposed to pursuing it aggressively."

I was prepared to provide examples as I thought clearly the questions were headed that way, but Levin suddenly changed direction.

One example I was ready with involved the Western District of Arkansas, where an accomplished FBI agent named Carroll Payne had obtained the conviction of a banking official. As part of a plea agreement, the official was to cooperate with the FBI in other related matters. One day I called Payne and instructed him to say to this banker, "Tell me about illegal campaign contributions made by the bank."

Payne contacted the former bank official, who stated that during the 1992 election he and his colleagues at the bank had all made contributions to the Clinton campaign, all of which were reimbursed by the bank, a clear violation of campaign finance laws.

Since U.S. Attorney Holmes had already told me he would recuse himself in any matters involving the president, I sent the information to FBI headquarters for coordination with Public Integrity. The response was not prompt, though there was a statute of limitations that required the matter be resolved quickly. Finally, the response came in the form of "twenty questions" that were clearly crafted to question the impact of what the former official had revealed about the administration. Payne immediately contacted the potential witness who not only reiterated his original statements but added that the practice had extended to the campaign of former Arkansas Senator Dale Bumpers as well.

This too was referred to Public Integrity, but the matter was never pursued; there was no indication that either the president or Senator Bumpers was aware of the practice. It would have been an easy case to pursue, with a witness who participated in the scheme and supporting documents from the bank itself, and could have sent a clear message to the Arkansas banking and business community that such practices were not to be taken lightly.

I came to regard the whole campaign finance matter as an assault on the political processes of this country. But as long as there are those who believe they have the right to govern, and that to govern they must win at any cost even if it means lying and cheating, the assault will continue. They assume the arrogant attitude that they know what's best for the American populace better than the people know for themselves. This is the attitude of the professional politician who never made a pretense of working at anything else, never made a mortgage payment, never put gasoline in his own cars, never mowed his own lawn, and never drove his own kids to soccer practice. This was the attitude of the Clinton administration and the story behind the campaign finance scandal.

I RETURNED HOME and almost immediately the phone began to ring. One call came from Fred Ansell of the Senate staff. He asked if he could give out my number to the media, as he was being asked for it. I told Ansell that he could, though I did not have a political agenda and didn't want to make statements giving an impression to the contrary. But the media had already found my listed telephone number. Though the calls continued for the next several days, I declined to make any further statements. After a few days the media interest died down. It was only after I decided to write this book that I decided to speak about CAMPCON and other matters. But the knives were out.

On March 9, 2000, an article appeared in the *Washington Post* entitled "FBI Lab Disputes Senator, Agent" by Lorraine Adams and David A. Vise. I recognized Adams as one who wrote frequently about the Department of Justice and Vise as a longtime reporter for the *Post* who had won the Pulitzer Prize. The article was misleading on its face for anyone with any familiarity with the FBI laboratory.

It was an obvious attempt to discredit not only Senator Fred Thompson but Special Agent Roberta Parker and the FBI as well. It accused Thompson of having "kept under wraps an FBI lab analysis showing the pages were never missing," a reference to Parker's testimony that twenty-seven pages of her spiral notebook were missing when it was returned to her after having been in the possession of the FBI and the Department of Justice. In an extraordinary breach of confidentiality, the article actually quoted from the lab report, including even the name of the examiner. According to the *Post*, the report stated that "nothing of significance was noted to indicate attached pages containing writing were removed from the Q1 spiral notebook." This conclusion was reached under the auspices of something called "indentation analysis."

What the article failed to note was that the analysis, based on selective comments from the report, did not preclude the fact that pages may have been removed or that pages were in the notebook at one time. It simply stated that there was no evidence pages were removed based on an examination of the remaining pages. This is something akin to a bogus burglary investigation. Using the standard of the article, in the absence of fingerprints no burglary could have occurred, even though jewelry and the big screen television were missing.

Further, the article indicated based on "two sources familiar with the test" that Parker had been polygraphed and the results "showed Parker was not being truthful about the missing pages." I feel certain that the writers of the article, both of whom cover the department, know the results of a polygraph are so unreliable that courts do not allow them as evidence in trials even after decades of their use in investigations. The article made it appear that the testimony of agents before congressional committees is the exception, declaring, "It is highly unusual for FBI agents to work investigations to testify before congressional committees. Keeping them insulated from political machinations has traditionally been considered paramount by the FBI." Apparently the reporters had not seen the virtual parade of FBI agents testifying on the Hill about Waco, Ruby Ridge, Wen Ho Lee, and even me when I testified about the White House Travel Office matter.

(Vise later wrote a best selling book, *The Bureau and the Mole*, about the Robert Hanssen investigation and the parallel career of Louis Freeh. The book, rushed to print without an index, clearly had the assistance of someone from within the FBI or the Department of Justice, assistance that was not readily evident in other books published about the Hanssen matter at the same time. In some respects it was as much a laudatory account of Freeh's tenure as FBI director as it was damning to Hanssen. However, Vise's zeal to create buzz about his book caused even the *Post* to question his tactics. For instance, he purchased almost twenty thousand copies of his book from Barnes & Noble and, in a convoluted series of transactions, returned them for credit, paying retail price when he could have bought them from his publisher at a forty percent discount. Many people suspected that Vise made the large purchases to manipulate the best-seller lists. Of course Vise denied that was his purpose, but in a series of confusing interviews, notably on *Imus in the Morning*, Vise came off as an absolute flake and Imus, as well as others, found his explanations unsatisfactory.)

Then there is the issue of who leaked the information in the *Post* article to the reporters. Adams and Vise not only had access to the actual lab report, but had at least two sources who claimed to verify the results of the polygraph. This breach of the confidentiality of the internal OPR investigation is a crime in itself and is again indicative of the extreme measures those aligned with President Clinton or the politicized Justice Department will go to besmirch the reputation of anyone who has the temerity to stand up to them.

I pondered who would have had access to the OPR investigation and basically identified three groups of people. There was Parker herself and anyone she may have revealed the results of the polygraph or the lab report to, even if she had known the results. But as the process works, Parker would not have been allowed to view the results of the polygraph or the lab report. I doubt she had seen them at the time of the *Post* article, if indeed, she has seen them today. Parker would have known only what she was told.

The second possibility was an FBI informant, either a lab worker or the polygrapher. Third there was the Justice Department. If I were conducting the internal investigation of this matter—and I suspect one never was initiated—the most likely suspect is readily apparent. The only one of the three that had a reason to publicly attempt to destroy Parker were those at the Justice Department. I would have lined up everyone with either direct or indirect access and had them submit to a polygraph in the same manner that Parker was subjected to that indignity. But I had no expectations that the Department of Justice would pursue this transgression with any more vigor than it had investigated the CAMPCON matter itself, if indeed there was an investigation at all. It had become glaringly apparent the Department of Justice had lost its way. Events subsequent to that hearing have only served to buttress my opinion—an opinion increasingly shared by the general public.

On December 9, 1996, Freeh related a conversation he had with Deputy Director William Esposito, who in turn described a conversation he had had with Lee Radek. According the memorandum, Radek told Esposito that he was "under a lot of pressure not to go forward with the investigation" because Attorney General Janet Reno's job "might hang in the balance." Later it was determined that Neil Gallagher, a deputy assistant director for the FBI's Criminal Division, had given him the warning. The memorandum further indicated that Freeh had met with Reno and expressed his concern for Radek's comments and "on that basis" had concluded that both Radek and Reno should not be engaged in the investigation of campaign finance matters.

Reno, of course, has no recollection of the conversation and Radek has stated, with typical legalese, the memo "has no basis in fact."

This memorandum of Freeh's was curious in some respects. While Reno recalled Freeh advocating the use of "junkyard dog" agents to investigate CAMPCON, the management team he had in place certainly did not meet that standard. I had never been told of Radek's comments, which makes the reticence of the FBI's management team to be aggressive in taking on the department's attorneys even more strange. But there is no doubt in my mind that Freeh's, Esposito's, and Gallagher's versions of the conversations with Radek and Freeh are the correct ones.

One member of the media who tried to persuade me to make further public comments about CAMPCON made note of my "unusual willingness to speak with such frankness." I told him that I considered that less a compliment than an indictment on life today, where one's willingness to tell the unvarnished truth is considered an exception.

Near the end of the CAMPCON hearings before the Senate Committee, Senator Susan Collins spoke with some clairvoyance. She observed, "This administration has a pattern of retaliating against civil servants who cooperate with congressional investigators. I am thinking of Mr. [Charles] LaBella, and I am thinking of whistleblowers at the Department of Energy." She can now add Roberta Parker to the list.

Senator Thompson returned to that theme with his closing remarks. He said that "if there is any intimation of any repercussions and intimidation from your coming here today, I personally want to know about it." He thanked the three agents for their being truthful and accurate, noting that they had been reluctant witnesses.

Then he turned to me. "Mr. Smith, you have retired now and you are obviously a man who probably would call it the way you saw it, even before you retired."

I responded, without giving much thought to what I said, "I did, and I paid for it at times, Senator."

Thompson looked at me a long moment before thoughtfully responding, "Well, I bet you did. But you have done your country a service by sticking to your guns and by being truthful and honest."

In retrospect I wasn't certain why I said what I did, but there were times when my career very likely suffered because I refused to place career enhancement before my personal convictions.

I could have told the senator that I didn't really have a choice, for that was the way my grandparents had reared me.

CHAPTER 24

THE MOLE

*"He's getting plenty of volunteers from among
both FBI and CIA operatives, the latter looking to
even things up after what the bureau did to them
following the Aldrich Ames spy case."*

Washington Post, "In the Loop," March 6, 2001

On the morning of February 20, 2001, I started the day as I have many since I retired by feeding our three Arabian horses. Then I got a phone call that Robert Hanssen had been arrested for espionage. Suddenly the other things I had planned for the afternoon seemed unimportant. I turned on the news to find the airways filled with accounts of the arrest. Soon I was getting calls from the media, which already had a lot of information, including a remarkably detailed affidavit.

I was not surprised that there was another FBI employee allegedly involved in espionage, nor was I surprised that it was Hanssen. While I had never suspected Hanssen of committing espionage during the time I knew him at FBI headquarters, I was certain that if I had been asked to choose someone from a list of those in the FBI headquarters who had done so, Hanssen would have been a likely suspect.

One of those calls I received was from *USA Today* and in an article by Traci Watson and Richard Willing, I was quoted, correctly, saying that Hanssen was "not your typical FBI agent." The article continued, "'He was kind of a loner, introverted, didn't laugh easily' I.C. Smith recalled,

'I could never figure out how he hung on as a headquarters supervisor.'"
I had known Hanssen for years and considered him arrogant, aloof,
introverted, totally devoid of people skills, and disdainful of authority.
Contrary to numerous news reports, he was not a "high-ranking FBI
official." Nor was his access "total," certainly not "everything—all
sources, all methods, all techniques, all targets," as one of his former colleagues and close friends, David Major, was quoted as stating. For
instance, I know he did not have access to the Aldrich Ames case as it
was being investigated, since he was not polygraphed as I was. He did
not have access to the Earl Pitts espionage case where, again, those with
access to the investigation were polygraphed.

His aloofness was legend. I can't think of a single employee who was
disliked as much as Hanssen. He tried to give the impression of a superior intellect and though in some respects he was bright, he was not the
intellectual heavyweight some would try to make him. I base that opinion not only on conversations with him, but also on having seen his
work. His had been a mediocre career, which likely aided his espionage
efforts as his mediocrity allowed him to avoid the inevitable transfers
that one expects when they move up through the FBI's ranks or receive
assignments to the most sensitive investigations where a polygraph
would be administered. He was not viewed as one who could be promoted to higher rank, and was in fact considered "unpromotable" by
various FBI career boards, an assessment I completely agreed with.

When I was responsible for formulating the FBI's National Foreign
Intelligence Program budget, where virtually all the managers in the
national security area provided input, I found his work to be average at
best. I often saw him hanging around analysts' workstations. On occasion I would see him in the FBI cafeteria with senior Chinese Analyst
Paul Moore and Unit Chief Ray Wichman, assigned to Chinese counterintelligence investigations, usually sitting away from others. I never
joined them, though Moore worked for me and Wichman had been a
longtime acquaintance.

I always found his secretiveness repellant and had the feeling there
was more to Hanssen than met the eye, though I hasten to add I did not

suspect espionage. As I had been quoted, he was not "your typical FBI agent," but clearly Hanssen had access that allowed him to exact a terrible price for his actions.

On October 4, 2001, Walter Pincus of the *Washington Post* outlined in an article entitled "Hanssen Gave Away Identity Of One of U.S.'s Top Sources" an example of the price paid for his treachery. Pincus reported that "according to lawyers familiar with the case," Hanssen provided the Soviets with the identity of one of the more storied FBI recruitments, Top Hat, the codename for Soviet Army General Dimitri Polyakov, who was also a member of GRU, the Soviet military intelligence organ. Top Hat was betrayed by Hanssen in 1979. Polyakov was suddenly recalled to the Soviet Union from his posting in the U.S. in 1980. For reasons still unexplained, the Soviet KGB did not arrest Polyakov until 1986; they executed him two years later. According to Pincus's sources, Polyakov was the third person betrayed by Hanssen that was put to death.

Hanssen exhibited many of the same characteristics as Aldrich Ames, whose 1994 arrest had eventually revealed his years of spying inside the CIA for the Russians: the social awkwardness, the intellectual arrogance, the mediocre career, the disdain for authority, a slovenly personal appearance with ill-fitting suits and unshined shoes. In retrospect, both Ames and Hanssen clearly gave warning signs that all was not right with them.

In the world of espionage there are risk takers and there are wimps. Ames fit the "wimp" category. He was dominated by his wife, Rosario, who never seemed to be satisfied with any amount of money he was able to obtain from his Soviet handlers. In some respects, Hanssen's wife dominated him as well. She insisted that he attend church every time the doors opened, made him help with the housework (though she never worked outside the home), and initiated an expensive remodeling of their home. But the fact that someone more appropriately fits the wimp category does not mean they can't undertake risks in conducting their illegal activities. Money drove Hanssen's treasonous activities, but a true risk taker would not have been preoccupied with the money. It would have been an afterthought, and then only from the standpoint that taking and concealing the money was part of the risk itself.

While I never knew Ames, there were times when Hanssen exhibited a barely concealed and groundless anger. He seemed to have a particular anathema toward women, especially women employees of some rank. He did not think there was a place for women as FBI agents. It was an interesting contradiction that Hanssen's wife clearly dominated his activities at home, while at work he showed his considerable disdain for females in positions of authority.

But the similarities between Hanssen and Ames were not the cause for my concern that afternoon as I sat watching the news and receiving the telephone calls. I knew without question that there was going to be payback for the way the FBI had handled the Ames revelations at the CIA years before. And paybacks can be hell.

In Freeh's press conference he made reference to the investigation being in part "a counterintelligence coup," which I found astoundingly naïve based on the reports I had heard. It could be a "counterintelligence coup" only if the information leading to Hanssen's arrest was the result of an FBI recruitment-in-place or an FBI-induced defection, which, according to the news accounts and the arrest affidavit, had not occurred. How could it be a "counterintelligence coup" if, absent that information from outside the FBI, Hanssen would have never been caught? Any claim of success, tenuous as it was, must be tempered by the fact the FBI, with principal responsibility for detecting spies in the United States, had not detected Hanssen for well over a decade. Indeed, it was a failure.

In the days that followed, I seemed to be the only former colleague who had anything negative to say about Hanssen. I had made the initial statement to USA Today and refused to make any further comments. Former colleagues of Hanssen, notably Major (who had ironically also been an friend of Aldrich Ames) and Moore, spoke of his considerable intellect, his deep religious beliefs, and the fact that he appeared to have engaged in espionage because of the "game"—the thrill of the risk, the excitement of the intellectual challenge, and the satisfaction of outwitting the other side. I found their statements puzzling. It was almost as if they thought the fact they were among Hanssen's very few friends was something to brag about. They were wrong about Hanssen's motivation. He was as mercenary as Larry Wu-tai Chin and Aldrich Ames. It was almost as if Major and Moore were attempting to provide Hanssen with an intellectual justification for his treasonous activities and, perhaps, for their association with him. Hanssen was not in it for the "game." Had the Soviets not paid him, he would not have continued to spy for them.

According to the affidavit, at the time of the very first contact with the Soviets Hanssen had asked for $100,000. If you consider all the reasons that might motivate an individual to commit espionage—revenge, ideology, the "game," coercion, etc.—Hanssen would not have continued his activities without the motivation of money. I suspect Hanssen was driven to act by his experience in New York. His assignment there was during a time when FBI salaries were lagging far behind the private sector and there was no differential pay for high-cost-of-living areas. Faced with a growing family, a mortgage that was straining his budget, a horrendous commute to work, etc., I suspect he looked to espionage as a means to keep his head above financial waters. It was the coincidence of being assigned to a Soviet counterintelligence squad that gave him the opportunity.

He may have rationalized his act, but he can't justify it. Indeed, Hanssen would have found other means to satisfy his deceit. This was evident from his secret relationship with the stripper Priscilla Galey, the obsession with pornography on the internet, and the rest of his whole life of deception. Hanssen is the type who, absent the opportunity to commit espionage, would have stolen from evidence in criminal cases or falsified expense vouchers. He was simply a thief.

THE PAYBACK I PREDICTED was not long in coming. Radio personality Don Imus, whose considerable pragmatism is frequently overshadowed by his bombast and parody, weighed in on Freeh's comments. Not only did he rail about Freeh's haircut, with sideburns shaved well above his ears, but he too questioned how it could be a "counterintelligence coup" when someone had been in place spying for over fifteen years. Imus recalled in vivid detail how the FBI had trumpeted the arrest of Ames, the innumerable articles and photo sessions by cooperating FBI officials, including Freeh, and the parading of Ames before the cameras. The FBI was arrogant then, and that attitude was coming back to bite them now. In some respects, the payback has never stopped. Even today Hanssen's treachery and FBI employment are mentioned more often than Ames and the CIA.

When it came to putting the Bureau in its place, Imus had plenty of company. In an editorial on March 6, 2001, the *Washington Times* observed, "While the good news is that Mr. Hanssen was caught, the bad news is that he was discovered only after a windfall of documents from Russia were turned over to the FBI. Certainly, Mr. Freeh has much thinking to do, and he will hopefully be just as critical of himself and the Bureau as he was of the CIA after the Ames debacle."

The same day, the *Washington Post* "In the Loop" segment reported: "Mike Shaheen, former longtime head of the Justice Department's Office of Professional Responsibility, has been picked by former FBI/CIA director William Webster to head his new commission to review security at the FBI and make recommendations for plugging up the leaky ship. He's getting plenty of volunteers from among both FBI and CIA operatives, the latter looking to even things up after what the Bureau did to them following the Aldrich Ames spy case."

When the FBI had the chance to be magnanimous, to be low-key, to not capitalize on the CIA's misery during the Ames revelations, it chose the opposite tack and there was consequently little sympathy for the FBI's own plight in light of the Hanssen revelations. I had cautioned Bob Bryant and John Lewis not to cooperate with the media beyond what was necessary, not to "jab a stick in the CIA's eye," not to capitalize on the Ames event, as the FBI was itself vulnerable to such acts of betrayal. I did not take any pleasure in being able to state, "I told you so."

Further embarrassments were not long in coming. On February 22, an article by Ed Pound in *USA Today* broke the story of Hanssen having hacked into a colleague's computer in the early 1990s. I was familiar with the incident, which had been the object both of great mirth and grave concern. As I recall, Hanssen had warned that the FBI's internal computer system for its National Security Division was not secure. When he was rebuffed, he hacked into the computer of Ray Mislock, the section chief who handled investigations involving Russia and the former Soviet Union. The amusement came from the fact that Hanssen had copied information from Mislock's computer to show its vulnerability and the document he had chosen to copy was one Mislock had written about his career aspirations. Given the fact that Mislock was unabashedly ambitious, the division found the whole incident immensely entertaining. Of course, Mislock was enraged and rightly so, but his was the only rage that I detected by those in a position to discipline Hanssen. Mislock's rage was not shared, for instance, by Pat Watson, the deputy assistant director of the division, a longtime associate of Hanssen's who should not have had a voice in considering disciplinary action.

There was no doubt that Hanssen had demonstrated the computer system was vulnerable. I had already decided not use the e-mail system for anything but the most innocuous information—information I'd be willing to post on a bulletin board—after I learned that such correspondence could be retrieved even after it was deleted. But inexplicably, Hanssen was not even disciplined. After all, the vulnerability that had been exposed was that the National Security Division's computers were only insecure from within!

The computer incident was followed by another revelation by Pound in *USA Today*. On February 23, the reporter detailed how Hanssen had been "suspended without pay for five days after an intelligence analyst alleged he had thrown her to the floor during a dispute at Bureau headquarters in 1993, according to the woman and U.S. officials."

I was familiar with that incident as well.

I had been working in my office late one afternoon when Peggy Mader, a capable and hard-working employee who handled budget matters, came into my office. She always seemed to know things almost as they occurred and on that occasion told me Hanssen had manhandled a female subordinate. I did not doubt Mader's information but found the whole incident incredulous. While I had a lot of misgivings about Hanssen and had noted the anger that sometimes seemed to be boiling just beneath the surface, I somehow never imagined he would resort to physically assaulting a subordinate. The next morning I wandered down the hall and raised the issue with Hanssen's supervisor, Section Chief Nick Walsh. He reluctantly confirmed the incident.

I left his office convinced that Hanssen would be demoted, if not fired. During a more than a quarter-century with the FBI, that was the single incident I had knowledge of involving the physical assault by an FBI manager on a subordinate. Even if the employee, identified in the *USA Today* article as Kimberly Lichtenberg, had spit in Hanssen's face, there was no justification for his grabbing her by the arm and literally dragging her down a hallway.

In the ensuing days I was again surprised at a lack of outrage by Hanssen's superiors. The fact that Hanssen, a manager in the FBI, had physically assaulted a female subordinate seemed to have been lost on them. There was actually an attempt to make Lichtenberg the villain. Even if she had incited the confrontation, which was caused by Lichtenberg's need to get to her carpool or avoid being stranded in Washington, the salient fact remained that Hanssen assaulted her. But Hanssen was only suspended for five days and, incredibly, according to the *USA Today* article, Lichtenberg was herself censured. I learned that one of the few close friends Hanssen had, David Major, weighed in with Doug Gow, the head of the Intelligence Division, on Hanssen's behalf, though there had been a recommendation for a much more severe penalty.

I have said in the past that the FBI's Soviet Section had taken on the characteristics of its principle target: it showed bureaucratic inertia, became insular, was slow to change and admit mistakes, and protected its own. It was clear that some of Hanssen's colleagues did not wish to see him punished for his actions, even though he was considered one whose personality flaws far overshadowed his contributions to the FBI.

The revelations continued. An article in the *New York Times* on March 4 by James Risen and Lowell Bergmann was headlined, "U.S.

Thinks Agent Revealed Tunnel at Soviet Embassy." I was advised that Risen had been working on a book, with the cooperation of the FBI, about counterintelligence in the Cold War. The FBI correctly declined to comment on the story, a throwback to the former days when the Bureau wouldn't comment on any matter involving national security. But not all current and former officials took that tack. In an article on March 11 by Vernon Loeb of the *Washington Post*, entitled "FBI Offered Officials Tours of Secret Tunnel Under Soviet Embassy," reference was made to "intelligence sources," "another former government official," and "current and former officials." But at least one article quoted an FBI official by name. The *Wall Street Journal*, in an article on March 6, 2001, quoted John Lewis, the retired assistant director of the National Security Division, saying, "We reached a point in the early 1990s where we were going to desert the thing because it wasn't producing." In effect Lewis, in contrast to the dictates of his past experiences in dealing with sensitive matters, had confirmed the existence of the tunnel and while this was not new reporting, by lending his name to the article he provided an official endorsement to the claim, a legitimacy lessened by the use of such terms as "intelligence sources."

The leaks to the press by FBI personnel, either retired or still on board, was virtually unprecedented. But I was aware of the frustration by many associated with the FBI for what was happening to the organization they had long served and revered. The frustration and dismay went beyond just the Hanssen case and included the seemingly endless series of allegations against FBI personnel such as John Connally cooperating with the Irish Mob in Boston, and Earl Pitts having committed espionage. Pitts was arrested at the FBI academy at Quantico after he had responded to a false flag approach by an undercover FBI agent pretending to represent a member of a Russian intelligence service after being dormant for years after the fall of the Soviet Union. However, when his wife, unlike Hanssen's, discovered his activities, she called the FBI. All had the effect of creating a heavy burden around the FBI in which the Hanssen case seemed to be a final straw.

The media used the Hanssen affidavit as a roadmap to pursue other such leads. The affidavit was, in my opinion, much too explicit and contained more information than necessary to establish probable cause to arrest Hanssen. For instance, in the *Times* article, Risen and Bergmann quoted from the affidavit itself: "[T]he government stated that Mr. Hanssen 'compromised an entire technical program of enormous value, expense and importance to the United States government.' Officials said that was a reference to the tunnel operation and related intelligence activities." That single reference does not provide a significant difference between sufficient probable cause to arrest Hanssen and insufficient probable cause; it simply provided accomplished reporters with additional avenues to pursue.

That wasn't the end of the revelations. On April 5, Dan Eggen and Vernon Loeb of the *Washington Post* detailed a story about Hanssen having taken a Washington D.C. stripper to church, buying her a car for $10,000, and buying her airline tickets to Japan. The trip had actually been to Hong Kong, where the stripper had accompanied Hanssen while he had acted as an inspector's aide, an inspection trip I had made several years prior. Somehow, again, I was not surprised. Typical FBI agents do not take strippers to church and buy them cars. The stripper, identified as Priscilla Sue Galey, was later interviewed by *Post* reporters Josh White and Brooke A. Masters. In an article appearing on April 19, Galey claimed that Hanssen had "showered her with nearly $100,000 in fine jewelry, a sparkling silver Mercedes-Benz sedan, a trip to Hong Kong, and cash." I did not then and do not today accept the explanation that he was simply proselytizing.

If you look at the history of espionage, almost all the cases made public have one thing in common: someone knew. Sometimes it was a spouse, other times a colleague, but the startling fact remains that those committing espionage almost invariably did so with the suspicion, if not direct knowledge, of others. If Hanssen's wife was truly in the dark about his activities as she was being portrayed, which I doubt, she was a stark exception to the rule. She admitted knowing about his initial foray into espionage, confronting him in 1980. Supposedly he gave the money he received from the Soviets to Mother Teresa after confessing to a priest. I still find it inexplicable that Bonnie Hanssen didn't know or at least suspect something when he renewed his spying and received large sums of money years later, used to pay for the extensive and expensive renovations of their home for instance.

The report about the stripper was different from other revelations in the press. While the story about Hanssen's hacking into Mislock's computer, his assault on Kim Lichtenberg, or even references to a tunnel under the Russian embassy could be attributable to former or retired FBI personnel, no one in those categories would have had access to the ongoing investigation. That information had to have been provided to Eggen and Loeb from someone "close to the investigation" as stated in the article. I viewed this with some alarm, but it confirmed what many of us had long suspected. The FBI's counterintelligence program was in complete disarray and the series of leaks of information is evidence of the deep disenchantment that existed in the aftermath of the daily revelations of the Hanssen arrest.

Apparently someone decided that Hanssen was a liability around FBI headquarters for, according to the affidavit, in April 1994 Hanssen was temporarily assigned first to the Washington field office and later to the office of the assistant director of the National Security Division. In February 1995 he was assigned to the Office of Foreign Missions at the Department of State, a liaison function used by the FBI to place individuals whose careers were at a standstill.

In *The Bureau: The Secret History of the FBI,* Ron Kessler wrote that, "In 1995, [Robert] Bryant transferred him [Hanssen] to work at the State Department's Office of Foreign Mission, where he had less access to secrets." That last assertion was largely wrong, for while at FBI headquarters, Hanssen had been a unit chief assigned to issues not involving Russia. The new assignment at the State Department actually gave him an excuse to make inquiries about Russian-related issues. The sentence also seems to infer that Bryant purposely transferred Hanssen because he wanted to limit his access to secrets in the FBI. If that was the case, and I don't believe it was, that would mean that Bryant had concerns about Hanssen's access. If he did have such concerns and his means to address those concerns was simply to transfer him to another agency, that would be the height of irresponsibility. I never heard anyone express concern for Hanssen's access or suspicions of his loyalty, though I did hear comments of uncertainty about exactly what to do with him due to his performance and personality. Hanssen was assigned to the Office of Foreign Missions simply to get him out of the building.

BY THIS TIME THE assistant director of the newly named National Security Division was Robert Bryant. In the past, there had been periodic meetings with the assistant director where sensitive matters involving personnel, administrative, and occasionally operations were discussed. The meetings would be attended only by the assistant director, the two deputy assistant directors, and the four section chiefs, all members of the Senior Executive Service.

However, under Bryant, who viewed security as a nuisance, the meetings were expanded to include not only those individuals on assignments outside the FBI in other agencies but also lower-ranking employees within the National Security Division. As the size of the group grew, the ability to discuss sensitive matters was inhibited and it finally got to the point where, along with other senior members of the group, I refused to raise sensitive issues in the meetings. I went to Bryant and told him that while I thought it was a good idea to have periodic meetings with those on assignments with agencies outside the FBI, to ensure they continued to feel they were a part of the FBI, their presence was creating a climate that inhibited discussion of important issues. Bryant apparently did not agree with me, for the size of those meetings continued to grow until literally every chair in the room was filled and the running joke was to get to the conference room early in order to get a seat.

Hanssen attended those meetings, but I suspect it was only on rare occasion that he was able to obtain any information of significance to pass along to the Russians. I never recall him making a contribution to the discussion. He sat along the outside of the group with his dark visage, seemingly alone in a room overflowing with fellow employees. But the meetings did give him the opportunity to return to FBI headquarters and wander among the agents and analysts and still have access to what was going on in the National Security Division. It is this indirect access that damage assessments cannot calculate.

Indirect access is information that is not in the course of one's assigned duties. For instance, while Hanssen may not have had direct access to a sensitive operation, by perusing the reports on an unattended desk, accessing a computer, or talking with someone in a hallway who trusted him, Hanssen could easily develop information of interest. But there are no footprints of his having knowledge of the operation, which makes a damage assessment virtually impossible. In Hanssen's case, the indirect access was likely as fruitful for him as was the direct access to information he had during the normal course of his duties.

It had the added advantage of directing no suspicion at him if the operation was compromised. The first rule of a compromised operation is to identify those who had official knowledge of its existence. Further, it is the rare individual with that direct access who will admit they may have inadvertently allowed someone to have indirect access to a file or computer, even if they knew it had occurred; and even rarer for them to admit that they had talked out of school. Robert Hanssen was protected by others who were protecting themselves.

CHAPTER 25

HANSSEN'S LEGACY

". . . an organization willing to expose past sources cannot be trusted to maintain the confidentiality of future ones."

I.C. Smith, in an informal memorandum to Robert "Bear" Bryant

Fresh details of Hanssen's activities and of the FBI itself continued to make news. On April 22, the *New York Times* ran an article captioned, "F.B.I. Rejected Spy Warning 2 Years Before Agent's Arrest," by James Risen and David Johnston, detailing how Tom Kimmel of the Criminal Division, at the direction of Deputy Director Bob Bryant (who had been promoted by Freeh to the number-two position in the Bureau), had conducted a damage assessment of the Earl Pitts espionage investigation. Pitts, a lawyer by training, had also undertaken espionage activities in New York, though he did much less harm than Hanssen. But unlike Bonnie Hanssen, Pitts's wife had told authorities of her husband's suspicious activities; unlike Hanssen, Pitts showed considerable remorse for his actions and agreed to cooperate fully with investigators.

I have known Kimmel for years and regarded him as a sound and tenacious investigator. Based upon that article, Kimmel uncovered clear warning signs of another FBI mole. He revealed that Pitts himself had told the FBI he thought there was another one, recounting how the Soviets had not asked him about specific information and seemed content with whatever he provided. But while Bryant had tasked Kimmel to conduct a damage assessment, he had been denied access to all the available information. In a meeting with Freeh in February 1999, Kimmel voiced his opinion there was probably a mole within the FBI. He also raised the issue of not having complete access to all the available material and being prevented from saying so in his written report. This is a remarkable omission for what was supposed to be an independent study and clearly indicates a report being edited before its final submission. There is only one person who could have done that, and that was the assistant director, Neil Gallagher.

Here, management failed again. If the FBI was serious about Kimmel's assignment, they should have directed Gallagher to give him full access to the available information, even if that meant Kimmel had to take a national security polygraph. Further, Kimmel should have reported directly to Bryant and his report should not have been subject to editing. This was a sound idea that failed due to a lack of follow-through.

In March, Kimmel met again with Freeh and stood by his original assessment that there was very likely another spy within their midst. But Freeh directed Gallagher to review the conclusions in Kimmel's fifteen-page memorandum. The result was that Kimmel "had failed to provide hard evidence or logical analysis" to support his conclusions. This begs the question, given the evidence that Kimmel's report was edited. I would venture that the report prepared by Kimmel was edited before its submission to Freeh in an attempt to lessen its impact.

But Kimmel continued with his usual persistence. After it was clear no one was accepting his logic, he maintains he wrote a personal letter to Freeh saying he had more details and was available to personally brief Freeh. He did not receive a response and, according to "FBI officials," Freeh did not recall such a letter. Well, I know Tom Kimmel, and if he said he wrote a letter, you can bet he wrote one.

Kimmel told the *Times* reporters that on the day Hanssen was arrested, FBI Deputy Director Tom Pickard (who had replaced the retired Bob Bryant) called and told him that he had been right all along. Pickard then ordered another review of Kimmel's original report. Not surprisingly, the same conclusion was reached. Any other conclusion would be an admission that they were wrong. Gallagher was quoted as stating, "He was right, but for the wrong reasons." This was a typical bureaucratic face-saving response. Perhaps he should have considered responding with, "We were wrong, but for all the right reasons." But that would have placed the focus on him.

On July 12, Robert Novak wrote a remarkable column entitled "The Hanssen Mystery" where, in an almost unheard of breach of a journalist identifying a source, he revealed that Hanssen had been his source for an article about the retirement of Ray Wichman and Freeh's assertion that he had nothing to do with it. (Novak was to later unapologetically publish the name of a CIA agent, Valerie Plame, but steadfastly refuses to identify the source of his information in that instance. Apparently he considers it acceptable to expose a former FBI agent as a source, albeit a treasonous one, but not those with political connections.) Freeh denied knowing anything about Wichman's sudden departure. Wichman, a Hanssen friend, longtime unit chief, and almost the sole "China hand" left at FBI headquarters still assigned Chinese counterintelligence matters, refused, according to Novak, to provide the Department of Justice with the identities of counterintelligence sources. This involved the CAMPCON investigation and, given my experience in dealing with DOJ in that investigation, I too would have resisted giving them those names. It would be an abhorrent violation of the strict sanctity the FBI traditionally affords its sources.

What I heard from an agent at FBI headquarters at the time of Wichman's retirement was that it had been prompted by a different incident. According to that agent, Freeh, Attorney General Janet Reno, and CIA Director George Tenet had testified on Capitol Hill, and Tenet had related some information, noting it had been reported by the FBI. Reno and Freeh were both irate and embarrassed that Tenet had access to that information but their own agent hadn't apprised them of it. Freeh, according to the headquarters agent, returned to headquarters demanding Wichman's scalp. Wichman retired the next day.

What is unsettling about the incident is that I was told Wichman *had* reported the information to his superiors but they hadn't passed it on to

Freeh. Of course those superiors had not admitted to Freeh what really happened. As a result, a good employee was unfairly maligned and retired at the very time his considerable expertise in Chinese counterintelligence was badly needed, simply because Reno and Freeh had been embarrassed, though their embarrassment was not of Wichman's making.

Finally on July 6, 2001, Hanssen pled guilty to multiple counts of espionage and will remain incarcerated for the remainder of his life. As part of the plea negotiations, he avoided the death penalty and his wife was allowed to keep about fifty-five percent of his pension, or about $40,000 per year. This agreement, while legally sound, did not sit well with the vast majority of retired FBI personnel with backgrounds in counterintelligence and presumes her complete innocence. I suppose she was given credit for confronting Hanssen years before, though she had not seen fit to notify anyone of authority. Then there were reports of Hanssen's obsession with pornography, the suggestive photographs of his wife he posted on the internet along with racy bedroom commentary, and the hidden camera he claimed was in their bedroom so guests on an adjoining deck could watch as they engaged in sex. It is difficult to believe that some of Hanssen's close friends, especially those who shared his passion for computers, had no indication of his deviant behavior.

Hanssen also has to provide the FBI with full details of his espionage activities. That could present another problem for the Bureau, for it was reported that Hanssen had provided the Russians with names of other FBI employees who might be vulnerable to an approach to act as spies.

THE EMBARRASSING REVELATIONS continued. David Vise completed his *The Bureau and the Mole*, which clearly had the assistance of Freeh or his staff, if not someone in the Department of Justice. The book, like the earlier *Killer Spy* by Peter Maas, clearly sets out to lionize Louis Freeh. In December of that year I had written an informal memorandum to Bryant about the "tasking regarding the Peter Maas book on Ames," and about the accompanying argument that had been made against a CIA request to confirm that Top Hat had been an FBI source. I noted it was a violation of an executive order protecting sensitive sources and methods, and that it violated "explicit or implied covenants" with the sources to protect their identities. I also noted it was unprofessional and that "an organization willing to expose past sources cannot be trusted to maintain the confidentiality of future ones." I concluded with the observation that "I assume if we discuss cases with Maas, it will appear (at some point) in the media, even if it isn't in the book." My concerns not withstanding, Maas got his briefings anyway, much to my discomfort and that of many who were made to cooperate with Maas and submit to personal interviews.

The result was predictable. Maas did write a book that included information about sources and methods that I had objected to and his book, like Vise's, was a fawning sop to Freeh. That was the price they paid for their access.

But there were new revelations—one in particular—that I found shocking both then and today. While a great deal of the publicity surrounding the book focused on explicit details of Hanssen's internet pornography, his stripper girlfriend, and similar things, the truly astounding news was the revelation of yet another warning of Hanssen's espionage activities that had either been ignored or consciously swept under a rug. His brother-in-law had reported suspicions that Hanssen was spying for the Soviets in the early 1990s, when he saw Hanssen with large amounts of money far beyond what could be expected on an FBI salary with six children in parochial schools. But that warning, if it actually came, was also ignored.

The *Richmond Times-Dispatch* reported on April 4, 2002, that the Russians had complained that a "'disaffected' FBI agent tried to give U.S. secrets to one of its military intelligence officers." Clearly this was when Hanssen had attempted to reestablish contact with his former handlers, a clumsy effort that belies the statements of former Hanssen associates of how smart Hanssen is. It was a clumsy attempt, so blatant, that even the GRU, the military intelligence arm of the Russians not known for its subtlety or caution, would have nothing to do with it. I thought it interesting that it was the GRU that Hanssen approached and not the more circumspect and careful KGB. If that incident was investigated, it too led nowhere.

Then the Webster report was released. Webster, who ironically was FBI director during much of the more damaging time of Hanssen's activities, concluded that the FBI had a "pervasive inattention to security" and that "security policies are too often viewed as a nuisance to negotiate around, rather than edicts with which to comply." The report revealed that in the late 1990s Hanssen had been caught with hacking software on his computer while serving as liaison at the State Department, but again, he was not investigated. There are undoubtedly revelations yet to come that will further erode public confidence in the FBI. The Webster report clearly took the FBI to task for its pervasive lax attitude toward security.

There should have been a thorough and public airing of what went wrong within the FBI that allowed Hanssen to serve in a position of trust and confidence for so long while committing espionage, though in the post-9/11 world and the current administration's obsession with secrecy, I am not confident that will occur. The FBI should follow the lead of the CIA in placing adverse letters of censure into employees' personnel files even after they have retired. For instance, who was responsible for investigating the allegations made by Hanssen's brother-in-law and who made the decision not to pursue them? Who made the decision to not discipline Hanssen when he hacked into Mislock's computer and was later found with hacking software on his computer? Were those decisions made by the Deputy Assistant Directors Pat Watson and Harry "Skip" Brandon, or by someone outside the Intelligence Division? Who made the decision to not demote and transfer Hanssen after he essentially assaulted a female subordinate at FBI headquarters? And who was on board when security within the FBI's counterintelligence program was deemphasized? Clearly this latter responsibility lies with Freeh and his assistant director, later deputy director, Bob Bryant.

In my view, the deemphasis of security can be traced to a series of individuals who were promoted to senior positions within the FBI's counterintelligence program without the requisite background for the work. This started with Doug Gow, a hard-working and dedicated FBI employee who had succeeded Jim Geer, a real professional in the world of counterintelligence with immense respect among his peers both foreign and domestic. Gow had virtually no background in intelligence matters.

He was followed, all too briefly, by Tom DuHadway, a counterintelligence professional highly regarded in the intelligence community and within the ranks of the special agents in charge as well. After all, he had been one of them. But his untimely death opened the door for Wayne Gilbert, also a seasoned and competent FBI manager, but whose exposure to intelligence matters had been limited to his time as the terrorism section chief when it was ensconced in the Criminal Division. His was a totally Criminal-Division approach to investigations.

Next came Bob Bryant, who had also developed in the Criminal Division, but who had gained exposure to counterintelligence in the Ames case. He was also the one who, while SAC in the Washington office, bragged about diverting foreign counterintelligence resources to criminal investigations. Bryant never understood the nuances of counterintelligence and that by its very nature, counterintelligence is a secretive discipline; espionage itself is only a small part of the overall program. He certainly did not have the awareness or interest in security.

Bryant's successor was his hand-picked subordinate at the Washington field office, John Lewis. Lewis had a sound background in counterintelligence, though his experience was the Soviet Union when the principal threat in the post–Cold War period was China, which had little in common with the Soviets. But to the detriment of the counterintelligence program, Lewis was promoted without ever having been an inspector or a special agent in charge. The FBI is something like the Navy in that one can be promoted to admiral through a series of Pentagon assignments, but he is looked upon with suspicion if he has never faced the demands of command at sea.

The FBI has traditionally placed great stock in its executives having demonstrated their worth as inspectors with demanding assignments and an SAC with the unique challenges of field command. Lewis had neither and thus never had the confidence of the field commanders. His promotion was certainly not unique with Freeh and Bryant in particular, who seemed to place more emphasis on loyalty than experience or fitness for the job.

As the Webster report noted, they viewed security as something to ignore more than they did as something to strictly enforce. All those individuals should have been identified and some price paid for contributing to Hanssen's ability to carry out two decades of undetected espionage.

WHEN THE HANSSEN investigation broke, one call I received was from a reporter who tracked me down through someone who had heard a lecture I had given at the Smithsonian Institution as part of the Smithsonian's "Cold War" series. He called about the stripper story, and I quickly told him I wasn't in a position to help him and could state honestly I did not know anything about Hanssen's personal life. I explained I had restricted my contacts with him to what was necessary to the job. But during the conversation, he mentioned that he had been told of comments I had made during the Smithsonian lecture, one I had termed "Punch and Counterpunch," that he found surprising.

I had discussed the Cold War as a period when adversaries, including the intelligence and counterintelligence agencies, had exchanged "blows." But I had concluded that intelligence and counterintelligence agencies had not been a determining factor in producing the end of the Cold War and the implosion of the Soviet Union. Certainly, there was a human cost for those activities, especially with Larry Wu-tai Chin and even Aldrich Ames and Hanssen. There are hundreds of graves and many casualties without graves that litter the world because of the life-and-death struggle between the competing ideologies of the Soviet Union and the West. The actions of the intelligence and counterintelligence agencies resulted in some of those graves, but in the final analysis, none made any difference.

Communism in the Soviet Union and its client states failed due to the weight of a flawed ideology, not because of the activities of the competing intelligence and counterintelligence adversaries. Hanssen and Ames did not cooperate with the Soviets due to a shared ideology, but rather for the most crass of reasons: money. They were simply unprincipled individuals who would have been thieves regardless of their occupations. It was unfortunate that they occupied positions of great trust and confidence within the very government they betrayed. I feel certain that they justified their actions, in part, due to their belief (correct as it turned out) that in the big picture their actions would do little harm to the U.S. and not tilt the ideological and economic battle toward the Soviet Union.

Even so, Hanssen, Ames, and their kind caused great pain, not only in the loss of human life but also within the CIA and the FBI, the organizations that entrusted their secrets to them and paid them well for their services. Still, none of what they did made any difference in the final outcome of the epic battle that was waged. They did what they did for money and money alone, and there is not a worse reason to commit espionage.

That is the legacy the Ameses and Hanssens have to live with.

CHAPTER 26

FIGHTING THE TIGER

*"If counterintelligence is for the long-distance runner,
then Chinese counterintelligence is for the
ultra-marathon runner."*

Retired FBI Special Agent T. Van Magers

C ounterintelligence has been the silent chapter in the FBI's history, but arguably it's also the single area where the FBI has had the greatest success and where it made its greatest contribution to the security of the United States. The art of counterintelligence was practiced by a relatively small number of employees and, due to its secretive nature, was largely misunderstood by a sizable number of FBI agents, both in the past and, I suspect, today.

Counterintelligence is not for the sprinter, those employees and managers with short attention spans who feel the need to accomplish short-term goals for instant gratification. Counterintelligence is very much an intellectual exercise and there is no place for those who seek publicity for their work, who expect every investigation to lead to an arrest with agents in camouflage and carrying automatic weapons, and who confuse the essential task of the counterintelligence agent.

I have defined counterintelligence as "opposing the acquisition of knowledge." It is the attempt to acquire knowledge of foreign enemies (and increasingly, foreign friends) while attempting to prevent them from acquiring that knowledge of the United States. The latter is virtually the exclusive domain of the FBI and its importance remains today. Spying is alive and well in the New Millennium.

In the wake of the implosion of the Soviet Union and the collapse of Soviet-dominated Communism in Europe, the FBI was caught up in the discussion of the "peace dividend," the idea that resources that for years had been used to counter the threat of the Soviet Union and its allies should be immediately diverted to other areas. At the time, the Bureau did not have a counterintelligence expert at the helm of the National Security Division, and counterintelligence had little influence on the seventh floor of the Hoover Building, where the director and the senior staff worked. Those with counterintelligence backgrounds were largely pushed aside in favor of nontraditional FBI objectives such as combating street crime.

The Russian (formerly Soviet) Section of the FBI made an ill-advised request for a large increase of resources even after the collapse of the Soviet Union left the KGB in temporary disarray. This led to the view among the hierarchy that the National Security Division was not serious about reducing resources and the resultant backlash encompassed other counterintelligence programs. Consequently, Congress demanded a massive shift of resources and the Department of Justice acquiesced, along with the leadership of the FBI, who saw an opportunity to grab counterintelligence resources and put them to work in pet areas within the Criminal Division.

The primary beneficiary was an ill-advised endeavor known as the Street Crime Initiative. This was followed by the early days of the Clinton administration, when there was little interest in foreign affairs; reports circulated that Clinton didn't bother to keep a daily schedule of meetings with National Security Council personnel. Even as the actual number of espionage investigations increased markedly due to revelations coming out of the former Soviet Union and Warsaw Pact countries, the reduction of resources had achieved a momentum all its own and couldn't be stopped. The Clinton administration, if it paid any attention to foreign matters at all, was prone to overlook or reject concerns about the two most important adversaries the FBI's counterintelligence program had to engage, the Russians and the Chinese.

The FBI moved swiftly so it could go to Capitol Hill and brag that it had reacted to the fall of Communism, a response that was premature given the large number of espionage cases being developed virtually daily. The Russian program then argued internally that it needed more resources to investigate the influx of espionage cases and they were successful in gaining additional resources, diverted from other areas, from an already reduced counterintelligence program.

A successful counterintelligence program has many facets beyond espionage. There must be an aggressive program to recruit members of the opposing intelligence services, there must be a double agent program to ensure the opposition is kept off balance, there must be proactive analyses that are predictive in nature. Espionage cases are the exception and not the engine that drives the counterintelligence effort.

However, the FBI did not understand that, and the single program that suffered the most was that involving China. At a meeting of the management staff, Bryant opined that the China program should be shut down. His handpicked assistant special agent in charge in the Washington field office, Steve Dillard, openly talked of stopping Chinese counterintelligence investigations, a position he continued to argue when he returned to FBI headquarters as a section chief with responsibility for the Chinese program. Ironically, he is now the head of the Department of Energy's counterintelligence office, where undoubtedly his greatest concern is the People's Republic of China.

The de-emphasis of counterintelligence, and of the China program in particular, continued in the early years of the Clinton administration without objection. Bryant was successful in having responsibility for the domestic terrorism program transferred from the Criminal Division to the National Security Division. This was another ill-advised move that has resulted in the FBI going full circle and, in the wake of the Wen Ho Lee debacle, having once again a National Security Division that deals with counterintelligence alone. Counterintelligence became a poor third priority within the National Security Division, after Domestic and International Terrorism. Chinese experts in counterintelligence, such as the talented and dedicated T. Van Magers, were transferred to other duties. There were many others who transferred, retired, or were removed from the area of their expertise and dedication that led directly to the embarrassment of the Wen Ho Lee case.

AT THE TIME OF THE Wen Ho Lee investigation, the FBI's counterintelligence program was dispirited, and the Chinese program had been diluted of virtually all the institutional expertise that had been nurtured over the decades beginning well before normalization of relations with China. I became acutely aware of this when I received a telephone call from Barbara Bradley of *National Public Radio* in the spring of 1999, who asked me to comment on the matter.

I had been retired for about nine months but had observed with increasing alarm the events surrounding the Lee case. I had no contact with anyone familiar with the investigation, but from the media reports I began to believe something had gone badly wrong. The fact that Lee had been targeted was not the issue; his being an ethnic Chinese was not a result of some attempt at racial profiling, for even a rudimentary understanding of Chinese intelligence and information operations led one to understand they almost exclusively rely on ethnic Chinese as sources.

Bradley told me the FBI had attempted a "false flag" operation. This demonstrated to me the depths of the destruction of the China program. A false flag—someone pretending to represent the government of a targeted country to a suspect to elicit some sort of cooperation or admissions—is a tried-and-true technique used against western countries, but never against the Chinese. The Chinese prefer to appeal to the ethnicity of Chinese Americans and discuss such issues as helping the motherland and scientific exchanges among academic colleagues; seldom is there an offer of monetary compensation. As T. Van Magers once observed, "If counterintelligence is for the long-distance runner, then Chinese counterintelligence is for the ultra-marathon runner." There is no sense of urgency by the Chinese. They have their contacts across the United States in the form of students, businesses, and most important, the overseas Chinese, all of whom they assume will help mother China.

The false flag attempt was compounded by the fact the agent who portrayed a visitor from Beijing making contact with Lee wasn't even a Mandarin speaker. Mandarin Chinese is the dialect used in Beijing and to have an emissary supposedly speaking for the government in China and not speaking Mandarin erodes the credibility of the messenger. The bungled false flag attempt was compounded by the results of Lee's polygraph results. According to media reports, Lee received two Department of Energy polygraphs that indicated no deception, but the FBI concluded that the results indicated he was lying. In one report dated December 28, 1998, from the DOE AAAP Test Center to Edward J. Curran, director, Office of Counterintelligence at the Department of Energy, the Wackenhut contractor specifically listed the relevant questions that Lee was asked. This document was declassified by the government and used as an exhibit by Lee's defense team.

The questions are as follows: Have you ever committed espionage against the United States? Have you ever provided any classified weapons data to any authorized person? Have you had any contact with anyone to commit espionage against the United States? Have you ever had personal contact with anyone you know who has committed espionage against the United States? Lee responded "No" to each of those questions, and the polygrapher wrote the "examination disclosed sufficient physiological criteria to opine Mr. Lee was not deceptive." Those are specific questions that go to the very heart of the allegations against Lee, yet the results were viewed differently by the Wackenhut and FBI polygraphers.

The Larry Wu-tai Chin case still offered a roadmap to success in planning the interview of an ethnic Chinese with strong emotional ties to his homeland, but all the agents with institutional knowledge of that case were long pushed from the program. The concept of *quanxi*, the reliance on relationships, was never utilized, and threats and bluster have not been successful in the past and will not be successful in the future in interrogating suspects with Lee's background. Often, ethnic Chinese who have provided information to unauthorized individuals simply do not believe they have done anything wrong.

Continuing revelations of the bungled Lee case are not surprising, as there was a conscious effort to dilute counterintelligence as a major FBI program. That has resulted in another reorganization being announced by the FBI without anyone publicly asking why the program was destroyed in the first place. The FBI's counterintelligence program today is a shell of its proud past.

The fallout from the Wen Ho Lee case was both intense and protracted and, in its own way, demonstrated how the leadership of the FBI in general and the counterintelligence program in particular suffered. In an article by Vernon Loeb of the *Washington Post* on June 29, 2001, entitled, "FBI Official Misled Congress About Lee, GAO Says", the *Post* reported, "[Neil] Gallagher told a Senate Committee . . . he had 'full confidence' in the initial investigation by the Department of Energy." But an official Government Accounting Office report said Gallagher had "ample opportunity to know, and should have known" that there was an FBI memorandum dated January 22, 1999, or more than a month before Lee was fired from the Los Alamos laboratory, expressing reservations about the investigation. The GAO report admitted it could not state that Gallagher's testimony was intentionally false and quoted Gallagher as admitting he "inadvertently gave incomplete testimony."

Senator Charles Grassley, a frequent critic of the FBI, went even further, stating in the *Post* article that "Congress should be suspicious of anything he (Gallagher) represents to us in the future." That was an absolutely chilling statement and went to the very heart of the credibility of the FBI. Gallagher had to admit the memorandum in question had been included in a briefing book he had been given to prepare for his testimony, but claimed to not have read the complete book. I found that an incredible admission and at odds with Gallagher's reputation for being very well prepared when testifying on Capitol Hill. Gallagher also noted that the initials on the memorandum were those of a subordinate, not his, so he couldn't be held responsible for the inadvertent misleading testimony.

This admission raised alarms for several reasons. If that was in fact the case, it was clear that Gallagher was not communicating very well with his subordinates. It is difficult to believe that a memorandum from the Albuquerque field office expressing severe reservations about the Wen Ho Lee case was not brought to his attention and that the subordinate who did initial the memorandum did not personally point out that startling information. Further, there is a time-honored, though increasingly ignored, tradition that those in command are responsible for the actions of their subordinates. Increasingly there is a tendency for those in command to have subordinates share, if not assume outright, the blame for their mistakes.

Instead of offering the tortuous excuse for his misleading testimony, Gallagher should have simply stated, "I did not properly prepare for my testimony, though I had all the pertinent information at my disposal. I take full responsibility for my misleading and incorrect testimony. It will not happen again." His attempt to deflect responsibility for his actions, an attempt completely consistent with his uneasiness with field command, only served to have his veracity questioned by a powerful senator and increase the public cynicism about the FBI itself. Gallagher retired at the end of November 2001.

THE FBI MUST REBUILD its counterintelligence program. It must reassert its leadership in the counterintelligence community. Agents must be encouraged to choose an intellectually challenging career in counterintelligence and, as Phil Parker so ably demonstrated when he assumed command of the Washington field office the day Ronald Reagan was shot, there must be a recognition that assignment to counterintelligence does not diminish one's ability to lead. There must be a program that rewards those whose career development choice is counterintelligence, and not permit it to be the detriment to their careers it has been in the past. And the FBI must promote senior personnel who have demonstrated leadership qualities, who are willing to tell the director what he doesn't necessarily want to hear, and who are chosen for high position because of their legacy of competence, not a fealty to those of higher rank.

In Sun Tzu's *The Art of War*, there is the following discussion of discipline:

"Tu Mu alludes to the remarkable story of Ts'ao Ts'ao (A.D. 155–220), who was such a strict disciplinarian that once, in accordance with his own severe regulations against injury to standing crops, he condemned himself to death for having allowed his horse to stray into a field of corn! However, in lieu of losing his head, he was persuaded to satisfy his sense of justice by cutting off his hair. 'When you lay down a law, see that it is not disobeyed, the offender must be put to death.'"

While I certainly do not equate the FBI's authority to the draconian methods advocated by Ts'ao, the story has important lessons. Ts'ao, a powerful general, readily assumed blame for his own transgressions and punishment was both swift and uniform. These are traits that are largely lost on the FBI today.

There is a direct correlation between discipline in the FBI and the career-development program. Discipline breaks down when there is a lack of confidence in leadership. Terry Neist, a longtime acquaintance and confirmed street agent who never loses an opportunity to voice his disdain for the FBI management, once observed that at some point, "The FBI began to confuse ambition with ability." He was absolutely right.

When I was an SAC, of the more than sixty SACs and assistant directors in field offices, I knew of only two who had any interest in returning to FBI headquarters. Those who were eagerly waving their hands to be recognized and get back to Washington were viewed with suspicion by their peers. The result is an FBI headquarters largely staffed with bureaucrats who feel uncomfortable with the daily responsibility of field command, if indeed they ever had field assignments in senior positions. There they can feel the comfort of surrounding themselves with various rules and regulations and issue edicts in the name of "The Bureau." The void between field offices and the headquarters hierarchy grows with each year.

The FBI has long had a "rabbi" system of senior officials looking after the interests of younger employees. It was in place in Hoover's FBI and did not disappear with his death. However, at no time in my career did

I see such blatant disregard for ability and performance as that occurring under Louie Freeh. Promotions were made on the basis of past personal friendships, and exceptions were made as to long established increments of career development and seasoning that allowed executives to perform at various steps along the process. Conversely, some excellent agents were denied promotions based on a whispered dislike by someone with Freeh's ear.

There has developed in the senior leadership the ability to surround themselves with self-serving sycophants who tell them what they want to hear and duck the responsibility of providing true and accurate advice. Decision-making was largely driven on the basis of career considerations, not advancing an investigation, not on what is in the best interests of the FBI.

Clearly SACs could not count on the support of Freeh, who did great harm to the FBI, undermining the traditional authority of senior management by going directly to street agents for advice and consultation at the expense of the SACs or headquarters managers. I personally experienced this at FBI headquarters, where Bob Bryant would contact subordinates routinely and ask for their input on issues without advising me of the meeting, though for the most part, the subordinates would advise me in advance if there was the opportunity. They recognized the chain of command, even if Bryant didn't. But if a subordinate begins to believe he or she has a direct pipeline to a more senior official, then there is an inevitable breakdown in discipline. Not surprisingly, those senior officials most inclined to ignore the chain of command had never served in the military and never been law enforcement officers.

Field offices no longer have the look of the professional work environment as in the past. Agents wear casual clothing to work routinely, personal grooming has deteriorated, work spaces are in disarray, and there is an overall erosion of the image of the FBI that for decades cast it in a different and better light than other law enforcement agencies. The exacting standards of the Hoover era have been abandoned.

Under Hoover, discipline was swift, sure, and perhaps, at times, unfair. But there was never any question that discipline was going to be the result of some infraction. When I came to the FBI, discipline was still being exercised with some degree of expediency and with a regard for equity. But that has changed too, and the current system is neither expedient nor equitable.

IF I WERE TO CHOOSE a single incident as a benchmark for the breakdown of an efficient and equitable discipline system, it occurred under the leadership of Director William Webster.

I had known Webster slightly in St. Louis where, as a federal judge, he had a reputation for being stiff and formal around FBI agents. He demanded that the letter opener on his desk be in the exact same location every morning but would wear suits with buttons missing. When he was named FBI director, the protection detail went to his house in a St. Louis suburb and noticed doors to the attic open and discovered they had been open for some time, leaving the attic exposed to the elements. Webster could not be bothered by such mundane things as an attic door open, regardless of the fact it could do damage to his house.

But while he could be unconcerned with such matters of a button on his suit or doors to his attic, he would labor for interminable periods over some decisions that were cut and dried. One involved the discipline of an agent who had been caught with marijuana. The agent, a black female from the northeast part of the U.S., was returning from the Caribbean and when passing through U.S. Customs was discovered to have a small amount of marijuana. Webster labored over the decision and finally concluded that since she was from the northeast where recreational marijuana use was socially acceptable, she would be able to remain in the FBI.

That decision caused a firestorm in the field offices. Tom Carson, who was on my squad at the Washington field office and originally from Alabama, said that if he had been caught with marijuana, he would have been fired according to Webster's rationale since in Alabama they looked with askance upon smoking pot. This single incident caused great harm to the confidence both management and rank-and-file agents had in the fairness of the FBI's disciplinary system, a suspicion that has not been overcome even today.

The current system has resulted in disciplinary matters being largely removed from the control of SACs and even the FBI itself in favor of the Department of Justice. Final action is seldom taken with any expediency and discipline is arbitrary. There were senior managers who committed felonies, yet not only were they allowed to remain in the FBI, they were promoted. This rightly feeds the perception by the rank-and-file agents that there are two standards for discipline: one for them and one for the senior management.

Promotion to senior rank carries with it an expectation that one will be subjected to a barrage of complaints by what I term "serial EEO complainers." That is, there are the same few employees who make the vast majority of EEO complaints that serve to only undermine the credibility of those with valid complaints. While there are strict guidelines for making a complaint based on time, the requirement was routinely waived. Further, there was no system that allowed for the manager to be advised of the disposition of the complaints.

An FBI organizational chart is unlike that for the military or even La Cosa Nostra. There is a pyramidal structure, altered to accommodate the SACs heading the various field offices. It is unclear exactly to whom SACs report. Freeh clearly felt uncomfortable with SACs. This is not surprising given his lack of management experience. But in their own minds, SACs viewed themselves as working for Freeh, not the assembled deputy assistant directors, assistant directors, and the deputy director in Washington.

This confusion was worsened when Bryant, as deputy director, insisted that each field SAC sign a personal "contract" with him, setting goals and objectives for the next several years, an absolutely asinine exercise that served only to confuse the command structure. Most SACs simply signed the worthless piece of paper, knowing they would be transferred or retired in the next year or so, that crime problems in field offices shift constantly with changing priorities, and that Bryant himself would likely retire before anything would come of these pointless objectives. I suspect that practice has been discarded in the wake of Bryant's retirement. I can't imagine Director Robert S. Mueller III agreeing to the practice.

THE OFFICE OF Professional Responsibility was for a long time part of the Inspection Division, headed by a career FBI deputy director. But increasingly, the FBI began to assign potential disciplinary matters to the FBI division where the alleged offense occurred. In 1986, as an inspector's aide, I helped prepare a Schedule of Findings, essentially a document outlining criticisms with solutions, for the assistant director of the Criminal Division.

The central issue was the Criminal Division's routine practice of investigating incidents of misconduct of its own employees. Bryant, as the inspector, would not allow the inspector aide authors of the document to place their names on it for he was all too aware that doing so could have career implications. His was the only name appearing on the Schedule "F," a courageous and principled act. This was especially true when the assistant director receiving the Schedule "F" was Oliver "Buck" Revell. Bryant very likely paid a price for the act of impertinence as his initial selection as SAC was considerably delayed.

Of course, the recommendation to move such investigations from the division was ignored. This resulted in the devastatingly harmful investigations involving the Ruby Ridge incident. Charlie Matthews, formerly a subordinate of Danny Coulson's, conducted the first inquiry. The second inquiry was conducted by Bob Walsh, also a product of the Criminal Division. While I'm not in a position to comment on the adequacy of either of those inquiries, the perception of conflicts of interest were sufficient to bring increased scrutiny and criticism and contributed to the notion that the FBI is incapable of disciplining itself.

There's also the matter of staffing the OPR. I have long maintained that no employee should be allowed to remain in that assignment beyond two years. Further, I have stated only half-jokingly that anyone wanting to be assigned to investigate complaints against their fellow employees should be immediately banned from such an assignment. There is no place in OPR for those who derive pleasure from the misery of fellow employees and OPR has had those individuals in its ranks.

What about failed managers? The FBI had increasingly taken those who have been promoted to senior positions and demonstrated an inability to perform at those levels, then moved them to "empty suit" assignments, usually at FBIHQ, where they performed mundane duties without suffering a reduction in pay. That too was a departure from the Hoover era. Those removed from senior positions should be demoted, absent their having committed a firing offense, to a level that allows them to perform with some level of competency.

CHAPTER 27

ARMED TO KILL

*"[T]he fact [is] that FBI agents act in self defense
and use firearms only as a last resort."*
J. Edgar Hoover, 1971

T he FBI's long and distinguished history in making arrests and suffering relatively low casualties has traditionally been due to both
superior planning and the fact that FBI agents seldom face the sponta-
neous events that are the primary cause of law enforcement fatalities. I
was at Quantico for an in-service when some of the first Special Weapons
and Tactics (SWAT) teams were being trained, and of course their training and utilization was the subject of considerable conversation. The
development of FBI SWAT teams was the direct result of the overwhelming firepower being utilized by the criminal element in the United States
and the indiscriminate firepower used by some of the 1960s domestic terrorist groups. The FBI believed it had to respond to this increased use of
force by creating a similar capability, but it was emphasized that SWAT
teams would be used only in exceptional cases. Initially they were made
up of senior FBI agents who had exhibited both proficiency in firearms
and coolness in arrest situations.

However, in the early 1980s the SWAT teams became convinced that
their capabilities had limitations, especially since each field office team
trained with their counterparts only sporadically and there would likely
be situations that required a larger, better-trained, and better-equipped

force. The Posse Comitatus Act would not allow for operations in the U.S. by U.S. military personnel without a presidential waiver, something presidents were loath to grant. So it was decided that the FBI should develop the capability to conduct larger-scale military-type operations. But the group was to be part of a law enforcement agency conducting a criminal investigation, preserving and collecting evidence, and viewing the area of operation as a crime scene, not a battlefield.

I was in the Washington field office when Danny Coulson was assigned there as the assistant special agent in charge of the newly approved Hostage Rescue Team. Coulson was one of those legendary figures in the FBI who always managed to be at the center of the action. He was an attorney with experience in the FBI's Legal Counsel Division and had been involved in the Iran–Contra investigation. It wasn't by accident that Director William Webster chose a lawyer to head the HRT. I am convinced that Webster had concerns for the establishment of a paramilitary force in the FBI and felt that ensuring the legality of its actions was paramount, not the tactical ability to accomplish an objective.

There was much discussion among the management about this new concept that would recruit fifty agents to serve as teams members, with additional staff for administrative and logistical functions. But Coulson made it abundantly clear that his first priority was to recruit FBI agents with a demonstrated ability to work cases first and to maintain a medium of physical fitness second. In fact, in Coulson's delightfully informative book, *No Heroes: Inside the FBI's Secret Counter-Terror Force*, he pithily observed, "I don't want anybody who blows through his cases so he can get in his ten miles a day." He even noted that when the first candidates for the team reported to Quantico, he had worn a coat and tie to reinforce the fact they were FBI personnel, not some hybrid military unit.

But over time, the original concept began to slip. SWAT teams were increasingly used for even the most routine arrests by timid SACs, much to the disgust of most street agents who had practiced hours at the Training Academy and at mandatory firearms training sessions in order to safely effect arrests. The HRT began to be further removed from the day-to-day operations of the FBI, and losing sight of its origins and motto, "To Save Lives," which led to the disastrous results of Ruby Ridge and Waco.

A successful operation by the HRT was to conclude a hostage or barricade situation without a loss of life, or without shots even being fired. The emphasis was on the ability of hostage negotiators to resolve a situation and to use the HRT only as a last resort. But there were increasing complaints by HRT members at the lack of deployment opportunities and that the constant training was becoming boring. So there developed a tendency to use the HRT individual members for operations far below the original standard. This was evident to me when HRT members came to Arkansas to participate in the arrest of Thomas Lavy, a single individual who was mobile and accessible, lived in a small house with no evidence of fortifications, and had espoused no views of hatred or overthrowing the government.

But the major crisis for the HRT was the crisis of leadership, and it was a failure of the selection process and of leadership that led to the events of Ruby Ridge and Waco that will haunt the FBI for generations.

When Richard Rogers was selected to head the HRT following the calm competence of Woody Johnson, there was surprise among those who knew Rogers. He had not been a member of the HRT or a SWAT team and had no experience in hostage negotiations or crisis management, though he had been a decorated Army officer in Vietnam. Coulson recognized that merely having served in Vietnam was in itself insufficient as a qualification to serve in the HRT. In his book he pointedly noted, "I didn't want any tortured souls lugging around unfinished business from Vietnam."

But Rogers had something more important than qualifications, he had the support of Assistant Director Floyd Clarke. And in the FBI's selection process, that kind of support overcomes other deficiencies. I recall the quiet concern for Rogers's selection, given his lack of background comparable to his predecessors, but none of us would have anticipated the disastrous results his assignment would have on the FBI.

The failures are well-documented. Rogers gave a command to shoot to kill, an order so alien to the FBI that I am told many of those at the scene in Ruby Ridge refused to implement it. In fact, in a speech the legendary J. Edgar Hoover gave in 1971 discussing the hazards of law enforcement, he observed, "[T]he fact [is] that FBI agents act in self defense and use firearms only as a last resort." The notion of shooting at someone who is not placing the life of someone else in immediate danger is contrary to everything that was reinforced in FBI agents' minds from the time of their arrival in training school.

Then there was the situation in Waco. After the horrific beginnings of the assault by the Bureau of Alcohol, Tobacco, and Firearms and the deaths of four ATF agents who should have never been placed in harm's way, the FBI was called in to assume responsibility for the protracted siege. It was here that the militarization of the FBI became apparent.

I first became aware of the assault at Waco when Harry "Skip" Brandon, the deputy assistant director of the National Security Division, stuck his head in my office and said, "You better turn on your TV." I clicked on the television that was always tuned to CNN and watched with horrified fascination as smoke began to billow from the building, the flag standing at right angles with the flagpole, and the tank beginning to punch holes in the side of the building. It looked like a scene from some foreign country, not Waco, Texas.

I wondered at the futility of inserting tear gas into the building, noting how strong the wind was blowing. At one point Brandon, or some of the others who were watching the scene in my office, commented that "some of the hostages should start coming out." I responded that they weren't coming out because they weren't hostages. David Koresh's people were there because they wanted to be there, or were convinced that they thought they wanted to be there. Instead of serving as a source of stress for Koresh himself, they were a source of his strength.

Later in the afternoon, after feeling numb on account of the events of the day and for what lay in store for the FBI, I walked across the street to Au Bon Pain for a cup of coffee and encountered an analyst who worked on domestic terrorism groups. I asked him what he thought of the day's events and he showed a rare flash of anger, commenting that it was "stupid" to plan an assault on April 19, a significant day for right-wing groups. It was the date the Battle of Lexington had commenced in 1775 and the day the federal government had started its assault on the compound of the Covenant, Sword, and Arm of the Lord in northern Arkansas in 1985, the paramilitary organization that had taken to living in a virtual fort in a remote part of the state. Clearly those engaged in the siege had not sought the input of analysts in their strategy sessions. By adding another significant event on that date, Waco helped lead to the carnage in Oklahoma City on April 19, 1995.

That evening, as I went to the garage after one of the longer days in my career, I encountered Mike Kehoe, the section chief at FBI headquarters responsible for the oversight of the Branch Davidian investigation. I asked if he thought what had occurred would be a problem for the FBI. He said it wouldn't be a problem because the FBI hadn't started the fires.

I was shocked. "For God's sake, Mike," I blurted out. "Women and children were burned alive, regardless of who started the fire."

Kehoe maintained he didn't think it would be a problem. It was apparent to me that he and whoever was directing the assault were either completely removed from reality or in complete denial. Incredibly, the single individual with the greatest tactical experience in the FBI, Danny Coulson, who had already been critical of Rogers and the situation at Waco, was not part of the command team that made the decision to implement the assault plan.

When the results of Waco became apparent, President Clinton went into hiding, and the next day Janet Reno walked before television cameras and took responsibility for the debacle. She received accolades, though they were short-lived, and stressed that her concern for the safety of the children compelled her to approve the assault. I was advised some time later, when there was a discussion of the White House's attempts to manipulate the media, that they were upset at the popularity of Reno's comments. It had been the White House that had pressured Reno to make the statement to take the heat off Clinton. This won praise for her "courage" in going before the assembled cameras, followed by questions from the media about why Clinton had disappeared.

In the inevitable after-action review, the first of several that was conducted, an agent who worked for me was part of the team. He returned from Texas and Quantico and as we visited, I asked about his impressions of what had occurred. He was firm in his conviction that the FBI had not started the fires, but made an interesting comment. He noted that the fundamental cause for the problems in Waco was a breakdown in discipline, especially among the tactical agents. He talked about how everything from dress to behavior had deteriorated during the siege. He pointed out the fatigue of the HRT was in part due to their refusal to be relieved by SWAT teams for a day or so to allow them to rest—SWAT teams deployed for that very purpose. He spoke of the "cowboy" attitude of the agents who drove tanks around the area, on one occasion running over a car, and how their behavior even raised the eyebrows of the local police.

But most troubling was the fact the tactical groups were allowed to completely get away from the motto of the HRT: "To Save Lives." The negotiators were effectively left out of the planning of the operation and when there was conflict—and conflict was considerable—the management at the scene invariably tilted toward the view of Rogers.

The FBI will for generations have to live with the results of an ill-advised plan that went awry after losing sight of its essential goal.

THE FBI WAS SLOW to learn the effects of Waco and Ruby Ridge. Sometime later, after I had been transferred to Little Rock, I was shown a new group of folders that were to be used for the recruitment of agent applicants and was amazed to see the cover design. Notwithstanding the disaster that had so tarnished the FBI's reputation, the front cover showed three agents, one white male, one black male, and a white female, in full SWAT gear, in a surreal scene, emerging from an alley with smoke or fog billowing up behind them. The back cover had a rear view of the agents, one brandishing an automatic weapon, also walking down the alley toward a billowing cloud. It was a scene not unlike some Kurt Russell movies that depict an apocalyptic world after a devastating war.

I called Weldon Kennedy, the deputy director who had replaced Larry Potts, and spoke to one of his assistants. I expressed my concern that after all that had occurred, someone at FBI headquarters had been so insensitive to approve a brochure that showed the FBI at its paramilitary worst, a minor part of the FBI daily mission even without the events of Waco and Ruby Ridge. Apparently someone agreed, for the brochure was recalled and, at the cost of thousands of dollars, reprinted with another cover.

On May 12, 1962, Army General Douglas MacArthur made a final trip to West Point to address the cadet corps. It was at that time he delivered his remarkable "duty, honor, country" speech. While many recall the sheer poetry of the last couple of paragraphs beginning with "The shadows are lengthening for me," and concluding with "[M]y last conscious thoughts will be of the Corps; and the Corps; and the Corps. I bid you farewell," there is another line that I always remembered. MacArthur observed in an earlier paragraph that "the soldier above all other people prays for peace." While I certainly can't equate the typical FBI tactical problem with a battlefield, I noticed that it was those who had never served in the military and seen the carnage of armed conflict, and never served as law enforcement officers and walked in the blood and gore of a homicide scene, who were the strongest advocates of tactical solutions to hostage situations.

Increasingly, SWAT teams were staffed with agents whose total experience was the relatively sterile law enforcement environment of the FBI, and it was those agents who were most prone to walk the halls of the FBI offices wearing SWAT gear and who looked for the opportunity to be in public wearing their military garb. They have forgotten that the FBI is foremost an investigative agency, not a paramilitary force. Their mission is to use the minimum of force.

It is imperative that the FBI relegate SWAT teams and the HRT to their proper position as alternative options in arrest situations, not the first choice. I am convinced one of the reasons many federal judges and U.S. attorneys increasingly issue subpoenas for indicted individuals is the FBI's increased penchant for agents in military garb brandishing automatic weapons for even routine arrests. Arrests should not be media events, but should be designed to take the individual into custody in a manner that will result in the slightest degree of disruption to the area. Further, an arrest is a part of an investigation and how it fits into the objectives of an investigation, to include potential for cooperation, should be paramount.

Closely aligned with the militarization of the FBI is the FBI's role in domestic terrorism, which the FBI officially defines as those acts committed by U.S.-based terrorist groups and does not, for instance, include such acts as the 9/11 attacks. The definition of terrorism, at the time of Waco, Ruby Ridge, and the Lavy case was, "The unlawful use of force or violence against persons or property to intimidate or coerce a government, civilian population, or any segment thereof in furtherance of political or social objectives." My thoughts on domestic terrorism evolved over time and became definitive when I was preparing to give a speech before the Radiological Emergency Preparedness Workshop in Eureka Springs, Arkansas, in April 1997. I viewed the definition of terrorism as having five essential elements. If an incident doesn't have all five, it isn't terrorism. Those elements are:

- *"The unlawful use of force or violence . . ."* This is what is stated, force of violence in violation of existing laws.
- *". . . against persons or property . . ."* This describes the necessary object of the unlawful activity.
- *". . . to intimidate or coerce . . ."* This describes the object of the illegal activity.
- *". . . a government, civilian population, or any segment thereof . . ."* This details who or what must be targeted for intimidation or coercion.
- *". . . in furtherance of political or social objectives."* Again, this describes the essential motive behind the activity.

Clearly the actions of Thomas Lavy did not warrant him being labeled a terrorist or the investigation being termed a terrorist investigation. But this did not satisfy the needs of a program that had oversold the threat to the United States posed by domestic terrorist groups resulting in a large and unjustified increase in resources.

I RECEIVED A TELEPHONE CALL one day from an acquaintance at FBI headquarters while I was in Little Rock and was asked how many additional resources I needed to work domestic terrorism. Based on crime surveys and the considerable travel and conversations I had across the state, I knew I needed no additional resources whatsoever. In fact, I didn't need all that I had. After I was told I would have to receive some anyway, I laughingly told the caller that I had some "terroristic health-care cases" that needed addressing.

There had been an absolutely irresponsible request by the terrorism sections in 1996 for an additional fifteen hundred agents to work both international and domestic terrorism, a request made without an intelligence or analytical basis. Even supporters of the program knew the request of that magnitude was absurd. Bryant, as the assistant director of the National Security Division, had finally decided that he would ask for five hundred additional agents, with expectations of receiving half that amount. He was advised repeatedly that there was no need for them. He ignored that advice.

I was not surprised at Bryant's position. When I was in the command post at FBI headquarters during the investigation of the Oklahoma City bombing of April 19, 1995, Bryant one evening stated he wanted a "full field investigation opened on every militia group on the United States." I pointed out that even if there had been such investigations before the bombing, it was unlikely that Timothy McVeigh would have been detected, for he didn't belong to any of those groups. Furthermore, there was a legal impediment to the demand. The standards that must be met in order to investigate domestic groups are exact. The FBI must show the group has advocated violence, has the potential to commit the violence, and have a federal nexus such as a threat to bomb an IRS building. The actions of most domestic militia groups in the U.S. fail to meet that standard by a long shot.

Besides, it had become apparent that most of the militia groups in the U.S. shared the revulsion of other Americans at the indiscriminate death and carnage caused by Timothy McVeigh's bomb. If anything, the pictures of the fireman carrying the severely injured baby from the wreckage, the public outrage at the incident, and the overwhelming law enforcement response diminished the probability of another such incident being committed by domestic groups in the immediate future, if ever.

I became convinced in domestic terrorism matters, it was the rogue individual the FBI should be worried about, not organized groups. Past history pointed out that fact with absolute clarity. But history did not satisfy Bryant. In meetings with the SACs, inevitably the Committee on Solidarity with the People of El Salvador (CISPES) was mentioned as an example of the FBI getting into legal and public difficulty by investigating a group on the basis of dubious legal authority. Finally, at one meeting, Bryant banged his fist on a table and said he was "tired of hearing about CISPES!" Well, he may have been tired of hearing about CISPES, but we weren't going to forget that example since it would be us, the field commanders, not those at FBI headquarters, who would have to justify any actions that would be the object of later scrutiny. There was no expectation that those at FBI headquarters would take responsibility for such a decision.

There was this strident approach toward the need to constantly display aggressiveness, and any perceived lack of aggressiveness in an SAC was viewed as a managerial weakness. While in the command post at FBI headquarters during the Oklahoma City investigation, I saw one exceptionally capable SAC, who should have been a deputy director in the future, savaged for his perceived lack of aggressiveness at investigating militia groups in his area. He was later proven right in his approach, both legally and tactically. But the damage had been done. He eventually retired prematurely and entered private industry, much to the loss of the FBI.

Some SACs without counterintelligence backgrounds or appreciation for its nuances quickly moved resources away from counterintelligence to domestic terrorism in order to curry favor with Bryant and Freeh.

One such office was Albuquerque, New Mexico, the scene of the flawed Wen Ho Lee investigation, where a lack of counterintelligence expertise in the field office, combined with a similar lack of Chinese counterintelligence expertise at FBI headquarters, made the result inevitable.

This situation was exacerbated by Freeh testifying on Capitol Hill that the increased number of agents were in place. Apparently no one at FBI headquarters was willing to tell Freeh otherwise. I specifically discussed that problem with Bob Blitzer, a terrorism section chief and he agreed that the resources were not in the field offices and Assistant Director John Lewis had not, and would not, advise Freeh of that fact.

I began to engage in a battle of wills with the Terrorism Section. I was already suffering from a resource drain caused by Whitewater and could ill afford to lose more agents to a nonexistent threat when we were solely pressed to investigate the ongoing corruption and other cases of higher priority in Arkansas. But I wasn't willing to engage in a subterfuge to give the impression I was going to use the additional agents that had been allocated but not received.

After the very successful inspection of the fall of 1997, we had been required to conduct yet another survey to determine the domestic terrorism threat in Arkansas. Those survey results revealed, as did the two previous surveys, there was no continuing domestic terrorism threat of consequence in Arkansas by organized groups, though there were several individuals that were perhaps capable of some act of violence. In June 1998, after we had reported the results of the survey and that we were not going to divert resources from other investigations to satisfy an under-utilization issue not of my own making, I received a response penned by a junior bureaucrat at FBI headquarters, but approved by Blitzer and, I assumed, then-Assistant Director John Lewis. This response took issue with the survey results, described Arkansas as a hotbed of terrorist activity, made reference to the "enduring" threat in Arkansas, and cited the Covenant, Sword, and Arm of the Lord compound in northern Arkansas.

The CSA had ceased to exist in 1985, its members were scattered, and one retired agent I personally discussed the group with and who had maintained contact with them, referred to them as "aging hippies." They didn't want to talk about the past and didn't associate with any other groups that embraced their former beliefs. I discussed the CSA with Bill Buford, the ATF resident agent in charge in Arkansas, who had been at the assault of the CSA compound with Danny Coulson in 1985 and was later wounded in the shootout at Waco. He agreed that the CSA had ceased to pose a threat. I even pointed out the compound had been abandoned so long that trees had grown up in the middle of it; I could have cut pulp wood where these supposed terrorists allegedly planned their evil deeds.

In my response I pointed out the fallacy of the argument about the threat in Arkansas. I resented the fact that a low-level headquarters bureaucrat who had never been to Arkansas was willing to talk about the "enduring" terrorism there. I added that the CSA members had apparently done nothing illegal, for they had all been found not guilty in a trial in Ft. Smith, Arkansas, prosecuted by United States Attorney Asa Hutchinson, later a congressman, head of the Drug Enforcement Administration, and current undersecretary of the Department of Homeland Security. But such legal niceties did not satisfy the FBI, whose need to hype the domestic terrorism threat included a continued reference to the CSA, regardless of the fact it had ceased to exist either as an organization or as a threat.

History has shown us that terrorism of any type is cyclical. There is a constant ebb and flow of threats by terrorist groups, both domestic and international. For instance, it's been some time since such groups as the Japanese Red Army, the Black Panthers, the United Freedom Front, even the Covenant, Sword, and Arm of the Lord posed a threat to anyone. As hard as it is to believe, at some point, al Qaeda will not be a threat, though I am not so naïve as to believe that terrorism of any kind will disappear. Terrorism itself is a constant, but the threat posed by different groups is anything but constant. And therein lies the great difficulty in the cessation of civil liberties in the name of combating terrorism. The FBI has, in the past, been goaded into conducting terrorism investigations by various attorneys general and senators and congressmen on

Capitol Hill, again CISPES comes to mind. But after a passage of time, those same politicians who demanded action, later, with convenient loss of memory, were at the forefront of denigrating the FBI for the very investigations they once lauded. Such is the nature of terrorism and the nature of many politicians themselves.

The great challenge for the FBI is to resist the political pressure to become a single-issue agency, and to resist the urge to, indeed, push the envelope in conducting terrorism investigations. This will take an FBI director who has the courage to stand up to an attorney general who seems to have taken a cavalier attitude toward civil liberties. Ashcroft will be long gone when, at some time in the future, al Qaeda is no longer the threat it is now, but the very activities he would want the FBI to undertake will inevitably be subject to review and criticism. I would urge the agents of the FBI, and especially Director Mueller, to remember the lesson of CISPES.

There are vulnerabilities inherent in our democracy and they will continue as long as citizens are allowed a freedom of movement, the freedom of association, and all the other guarantees of our Constitution. The Constitution provides would-be terrorists with the very freedoms that enable them to commit terrorist acts against the government and the laws they purport to loathe. But this does not allow the government to make exceptions to the safeguards of our Constitution in investigating our citizens. The FBI's domestic terrorism program, indeed all investigative programs, including the International Terrorism investigations in the aftermath of 9/11, should investigate only those matters that are in strict agreement with attorney general guidelines for both groups and individuals and with a full awareness of the potential for civil liberties to be trampled upon for the sake of national security. There is no place in the FBI, there is no place in this country, regardless of the attempts at justification by Attorney General John Ashcroft, to do otherwise.

CHAPTER 28

WHO'S THE BOSS?

"My God, you can't even get a velvet Elvis for two dollars!"

I.C. Smith to a reporter upon hearing a painting of President Clinton
stolen from the Arkansas Capitol was for sale for two dollars

Dealing with the press is often a problem for law enforcement because there's a fine line between the right of people to know what their government is doing and the government's need to conceal certain information in order to accomplish its goals. I decided long ago that if I was to err it would be on the side of disclosing information through the media rather than withholding information the people have a right to know.

The tendency to mistrust the media is certainly justified at times, but that mistrust should not manifest itself by halting the flow of information to the public. I have found that being overly restrictive with the press inevitably leads to leaks, and press leaks—especially if they are erroneous—can be devastating. An erroneous press leak is just as bad as a premature release of information.

While I recognize the need to keep some information secret, especially in the area of national security, I am also convinced that many individuals and agencies hide behind a cloak of secrecy only to obscure their own mistakes and misconduct. There is a tendency to over-classify information to the point that it is virtually useless. But remember that in governmental bureaucracies, information is power.

I recall one study when I was on the National Foreign Intelligence Board concerning a criminal problem. Its distribution was so severely restricted that only about ten copies were printed. Yet an FBI review of the completed report disclosed that well over 75 percent of it came from open-source and unclassified FBI information, and the rest was of dubious value. Further, its classification was so restrictive that if the information had been of any value to law enforcement (which it wasn't), it could not have been used even as a basis for a criminal investigation, much less for prosecuting an alleged offense. Arthur Hadley had it right when he wrote, "The possession of secrets enhances the power of those who know them. Intelligence information is often unnecessarily restricted for reasons of bureaucratic prestige rather than national security."

Certainly Paula Casey and I had different views about the press, though I do know Casey wasn't above assisting with a well-placed bit of information. I judiciously declined comment on such areas as indictments or details of an ongoing investigation, regardless of the accusations she and Michael Johnson leveled against me, but I also believed it was foolhardy to make "No comment" when it involved the obvious.

For instance, if a reporter asked that I comment on the fact that FBI agents were serving a search warrant at a specific location, it was ridiculous for me to respond with "No comment." I believed my office would be better served if I acknowledged that, "Yes, the FBI is in a process of conducting a search warrant, but I am not in a position to provide any further details." When the press receives a quote beyond the cryptic "No comment," that infers a measure of cooperation which avoids the ill will that develops from failure to confirm what the reporter could visually observe.

This philosophy was borne out when I met with the editors of the *Arkansas Democrat-Gazette* after the paper had run a couple of tough editorial cartoons regarding the FBI. I was in Phoenix attending a meeting of the International Association of Chiefs of Police and had copies of the cartoons with me. I showed them to Deputy Director Weldon Kennedy and Freeh, with the suggestion that I meet with the editors to ascertain if those cartoons reflected their collective view of the FBI. Both agreed to the proposal, and I arranged the meeting upon my return to Little Rock. There I raised the question: Did those cartoons reflect their views of the FBI? The reply was unexpected but also gratifying.

One editor said he had two views of the FBI, a generally positive one of the Arkansas office and a contrasting, not-so-positive one of headquarters. He mentioned the accessibility I had granted reporters and while there was no expectation that I would divulge internal information, the fact I made myself readily available was a source of goodwill far different from what happened when he placed a call to FBI headquarters. There, he said, the inevitable response was a "sh—y 'no comment.'"

I asked the editors if I could pass their sentiments on to Freeh and they agreed. I wrote a letter to Freeh detailing the conversation and urged him to appoint a national spokesman to respond to media inquiries and to establish a platform for providing good news to the public about FBI programs and successes. I had discussed the matter with Kennedy, who had also been urging Freeh to have more contact with the media. A few weeks later, Freeh did appoint an old friend of mine, Tron Brekke, to that position.

Some reporters called me frequently and more times than not, we would just visit about some news of the day such as speculating who would be the next University of Arkansas football coach, would Governor Mike Huckabee get the much-desired 60 percent of the vote in the general election (he didn't), what was the national news of the day, etc. These routine contacts built a bridge of trust that often had positive results for the FBI.

On one occasion the media had gotten information about an ongoing investigation outside of Little Rock and were going to run a story that had the potential of harming an ongoing investigation by the DEA. Through my contacts I was able to delay the story. This allowed the reporter to later write a more complete and more accurate account of the investigation, and also protected the integrity of the investigation that would have been lost with a premature story that was also erroneous. There were many other similar occasions.

I also was not hesitant to call the media when something misleading or inaccurate appeared. One example involved a candidate for the archaic position of constable who had publicly stated he had given the FBI information that reflected badly on his opponent. He explained how he had spent time in the office, the nature of the information he provided, and so forth. I checked the office log for visitors and noted he had embellished on the length of time he was in the office. When I talked to the agent who had talked with him, I learned he had exaggerated the content of the conversation.

I called the reporter, who had run the story without asking me for a comment from the FBI, and gave her an accurate account of what occurred, noting, "I don't want to get involved in the politics, but at the same time, I don't want to get used in the politics."

I relied on the media as an outlet for advising the public on other issues. Once there was a rash of letters coming into Arkansas from Nigeria with fraudulent offers, so I asked the media to warn the public to avoid responding to the letters. Another time there was discussion of the exploding methamphetamine problem in Arkansas.

In June 1997, there was a large exercise in Memphis, Tennessee, that involved several field offices and their SWAT teams. The Little Rock team members had worked a normal day, then driven a vehicle loaded with SWAT equipment to Memphis. There they learned the reservations at the hotel had not been held, so the agents had searched for an alternative. By this time it was approaching midnight.

They located another hotel, but rather than a motel-style layout where every room had a door opening onto the parking lot, the rooms opened into an enclosed hallway leading to the lobby. Since the agents couldn't offload the weapons and ammunition without walking through the lobby with them, they left them in the vehicle. That night the Little Rock vehicle was stolen, torched, and the weapons stolen.

There was a national media frenzy. FBI headquarters was looking for a scapegoat, questioning why the teams were there, why they had weapons and live ammunition (there was to be a live firing exercise that had been approved by FBI headquarters) and asking other questions designed to fix blame immediately.

John Hancock, the SAC for Memphis, had already called a press conference to address the exercise, and I argued that there should be some separate comment about the stolen vehicle, a suggestion he rejected. Of course, most of the questions concerned the stolen FBI SWAT van, detracting from an otherwise good story regarding the exercise. Since I was in his territory, I kept my mouth shut.

However, when I returned to Little Rock the phone was ringing, and I talked with Judd Slivka, a reporter from the *Arkansas Democrat-Gazette*. I made it clear I was ultimately responsible. I was correctly quoted saying that I was "not in a position to know what each of my employees is doing at each moment of the day. But I'm ultimately responsible for what my people do. I'm ultimately responsible for what happened to the van."

The media frenzy quickly died down, simply because I addressed the issue head-on and made what some considered a definitive statement that didn't allow the story to continue to, in media parlance, "have legs."

I also believe the media can be a good source to put a human face on what is often a faceless organization. On one occasion, I had just returned from a weekend out of town with Carla and as we walked in the house, the phone was ringing. While still holding bags in my hands, I answered the phone and learned a reporter was looking for information regarding the theft of a painting of Clinton from the Arkansas State Capitol. The painting, which was U.S. government property, had been discovered missing while I was gone, had been the object of quite a search, and the media interest was high. Arkansas Secretary of State Sharon Priest had finally advised the public that since it was government property, the investigation had been turned over to the FBI. I hadn't been informed of the referral. However, the reporter also told me that the painting had already been recovered when a homeless man tried to sell it on the street for two dollars. I responded, "My God, you can't even get a velvet Elvis for two dollars!"

That line was picked up by the wire services and received widespread play across the United States, much to the amusement of my colleagues who called me for the next several days laughing about the quote.

On another occasion, I received a telephone call from Meg Jones, a reporter from the *Milwaukee Journal Sentinel*, after Wayne Edenfield, the senior agent in Fayetteville, Arkansas, had caught a fugitive, Steven Rowe, in southern Missouri. The apprehension involved a chase through the woods, followed by an attempted carjacking of a vehicle with a six-year-old boy in the car. The boy's father jumped in the back of the truck, reached through the rear window and choked Rowe into submission until Edenfield arrived on the scene.

I gave a brief account of the incident, knowing she had already talked to local authorities. When she persisted in wanting to know more details of the chase, I likened it to Arkansan Jimmy Driftwood's song, "The Battle of New Orleans," recorded by Johnny Horton, where "they ran through the briers and they ran through the brambles and they ran through the bushes where a rabbit wouldn't go." Jones used the direct quote in her article, which served to provide a good description of the event, as well as add some much-needed amusement to a business that is all too often humorless.

I do not regard the media as the enemy. In fact, their role is absolutely essential. But the media are not blameless. Like the FBI, the media world is made up of individuals with their own biases, agendas, and fears who can display great personal courage but are also susceptible to human failures.

Clearly there were some members of the media who failed to adequately report the antics of Bill and Hillary Clinton in Arkansas, and even today find themselves too closely aligned with certain politicians to provide in-depth and insightful reporting. I know one senior member of the media in Arkansas who, when he heard that State Senator Nick Wilson was the object of FBI search warrants, said he hoped "Nick is not in trouble because we have been friends for a long time." Clearly this reporter, who has been on the Arkansas scene for years and was a personal acquaintance of Bill Clinton, was not in a position to provide tough reporting on either Wilson or Clinton.

Had the media in Arkansas done its job, there would arguably have never been a Clinton presidency. If the country knew then what it knows now, the history of the 1990s in America might have been far different. But local reporters didn't report. Instead, outside members of the media went to Arkansas and scooped their local colleagues. And so the most insightful reporting of Clinton's travails in Arkansas over the course of his presidency, all of which was in the public interest, was done by outsiders.

Given all that, it is absolutely essential for the sake of its own credibility that the FBI maintain a press posture separate and distinct from that of the Department of Justice and local United States attorneys. The FBI is better known, and the public still holds the FBI in higher regard than it does the USAs. Special agents in charge who hide behind the shadows of their media coordinators, who refuse to return calls from the media and who abdicate their office's relationship with the local U.S. attorney's office, aren't displaying leadership and are shirking their managerial responsibilities.

FEARLESS MANAGEMENT is the most acute need in the modern FBI because politicization—the shameless attempt to influence management decisions for political purposes—is the single greatest danger to the criminal justice system. The Clinton administration did not invent this situation, but, as with many things, they refined it to a degree unprecedented in the annals of American politics.

This was clear when the administration summarily fired all ninety-seven United States attorneys in the United States within days of assuming office. The manner in which this was done was unprecedented, and while there was always the recognition that United States attorneys served at the pleasure of the president, the firing of every one of them in the country left frighteningly huge management voids. Replacements had not been identified, vetted, and approved by the Senate and no attorney general had even been named who could aid in the search for replacements.

The administration went through the embarrassing and even bizarre search for an attorney general, suffering setbacks by publicly naming

Kimba Wood then Zoe Baird before, in what was in all appearances an act of desperation, settling on Janet Reno. I had met Reno in Miami when I served as ASAC and where she had a well-deserved reputation as one who had greater interest in prosecuting deadbeat dads than drug dealers.

The criteria for appointments for both the attorney general and the United States attorneys was never competency but instead race, gender, and—most important of all—political affiliation and loyalty. Credentials as a prosecutor were never a factor.

The result, in the view of many of my colleagues and based on our collective decades upon decades of experience, was that Clinton appointees were the weakest group of United States attorneys in our memory. Simply stated, the management of the criminal justice system was conducted by many who were poorly prepared to occupy those positions and who, even at that, were in many cases second or third choices.

Any career investigator would prefer that all prosecutions be handled by career prosecutors, who, like the investigator, keep their politics to themselves and are publicly and privately apolitical. But ours is an imperfect system. All we can hope for is a level of competency and willingness in political corruption cases to overcome past political affiliations and, for the time they are serving as the principle prosecutors for the federal government, remain politically neutral.

I recall one day during the investigation of Nick Wilson when Paula Casey lamented the fact that after the prosecutions of Wilson and other legislators, no one would want to hire her. I admired her courage and had compassion for the predicament she found herself in prosecuting powerful members of the political system that produced the president of the United States and appointed her a U.S. attorney. However, I had no real sympathy beyond that, for she had an obligation to fulfill the oath of her office when she agreed to take the job.

Janet Reno was the third choice, at best, to be attorney general. I know that P.K. Holmes III was not the first choice to be United States attorney in the Western District of Arkansas, and this applied to Paula Casey as well. Holmes had a lucrative practice in civil law and was best known for serving as Democratic Party chairman in Sebastian County, Arkansas, and being an avid supporter of Senator David Pryor. Casey was a teacher at the University of Arkansas at Little Rock Law School after being a legislative aide to Senator Dale Bumpers. Neither Holmes nor Casey had spent time in courtrooms engaged in criminal trials as either a prosecutor or defense attorney, and neither had experience in managing large staffs.

It was clear in Little Rock that the only people being considered for the position of United States attorney were females. This was at the dictates of Hillary Clinton and while Casey was, in a real sense, not ready to assume the position she ultimately agreed to assume, she was no worse than any number of candidates who may have been considered.

Holmes worked hard to overcome his lack of criminal courtroom experience and emerged as a likable and competent prosecutor, though his past political affiliations made frequent recusals inevitable. Casey handled the brunt of the politically sensitive cases with varying degrees of success and enthusiasm. She too found the need to recuse herself from cases with some frequency and overall, I am convinced the political nature of the appointments of Casey and Holmes resulted in cases not being pursued. This was especially true given the politicization of the Department of Justice. Basically, the department did not offer a viable alternative for prosecuting those cases that were referred due to Casey and Holmes's inability and unwillingness to handle the investigations because of past political affiliation. To me, this was not a valid and responsible stance, for they should prosecute any and all worthy cases with expediency and vigor, regardless of past political ties and regardless of public perception. Had there been more apolitical appointees and appointees based on merit in lieu of political affiliation, gender, or race, this wouldn't have been an issue.

Without the work of the independent counsel, I believe Webb Hubbell, who stole money from both his clients and law partners, very likely would have been the deputy attorney general, if not attorney general itself. It is hard to imagine a greater travesty to the criminal justice system than having such an unprincipled individual at such a high position, where the enduring symbol is of a blindfolded woman holding the scales of justice. There was the picture of a virtually grieving Janet Reno lamenting Hubbell's departure in a public ceremony while all knew he was in ethical, if not legal, jeopardy. In hindsight, there is no doubt in my mind that Hubbell was placed at the Department of Justice to serve as a watchdog for a White House that had every reason to fear an impartial and unfettered Department of Justice. This was especially important when they were forced to appoint Janet Reno, a political unknown for the Clintons.

There is little the FBI can do to avoid the political spoils system that has evolved in the criminal justice system beyond ensuring there are complete and thorough background investigations of all individuals being nominated and ensuring that all information is contained in the report. I recall when I was in St. Louis conducting the background investigation of William Webster for FBI director. While in Clayton, Missouri, interviewing a reference, another attorney who obviously knew what I was doing asked if he could make an unsolicited comment. When I told him he should, he said, "Bill Webster takes eight hours to do what most attorneys do in four," but went on to add that Webster was of high moral character, etc.

I returned to the office and wrote my report, including the unsolicited comment. The supervisor deleted that addition stating it wasn't from someone on the reference list and may be viewed as negative. I argued, "So what?" but the supervisor prevailed, and that comment, which was prophetic for those who later worked with Webster, was not included. I always viewed the background of Webster as being incomplete without that tidbit of information, though it certainly would not have altered his subsequent approval as FBI director.

Future backgrounds of prospective United States attorneys and attorney generals must contain all the available information, and if unqualified personnel are ultimately selected for those positions, as was done in the Clinton administration and from all appearances the Bush administration as well, it will not be because the FBI succumbed to political pressures.

The FBI must remain clear of political interference. One of the great concerns I have is the greater interference by the department in not only the FBI's conduct of criminal investigations such as CAMPCON, but in the internal administration of the FBI itself. It is absolutely absurd to think career DOJ employees are not susceptible to political pressures. The comfort of their positions, their assignments, and their promotions are all tied to the ultimate decision-making of political appointees within the department. Increasingly, there is sentiment to "bring the FBI under control," an euphemism for bringing the FBI under the dominance of an increasingly politicized Department of Justice. From all indications, the FBI under Director Mueller, certainly at the dictates of Attorney General Ashcroft, has greatly centralized control of investigations. This has had the effect of greatly diminishing the authority of individual SACs and the agents conducting the actual investigations. In effect, the very problem that was readily evident in the Whitewater and CAMPCON investigations is likely occurring within the FBI. As the bureaucracy in Washington debates strategies, agents in the field, those most familiar with the individuals and issues surrounding the investigation, are left to while away their time awaiting some decision from Washington where decisions and initiatives are seldom done with any dispatch. This has the inevitable consequence of impacting, adversely, morale and further lends itself to politicizing the investigative process.

AS THE LEGACY OF Louis Freeh evolves, one of the negative aspects of that legacy has been the encroachment of the department in such areas as the discipline of FBI personnel, promotions, and assignments of ranking FBI officials, a practice that has continued under Director Mueller and Attorney General Ashcroft's Department of Justice. Further, the degree of friction between the FBI and the department, during Freeh's tenure, was both unprecedented and unhealthy. Freeh, to his credit, demonstrated courage in confronting the department in some areas, notably the CAMPCON matter.

Mueller certainly has the background to be the FBI director, though running a USA's office is a far cry from managing 30,000 employees with a four-billion-dollar budget. He is an experienced prosecutor and from all accounts is unafraid to act quickly and decisively in removing poorly performing employees. Clearly Mueller was the early favorite of Attorney General John Ashcroft for the job. When he emerged as one of the three names on the attorney general's "short list," it was apparent Ashcroft meant for Mueller to rise to the top. George Terwilliger would have encountered opposition in the confirmation process due to the prominent role he had played in the disputed Florida ballot contest. And Judge Sterling Johnson, a distinguished African-American jurist, could not be considered a serious candidate for a ten-year term given his sixty-seven years of age. Indeed, I viewed his placement on the short list as tokenism.

Mueller received considerable kudos for having given up a lucrative law practice in Boston to prosecute street crimes back in Washington, D.C. No one is going to be criticized for prosecuting Washington-area gang bangers and drug dealers. But while those prosecutions are certainly needed, they are politically safe.

I am certain the obvious close relationship between Ashcroft and Mueller pays dividends in such matters as the mammoth investigation resulting from the attacks of September 11, 2001. The country and the FBI benefit from the FBI director and attorney general having that type of relationship in contrast to the uneasy truce between Freeh and Reno. But that is not the true test of Mueller's courage and independence. At some point, if it hasn't already occurred, there will be a need to conduct an aggressive investigation that is also politically sensitive. The true test for Mueller will be his courage to do so and whether he has the independence from Ashcroft to aggressively and thoroughly conduct an investigation that may have adverse political impact. I am not especially optimistic that will occur.

Indeed, it is the perception of many both inside and outside the FBI that it is Ashcroft, not Mueller, who actually runs the FBI. That perception has in fact been the object of some ridicule. One story widely circulated among past and current FBI personnel was that Mueller had participated in a press conference and "you could hardly see Ashcroft's lips moving."

However, Director Mueller and future FBI directors, if the trend of politicization continues, must demonstrate courage and independence in conducting politically sensitive investigations. There is no longer an independent counsel's law that offers an alternative avenue for such investigations. It is left up to the Department of Justice and its principal investigative agency, the FBI, to ensure that such investigations will occur. This will require greater political independence than has been demonstrated in the recent past.

The very future of the criminal justice system depends on it.

EPILOGUE
Preventing 9/11: Where the FBI Went Wrong

"Someday someone will die—and [legal] wall or not—the public will not understand why we were not more effective in throwing every resource we had at certain 'problems.' Let's hope the National Security Law Unit will stand behind their decisions then, especially since the biggest threat to us now, UBL [Osama bin Laden], is getting the most 'protection.'"

An early September 2001 e-mail from an unidentified
New York FBI agent to the FBI's National Security Law Unit

"We're like a soccer goalkeeper," the FBI's Dale Watson told Congress in September 2002, one year after the worst terrorist attacks in American history. "We can block 99 shots," Watson complained, "and nobody wants to talk about any of those. And the only thing anyone wants to talk about is the one that gets through." I have known Watson for probably twenty years, since he was an agent working Soviet bloc counterintelligence, and while not surprised, was still profoundly disappointed in his statement.

Watson, then the outgoing FBI chief of counterintelligence and counterterrorism, saw his whining fall on deaf ears—and rightly so. Regardless of his statements, the central issue remains. The September 11 attacks occurred on his watch and he, like the rest of his contemporaries in the Bureau's upper reaches, have never been able to cite any examples of the "99 shots" the FBI and the rest of the intelligence community supposedly blocked, certainly nothing that had the potential to be as damaging as what occurred on September 11, 2001.

Nor can Watson argue that the problem is just a single stray shot that swept past the goalkeeper on that tragic day. While it may be convenient to deny responsibility, any official speaking candidly would admit that longstanding intelligence failures on the part of the FBI, not fate or flukes, helped pave the way for the decades of terrorist atrocities that culminated in September 11. The examples are legion: the bombing of Pan Am Flight 103 over Lockerbie, Scotland, in December 1988, the first World Trade Center bombing in 1993, the bombing of the U.S. Marines at the Khobar Towers in Saudi Arabia in 1996, the bombings of U.S. embassies in Kenya and Tanzania in 1998, and the bombing of the *USS Cole* in 2000. Even the foiled Millennium bombers, caught when crossing the Canadian border in December 1999 as they prepared to blow up Los Angeles International Airport, owe their capture not to an intelligence success, but to the vigilance of an obscure agent at the U.S. Customs Service named Diane Downs.

However, we must also recognize that the fault for failing to respond to these warning signs lies not just with the FBI—not even just with the United States intelligence establishment. True, the Central Intelligence Agency, the National Security Agency, the Defense Intelligence Agency, and the intelligence services of the Army, Navy, Air Force, and Marine Corps collectively failed to prevent any of these calamities from occurring. But so did the famed British MI-6, the German BND, the French DGSE, and yes, even the Israeli Mossad.

But to the extent the FBI deserves the criticism it has received, and it is criticism that is certainly deserved, much can be explained by the checkered history of the Bureau's international terrorism program. The Bureau's efforts got off the ground in 1980, in the wake of the Shah of Iran's fall and the concomitant rise of the Ayatollah Khomeini, who was promoting his own brand of radical Islamic fundamentalism. At the time I was at the FBI's Washington field office, and remained there as the fifty-two U.S. embassy personnel were held hostage in Tehran for

444 days. The FBI's knee-jerk response was to form "terrorism squads" around the country and a Terrorism Section at FBI headquarters. I noted that virtually all of those initially involved in managing the terrorism program were drawn from criminal investigations. Further, most of the people assigned to the terrorism effort were not considered the best and brightest of their squads. Typically, when there weren't enough volunteers to staff the special terrorism squads, supervisors kept their best agents and sent others to the terrorism operation; usually they sent the poorest performers. And the vast majority of those came off squads that handled criminal investigations, not counterintelligence.

Therein lies the problem that would plague the FBI's international terrorism program for decades—until September 11, when the nation's intelligence community could no longer ignore the Bureau's bureaucratic and strategic failings: The FBI had long approached international terrorism investigations as if they were street crimes, never mastering or even assimilating such intelligence techniques as the use of analysts, foreign intelligence wiretaps, informants, information-sharing, or synthesizing all of that information into hard and fast predictions that could get us one step ahead of the terrorists.

There's an inherent paradox in the fact that the people who ran the FBI's terrorism investigations bragged that they, unlike their counterparts in foreign counterintelligence, actually prosecuted criminals and put them in jail. That was the primary basis for the failure of the terrorism program. Criminal investigations are inherently reactive in nature. While the occasional criminal conviction may score points with the press and Capitol Hill, and satisfy the FBI brass who used statistical accomplishments as a measure of efficiency, the fact remained that they didn't really prevent future incidents. The result of this misplaced focus on criminalizing terror after the fact rather than beating the terrorists at their own game: hundreds of lives needlessly lost to terrorist atrocities long before September 11.

Another flaw with the FBI's terrorism program is that it lacked the skilled core of professionals that populated the FBI's counterintelligence program and even its organized crime and white-collar crime programs, where street investigators immerse themselves in the geographical area to which they are assigned, becoming familiar with their targets' religious and cultural backgrounds, even growing fluent in their native languages. Counterintelligence investigators, for the most part, rose through the ranks as their skills developed, as their expertise became recognized, and as they demonstrated their ability to manage complex investigations that oftentimes, if they involved an espionage investigation, combined both the criminal and counterintelligence responsibilities of the FBI.

That was not the way the terrorism program began, and it was not the way it was managed on September 11. But even with its misplaced focus on criminality rather than intelligence gathering, the program started off strong after it was conceived in the early 1980s. However, the stakes were much lower then. The FBI busied itself with investigating domestic groups that look like child's play compared with al Qaeda and its ilk: the Puerto Rican Army for National Liberation, known as the FALN; Omega 7, an anti-Castro group; Croatian nationalists bombing Yugoslavian missions; the Jewish Defense League; and the Weather Underground. Under the watchful eye of Oliver "Buck" Revell, the two FBI terrorism chiefs who ran these investigations, Wayne Gilbert in the 1980s and Neil Gallagher in the early 1990s, developed expertise in terrorism and emerged as credible leaders. Unfortunately, not even they were able to shepherd the FBI away from its domestic and criminal focus and toward the indispensable task of gathering intelligence abroad—not even after Libyan terrorists blew up Pam Am Flight 103 over Lockerbie, Scotland, in 1988.

THE PROBLEMS ONLY GOT WORSE upon the arrival of Louis Freeh as director of the FBI and Bob Bryant as assistant director of the newly-formed National Security Division. In a display of the cronyism that would become a defining feature of Freeh's tenure, he reassigned Neil Gallagher to the FBI's New Orleans Division, where his considerable terrorism expertise was largely wasted, and replaced him with Dave Tubbs, a Bryant crony from his Salt Lake City days with virtually no experience handling terrorism investigations. Then just six months later, an unusually brief time, Tubbs was promoted, again at Bryant's behest, to Kansas City as special agent in charge and replaced with John O'Neill, then an assistant special agent in charge in Chicago.

Many were shocked at the choice of O'Neill, who also had limited exposure to international terrorism and had been considered "unpromotable" by various career boards, in part because of his overbearing management style. Bryant persisted, even in the face of advice from his fellow assistant directors, and eventually O'Neill took over the reins. I called O'Neill and offered my assistance in navigating the FBI bureaucracy and the rather complex budget issues he would have to deal with, but O'Neill never responded. He dealt almost exclusively with Bryant, bypassing Bryant's handpicked deputy, John Lewis, and had virtually no interaction with his fellow section chiefs.

A brilliant and dedicated man conversant on everything from Broadway shows to fine wine—I spent a couple of long evenings with him—O'Neill eventually retired in August, 2001, about two weeks before the 9/11 attacks, under a cloud of allegations that he had been careless with classified documents. He had also fallen victim to other personal qualities not appreciated in the FBI culture, including a penchant for expensive suits and carrying on torrid affairs with several women at a time. In part to pay off the debts that he accumulated in pursuit of his lifestyle, O'Neill took a high-paying job as the World Trade Center security director. When the planes crashed into the twin towers on September 11, O'Neill predictably stormed into the building to try to save as many lives as he could. He died when the North Tower tumbled to the ground.

O'Neill was replaced by Dale Watson, a Tubbs and Bryant protégé in Kansas City and the man who later complained to Congress about the "99 shots" that the FBI had allegedly blocked without receiving any credit from an ungrateful public. A specialist in Soviet bloc counterintelligence, Watson was yet another appointee who lacked terrorism experience. He had never even worked as an FBI inspector or a special agent in charge, developmental steps that are essential for senior executives—

though none of that later stopped FBI Director Robert Mueller from appointing him the head of the FBI's entire counterterrorism and counterintelligence operations.

In that sense, those like *Newsweek*'s Evan Thomas who claimed the FBI's terrorism program has long been a backwater assignment with little prospect for advancement are dead wrong. To the contrary, throughout the 1990s the program was characterized by the worst kind of cronyism, one in which assignments were made based solely on a loyalty and past association to either Bryant or Freeh—and in which the hasty promotions of those like Tubbs with no terrorism background and with too short a tenure to bloom kept the program from fighting terror.

THE CRONYISM THAT GUIDED appointments to key antiterrorist posts was not the FBI's only problem in fighting terrorism, though there is a relationship. The fundamental failure of the terrorism program was its failure over the years to develop either an appreciation for information analysis or a cadre of skilled analysts to concentrate on terrorism investigations. By analysis I don't mean a piecemeal study. I mean taking raw data, submitting it to thoughtful and rigorous review, and drawing predictive, pragmatic, outside-the-box conclusions. That sort of analysis, so essential to predicting and forestalling imminent terrorism incidents, was alien to the FBI's terrorism program.

I have always believed that analysts should work with operational units—but never *for* them. When the National Security Division was formed in January 1994, the new division consolidated the FBI's antiterrorism and counterintelligence programs, in part because the FBI's counterintelligence efforts had shrunk dramatically since the end of the Cold War. Neil Gallagher, who had headed the antiterrorism section, fought to keep his section in the Criminal Division because he shared the widespread disdain for counterintelligence (though oddly enough, he would later be named the chief of the Counterintelligence Division). Over Gallagher's protests, however, the consolidation moved forward all the same.

At the time, I headed the National Security Division's Analysis, Budget, and Training Section, where all the counterintelligence analysts worked. I argued that we should gather all the terrorism analysts splintered among the various terrorism operational units and reassign them to my section. My reasons were simple: analysts must work closely with but independent of the operational experts who are supposed to act on their advice. Analysts are useless if they are tempted to "cook" their analysis to suit the preconceived ideas of the very operational agents who decide when to hire, fire, and promote them.

In that sense the CIA was ahead of us, for the CIA had always distinguished between operations on the one side and analysis on the other. But the FBI's Terrorism Section, never on the vanguard of integrating intelligence information with its criminal investigations in the first place, had somehow muddled that key point along the way. I had dealt with the CIA's analysts over the years and was always impressed with their professionalism and academic curiosity and used their experience as a guide in developing a counterintelligence analytical capability that was up to the demands of the operational responsibilities of the FBI. I wanted to use that same approach in developing the FBI's analytical capability in dealing with terrorism as well.

Grave consequences arose from the FBI's poor treatment of its analysts. For instance, I was dismayed to learn that the FBI had never even developed a basic antiterrorism training course for analysts and the agents assigned to terrorism investigations. I had to ask Ken Schiffer, an old colleague at the Washington field office and an expert in Chinese counterintelligence who was assigned to my training unit, to develop such a course, which we soon made available to analysts, the new agents at the FBI academy, and even to the experienced agents newly assigned to terrorism investigations.

The course didn't solve my problems with the analysts, however. As a group, they were ill equipped to draw any useful conclusions on which our government might act. Lacking the academic backgrounds and sheer intellect to conduct high-level analysis, they also lacked any cultural understanding of the Middle East or any Arabic language skills.

Unlike the counterintelligence program, which recruited top talent from academia and industry, the terrorism analysts were largely bureaucrats promoted from clerical and secretarial positions. It turned out that their clerical backgrounds provided good training for what they had been doing at the Terrorism Section: making overheads for briefings, copying documents, writing random speeches, and drafting country overviews not even as sophisticated as what you might find in *National Geographic* magazine. Their job description didn't mention reviewing raw data gleaned through terrorism investigations, information from domestic and foreign intelligence agencies, or anything else for that matter. And yet these analysts were all we had.

I knew I had to act fast—and that simply creating a terrorism course wasn't going to cut it. I chose some of the FBI's best counterintelligence analysts and lured them into the terrorism program. I also did whatever I could to protect my analysts from their former operational supervisors. Yet just as I started to see real progress, I was dealt a blow that was simply unforgettable.

One afternoon in late 1994, the National Security Division's John Harley informed me that Bryant, under pressure from Tubbs, had decided to repatriate all the terrorism analysts into the Terrorism Section—in essence, to replicate the very organization that had failed so miserably in the past. I snapped that the Terrorism Section must have had a large backlog of photocopying requests if Tubbs and Bryant believed that was the best way to use the analysts. Bryant, I had learned, had no inkling of how essential serious analysis is to counterintelligence and to fighting international terrorism. As one terrorist analyst told me after Bryant announced his plans, "Any chance we had to become real analysts is gone." How right she was.

It wasn't my last run-in with Bryant on this subject. At a section chiefs' meeting a day or so after Harley advised me of Bryant's decision, where I took my usual seat at the far end of the table from Bryant, Bryant announced that the analysts were going to be shipped back to the Terrorism Section and integrated into the individual terrorism operational units. Bryant hesitated a moment and then looked at me. I said I disagreed with the move. He responded, "Your deputy [John Harley] told me you agreed with the move." I replied, "No, I don't agree with the move, but I'm told your mind is made up and nothing I can say will change it." It was a tense moment for all of us, but I wanted everyone to know how strongly I felt about the issue, regardless of how defying Bryant in public could hurt my career.

MY CONCLUSION THAT THE FBI's terrorism program failed to appreciate the usefulness of analysis was not just conjecture. It was based on actual incidents. Buck Revell explains in his book *A G-Man's Journal* that in the wake of the 1993 World Trade Center bombing, the FBI became aware of a New York terrorist cell that should have been detected long before. Back in November 1990, in fact, the FBI and local authorities made a shocking discovery when they searched the home of El Sayyid Nosair, a suspected accomplice in the assassination three days before of Rabbi Meir Kahane, the founder of the Jewish Defense League. A gold mine of terrorist documents awaited them: forty-seven boxes of evidence, including a diary written in Arabic.

And what did the FBI do with these documents? Most of them collected dust for years, untranslated and unheeded. The diary, however, which the Bureau did take the time to decipher, provided a treasure trove of detailed plans to terrorize the New York area, including the World Trade Center. More important, it detailed the existence of an entrenched international terrorist cell based in New York—a cell the FBI didn't even know existed. As a result, when Nosair was later shipped off to the Attica prison, the FBI sent in an Arab informant to infiltrate. Nosair fell for the bait and bragged to the informant about the burgeoning Islamic cell in New York. Although the informant passed on the information promptly, it languished, unanalyzed, until long after the 1993 bombing. By that point it was far too late, of course, but not even that bungle could force the Bureau to question its failed approach to terrorism.

It will be many years before historians can evaluate Louis Freeh's performance as director and, more specifically, his performance fighting terrorism. When Freeh was first appointed director, he'd been an FBI agent for only six years. He was a hard worker, resourceful, and dedicated. But he was not, despite his media-fed image, a "law enforcement legend," a phrase applied to Freeh by President Bill Clinton the day he was sworn in as FBI director. I was sitting in the audience at FBI headquarters when I heard the phrase and wondered how someone could be considered a legend when I had never heard of him until his appointment was announced with much fanfare. It's ludicrous to put Freeh in the same league as, say, a Joe Sullivan, who took on the Klan in Mississippi, investigated Nazis in South America, defused bombs himself during a union dispute, and investigated 1960s antiwar protests. That's not to say Freeh didn't throw himself into the minutiae of the Oklahoma City bombing and other catastrophes, such as the bombing of the Khobar Towers in Saudi Arabia. But his case-by-case focus didn't make for a great FBI director and even undermined his ability to develop strategic solutions to the Bureau's most pressing problems, including the need for enhanced automation, the use of strategic intelligence in terrorism investigations, and an equitable disciplinary system.

In that sense, then, Freeh's testimony on September 11 was like his testimony every other time he was in the hot seat. Freeh would "take responsibility" for what happened, only to shift blame to outside influences. The litany was always the same: Congress hadn't appropriated enough money, fighting terrorism was the job of the military and the State Department, Janet Reno's Justice Department prevented agents from investigating terrorism effectively, or whatever the excuse of the moment happened to be. But when it comes to September 11, nothing can change the fact that highly-qualified agents in Phoenix, New York, and Minneapolis tried to curb terrorism through existing laws using existing resources and without the help of the State Department or the military. What hurt those agents was one thing and one thing only: the bureaucracy that Louis Freeh built.

Freeh did many good things for the FBI and infused the organization with new energy after the protracted dismissal of William Sessions, his predecessor. Freeh also showed courage in the CAMPCON investigation when he recommended naming an independent counsel to investigate fund-raising by the very president who had appointed him FBI director. And Freeh expanded the role of the FBI abroad, though he often sparred with foreign diplomats and sent inexperienced agents to Saudi Arabia, Tanzania, Kenya, Yemen, the Philippines, and Pakistan, where they learned the hard way that they could not brandish weapons and pull people off the street for interrogations.

The biggest international debacle of Freeh's tenure occurred in Yemen, where the FBI insisted on carrying weapons and bypassing the Yemeni police—and eventually was banned from investigating the bombing in Aden of the *USS Cole*. The late John O'Neill, who headed the operation, was even ordered out of the country by the U.S. ambassador. He was praised upon his return for standing up to the diplomatic corps, but meanwhile, the investigation of the bombing languished and the victims' families never got the answers they so desperately sought.

To my mind, this episode was a symptom of a larger problem. The FBI had become so enmeshed in its overseas investigations that it ignored the very real possibility that the same terrorists it was tracking abroad could commit even more devastating acts of terror here in the U.S. Even after the failed attempt in late 1999 of the Millennium bombers, who sought to blow up Los Angeles International Airport, the FBI dug in its heels, focusing as it long had on terrorism committed against embassies and other U.S. targets abroad. Just as in 1993 when the existence of a New York terrorist cell emerged only after the World Trade Center was bombed, so history repeated itself on September 11 while the FBI still had its blinders on when it came to domestic activity by international terrorists.

THE TERRORISM PROGRAM has been fraught with other systemic problems. "Reprogramming" has been the norm. As investigative reporter Bill Gertz explained in his book *Breakdown*, millions of dollars budgeted for intelligence were spent instead on a crime laboratory, and tens of millions of dollars allocated to hiring agents to conduct criminal investigations, not terrorism matters. All the same, hiring more terror-ism agents is not the answer. Freeh always asked Congress for more money to hire more terrorism agents, but he never specified the precise threat to which those agents were intended to respond. Even when the FBI incorporated international terrorism investigations into the newly formed National Security Division, the Bureau failed to treat intelligence gathering and analysis with appropriate seriousness, then compounded the problem by incorporating the investigation of domestic terrorism—primarily anti-abortion radicals and militia groups—into the National Security Division as well. Domestic terrorism investigations rose in prominence, with international terrorism and counterintelligence falling behind, even though the U.S. had seen dramatically reduced activity among the militia groups after the Oklahoma City bombing.

In November 1999, Bryant proposed another reorganization plan to Freeh, this one in two parts: a separate Terrorism Division and an all-encompassing Analytical Division. Most of the National Security Divi-sion's senior staff were wary of both. What Bryant really wanted to do, they realized, was to consolidate all of the Bureau's analytical resources into a single division, which would enhance the weak analytical capabil-ities of the FBI's Criminal Division. I had retired by that time, but a for-mer colleague called me advising me of the plan and I concurred with his view of the underlying purpose for Bryant's proposal. Once again I feared criminal investigations would drown out counterintelligence and international terrorism programs. I was even more concerned because the new head of the Investigative Support Division was Dave Alba, the special agent in charge of the FBI's El Paso office. Alba, plagued with management problems in El Paso, had virtually no background in intel-ligence or analysis. The result was predictable: valuable intelligence information never reached the analysts from the operational units and the analysts themselves were often diverted instead to further the FBI's persistent focus on criminal investigations at the expense of counter-terrorism.

Bryant's reorganization did create a new and independent Counter-terrorism Division. Its real purpose was to satisfy congressional critics angry over the Wen Ho Lee and Robert Hanssen debacles and who believed the counterintelligence program had been so eviscerated that "something" had to be done. So counterintelligence once again became an FBI mission with a single purpose. That said, my former colleagues in the National Security Division told me they believed this was also a ploy on Bryant's part to create a bureaucratic entity that could be headed by Dale Watson, Bryant's protégé. Neil Gallagher, who had been a terrorism section chief for five years, lobbied for control of the Counterterrorism Division and was considerably more experienced on paper than Watson, but he did not have either Bryant's or Freeh's confidence and thus lost the battle. Gallagher remained as head of the National Security Division; the staff knew his real interest was in terrorism and that their work, counter-intelligence, was of secondary interest at best.

MY CONCERNS ABOUT THE Investigative Support Division, which Freeh had claimed would "substantially strengthen" analysis, were soon echoed by others. Two weeks after the September 11 attacks and three weeks after he became director, Robert Mueller disbanded the entire division, convinced it was a disaster that had contributed in part to September 11.

In the days and weeks following the attacks, I received telephone calls from former colleagues who expressed their considerable dismay with not only what had occurred, but how the investigation was being con-ducted. One former colleague told me that those at FBI headquarters seemed to be as interested in "circling the wagons," to avoid blame as they were investigating the crimes themselves. Another told me of the sheer incompetence of some of the senior officials managing the inves-tigation, officials who had been promoted by Freeh based on cronyism and as much for their gender as any demonstrated competence in man-aging complex terrorism investigations.

One longtime friend, a street agent, had told me of his plans to remain in the FBI for a couple more years, but he had become so dis-gusted with the leadership that he decided to retire at the end of the year. Others expressed no confidence that anyone would attempt to fix responsibility for the September 11 intelligence failures. Those whose bureaucracy was in place when the attacks occurred—Freeh, Bryant, and others—simply avoided the media and were not called before Congress until Freeh's brief appearance a year after the event. Developments since my conversations with those employees who felt no one would be specifically blamed for the failures have borne out their predictions. In this country's worse calamity since Pearl Harbor, not a single person with responsibility for the FBI's counterterrorism effort has even been given a slap on the wrist, much less censured or demoted for their management and operational failures.

An FBI director is not omniscient and is not endowed with eternal wisdom at the moment he is appointed. Like any manager, he or she depends on subordinates for advice and counsel. Freeh promoted me and I am grateful for his trust. But after September 11, I can longer be an apologist simply by remaining quiet. Freeh, it must be said, was badly served by some of those he promoted. Cronyism played too big a role, and he justifiably bears the brunt of his bad decisions. I've always given my opinions of Freeh openly. That was an added benefit of not being a "friend of Louie." But the backstabbing has already begun by many who were promoted by Freeh and it won't end anytime soon. The exceptionally harsh view of Freeh that emerges in Ron Kessler's book, *The Bureau,* was fed to the author in part by senior FBI managers speaking anonymously. They did not have the courage to speak on the record, which comes as no surprise. By hiding beyond anonymity, they're displaying the same lack of courage that helped allow September 11—and these managers, along with Freeh himself, have to live with the consequences.

There are no quick fixes for the FBI's decade-long mismanagement of its terrorism program, but Director Mueller has made some long-needed changes. He has named terrorism and counterintelligence as the FBI's highest priorities, followed by cyber crimes, and then public corruption (the last one a priority in name alone). But this means Mueller had to replace the crony-hires with new talent and probably find a whole new way to hire and evaluate key personnel based on what they contribute to intelligence operations, not based on how many criminals they put in jail.

A growing chorus, particularly on Capitol Hill, has called for removing counterintelligence and international terrorism from the FBI and placing those responsibilities in a new agency modeled after the British MI-5. Here, the facts should get in the way: The MI-5, an agency with internal security responsibilities but no law enforcement powers, hasn't exactly been a model of success, and it certainly hasn't been able to prevent terrorist acts by the Irish Republican Army. Indeed, on several occasions, acquaintances of MI-5, as well as similar security agencies from Canada, Australia, and New Zealand, voiced their preference for a structure like the FBI, where internal security and law enforcement functions are embodied in a single agency.

In addition to reorganization, there's that other familiar standby: just throw more bodies at the problem. But new agents can only do so much. It will take years for the FBI to develop an adequate expertise in terrorism and counterintelligence. In the meantime, the FBI must become willing to admit its errors and not hide behind its cloak of secrecy and "national security." I am certain that further revelations in the next few years will create even more anguish over the FBI's failings, but the FBI will also be judged on its willingness to put out embarrassing information itself, along with its plans to rectify any mistakes, instead of continuing to "circle the wagons."

The reasons for the FBI's failure to prevent the attacks of September 11, 2001, were managerial, not structural. The current knee-jerk response, though essentially a political one, is to create a new bureaucracy or, at the minimum, reshuffle the old one. But those are shortsighted solutions that only satisfy a political moment but will never lead to the results that are so desperately needed, neither in the short term nor for the long haul. True reform is not the result of an event. It is a process that requires time, patience, and a commitment to a course or action that leads to an accomplished and energized FBI that will be responsive to future terrorists' threats. But there is an unwillingness to fix responsibility for the failures of the past, and there is no interest in having those who failed in their responsibilities to pay a price for their failures. And this failure to adhere to a fundamental tenet of command, that command has both its rewards as well as its perils, practically ensures that at some point in the future, terrorists will strike, fingers will point, politicians will posture, and we will revisit the same process again. That is the historical consequence of failing to come to grips with mistakes after they occur, and history tells us it will be the consequence we will pay in the future.

APPENDIX A
Arkansas Democrat-Gazette Editorial

A few days after my retirement, under the headline, "Mister FBI retires," the *Arkansas Democrat-Gazette* editorialized: "The agent in charge of the FBI's offices in this small, wonderful and highly investigated state retired Friday. I.C. Smith will be missed for his skills in catching bad guys, and for a lot more. Like his unusual way with a police communiqué. There was the time a bum—excuse us, a transient, as they say on police reports—stole a portrait of Bill Clinton from the state's Capitol and sold it for $2. Agent Smith was shocked, simply shocked. 'My God,' he said. 'You can't even get a velvet Elvis for $2.'

"Here was one FBI agent who was quotable. They're an endangered species. And he was reachable, too. Come to find out, he'd told his secretary on his first day on the job not to screen his calls. Who knows how many he got from reporters and other degenerates?

"I.C. Smith fielded all kinds of inquiries over the years. There was no hiding behind closed doors or neutral statements for him. Remember when a local constable running for re-election, and rather ludicrously at that, took some allegations about his opponent to the FBI? Remember how said constable solemnly reported that the agents had taken his claims seriously? That they were investigating them posthaste? Not so, said I.C. Smith. If anything, the investigators found the constable's story 'farfetched.' Rather than keep that impression to himself, I.C. Smith let the public know, too. He didn't want to get involved in local politics, but he wasn't about to let his office be used for politics, either. Good for him.

"There seems to be only one embarrassment on the FBI's record during I.C. Smith's watch here in Arkansas. That was when some of his agents had their van and its high-powered weapons stolen during an overnight stay in Memphis. Mr. Smith offered no excuses. 'Obviously, this is not a banner day for the bureau,' he said. 'The FBI is made up of human beings, and we have human successes and human failures.'

"Those successes are many. They include: Dan Harmon's downfall. And the dismantling of notorious gangs in Little Rock like the Oak Street Posse and the 23rd Street Crips. But the best praise of all comes from those who knew him best, his peers in law enforcement. They're going to miss his skills—and lots more."

© Used with permission, *Arkansas Democrat-Gazette*, 1998.

APPENDIX B
Retirement Dinner Speech

One book I have managed to reread is *The Old Man and the Sea* by Ernest Hemingway. This is a sparse and beautifully written book about the old man, Sanitago . . . [who] is beset by sharks, and though he fought them valiantly, when he arrived back in Havana, all that was left of the giant fish were the skeletal remains. He staggered to his hut and went into a sound sleep and began to dream. But the old man did not dream of the battle with the fish, nor did he dream of the savagery of the shark attack. Instead, he dreamed of a time in his youth when he traveled to Africa and of the wonder of the evenings when lions would play along golden beaches by the ocean.

Now, I'm a long way from an old man, but perhaps at some time in the future I too will dream. And I would like to think, just as the old man in Hemingway's novel, that I will dream of pleasurable experiences, not those directly associated with work. I think I will dream of Mike's Bar in St. Louis where I learned of the comradeship of this wonderful Bureau and the resultant identity with the organization. I will likely recall the assignments in Washington D.C., where we witnessed history and attended social functions and ate in good restaurants where the food was good, but the conversation was so stimulating it overpowered the menus. I think I will dream of the sheer energy of the most dynamic of American cities, Miami, so aptly named "America's Casablanca," and will hear the melancholy cry of the kookaburra in Australia and feel the tradewinds of soft summer nights in the South Pacific. And I will remember not only the natural beauty of this wonderful state, but the fundamental goodness of its people that I have been privileged to have served. And all these dreams were made possible by the Bureau. . . .

Just think, a country boy of very modest means has walked on the Great Wall of China and the edge of the Grand Canyon. I strolled around the Kremlin while it was still the Soviet Union, and into the very core of the Central Intelligence Agency, the National Security Agency, and yes, the White House. I explored the great cathedral in Cologne, Germany, was on the roof of the Reichstaag in Berlin during the Cold War and ate dinner where Joey Gallo was killed in New York City. But it isn't the places that I remember so much as the people. I remember the service station attendant in Narrandara, Australia, who told me what his battle-scarred dog was good for and for good measure, volunteered what was wrong with America. I remember the peddler along the Arbat in Moscow who was trying to sell me a set of those little dolls that are placed inside one another, that included all the Soviet Union leaders form Lenin to Gorbachev. He described Lenin as the "first Communist" and I pointed to Gorbachev and asked if he was the "last Communist." I remember a young boy in the Cook Islands who I photographed and of all the photographs I have taken, it is my favorite, and while he had heard of America, he didn't know where it was. And I remember the old "aunt" in St. Louis who I would drink coffee with on her front porch after I would take her a mess of collard greens and who insisted on calling me the 'man from Texas' though I told her I was from Louisiana, but who would also give me a whispered call when her nephew would run away from the Army. Then, of course, there was the old gentleman in a store up near the Buffalo River who, over biscuits and gravy, went into great length telling me the difference between elk meat and deer meat, while all the time I had the distinct impression he was basing his views on personal experience, even if elk were protected and he didn't really know who he was talking to. I didn't tell him, for I didn't wish to ruin a good conversation. . . .

It isn't easy being a spouse and family of a law enforcement officer, and years ago I made the conscious decision to keep my work and family largely separate. I'm not certain that was always the correct thing to do, but at times it was necessary. . . .

[I've been] blessed with a wonderful wife and daughters and now two sons-in-laws and a grandson, and for that I am quite grateful. The hours were long, and there were many times my absences were not readily explainable, but I did have the safe haven of a warm and loving family to return to that allowed me to recharge and start another day. They were very much a part of any success I have enjoyed, and Carla in particular, who has taught in five states and essentially put her family and my career before herself, has paid a price for being married to an FBI agent. I love them all very much, and being around them more often than I have in the past is in itself an incentive to call it a career.

As I look back on my career in law enforcement, well, it's been quite a ride.

You have all honored me with your presence this evening and for that I am eternally grateful.

> Ivian C. Smith,
> Retirement Dinner
> August 28, 1998

INDEX